FÜHRER-EX

RANDOM HOUSE
NEW YORK

FÜHRER-EX

Memoirs of a Former

Neo-Nazi

∎

INGO HASSELBACH

WITH TOM REISS

Führer-Ex grew from *Die Abrechnung: Ein Neonazi steigt aus*,
by Ingo Hasselbach and Winfried Bonengel, published in Germany in 1993
by Aufbau-Verlag GmbH.
A portion of the introduction was originally published in *The New York Times*.

Some names in this book have been changed; they appear on page 388.

Library of Congress Cataloging-in-Publication Data
Hasselbach, Ingo, 1967– .
[Abrechnung. English]
Führer-Ex: memoirs of a former neo-Nazi / by Ingo Hasselbach
with Tom Reiss.—1st ed.
p.   cm.
ISBN 0-679-43825-4
1. Hasselbach, Ingo, 1967– . 2. Fascists—Germany—Biography.
3. Fascism—Germany—History—20th century. 4. Germany—Politics
and government—1990– . I. Reiss, Tom. II. Title.
DD290.33.H38A313   1996
943.087'092—dc20   95-31751
[B]

Printed in the United States of America on acid-free paper
24689753
First Edition

Contents

Introduction:
A NEW WORLD

I happened to arrive in the United States from Germany for the first time two days before the bombing in Oklahoma City in April 1995. I was sitting in a hotel room in the middle of Manhattan finishing work on the pages that follow. It was one of the first times I'd had a chance to rest and pause in the two years since I'd left the neo-Nazi movement. America represented everything I'd come to love since quitting—a society of all nationalities, a strong democracy, a land of liberty—everything I'd worked to destroy when I was in the Movement.

The news in the weeks that followed linked the bombing with the existence of a far-right subversive movement, fueled by paranoid conspiracy theories and hatred of the federal government. That there was such a movement didn't come as news to me. As the founder of the former East Germany's first neo-Nazi political party, I'd been the main contact for several American far-right organizations in Europe and one of the main distributors of their propaganda. Before I got out of the Movement in 1993, I organized teach-ins, ran paramilitary camps, and indoctrinated young people at marches and meetings.

I began developing right-wing extremist ideas in 1987, when I was nineteen years old and sitting in an East German prison for shouting "the Wall must fall!" in a public place. When I got out, I began working secretly with a small militant group opposed to the Communist government.

After the government fell, I didn't simply quit being a troublemaker and rejoice in my newfound freedom. Prison, youthful rebellion, and the intense study of the most evil ideology known to mankind had already begun to change me. The peaceful revolution going on in the streets of Berlin in November 1989 had nothing to do with the violent revolution going on in my head. I didn't want a part of this capitalist West Germany where I could buy a Walkman or a bunch of bananas. I wanted the German empire a former Gestapo officer had told me about in prison, the one whose medals and slogans and insignia were the ultimate taboos in both East and West Germany—and whose embrace confirmed my opposition to both those systems.

My "Kamerads" and I had been beaten and warped into what we were by the bizarre, disappeared system of Communist East Germany. But oddly enough, we found our vicious, ornate code of hatred gained us entree into a growing circle of groups in West Germany and around the world. That we were East German only seemed to endear us further to them—as if our being raised in the failed system of German communism somehow made us less domesticated, less corrupted by the past forty years of German democracy. Those looking for a new Führer saw me as a pure "blond beast" risen from the ashes of the Iron Curtain, and, along with the drug of never-ending rebellion, I began to crave the fix of power I got from handing out hate literature, planning attacks, and standing at the head of hundreds of other equally angry young people, egging them on, pushing them further over the edges of decency.

I made contact with a flourishing international network of neo-Nazis and racist movements and began building up caches of weapons and starting paramilitary camps. Like the extremists in America, the common attitude we shared was a hatred for the government (especially federal government agents), a belief that our freedoms and traditions as white men (or, as we said, Aryans) were being infringed on by a multicultural society, and a general anti-Semitism that held that the Jews ran a conspiracy that emanated from New York and Washington.

While most of these ideas could have come from European anti-Semitic tracts from before World War II, they didn't. Virtually all of our propaganda and training manuals came from right-wing extremist groups in Nebraska and California. Such materials are legal to print in the United States under the First Amendment. In Germany they are not, under the Constitution passed after the defeat of the Third Reich.

We also received illegal materials from our friends in Nebraska—the world headquarters of the NSDAP/AO, the successor to the original National Socialist German Workers' Party, or Nazi Party—

like a U.S. Army training manual entitled *Explosives and Demolitions,* which has since been copied and circulated (still with the TOP SECRET stamp across the title page) to thousands of right-wing extremists all over Europe. A computer program we received from the NSDAP/AO, entitled "A Movement in Arms," described how to build bombs and wage a war of right-wing terrorism against a democratic government. Before I quit, I'd become the leader of an NSDAP/AO terrorist cell, taking my orders directly from Lincoln, Nebraska.

I'd had plenty of contact with America. But it was an America populated by men who hated their country and found the swastika a more appealing symbol than the Statue of Liberty, who saw great affinities between their Founding Fathers and Adolf Hitler. It was an America oddly obsessed with Germany and the Third Reich. But it was not this America that I'd come to see. I was coming here to get away from eighteen months of running, always looking behind me, never having an address or a telephone number for fear it could lead my former Kamerads to me.

That week in New York I'd ridden public transportation for the first time in two years. I couldn't do so anywhere in Germany because someone in the Movement might recognize me. I'm easy to recognize. I'm blond, blue-eyed, and so tall—about six foot six—that I stick out even in Germany. In the Movement I was considered the ideal, the ultimate Aryan type. I was famous in the national media—first as a neo-Nazi leader and then as a quitter and a voice against extremism. In New York, I could finally be an anonymous person again, in a city where people of every nationality seemed to live peacefully with one another.

And then, two days after I first set foot on American soil, the worst act of terrorism in U.S. history was committed.

I don't know if whoever blew up the Alfred P. Murrah Federal Building in Oklahoma read the army manual we worked from. If they didn't, I'm sure we had some other reading material in common. The right-wing extremist movement is a loose network of people with a great deal of hatred and potential for violence, and all over the world they are constantly exchanging information. Of course, lots of people in the Movement may have been horrified by the sight of burned children in the Oklahoma bombing, but my experience as a neo-Nazi taught me that enough militant ideology and conspiracy thinking can destroy even the most basic human sympathy.

I began the slow and difficult process of getting out of the Movement after the fatal firebombing in 1992 of a Turkish family in the city of Mölln in northern Germany by two young men in the middle of the night. It had killed two young girls and the grandmother of one of the girls. My group had had nothing to do with the attack, but for the first time the deadly potential of our rhetoric was driven home to me. The police investigation showed that the perpetrators had connections with and had received propaganda from a group like mine in Hamburg, as well as from an American neo-Nazi group. Yet in prosecuting the case the authorities viewed these connections as secondary and treated the bombing as a case of isolated, if deadly, juvenile delinquency.

I never personally built a bomb or set fire to anyone's house. I justified my role in the Movement much as the leaders of the American militias or any of the other militant groups do. I was trying to "defend" my society against rampant crime, too much immigration, racial and cultural "alienation," and control by a world conspiracy. I organized paramilitary camps and taught guerrilla warfare only to prepare Germans to defend themselves and the cultural traditions of northern Europeans. I knew the arguments well, and I taught them to many others.

I know now that during all that time I was deceiving myself. Morally, I was just as responsible as anyone who planted a fuse or drove a truck with explosives in it—because my messages of hatred against the larger society influenced who knows how many potentially violent young men. The first step for me in rejoining the civilized world was realizing that.

BUT IT IS not so easy to rejoin the world above ground when you have been living in the subterranean world of fanatics. Groups like the one I was part of watch their enemies—whether Jews, foreigners, the government, or traitors like me—from a distance. They are afraid of getting close because if they do it might defuse the hate, or at least corrupt it with firsthand knowledge and second thoughts. They want their hate pure.

As the "Führer of the East," I had walked as if sealed inside an ideological space suit, treating my enemies as if they were deadly viruses. The suit kept the virus from infecting me and killing the hate. To take this suit off and approach my enemy without my ideology on was to risk discovering him as a person. My neo-Nazi Kamerads and I would go to a Jewish community open house and act utterly calm and normal, perhaps smiling or looking blankly on, safe in our space suits, until we struck.

This is what distinguishes a true ideological hate, I think: its intense power and the way members of the group carry it so carefully, keeping it sealed against all corruption. What makes them different from casual bigots or ordinary nationalists is the way the hatred is so carefully prepared and maintained. They spend all their free time concocting new recipes for it, learning how to transfer it to the widest group while keeping it pure.

This is why bombs are such a perfect weapon for terrorist groups—they allow you to maintain a cleansing distance from the target, and the violence is sudden: there is no time for thoughts, arguments, or counterblows. Fanatics like feeling that hatred and violence are almost acts of nature over which they exercise only the most perfunctory control.

THE BOMB MY former Kamerads sent to my mother's apartment in Berlin after I went on TV to renounce neo-Nazism was powerful enough to have blown off four stories of the building, the police said. But there had been a problem with its construction; a scrap of metal had been left touching one of the wires, and the battery had drained itself in the mail. Had it arrived a day earlier, the police said, it would have worked. But after the bomb, I had to live in a new world. These were the same streets, the same city I'd grown up in, where I knew every crack in the pavement, but it was different. My familiar Berlin had become a place of constant danger. In every bar I'd ever drunk a beer in, in every subway I'd ridden, I now saw the faces of right-wing youth who saw me as the great betrayer and who would eagerly kill me for the glory of the Movement.

My first reaction was that I would kill them first. But my hatred and vengeance toward my former Kamerads quickly gave way to grief and shame—shame over the pride I'd taken in what I now knew was an ideology of pure hate. I'd justified it with arguments about what was good for the German nation, the environment, the unemployed youth. But if an organization aims to employ the youth, the first question you should ask is: to what end? These causes are just window dressing for the goals of all serious neo-Nazis: to restore the Nazi Party and to once again make the arguments of biological racism and anti-Semitism powerful and legitimate political forces. The basic goal, in other words, is the justification, mobilization, and *organization* of pure hatred. Now I had experienced firsthand what it was like to be on the receiving end of this explosive hatred.

There are stages you go through when trying to get out of any extremist movement or cult, and even when you are out, that does not necessarily mean the movement is out of you. The bomb sent to my mother, intended for me, was the last stage of my own internal accounting. Even though it did not explode, something inside me did. The feeling of empathy I'd had for the Turkish families was now made palpable for me, for I knew what it felt like to be struck at through innocents, through those you loved.

The bomb was also the final step in making me realize that any feelings of camaraderie or friendship that had survived my renunciation of the Cause were false. My friends were neo-Nazis first. They'd kill me and my family and anyone else without blinking if they thought it best served the Movement. So I could have only one purpose—to fight them and to fight the Cause. And the first step in fighting them was to tell the story of what made me one of them, of how I pulled others in, and of how a sewer of Third Reich wastewater flows beneath the clean streets of modern Germany. I've climbed out of that sewer, and I will now tell you what's down there.

FÜHRER-EX

1

COLD INNOCENCE

My FATHER IS from Düsseldorf, in the westernmost part of Germany, on the Rhine. He was born sometime in the mid-1930s and soon became an orphan. He lost both his parents to the war: his father was killed in action, and his mother was killed in an Allied air raid. My father always hated the Nazis. After the war, he joined the German Communist Party, the KPD; by then, he was a committed Communist, a Stalinist. In West Germany, which was then named the Federal Republic, the KPD was outlawed, but my father continued his activism in secret. His ideology was more important to him than anything—wife, children, work. In 1961 he was caught and thrown into prison for illegally promoting an "anticonstitutional" organization—the same law now used against the neo-Nazis.

In 1964 my father was released from prison and went over the Wall in what you'd call the wrong direction—east. People didn't realize at the time how impossible it would be ever to escape once you were inside the "real and existing" socialist paradise that was East Germany—that the pretty rhetoric belied a state at least as Stalinist as the USSR was at the time. Still, you had to be a fanatic to make that decision. But hadn't my father been willing to go to jail for his

3

political beliefs? Now he was willing to enter a nation-sized jail called the German Democratic Republic.

On the other hand, he had few options other than to go over the Wall, for even after his jail term was up, he was a victim of one of Germany's most effective laws for stifling political dissent: the *Berufsverbot,* or "profession ban," which allows a court to forbid a citizen to practice his chosen profession because of his political activities or background. In practice it was only ever applied to Communists in the Federal Republic, but since the fall of the Berlin Wall and the rise of the neo-Nazis, it has been applied against some of us, too.

My father had a wife and children in Düsseldorf, and life became difficult for them when he was sent to prison. It didn't make you popular to have a husband in jail as a dangerous Communist at the height of the Cold War, so in 1961, only a few months after my father's imprisonment, his wife defected to the East. She was also a devoted Communist. This woman brought their five children with her across the Wall, and the whole family is still living in East Berlin today, even though the country of their dreams is gone.

MY FATHER MET my mother in East Berlin in 1964. They were both working as journalists at the East German press agency. My father had landed the coveted job easily. While he had worked briefly as a journalist in the West, his main qualification was that he was a "hero of the fight against fascism." He had served time in a West German prison, and to the state that would later put his son in prison, this was the highest honor one could get, the equivalent of having saved a battalion on the battlefield. He'd struck a blow against the capitalist-Fascist Goliath, for East Germany made no clear distinction between the Third Reich and the Federal Republic. It was all Western, capitalist fascism. My father's four-year imprisonment was seen as similar to having survived a Nazi concentration camp, and he was accorded lavish treatment in the spartan new society.

My mother had grown up in East Berlin and had studied journalism in school. By the time she met my father, she had worked her way up from apprenticeship to being a full-fledged journalist for the East German press agency. My mother was never a particularly convinced Communist. She always was and remained skeptical, removed. She just happened to have been born and raised in East Berlin, and she didn't feel strongly enough about politics one way or the other to leave her friends and family behind by fleeing to the West. So she was an East German journalist. But in the GDR it was better to achieve your position through ideology rather than through simple hard work. Although my parents started with similar assignments, my father rose to be chief of the official state radio of the GDR, while my mother stayed in the same position at the press agency for twenty years.

My parents' affair began in late 1965, and it didn't last more than a year. I think they even loved each other, but my father had a wife and five children who had followed him across the border. It was clear that he and my mother couldn't stay together, though they stayed in contact for the next twenty years because of me.

As a boy, I knew my father as "Uncle Hans." I had no idea that he was my father; at the time it never occurred to me that I had or needed a father. When Uncle Hans visited, he always brought me presents. He was friendly to me, and he got along well with my mother. I liked Uncle Hans. We played games together, and he seemed friendly and very interested in me. He was tall and thin and had hair that was gray like cement. He always smoked a pipe that smelled delicious.

Not only did I not know that Uncle Hans was my father, I also didn't have any idea that he was such an important man in East Germany. His job and title of "honorary" citizen gave him more or less free access over the Wall—a privilege mere mortals in East Germany could only dream of. After all, my father was someone who'd come of his own free will to build socialism, and a hero to boot.

My mother had one son older than me. When I was born he was in school, he was already very independent, and I never got to know him. He was the son of my mother and a man she'd met several years before. The GDR authorities found it quite incorrect that my mother had had two children out of wedlock, but, as I said, I never even noticed that I didn't have a father.

SINCE MY MOTHER was usually at work and often away on assignment, I spent most of the first years of my childhood with my grandmother and grandfather. They lived in one of the old apartment houses in Prenzlauer Berg, an old neighborhood of East Berlin directly bordering the Wall. It was the section of the city that had been left most intact by the war. My mother had spent her whole life in this apartment, where my grandpa still lives today.

Prenzlauer Berg was one of the only neighborhoods in East Berlin that was never fixed up to modern Communist standards. The small apartment building my grandparents lived in had been built around World War I, and it still had bullet holes from World War II scarring its concrete façade. Like most of the buildings in Prenzlauer Berg, it was a five-story walk-up. It was gray and had bay windows with balconies running around them. I'd sit on our balcony and throw my plastic cowboys over the edge onto the street below.

My grandpa was a postman, and he loved his work. He began working at the post office in the early 1930s; before that, he had worked as a mechanic at AEG, Germany's largest electric company. He delivered mail for most of the war. He was drafted into the Wehrmacht in 1944 and served for about a year, during the final defense of Nazi Germany, when most of the soldiers were either over- or underage. After the war he worked as a postman again until he was seventy-five, ten years longer than he had to.

Every Saturday until three in the afternoon, I went with him and helped him deliver the mail. I was about five or six, and he would lift me up to reach some of the higher mailboxes so I could shove in the letters, packages, newspapers. He watched that I didn't make a mistake and put the mail into the wrong box. He worked in what seemed to me a huge post office—and no one minded that he brought his grandson along to help on Saturdays.

Prenzlauer Berg fascinated me. Each old house with its courtyard was another universe. On some streets one could walk for really long stretches over the roofs, and I often ran across them with a pack of neighborhood kids, looking down at all the life in the streets and courtyards. We had our own world up there. We also played on the S-Bahn bridges, above the train tracks, throwing rocks down onto the trains.

At night I played around my grandma and listened to her telling stories as she cooked. She told me how she had once been arrested by the Gestapo and nearly sent to a concentration camp because she looked Jewish. Eventually they had found out she wasn't a Jew and had let her go. She told me how SS men had come to the house and threatened to arrest my grandfather when he refused to hang a flag with a swastika out the window. I have no doubt that she was telling the truth about this because I knew my grandparents refused to hang a GDR flag out the window; while no one came to arrest them about it, some of the neighbors had made a fuss. My grandparents didn't want anything to do with any ideology, whether Left or Right.

My grandma was the only one who ever told me about the Nazi years, and I remember thinking only that these events had happened an eternity ago, in another world. I grew up in another civilization with its own problems, and I didn't care about the Third Reich. I know that seems funny coming from the mouth of someone who was later to start the most successful neo-Nazi movement ever in East Germany and recruit thousands of young East German kids into the ideology of Aryanism, Jew hate, and murder. But I only thought about what she said to me years later, after I'd renounced neo-Nazism and dropped out of the Movement. My grandma was dead before I even became a neo-Nazi—and thank God, for it would have pained her. My grandfather stopped speaking to me then and only resumed communication after he found I'd quit, when he told me how happy he was about my decision.

I think my grandparents meant so much to me because at heart they were the least ideological people I knew, and the most human. Just as they had never been Nazis in the Third Reich, they were never Communists in the GDR. They were always just people. And in my life that has been a rare quality.

When I was four, my mother married her boss at the press agency. By then my father, or, as I still knew him, my Uncle Hans, had moved to the radio station.

My stepfather, Edgar, was the opposite of my Uncle Hans in every way. He was a short, bald man who looked a lot like a pig, with thick, round glasses. He smoked cigarettes, not a pipe. What I was most conscious of was his lack of personality. There was no atmosphere around Edgar, as there was around the other adults I knew. He was very bland, almost easy to overlook, except that he was very authoritarian. After Edgar moved in, for the first time in my life, I was hit.

But perhaps the biggest change, the worst blow to me, was that after my mother married Edgar, we moved out of my grandparents' flat into a newly built apartment building in the Lichtenberg district, at the very heart of Communist East Berlin.

Just as Edgar was different from the other adults I'd known, Lichtenberg was very different from Prenzlauer Berg. While each house in Prenzlauer Berg was a little community around a courtyard, the houses in Lichtenberg were prisonlike complexes built on a vast scale. These were the ultimate architectural product of East German communism. They took up whole blocks, and the parks between them were shared by hundreds of families—inhuman concrete abstractions with meager smatterings of green.

I made a couple of new friends, and we ran around the concrete jungle exploring. It was fun for kids because apartment houses were just being built when I moved in, and the whole neighborhood was one big construction site. We used the cranes as tree houses. We ran through the streets when they'd just put down concrete—you can still see my footprints. Uniformed cops and watchmen always came immediately and chased us away, but they seldom caught us, for we were fast at running through the construction sites and good at hiding. It was a big game of hide-and-seek.

But the people in my new neighborhood were always stopping us and saying, You can't do this because it hurts the State or it hurts socialism. I remember one day my friends and I stumbled into paradise: a cake-making factory. We noticed that the workers would put trays of cakes outside to cool and then would leave the cakes unguarded. There was a chain-link fence separating us from the cakes, but it wasn't hard to scale. I'd go over first and lob the cakes back over to the kids on the other side, who'd catch them. Actually, those cakes were lousy. Sweet-tasting garbage, so bad that even at six we weren't tempted to eat too many. Instead, we used them as bombs and missiles and threw them at one another. Once I was caught by a man with a grave expression who told me I mustn't steal cakes because it would "hurt the People's Economy." That was typical of the atmosphere in Lichtenberg. But I didn't care. Why should I? I had no idea what the People's Economy was or why I shouldn't hurt it.

A child notices when adults are fearfully trying hard to behave, and I noticed this atmosphere in Lichtenberg in a way I'd never noticed it in Prenzlauer Berg. You felt that something was wrong, that your parents could get into trouble for something you did. I would later find out that half my neighbors here had worked for the Ministry of State Security—the Stasi—spying on one another and that my family was actually part of a tiny minority in the building that had no Stasi agents, officers, or informants in its ranks.

My first encounter with the Stasi happened another way.

Directly across the street from my family's new apartment, an enormous complex was being built. Once my friends and I were playing soccer and the ball flew over a metal fence into the construction area. We crawled under and found ourselves in front of some big metal objects—I still don't know what they were, perhaps some sort of bunker. Anyway, we used them as goals and continued our game inside the complex.

Suddenly, in the middle of a play, I found myself surrounded by people other than my teammates. They were gray-uniformed soldiers holding guns. I looked at them with awe. I don't think I knew enough to be afraid, but the men looked cold and machinelike. They didn't do anything to us. One of them simply said, "You need to run away fast, or else you'll get into a lot of trouble." They didn't say who they were, and we didn't have any idea. Much later I understood: these were soldiers of the Stasi, the secret police.

At that age I was really innocent about the Stasi, but I had no excuse to be. We were living across the street from the future headquarters of the entire East German secret police. The construction site where we played soccer would soon strike fear and pain into the hearts of millions of people.

BECAUSE MY MOTHER worked from Monday to Friday, I was put into a child-care center, called a "home." It was about forty miles from Berlin. We were taken there every Monday morning in a big bus from my mother's office, and we couldn't come home until Friday afternoon.

I hated the home. The kids were all so dense. I had no friends. Mostly we went into the woods with the caretakers, wandered, played. The caretakers were very harsh young women, very strict. As in Lichtenberg, everything was forbidden, everything would hurt the People or the State or ourselves. You couldn't play in the water, you couldn't do this, you couldn't do that; everything that one can forbid a kid from doing, they kept us from doing. Everything that was any fun was unhealthy, either physically or socially.

There were no uniforms. I always had nice clothes because my
mother often went to West Germany. She was allowed to travel only
for business, but she could go practically anywhere to cover a story.

We all slept together in a big room on cots. I didn't mind sleeping
with the other kids so much, and I don't remember being very home-
sick at nights. It was only the constant control that bothered me. If
we didn't sleep, we were told that we were hurting our bodies and
strictly punished. The worst punishment was having to stand in the
corner for an hour. That happened to me a lot. Some of my earliest
memories are of the solitude and oppression of having to stand there
when I just wanted to move, to leave, to go play.

UNCLE HANS STOPPED coming to visit me when we moved to Lichtenberg, and I had no relationship with my stepfather, Edgar. The only
older man I remember playing with in those first years in Lichtenberg
was my older brother, who seemed like an adult then; I lost contact
with him very shortly after, and to this day I barely know him.

I remember one year, the first winter after we moved to Lichtenberg, when I really enjoyed snow for the first time. It was gray snow,
dirty city snow, but you could do things with it just the same. My
brother and I threw snowballs at each other and built things. The
construction site had become even more mysterious, shrouded in this
gray icy stuff. But it was also dangerous to play in the snow, for you
never knew what was buried underneath. Junk was lying all over the
place—either rubble from the war or new construction.

My older brother and I learned this the hard way. He was climbing up on a snowbank, when suddenly it collapsed a bit and his leg
sank in. Then he screamed. The snow had accumulated over a large
pile of broken glass. When he'd gotten out, we dug in the hole where
he'd fallen and it was beautiful: like a cave filled with buried treasure, jagged green and red and yellow jewels. We reached in, pulled
out some pieces, and cleaned them off. But around us huge red
patches appeared everywhere in the gray white snow. My brother's
legs were bleeding furiously through his pants. I looked at them and
began to laugh. Somehow it struck me as so funny to see the blood
all over the snow. My brother found it funny too. He must have
been in some pain, but he didn't cry. We both sat up there on the
snowbank laughing.

A while after that, I stopped seeing him at all, and I got a baby brother named Jens, the child of my mother and my stepfather. Three years after Jens would come my little sister, Jana. When Jens was born I started going to school.

It was called "Oberschule," and you stayed in the same building for ten years. What I most distinctly remember about school was the smell of cleaning chemicals. The building was white and cold and always smelled of them.

My grandparents' home always smelled of beeswax. Their whole apartment building smelled of it—and of delicious food—and my grandmother was responsible for both these scents. She polished the wooden staircases, just as she took care of the courtyard, sweeping up and planting flowers. She was an informal sort of concierge, not paid by anyone.

I was allowed to visit on weekends, and, as Jens began to occupy more of her time, my mother let me spend evenings at my grandparents' during the week. Even though I was only six, I got used to riding the subway between Lichtenberg and Prenzlauer Berg alone.

I lived for my grandparents' home and the old neighborhood. Running along the flat roofs of the old houses, you could see much of East Berlin and the television tower in the middle of Alexanderplatz. I knew my mother worked near there.

I knew there were ABV men around me, watching what we did— every block in East Berlin had its ABV, or *Abschnittsbevollmächtigter*, which meant, literally, "person with all power in the district." The ABV man was a sort of neighborhood sheriff, a representative of the People's Police, the Stasi, and the State, there to keep an eye out on the smallest unit of the socialist paradise.

But I didn't seem to notice or care about the ABV in my grandparents' neighborhood, as I did in Lichtenberg. I loved the feeling of being up on the roofs more than ever. I didn't have any particular friends around, but it was much easier to join the neighborhood pack than in Lichtenberg, where the children were not as relaxed and came from Stasi families.

At that time, there was a commune in my grandparents' building. It seems strange now to think that there could have been hippies living a few blocks from the center of East Germany, but protest culture was a reality of life in the GDR. It was tolerated because the government thought it more profitable to spy on these groups than to ban them.

The hippies often invited me into their apartment. The members of the commune all ran around practically naked the whole day, and the windows had no curtains. Every once in a while, you saw a Peeping Tom who'd stop right in the middle of the street and stand staring at all the naked women. I was fascinated with the lifestyle of these people, who really spoiled me. I smoked my first cigarettes there.

My grandmother got along with the hippies. She liked them, and they appreciated her for cleaning the place and bringing them cookies.

Long hair was forbidden in the GDR, but the State had a conflicted attitude about it. Long hair and hippie culture came from the decadent West, but there it had been a protest culture against U.S. imperialism and the Vietnam War and often rather in favor of the Communist bloc. The government tried to co-opt its own hippies, sponsoring peace-protest rallies against the West and allowing hippie rock bands to produce albums with songs that had lots of lyrics decrying the West. (American and European rock albums were allowed if they contained a strong element of protest against capitalist culture. They were pirated by Amiga, the official record label of the GDR.)

The government soon realized that the hippies in East Germany were mostly protesting against their local oppressor, the Communist state, not the West. But the government was also rather overwhelmed by these people, who had no strong ideology and just wanted to live a laid-back lifestyle. And because they nominally represented a movement the GDR felt was, in the international arena, on its side, often the State let them live their own way, somewhat outside the system; often they were allowed to leave the country or be "bought out" by the West.

The system of cash payments for dissidents was one of the most bizarre aspects of the relationship between the Germany my father had abandoned and the one I grew up in. The Communists had spent huge sums building the Wall, and now, twenty years later, through the finagling of lawyers on both sides, they were selling their own citizens' freedom for cold hard currency. In some ways I have to laugh at my later career—no wonder I eventually was drawn to terrorism; I was living in a state governed by people who behaved like a giant bureaucratic terrorist gang, holding 16 million people hostage and releasing them one by one. As I grew up over the next ten years, these ransom payments would become East Germany's major source of hard currency.

* * *

BACK AT HOME in Lichtenberg, though, I'd begun to fight with my stepfather. He seemed to love me so much less than his other son, Jens. Everything that I did got on his nerves, everything Jens did was fine.

My first distinct memory of him beating me was on the back with a clothes hanger. It had been going on for a long time before that, but it hadn't hurt so much. Usually he just hit me with a belt or a shoe on my behind. He only did this when my mother wasn't around. Edgar came home from the press agency at four while my mother would get home at six, so this gave him two hours to terrorize me. When she came home, he'd act as though nothing had happened. I was scared to tell my mother, because I thought I'd get it from him again.

But one day I told my grandma about it. I must have been almost seven. Edgar had beaten me particularly severely, and I took the S-Bahn from Lichtenberg to her house in Prenzlauer Berg and sat crying in her lap. I always talked about everything with my grandma, because, for the first twelve years of my life, we were closer than my mother and I. My grandma hated Edgar too, and this made her really furious, which was truly a rare sight. She patted my back and soothed me in that gentle way that she had.

"Don't fret about it, Ingo," she said. "Edgar isn't your real father."

This was the first I'd heard of this. I'd never doubted that Edgar was my father. For almost as long as I could remember, he'd been there. The news took a while to sink in, as my grandma explained a few more details to me.

My grandma told me that Uncle Hans was actually my father. This confused me a little at first, but I was so happy to be rid of Edgar that I didn't much care. Suddenly it became clear to me why he always favored Jens and beat only me. He had treated me completely differently from his real son, which was one reason why I could never forgive him now.

"Oh, this is so good!" I said to her, bursting with happiness. And she hugged me and said it was good and that I shouldn't let what Edgar thought upset me.

I didn't think to ask her why Uncle Hans wasn't there then. Those questions only came to me much later. My mother should have told me herself that my so-called father wasn't really my father.

From then on, I came home to Lichtenberg only to sleep and so avoided all confrontations with Edgar. My life was played out on the streets or in other people's apartments. I was always tall for my age— by the time I was twelve, I could pass for sixteen—and this helped me get around East Berlin with less trouble. I spent most of my time at this age over at my grandma's with the hippies.

The hippies were the first truly free people I'd met in the GDR. They did only what they really wanted, and this suited me perfectly. They had no interest in work. Everyone had a bit of money that they got from relatives in the West. The exchange rate was 1 to 10, as I re-call; for 50 West marks, you got 500 GDR marks. That was a lot: you earned a good salary in the GDR if you made 1,000 marks per month, and you paid, say, 37 marks for a three-room apartment. This was the late seventies, but prices in the GDR never changed much from decade to decade. Everything was always cheap. If you had a friend or relative in the West, you had it made. Not all the hip-pies did, but they believed in sharing their wealth with the group, so if one person got some West money, it would keep the commune par-tying for weeks.

I was always going places with the hippies. On weekends we al-ways went to some concert or other, and in summer we always went to the Ostsee. Everyone looked after me because I was the youngest. Sometimes they made sure that I didn't drink too much; other times, that I had enough to drink. After the concert, we usually built camp-fires and slept on the beach.

I had my first girlfriend when I was eleven. She was in the hippie commune and must have been twenty-five or twenty-six. Her name was Elke. We were friends first and then started having sex. I liked it a lot, and all the other hippies thought it was cute that I was sleeping with Elke. I was like a child for the whole group of them, their little hippie kid. Elke was like my mother or aunt, but my having sex with her didn't strike anyone as strange. The hippies didn't really have morals or taboos about things like that, which was what made them so wonderful. Even though it should have been a problem, I remem-ber only good things about my relationship with Elke.

I had to be careful that my stepfather didn't catch on, but by this point he and my mother had pretty much lost control over what I did after school and I was always allowed to sleep at my grandparents'. I'd pretend to be sleeping at my grandparents' and then actually go upstairs, either to sleep with Elke or just to hang out, drinking and listening to music. The idea that I'd one day grow up to be a hippie and live like them made me happy.

A hippie named Ulf turned me on to what is still my favorite music today: Neil Young. I have every album he ever made. I once paid a month's salary to get *Decade,* his greatest-hits collection, on a black-market original from America. (The state-owned Amiga label did not think it was politically correct enough to bootleg.) Even later, when I became a punk and then a neo-Nazi, the only thing I kept listening to over all those years was Neil Young.

Whenever my neo-Nazi friends came into my room and heard "Heart of Gold" or "Like a Hurricane," they would get all excited and upset. "You have the most impossible musical taste, Kamerad Hasselbach," they'd say. "Really decadent and depraved." They all listened to racist bands like Screwdriver, Destructive Force, and Blood and Honor. But if I was depressed, Neil Young was the only thing that brought me back, and whenever the scene became too much for me, Neil could always ease me down.

Anyway this hippie, Ulf, who turned me on to Neil Young even looked a bit like him. He taught me a very important lesson: Do what you want. When you want something to eat, take it. When you want to leave, go.

Once, years later, I was in prison in Keibelstrasse, and I got stuck in a cell with an old hippie. It was Ulf! He gave me a friendly hello, even though I was a well-known neo-Nazi by this time. He didn't care that I fought the socialist state with a swastika—this was right before the Wall came down, and it was every man for himself. Whatever worked against the State, whatever provoked the socialist masters, was fair.

Ulf, the man who'd taught me to love Neil Young and do what I wanted when I wanted, simply said, "I always knew we'd meet again here."

"Why?"

"Because you belong here," he said, laughing in an oddly self-satisfied way. "We all belong in prison here."

"POTENTIAL DISTURBER OF THE
SOCIALIST PEACE"

JUST AFTER JENS was born, I entered the first grade. I attended
Oberschule 31: Hilde Coppi. I liked school better than the home,
though there were many similarities. Most of the teachers were as
harsh as my caretakers had been. They wanted us to learn to live
for our own good, which was for the good of the community and
society, which was for the good of socialism, which was good for
the heroic, never-ending struggle against the forces of capitalism,
Western decadence, and . . . fascism! The GDR had adopted much
of the feel of the previous Fascist society. Yet we were never allowed to forget that *this* Germany—made up of Communists—had
provided the only true resistance to Nazism. We were all anti-
Fascists here.

Our school was named after a German anti-Fascist Resistance
fighter named Hilde Coppi, who had been killed by the Nazis. She
had been executed in the notorious prison at Plötzensee—beheaded
with a guillotine. Many were guillotined in Berlin; you might say it
was our local method of execution. In other cities you were shot or
hung, but in Berlin it was always the guillotine. There was a big
room, and in the middle was the guillotine, looking as fearful as the

pictures of the electric chair from the United States. It was scary to hear about, but at seven you don't think too hard about what it means when someone is executed. I had no idea what death meant, and the teachers never showed us pictures of anyone with their head cut off, though we'd have been interested in that.

Hilde Coppi had a husband named Hans and a son who was also named Hans. The husband Hans was executed, and the son Hans was born in Plötzensee Prison. The Nazis forced Hilde Coppi to bring him to term before guillotining her. I think we were supposed to understand this as another bit of gratuitous cruelty, but in the Third Reich they never killed children or babies of German blood, no matter what their parents did.

The son was still alive, and he would always visit us in the school named after his mother, to try to teach us how to all be good anti-Fascists. The implication was that it ran in the blood, like a gift for music or science. As Young Pioneers—the East German equivalent of Cub Scouts, a required activity—we all had to become good little anti-Fascists. "You *must* do it!" Hans Coppi the Younger would say to us, his voice trembling. He would run his wide hand through his black hair and move his muscular frame around dramatically in front of the class. "You must fight fascism all around you and for-ever. You must fight because of my mother, my mother who was guillotined for your right to live under socialism! The Nazis exe-cuted her, and therefore it is your *duty* and your *responsibility* to keep fighting for her."

I hated Coppi's lectures. He was arrogant, and his every gesture had an air of smugness about it. He came once a week, mostly with the same speech, about the duty to be an anti-Fascist. The more I lis-tened to this boring, repetitive, and wooden little fellow, the less at-tractive "anti-fascism" seemed, the more like a form of oppression. Most of the rest of the class swallowed it hook, line, and sinker, but there was a small group of kids upon whom, like me, Coppi's lectures had the opposite of their intended effect: we were being turned *against* the idea of "anti-fascism."

There was something called the "class book." It was like a direc-tory for the whole school. In it were the names of all the students, their addresses, and their parents' jobs. In our class, however, under the "parents' jobs" column, nothing was printed except next to the names of six kids. By my mother's name it said "journalist," by someone else "cleaning woman," one father was a locksmith, another a garbageman, and so on. But by the names of all the others there was a blank, and it was clear to anyone what the parents of these kids did: they were employed by the Stasi.

I sometimes couldn't believe that they didn't at least try to give them a fake profession or something. Once I asked a couple of kids in the class what their dad did and they said, "I don't know."

"Shall I tell you?" I said cheerfully.

"How would you know?"

"Your father is with the Stasi," I said.

"That's not true, that's not true!" they screamed.

Today we all know it was true. These kids knew at the time but they couldn't say, they'd been instructed many times never to admit it. And besides, they were all little straight arrows. All except one, that is.

There was one Stasi kid who was as bent an arrow as any of the rest of us.

FRANK LUTZ, WHO would go on to become one of the most brutal neo-Nazis in all of Germany, had two parents who worked for the Ministry of State Security. He was a "super" Stasi kid. When I first met him in my class at the Oberschule, he was what we called a real "little Stalinist brat." He even looked Russian, with his round, fleshy face and washed-out blond looks.

His parents were both high officers in the Stasi. He wanted to grow up to get a useful position in the security service himself and work for the safety and security of socialism. He quickly became a Gruppenrat, or group leader, in the Pioneers.

Somehow, despite his despicable background, I managed to be friends with Frank Lutz because he was a fun guy. I met him one day before school started, and he became my best friend.

We didn't hang around so much in school because while he was busy leading the Young Pioneers, I and the other six kids whose parents had ordinary jobs were busy tyrannizing the Stasi brats. They were always dressed neatly in white shirts and pressed slacks, and wore little badges with some socialist father figure on it. The six who weren't Stasi wore torn T-shirts, jeans, and earrings. We were oppositional from the beginning, and even as little kids we saw ourselves as "the Front." The teachers would say, "Take an example from the others"—the Stasi kids—and I'd always say, "Thank you, I'd rather not."

The Stasi kids saw life as one long duty to socialism and the State. For them, it was a holy duty and a great honor to learn Russian, the language of the Soviet liberators. We, on the other hand, didn't feel the duty to learn Russian. I found it fun to learn to speak other languages, but I didn't see it as a duty. I often came to class without memorizing the vocabulary, and I didn't think twice about it. But my classmates all practically cried when it was shown that they hadn't learned the vocabulary or when they were in some other way not given the best marks.

The Stasi kids would come up to you when there was an exhibit about Lenin's childhood in the school auditorium and say, "Oh, I was already there on the weekend with my parents, they took me early." "You went to a Lenin exhibit, you little Red brat? Well, we went to a party!" The teachers constantly punished us for teasing them, but we never stopped. We were already building up deep hatred for the totalitarian state, and these little scions of the state security apparatus were the easiest targets for venting it.

We threw their notebooks out the windows. They always had "1"s all over them. The Stasi children always got "1"s, while we'd get "3"s and "4"s. I remember a Stasi kid holding up his notebook and saying to me, proudly, "Hey Ingo, look, I got a '1'!"

"Oh, fine!" I said and threw it out the window.

One day I noticed another boy in the class above us who was even more rebellious than we were. He actually seemed a little crazy. His name was Frieder Meisel, and everyone called him Freddy.

Freddy was considered one of the worst delinquents and the school had mostly given up on him, but our gym teacher thought he could bring Freddy back into the group. That was the day Freddy shocked all of us: the gym teacher asked him, in front of the class, to bring his sports things with him next time in order to rejoin the team; he hadn't been participating, and usually the teachers didn't bother to force him. In response, Freddy snapped to attention, raised his hand in a Hitler salute—a gesture I'd never seen in my life—and cried, *"Jawohl, Herr Obersturmbannführer!"*

I was impressed. By making a Nazi salute and calling his gym teacher by an SS title, this guy had instantly created a serious Stasi file for himself, possibly even grounds for a jail sentence. Freddy had balls, and I wanted to get to know him.

*   *   *

THERE WERE NO drugs in the GDR, but there was a lot of grain alcohol. By the time I was twelve, I'd become an expert at stealing it. At first I stole mostly for the hippies. I'd spend my afternoons stealing from department stores and supermarkets—anywhere that had liquor—and bring it back and drink it with them. By now there was a substantial punk scene and I'd taken to hanging out with them during the week, when I was at my mother's house.

I'd spend weeks with the hard-core punk crowd in Lichtenberg and then have pastoral weekends with the hippies and my grandmother in Prenzlauer Berg. It wasn't considered a problem to hang out with both of these apparently radically different groups. All the "opposition" groups were still on good terms: the hippies and the punks would go to the Ostsee together, just as later the punks and the skinheads—or "skins," as we called them—would hang out together.

But at the same time there was an undercurrent of violence that I now realize was the beginning of what would happen over the next ten years. Even when I was with the hippies, if an ordinary guy came along, a type wearing a nice shirt and tie, we'd throw him down in the dirt. And these were hippies, who were supposed to love peace and love. But everyone in the GDR was somehow hard. They were all prepared to oppose a society that pretended to be benevolent in order to hide the ruthless violence at its core. Every group wanted to fight with the cops, but nobody could so we fought with each other. The hippies were used to being hassled about their long hair by the cops, so when they saw a regular guy with well-kept hair and tie, they'd attack him.

I began to fight a lot in school when I was eleven. I can't really remember my first fight—I have no idea why it happened or whether I was dressed more as a punk or a hippie then or what my opponent looked like. I don't remember who won, either. None of that mattered. He taught me the first rule of fighting—hit to the nose. Almost any blow to the nose was guaranteed to blind your opponent for an instant—the effects of automatic tears and pain—time enough to get in the next blow and the one after. We both looked good and beat up at the end, with bloody noses and black eyes. It was always for some "serious" thing—because of a girl I liked whom someone else had insulted—the sort of thing that goes on with boys the world over. Later fighting would become a way of life for me, and I would become deadly at all manner of hand-to-hand combat with punks, leftists, and anarchists.

With the punks, I soon improved my understanding of gang fighting, group fighting, which I'd already had a taste of with the hippies. The fights would often happen in discos. It was still ostensibly about someone's girl or because someone had spilled his drink on someone, but then there'd be a rumble and you'd beat up everyone who was dressed differently from you. I started to really learn the fun of violence, especially crowd violence. There's a unique thrill to being in the middle of a violent, dangerous crowd and slugging, slamming, and kicking your way to victory. Each group got more violent. The punks were harder than the hippies, and the skins were harder than the punks, but there was no definite boundary. Still, beneath all the obvious differences in ideology and appearance, it was not about Right or Left. It was about the State.

For my parents' generation it had been different—for them, the GDR had been about striving to establish the first socialist German state in history and make it work—a state of justice and "anti-fascism." But in the state they created—the state I grew up in—there was nothing to strive for except conformity. And if you didn't conform, this "anti-Fascist" state would come down on you with a brutal force reminiscent of the very Fascists they supposedly were protecting you against.

Each youth group had a basic way of fighting the State: the hippies had their lifestyle, the punks stole like maniacs, and the skins used raw, sadistic violence. Three steps to rebellion. The state that oppressed us was literally the extension of the will of our parents, whose generation had established "real and existing socialism."

In my case this was especially true. My father had gone over to radio in about 1970, and he had his own show. He was thus something of a Communist celebrity before becoming the chief editor and the director of all GDR radio. I heard his programs sometimes, but I was never impressed. His programs were for the youth of the GDR: dry, boring reports about what Communist youth groups were doing to help the People's Universe: Today the Social German Youth went to the forest to work out some plan for the good of the People; they achieved what they set out to do and struck a noble blow for the Socialist Youth Movement. . . .

It was pure propaganda—party-line bullshit. I remember listening to it with my punk friends. Kids would come up to me and say, "Hey, man, hear your dad talks real shit on the radio." And I'd nod and say, "Yeah, man, total shit—for the Fatherland." I would say, "Yeah, that's my old man and I don't know him at all. I've never hardly seen him in my life, but I hear him talking shit on the radio all the time." I never thought about it long enough to really get disgusted. It wasn't like it was my dad or even Uncle Hans. It was like this disembodied voice that I knew was my father, trying to brainwash all the kids in the nation even though he never had any part in raising his real son. My father's voice *was* the State, and I directed all my rage at it, rather than at him. He barely existed for me.

GRADUALLY, THE PUNKS split permanently from the hippies, and I went with the punks. The hippies had simply become too "good" for me. It wasn't enough to just protest by waking up when I wanted and sleeping with whomever I wanted and never reporting to work. I wanted to go outside and make a statement.

As a punk with a mohawk, I'd walk down the street in Lichtenberg and the orderly socialist citizens would call me names:

"State enemy!"

"Pig, dirty pig!"

"Rabble!"

It was clear I was making a statement and that they wanted me out of their perfect society as soon as possible. We were already out, we were total outsiders to them, and, ironically, considering we were the ultimate product of the GDR, they saw us as invaders from the West—raving capitalist-anarchist-decadent "West" people. They were terrified of us.

It was while hanging out with the punks that I became friends with Freddy Meisel, the boy who had given the Hitler salute to his gym teacher. Even though he was about my age, younger than most of the other punks, he was by far the toughest of the bunch.

We actually met while stealing. Both of us stole a lot for the older punks, being fast and cagey, and one day we realized that we stole well together. That was the beginning of a long friendship.

We were about the same height and build, Freddy being a bit shorter than I and dark rather than blond. But at night the cops would always mistake us. I was often arrested when they were looking for him, but they would finally recognize him by his tattoos—the swastikas he had gotten in prison and the big "D" on the back of his neck, with the words *"Deutsches Reich"* beneath it. Freddy was a brutal type. Not so intelligent. But he was a tough, funny guy and totally nuts.

Once Freddy and I walked into a zoo with a bottle of vodka and poured it all into the wild pigs' trough. They went at it like alcoholics, and within ten minutes they were staggering around their pen. "Hey, Ingo, that one looks like your stepfather!" Freddy said, and the one he'd pointed at promptly fell down in the mud. A few minutes later another stumbled over him and was also down. We laughed ourselves to death.

When we were thirteen we began to sniff—mostly spot remover or gasoline. We'd start the day by sniffing some gasoline, go out and steal, and then find some hangout to drink our booty in. Most evenings we were too trashed to walk.

When I went home, I always went straight to bed. My stepfather had stopped beating me by this age because I was too big, and I don't think he or my mother even noticed anything. They were both too busy with their work.

At first it was enough for me to run around with green pants and weird hair. After a while I got more into it. I put sayings on my jacket like "Destroy what you destroy," "No one helps anyone," and "You're free when no one is watching you."

It made me happy to see the shocked faces of my neighbors, whom I took mostly for Stasi agents anyway. I felt strong, and I liked belonging to a group that wouldn't take shit from anyone and couldn't be shocked. Once Freddy and I stole some spaghetti with tomato sauce from a store, poured it onto a concrete table at the playground, and ate it with our hands. I'll never forget the faces of the mothers frantically pushing their baby carriages as they rushed off at the sight of us.

It was utterly unpredictable how Freddy would get his kicks. One time he bought a bottle of black-market vodka for 18 marks, a huge sum, because it was Sunday and the regular stores were closed. He threw the bottle into the air and watched it smash to pieces on the sidewalk. He just laughed when I asked him why he'd wasted that perfectly good and overpriced booze.

Freddy and I were often picked up by the cops or an ambulance because we had alcohol poisoning. It's not an exaggeration to say that for six years I was drunk most of the time, when I wasn't high from sniffing glue. Mostly I was both. My stomach was pumped many times.

WHEN I BEGAN my first spray-painting actions, Freddy was with me. We first sprayed near Strausberger Platz—two U-Bahn stops from Alexanderplatz, where my mother worked—on the walls of houses in a fancy residential neighborhood. We sprayed a capital letter "A" with a circle around it: the symbol of anarchism.

After a few weeks, we began spraying swastikas next to our anarchist "A"s. We didn't know then exactly what a swastika meant, but we knew it was the most forbidden of all symbols. We'd never worn a swastika patch or symbol because you couldn't, it was too dangerous, so we had no idea what might happen if one painted this taboo symbol. It had been completely kept out of our lives. The next day, our symbols mysteriously disappeared from the walls.

I was still a punk and following a maxim of Johnny Rotten: "Provoke with all means." Johnny Rotten had once stood with a swastika in front of Buckingham Palace—he was the ultimate star for us, we had all his tapes from the West radio. Both Freddy and I wore mohawks. While we couldn't tell exactly how the good citizens of East Berlin reacted to our swastika graffiti, we could tell exactly what they thought of our hairdos. And our hair annoyed the cops and the ABV men even more.

Every time we weren't looking, an ABV guy would nab us and take us into the local office for a working over. They had these little ABV barracks on every block—a table, a chair, a typewriter, a picture of Honecker—and there was always just one cop in there. He was dressed like a normal cop with a gun, a pad, handcuffs, and a billy club. One of the big goals these cops had was to "scalp" punks, shaving off their mohawks, and one ABV man had his eyes on Freddy.

One day, this ABVer nabbed Freddy, pulled him into his office, and pulled out a big shears. I watched through a window as the cop with the shears in his hand chased Freddy around the desk. Freddy ended this comical game when he grabbed the billy club and tapped the ABV man on the skull with it. The police only carried them along for soccer games or demonstrations and didn't expect to meet serious resistance with the weight of the omnipresent state security forces behind them; for the same reason, the ABV didn't need more than one guy in a little office to terrorize a whole neighborhood, because everyone knew the State stood behind him.

A bunch of other punks and I looked in through the windows and laughed our heads off. We couldn't believe it. It was so excellent. It never occurred to us that this would mean prison for sure for our friend Freddy. The cop wasn't hurt, it was just a light bang on the head. But he was in such shock that he fell back on the chair and sat there dizzy and looking petrified. Then he pretended to be badly wounded, to get Freddy into as much trouble as possible. And fourteen-year-old Freddy Meisel got his first prison sentence. He was locked up for three months. After that, the ABV offices in Lichtenberg always had two men in them.

Our attitude was getting more belligerent. Dead drunk, we hung out in Alexanderplatz and cranked the music of the Sex Pistols, UK Subs, Plasmatics, Fehlfarben, and Hansa Plast. We provoked tourists and policemen. We didn't think about consequences, we didn't care at all.

Naturally we could recognize West Germans easily from their manner and clothes. After he got out of prison, Freddy and I had fun following well-dressed, older men to the bathroom at the U-Bahn stations. Usually at the moment when the man was most occupied, we would jump him from behind, so that, frightened, he would fall against the dirty wall and often lose his wallet in the process. These guys were tourists, and we had a special kind of contempt and resentment for rich West tourists. They came over to East Berlin to take advantage of the exchange rate for a cheap meal and to gawk at the capital of totalitarianism. We always took their money and threw away the credit cards and passports. It was too dangerous to try to use them in the GDR. The Volkspolizei—or Vopo, as we called the green-uniformed People's Police—could stop you and search you, and if you were found with West stuff like that you were really fucked. But the Vopo didn't seem too interested in a basic mugging. One time we saw one of our victims complaining to a policeman, who just shrugged his shoulders. If we'd robbed an Easterner, it would have been more serious. It was one moment when the police and we had something in common: contempt for the Wessie.

*   *   *

DURING THIS TIME our local bar was a place called FAS. Punks, skins, hippies, and hooligans all hung out there. The bar was the property of the State. The same could hardly be said of the people who went there and worked there.

The *Wirt*—the bartender—was a funny guy. There was, for example, in the GDR a brand of popular cigarettes called "Karos" ("Plaids") because they had a plaid pattern on the box. They were strong cigs, really good. They cost 1.60 marks. And one day I asked the *Wirt,* "Do you have any Karos?"

"Yes, but only my own."

"What do you mean, only your own?"

"Yeah, they cost three marks." He was really an okay guy. He always gave us beer and stuff, so it was cute that he went in for a bit of capitalism. There was something vaguely subversive about pretending we could actually barter and set our own prices in a world where everything was fixed.

"Okay," I said, "then I'll buy a pack of Cabinets"—this was another kind of cigarette that cost 3.20 marks.

"Those are also mine," he said, "and they cost six marks."

This *Wirt* had been in jail many times, and he always had a request to leave the country on file. His pub was the sleaziest in Berlin. A lot of the waiters were ex-cons, too; the State sent them because it was thought that there they couldn't be a corrupt influence on anyone but themselves. (The *Wirt* was run over in a car accident and died shortly before the Wall came down. It was sad, he would have loved to have seen that.)

The bar was attached to a larger room that served as a disco. There were about five or six waiters who were always drunk. A pint of beer cost a mark. And you'd always drink ten beers and get drunk. They'd bring food, too, but you had to be careful to order your food from a waiter who wasn't too smashed. One day I ordered a steak with fries and beans. The waiter came with the plate, and he was holding it so slanted that between the kitchen and the table all the beans and fries fell off. Once a waiter was standing about ten feet away from the bar and he called to the bartender, "Hey, I need a bottle of wine." And the *Wirt* just took a bottle of wine with no cork in it and threw it to him, spilling half the bottle on the customers.

*   *   *

BUT THE CLUB was our turf, and even the scruffy staff learned that to mess with us was dangerous. There was a rule that you weren't allowed to stay after 10:00 P.M. in a place that served alcohol if you were under sixteen. Of course, the *Wirt* and his boys had never followed the rule. But once there was a new waiter and he tried to enforce it. We had to make an example of him. We all crowded around the guy when he asked for our IDs, and practically lifted him off his feet to take him into one of the corner booths that couldn't be seen from the bar; then we punched him for about fifteen minutes—nothing permanently damaging but enough for him to remember for a long time. I beat him like a sack of potatoes, like a punching bag—it was fun to practice on somebody like this. As a coup de grâce, Freddy smashed him over the head with an ashtray, and we left him with his head bleeding in the booth like that. It was the first time we'd beaten up an older guy—he must have been almost twenty-five—and it seemed like a real accomplishment. He wasn't seriously injured, but he quit the next day, and the other waiters kept their distance from then on.

Soon after, we started practicing on soldiers who'd come into the place. We had nothing against army people as such—military service was compulsory and everyone had to do it sometime—but the guys who came in wearing their uniforms were making a political statement, as far as we were concerned. You weren't required to wear your uniform on furlough, so those who did we branded as real straight-arrow, party-line, Communist People's Army pussies. And we hated them.

Whenever one of them would come in and walk up to the bar, one of us would walk up to the bar at exactly the same spot, making sure to muscle our way by the soldiers, thereby spilling a drink all down the front of their perfectly pressed uniforms. We also deliberately dropped ashes on them. And when we were feeling real cocky and real drunk, we just walked up and spat at them. Anything to give them a reason to start a fight. After I'd spill a drink on them, one might say, "Hey you asshole, why don't you watch where you're going!"

"Ah, so you come in here looking for trouble?" I'd say.

"Just leave him alone," another soldier would invariably say to his friend, trying to calm things down. Of course we wouldn't let them back out.

Another of our gang would come up: "Are you pushing my friend around, you militaristic faggot?"

At some point the soldiers would feel obligated to defend their honor and a fight would start. Then we could do what we wanted. There was never a risk with soldiers, as long as you could get them to throw the first punch in front of witnesses. Even without witnesses, it didn't matter. Being beaten up by a bunch of fifteen-year-olds was not the kind of thing they would report to their commanding officer. And then there was the problem of jurisdiction: the regular police would be very hesitant to get involved in a military matter because of the bureaucratic complications involved. The soldiers were only under the jurisdiction of the military police, after all. Anyway, we knew the MPs wouldn't do anything to us. We had them between two competing state ministries: the Ministry of State Security and the Ministry of Defense.

Whenever the *Wirt* saw that there would be fighting with the soldiers—he knew our game—he'd say, "Ingo, do me a favor, go outside with them. I don't want any fresh blood in my restaurant."

"Okay, we have to go out now," I'd say cheerily to the soldiers.

If they tried to protest that they didn't want any trouble, we'd grab them by the shoulders and carry them out, saying *"Raus, General, raus!"* Part of beating up soldiers was tearing up their uniforms. We took an almost ritualistic pleasure in this desecration of state symbols. Rip off their medals, walk on their ribbons, pull their damned East German Army pants below their knees. The soldier would then get such shit for coming back with a torn, bloodied uniform that he'd lose his vacation. A German soldier is supposed to be able to protect himself! Especially from fifteen-year-old boys. It made us feel pretty tough. We could take on soldiers of the East German Army.

Once I remember that I personally took on an even older guy in the club and it made me feel especially tough, though there's no real reason why it should have. It was an act of pure bullying and sadism, which acted as a lightning rod for all my hatred for adults and the "respectable" people of East Germany. Normally only the under-twenty crowd hung around and drank in our disco, but one day this older guy came in with his wife. He was a well-groomed, spit-and-polish type, and his wife also looked very proper. They were too obvious to be Stasi; I figured they were just nice boring geezers out to get a little fun by watching the kids cavorting around. I was in the club with Judith, my girlfriend at the time, a huge girl, over six feet, with a great figure—a "super bride," as we called attractive women back then. Judith and I sat down at the table with these geezers, and after five minutes, without any encouragement from me, Judith started to provoke them. "What do you want here, Grandma?" she said to the woman. "Why don't you and the fossil go home and watch TV?"

"Hey, get lost, you silly kid," said the man to Judith.

This was my cue.

"Whoa, are you looking for trouble, Pops?" I said, and before he could answer I emptied my beer glass down the front of his shirt. It felt more refreshing than drinking it. His wife tried to get between us, and that was it.

Judith threw the first punch. She punched the woman in the nose. When I saw how Judith socked the old bitch in the nose, I thought, "Now *this* is a *super bride*!" I grinned and took care of the male side of things, knocking the table over on top of the guy and pinning him to the floor. When I had him down, I beat him and kicked him all over—legs, back, ass, head—until I had to remind myself that if I murdered him in front of a hundred disco goers, it would be hard to cover it up. But I really enjoyed every minute of it. I achieved a rare moment of completely shameless fighting, as if I were Frank or Freddy, thinking only: "You stupid old asshole! You stupid Communist Party conservative bastard, you had no business being here!" I don't know, maybe it was a chance to get my father back for all the beatings he'd given me. God knows, they didn't look all that dissimilar.

Yet at the same time, I remember distinctly that his age, rather than making him seem more fragile, somehow had the opposite effect: it made it seem less possible to me that I could hurt him—and more possible that, if he got to his feet, he could hurt me. If he ever got up, I felt, he could do a lot to me. I don't know why. It was ridiculous. But there it was. Despite the well of meanness and hardness that had been building up in me, I still felt vulnerable when confronted by an ordinary middle-aged East German man. And that made me want to kick him even harder—to neutralize him before he could get up and do anything to me, to beat and kick him so far down that when he got up he couldn't retaliate . . . and, more, so that he would regret ever for one second feeling superior to me, so he would pay for how men like him made me feel every day of my life. He was bleeding all over his face and neck, but I kept kicking him.

There were more than two hundred people in the disco, and they were mostly watching us now, mostly laughing at these two teenagers doing this to the older couple: me pounding the man, Judith doing the same to the woman. The management, the waiters, the bouncers all watched as well. Nobody did anything, for they knew they'd get more problems from the police and the Stasi if they reported something. Then they'd have to testify against us, and they'd get problems from us later. The waiters went on about their business, they didn't see anything.

Finally, we left the two in a bloody heap and went off to dance. Some people in the club helped take them to a hospital. Four days later I got a summons for assault and battery. When the cops said that it was a forty-year-old man who was making the complaint, I broke out laughing. "Is this a joke or what?" I said. "How often do you think young kids like me go around beating up forty-year-old men in crowded public places?" His wife was the only witness. Everyone else in the disco backed up my story, including the people who had helped the couple get up and go to the hospital. The guy had to drop the charges. The club was our turf, and outsiders had to be careful there.

ONCE ONE OF the hard-core punks went too far. Freddy and I were called in as witnesses at his trial. We were supposed to testify against him, but after I'd given my testimony the judge asked me whether I'd been a witness for the prosecution or the defense. At such times I would always mention the honorable qualities and unimpeachable lifestyle of the accused. Most punks stuck together at such moments.

It was clear that there were a lot of us, that you were never alone. When you were imprisoned, and taken to your cell, in six neighboring cells you'd find exactly the same kind of people as you—your friends because you shared a common enemy. It made you stronger. Still, you didn't think what it would be like to get a real sentence. It was like a game.

At sixteen, instead of staying in school, I got an apprenticeship as a bricklayer. Freddy also got an apprenticeship. But we both soon stopped going to work and simply stole as much as we could.

The Vopos checked our IDs all the time. Freddy and I had a standard smart answer when the police asked for our papers: "You can have my ID, it doesn't belong to me anyway. It's *your* ID."

"What does that mean?" the cop would say, annoyed. "It's yours."

"No, we're sure it's yours," we'd say, and then we'd show him inside where it said, in every GDR ID, "This is not the property of the card bearer but of the State."

We'd go back and forth with some of the thicker ones, explaining, "It says it's 'property of the GDR.' Well, *we're* not the property of the GDR!" The implication was that he was. There was always a bit of double meaning to being a GDR citizen, at least in the eighties—even these Vopos knew that it meant they were part of a system that kept them prisoner. They needed to crush us because our defiance was a reminder of their imprisonment, and this sort of reminder usually got us twenty-four hours.

You could fuck around a lot with a cop but never with a Stasi man. That was absolute power, and you knew it. If you fucked with one of them, you'd never get out of prison in this lifetime.

You could easily spot a certain type of Stasi man in Lichtenberg: he would be wearing a suit with a trench coat over it, holding an umbrella. You saw someone standing in a corner for no reason, you felt it. He was usually reading a paper. It was like in a bad film. But it wasn't a blunder that they looked so obvious. This was the strategy, as if they were beat cops. They wanted to let you know they were everywhere.

For every one of these film-spy Stasi men standing on the corner, there were ten who looked perfectly normal—like your mother or your best friend—or who *were* your mother or your best friend. Young people, people with the same rebellion and anger and dreams as you—only it was all a game, they were only doing it to elicit and record your reactions. At my first trial, I met six witnesses to my bad conduct who I never would have guessed were not just ordinary kids. Much later I read in my Stasi file that since the time I was fourteen, I had been watched and followed as "a potential disturber of the socialist peace."

We used to spit at the Stasis' backs when they walked by. They never knew it, but you could feel like you'd attacked them a little. Once or twice I'd called somebody on the street or in a pub a Stasi asshole. Years later, when they had me in jail, the Stasi showed me the places in my file where they'd recorded every such remark.

If you did mouth off to a real Stasi guy, he couldn't arrest you just for insulting him. But I remember one saying to me, "Don't worry, we'll get you. We'll get all of you one day." He was right.

3

MY FATHER'S HOUSE

WHEN I WAS in my mid-teens, a lot of punks started getting thrown into jail. We were all being watched by the police and the Stasi all the time. One of the punks got scared and told the Kriminalpolizei—the Kripo—everything about our petty thefts, and the police arrested Freddy and me. They went nuts when they saw Freddy's black, red, and gold mohawk—the stripes of the West German flag. I also had a big black, red, and gold pin on my jacket. The East German flag was also black, red, and gold, but it had a Communist emblem in the center, and if you wore these stripes, it was clear which flag you were referring to—no one wore the German colors in honor of the GDR.

The Kripo beat the hell out of us; then they cut Freddy's hair and tore up my jacket. After beating us, they booked us for theft amounting to about 5,000 marks. In my case, my family was told that, if we could pay back the entire sum, it could keep me out of jail. My mother came up with 2,500 marks, and my grandmother put us over the top by contributing everything she'd been saving up for my future: 2,700 marks. My inheritance went to one police payoff.

In Freddy's case, things were a bit more complicated. He was a year older than I was, and he had an apprenticeship as a tile layer while I was learning to be a mason. Freddy had been skipping work on an even more regular basis than I had. He always said he figured that the money you could make was useless anyway, because you couldn't buy anything with it.

But in the German Democratic Republic you were not allowed simply to skip work. Everyone had his scheduled workplace, and if you didn't show up, you weren't only fired, you were arrested. So Freddy was prosecuted for "slacking," as well as for theft and a number of other crimes, such as "rowdiness."

The judge asked him before sentencing if he had something he wanted to say. He stood up and said, "I ask for the death sentence for myself."

He was given a year in a prison camp.

I was too young for prison. Instead, I was banned from Lichtenberg, and I got one year's probation from a three-year sentence in a juvenile prison. I was put under the care of the Jugendhilfe, the State Social Youth Service. The Jugendhilfe guys were regular middle-aged types who acted like they were really concerned about turning me around. One of them tried to give me advice about how I should use my free time differently. "You should start hanging around with a different group of people," he said. "Meet a new crowd of young people, not those good-for-nothing punks."

"Sir, I've already done it," I said. "I'm no longer with the punks; as of a week ago, I'm back hanging out with the hippies again."

"But you're going back and forth between two terrible groups," he said, not realizing that I was shitting him, that I'd broken completely with the hippies long before. "They're both terribly antisocial and nihilistic and Western."

I decided to play with them awhile. One time I came in to report to my case officers wearing a backpack that said "USA." The little men flipped out.

"Oh, God, back with the USA and Woodstock! A completely decadent, nihilistic, capitalistic, *kaput* society!"

My antics had convinced them that I needed to be assigned to a work camp. But then I was offered something very unusual in the GDR: a choice. I could choose between a public and a private prison: I could go to a work camp, or I could live in the house of my father, the radio hero of the GDR.

Under the circumstances, I chose to be reunited with dear old Uncle Hans.

I HARDLY KNEW anything about my father, except that he was a well-known journalist. I had no idea how I should behave with him. I didn't know him.

From a circle of completely undisciplined, asocial hippies and punks I moved overnight into an orderly socialist family. Nothing about my life so far could have prepared me for the way my real father lived.

At first I thought I could get used to my father and his wife. But very soon I noticed that they had it all planned out to reeducate me. "What's going to become of you, then?" was one of the questions my father shot at me so often that I could no longer hear it. This question really made me sick: on the one hand because I really couldn't care less about the answer, on the other because I didn't *have* an answer. "All for socialism" was their answer to everything.

My father's wife tried to act like my mother, but it didn't work. To her, I was a sick, capitalist-influenced boy who needed "reeducation," and everything she thought, said, and did around me was directed toward this goal—toward providing the proper socialist model.

My father advised me to pay attention to GDR radio and television so that I would learn about the virtues of our society. I watched and listened, but I couldn't begin to understand what there was to it all. It just sounded like cheap propaganda, the same stuff I'd been fed in school.

For music, they mostly listened to old Communist *Kampf* music— folk songs from the Spanish Civil War. I also enjoyed this music, for there was a fighting spirit in it that I liked.

There was also a fighting spirit in my father that I liked. I'd get glimpses of it sometimes, when he reminisced about his years in prison in the West. I admired what he'd been through and what he'd done in the 1950s—that he'd been an idealist and gone to jail for it. It was fun to argue with him and see his enthusiasm for the Cause: the right to be different, to pursue his noble ideals against a corrupt, oppressive community. It was fun to momentarily see it as he had seen it—and still did see it—even though I knew that now the Cause had come to stand for that oppressive sameness he once had fought. My stepfather, Edgar, on the other hand, was really the "man in the gray polyester suit"—the perfect Communist bourgeois, the total socialist—someone who would never have fought for communism in the West but rather would have become a banker, the same brain in a different suit. My father was the sort needed to found a society like the GDR, but my stepfather was the sort needed to sustain it.

My father had been brave and rebellious when he was young in the West. But since coming to the East, he'd become an upstanding citizen through his propaganda radio show. He resented the West system for what it had done to him, and now his whole identity was bound up with the success of communism in East Germany. He worshipped the state that had respected and elevated him. And so my rebellion against it was the ultimate personal insult to him, a real slap in my father's face. He could never see any parallels between us, even later, after I'd been in jail and been prosecuted by the Federal Republic under the very same laws he had been.

"Ingo, when I was your age, I fought for something important, for socialism," he'd lecture me. "When I was young I was put in jail but for a good cause."

I tried talking with him about why kids in the GDR were different today, so different from the way he'd been or wanted us to be that we felt trapped in the only German state with "real and existing socialism"—the standard government accolade for this ideologically programmed prison in which we lived.

But we couldn't even begin a conversation. To my father, we were all children corrupted by seeds of capitalism, case closed. For him there was nothing revolutionary about the alternative people in the GDR. We were simply anarchists, destroying everything he'd fought to build.

He wanted to make me realize that it was important to live for this society and to fight for it. He wanted me to be a construction worker, because "everyone does what he can" and he himself had been a mason before becoming a journalist.

It's not that I minded manual work—I like masonry to this day—but I also admired his other profession and I wanted to be a journalist as well. I think I would have been good at it. I was always attracted to reading and writing, but I knew there was no point in doing it there. I resented the fact that my rebellious background had

already closed this career path for good, when my father's rebellion
had helped make him a journalist. In my father's socialist paradise I
couldn't even get a job as a copyboy.

At that point, though, I think our relationship might still have been
salvaged. While I hated being in his house and away from my friends,
it was kind of interesting finally to be with the man whom I'd only
known as Uncle Hans. And despite his wooden communism, my father was a funny guy, because he was from the Rhineland.
Rhinelanders are always a bit funny—we Germans usually say it has
to do with the Carnival spirit, because Rhinelanders have the most
raucous carnivals in northern Europe, very Latin and non-German.
Hans could be a jolly beer-drinking partner, when he would loosen up
and make fun of German politics—*West* German politics, never East.

These nights would give me hope that we could eventually get beyond politics. And for quite some time after I arrived in his house, I
had a burning urge to talk to my father on a human level. I don't
know what we would have said exactly—I don't know what a nonpolitical discussion with one's father sounds like because I've never
had one—just normal little things that become important because
you are father and son. But it never happened. Instead he pressed on
trying to make a good Communist out of me, and I gradually lost all
interest in developing a relationship with him.

My father never gave me books to read, but they were all over the
apartment, and I used to read them just to distract myself. There
were novels by Ludwig Renn, an anti-Fascist fighter against the
Nazis. Most of his other novels were also about Communist resistance movements or other left-wing themes. They mostly were disap-
pointingly bad, and, anyway, I already had to read that sort of thing
in school. One I particularly remember liking was *The Moor Soldiers*
by Wolfgang Langhoff; it was about a concentration camp in Burg-
ermoor in Holland. The title was sadly ironic, for these men were not
soldiers but slaves. There was also a famous Communist song of the
same title that we sang in school. It had an oddly cheery, defiant
melody, considering it was sung from the perspective of concentration camp inmates: "We are the moor soldiers, we're marching all the
day—to the moor, to the moor . . ." The Communists always made
everything into a heroic struggle.

In addition to this novel, I also enjoyed some of the plays and poetry
of Bertholt Brecht. But thank God there were also a few adventure

writers on his shelves, or I would have gone crazy. I devoured everything by Jack London with special pleasure. My father liked London because he'd been one of the first socialists in the West—a socialist and a nonconformist, a rebel. It was a socialism exactly the opposite of what I'd grown up under, and I admired it, too: in Jack London you saw socialism before it had become institutionalized. I wouldn't say I liked London primarily for this. His books were mostly good stories, and also I always liked the northern settings of such books as *The Call of the Wild, The Sea-Wolf.* I loved cold, icy climates, and I liked reading about the challenges to a man who tries to survive in them.

Still, the apartment was like a prison. I'd fought the State, and now the State had put me in with its ultimate embodiment: my father. A man who lived, breathed, and farted GDR.

I just wanted to get through my year there and get out.

"INGO'S SLEEPING," MY father said one day when my friend Silvio and another friend rang the doorbell and asked urgently if they could speak to me. My father refused to let them in. They tried to convince him to wake me up, but he sent them away. I wasn't sleeping, but he never told me about their visit. He didn't want me to hang around with "such people."

I only found out through other sources that Silvio Baumann fled to the Federal Republic a couple of days later. If I'd spoken with him that night, I'm sure I would have fled with him. And I would have never seen my father again. I only saw Silvio again in the West in early 1990, almost four years later.

MY FATHER ALSO forbade me all contact with my mother. Today I understand very well why he wanted to prevent me from seeing my punk friends—and I can even see some sense in it, though it actually made things worse—but I still can't understand why he wouldn't let me see my mother. I suppose on some level he blamed her for how I'd turned out. Although she had a helpless, passive attitude toward me and my troubles, she never actively pushed me away. It hurt her deeply when I moved out and cut off contact with her.

After I'd lived with my father for about nine months, I met her secretly one day, and when he found out he got furious and tried to

keep me from ever leaving the house except for classes. This was finally more than I could take. We fought, and he threw me out. I was
relieved to be chucked back out onto the streets the way I had been
when he took me in, having lived all that time with him without having depended on him or learned from him. I was my own man again.
He would have gotten in trouble with the State Social Youth Service
for throwing me out, but we made an arrangement so that the authorities would think I was still living there for the final three months
of my probation.

I went first to my big sister's in Pankow, and the same night I was
back with my old friends in Lichtenberg.

The scene had changed a lot during the time I was away. Many of
the punks had shaved their heads and adopted right-wing poses. The
ones who were left were now fans of new bands like the Böhse
Onkelz, the Bad Uncles—a right-wing band from Frankfurt am Main
that sang songs about football, women, violence, and German nationalism. Later, they were often called a neo-Nazi band, but they
weren't really. It's true that the music was very violent, like everything the skinheads liked, but for us in East Berlin what was important was that it was the newest protest culture from the West.

Many of the East Berlin punks had shaved their heads and become
skinheads. It was a fashion wave from the West—from England, then
through the Federal Republic, and now it had washed up on our
shores, where it was to take its most radical form. It wasn't political
at all but pure fashion. I shaved my head and went along.

I and some other former punks had taken to watching the *German
Weekly Show* from the Nazi era—we didn't really know what we
were doing, it was simply another way to rebel. We had taped them
from West television. They were scenes from the war—the invasion
of Poland, the Russian field campaign, the speeches of SS General
Otto Ernst Remer after he suppressed the plot to kill Hitler in 1944.
It was cool to watch weapons being used and fascinating to see a time
when German men had been on the move. It was the opposite of the
stagnant national pool in which we'd grown up.

The music was always stirring, often Wagner, gigantic—as vast
and ethereal as the concepts the newsreels reinforced: camaraderie,
patriotism, dreams of conquest. There were also some Nazi political
speeches in the weekly shows, some scenes of Hitler, but these
weren't so important. It was more about the soldiers and the music

and the reports from the front. Our crowd wasn't yet really interested in the Nazis; that only started much later. Sometimes someone
would raise his arm high in a Hitler salute, but it was basically a joke.

Most of the people who taped these shows from radio and television were already pretty militant and wanted to go into the army. It
may seem funny that these right-leaning guys would want to go into
a "people's army" that was the embodiment of the State, the Communist vanguard. But that's not how they thought of it, and often
that's the way with guys who like the military. The East German
Volksarmee was a strict, hard army. It was a strong army. It was also,
finally, a *German* army, and this fact carried a lot of weight. The
troops still goose-stepped the way the Nazi armies had. After the
Wall fell some of them stayed with the army. Some went into private
life. And some came to the neo-Nazis.

IN THE MIDDLE of 1986, after I left my father's, I drove together with
Frank Lutz and another pal to the Riviera, an old garden restaurant
in the Grünau quarter and at the time a meeting place for all possible
shady types from East Berlin. We drank a lot and took a lot of
painkillers.

A couple of hours later the police busted us as we were about to set
the Grünau woods on fire. We were immediately arrested—six future
neo-Nazis, including me, Frank Lutz, and Freddy. The others were let
go after a couple of hours, but I was held for three days. We got a so-
called fast trial, where you don't have a lawyer or a real chance to
argue your case but you're also guaranteed not to be sentenced to
more than a year. I got a fine of 1,200 marks. I discovered for the first
time all the things I'd "done" when they read us the court verdict.

I don't believe we did it all, but what can I say? I was so drunk and
high that when I woke up twenty-four hours later in a police cell they
could have told me I'd killed somebody and I wouldn't have known
for sure if they were lying. I don't know now why we would have set
the woods on fire, but I can't say there was a logical reason for much
of what we did back then. I had to take the cops' version of the story,
and they said we'd been trying to do it. They kept me there the
longest because they said I'd been the ringleader. My father didn't
help me this time; he'd thrown me out, and as far as he was concerned his responsibility was over.

*   *   *

AROUND THIS TIME I met Christine. She was a tall, slim, punky girl with long black-brown hair. A few months later, in the fall of 1986, we were married in Lichtenberg. I liked Christine more than any girl I'd ever gone with, but I don't think either of us was exactly in love. There were simply advantages to getting married in the GDR. We got a marriage credit of 7,000 marks from the State, for example, and we got an apartment that would have taken years for an unmarried couple to get. It was a fast way to become independent from your parents. Christine also needed to get out of her house in a hurry because she was having problems with her mother.

For me, it was also a chance to get rid of my name. In Germany you can't change your name as you can in the United States and other countries, but a man can take his wife's name when he gets married. I didn't want anything to do with my stepfather or my father anymore, so I wanted to be rid of both their names. I took Christine's name, which is why I'm called Hasselbach.

4

"THE WALL MUST FALL!"

ONCE A YEAR, in Lichtenberg Park, the government sponsored a festival in tribute to our occupiers: "The Honorary Friendship Festival to Honor the Soviet Troops." In 1987 Freddy and I decided to attend.

Lichtenberg Park was the biggest piece of green in our concrete jungle, and the music, both Russian and German, sounded inviting. Also, we knew there'd be lots of beer. The park was full of scene kids—punks, hippies, skins—normal people, police, Stasi, and Russian soldiers. Somehow, though, it managed to be a relaxed, friendly atmosphere, even though there was hardly a real friendship between most Germans and their Russian occupiers. It was simply a party with free beer and music.

Freddy had just gotten out of jail, doing time for "attempted republic flight" and "slacking/not working," and this was a welcome-home party of sorts. We drank a few beers. An "*Ost* band"—a band from East Germany—was playing, and it actually sounded good. That was a surprise because there weren't many good East German bands; the one exception was the Puhdys, who copied a lot of their style from the Beatles and the Rolling Stones, added lyrics about living in East Germany and freedom and love, and managed to make this absurd mixture sound really good. The band in Lichtenberg Park was one of the many who copied the Puhdys. We drank a lot and began to make wisecracks to people, including cops.

Oberleutnant Schuchard, the neighborhood cop who had often busted us, pulled his enormous frame up—he was almost as tall as we were and twice as wide—and said, "I don't want to see you boys here anymore today. Get lost."

Schuchard was a lieutenant with the Kripo, but he had close connections to the Stasi, and he was responsible for keeping tabs on all the youth gangs. He always knew which bands which groups were into and who was dyeing his hair what color. No doubt Schuchard got word from Stasi informants, but he was also just very interested in what was happening with teenagers. He was sort of a fatherly type. When we'd done some shit in Lichtenberg and got arrested by the Kripo, we always landed up in front of old Oberleutnant Schuchard.

"Yes, yes, Herr Oberleutnant," we said. *"Jawohl!"* We started to make our way toward the gate, but as soon as Schuchard's huge, trench-coated figure had disappeared into the mass of revelers, we went to one of the stands and downed more beers. That was when I did one of the braver and stupider things I've ever done. I walked into the middle of a group of our "liberators," took a deep breath, and shouted, "The Wall must fall!"

Everyone within hearing distance turned to see who had yelled this heresy. Others who probably hadn't heard turned to see why everyone else was looking. The Russian soldiers who spoke German looked outraged. Drunk and thrilled by my own effect, I shouted it again and again. It felt great.

I looked at Freddy, who grinned and held up his beer bottle. "The Wall must fall!" he shouted back, as a sort of toast. It felt like what I'd always wanted to say, and here I was saying it right in the middle of this crowd of assholes.

"The Wall must fall!" I shouted, as though I expected the gawking Lichtenbergers to suddenly rise up and head for the barricades.

Nothing of the kind happened. Everyone kept looking at me. Then suddenly I was grabbed by cops descending from all directions and hustled off out of the crowd, leaving my neighbors to go on partying with their Russian occupiers.

* * *

TWO HOURS LATER I was sitting in handcuffs in front of Schuchard. We were in the cellar of the police station on Keibelstrasse. Schuchard was as furious as I'd ever seen him. Not only had I spoken the ultimate heresy, I'd said it in front of the Russians.

But the old bull wasn't doing the interrogation this time. The crime was serious and political enough that it was a Stasi interrogator. First they took Freddy, and I sat in the holding cell for twelve hours waiting my turn. Finally I was taken into another basement room, filled with smoke.

The Stasi interrogator was a fat little man with glasses in a tight-fitting, maroon polyester suit. He reminded me of my stepfather. He sat in front of a huge picture of Honecker. On the lapel of his old-fashioned suit he wore a Communist Party pin.

"Now, don't *you* make a circus here, or all hell is gonna break loose!"

I had to grin, because I knew Freddy had been here. I knew this look on older people's faces when they'd had a bout of trying to deal with Frieder Meisel. Even though he was my friend, I myself sometimes had problems standing him for twelve hours at a stretch.

"No steam, no struggle," I said cheerfully.

He frowned and offered me a pack of "interrogation cigarettes." While we didn't have a Bill of Rights protecting our freedom of speech or freedom from self-incrimination in the GDR, a prisoner did have the State-given right to drink coffee, smoke, and eat during an interrogation. This was important, as in our society you might spend a fair amount of your life in interrogations. Of course, this is also a standard bit of police procedure that helps to relax prisoners and convince them to spill their guts. I always found it especially sinister, though, that the State provided special cigarettes and coffee for these occasions, and, like everything else, I saw it as a way of getting me to imbibe their system—to make it part of me, to make me accept it by inhaling their smoke and eating their food.

"Thanks," I said. "I only smoke my own brand."

He looked disappointed and then, breathing in as though he were bone weary, he said dead seriously, "Have you ever thought that you could completely destroy your family with these stunts of yours?

Have you thought of the consequences for your mother? And how will things go for you?"

"Well, hopefully I'll be out in time to attend next year's 'Thanks to the Liberators' festival," I said, because for me the whole thing was still a joke. I'd gotten so used to being hassled by the authorities, it was hard to remember what the worst consequences might be. This Stasi man was an extension of the teachers in Oberschule, who were an extension of the caretakers at the home, who were an extension of my stepfather and my real father, and everybody was saying the same thing: conform for socialism.

The Stasi man then made a big show of looking through my file.

"This could really make someone sick," he commented. "What should we do with you? We've worked our asses off our whole lives for guys like you. And now this! If I so much as look at your colleague Meisel, I want to puke."

"Look," I said, staring him in his bloodshot eyes, "I've just sat around twelve hours so I could get a speech on what makes you ill?"

"What did you think? That I'd be waiting here with roses for you?" He was furious now, and I thought, Yes, this is where I want him.

But then he suddenly seemed to have had enough. He jumped up, gathered his papers, and walked to the door. He turned as he was leaving and shot a final blow at me.

"You're going to feel the full force of the law, Ingo Hasselbach. Thank God we in the German Socialist State have ways and means against people like you."

I just grinned at him. I wasn't really scared yet, but I was definitely not as confident as I'd been a minute before. The meeting was ending more abruptly than I'd thought. I'd been counting on twelve hours of back-and-forth, feeding off his fury and trying to play games with his expectations.

But then he simply closed the door and left me sitting in the smoky room, alone with the portrait of Honecker. I lit up one of the interrogation cigarettes he'd left on the table and listened to his footsteps recede down the hallway and others, of more men, approach the door.

WHILE I'D FOLLOWED the path that had led me into this situation, many of my schoolmates had, as might have been expected, gone into the Stasi. It was my luck that one of these boys, whose notebooks I had heaved out the window with such joyful abandon, now appeared at the door with three other Stasi guards to take me away.

Frank had always been a blond, big-eared earnest young Communist. After school, at seventeen, he had entered the Ministry of State Security. After three years of that, he had been assigned here, to guard duty in the Stasi wing of the Keibelstrasse jail.

"Hey, hello, Frank!" got me a kick in the back with his leather boot. The other guards pulled me off the floor. Either out of a sense of responsibility to socialism or simply to impress the other guards, Frank told me what a piece of degenerate capitalist swine I was as they dragged me down the hall and locked me back in the cell.

"I missed you too, Frank!" I shouted as he and the other proud young Stasi guards marched back down the hall.

KEIBELSTRASSE WAS AN old jail. It had been used by the Gestapo, so the Stasi were following in good police tradition. I was being held in protective custody in a small six-story red-brick building inside the courtyard of the complex.

Sometime during the next twenty-four hours, I figured out a neat trick: if you pumped out all the water in the cell's toilet, you could speak through it. You pumped it really fast with the toilet brush and it formed a suction and all the water went away. It took a long time for the water to come back, and in the meantime the empty toilet bowl became a receiver and the pipe became a kind of phone line. I talked to somebody a few stories above me on the toilet line, a woman. I knew the prisoner must be on the sixth floor, because that's where they held all the women.

After a few pleasantries, I asked, "What's your name?"

"Birgitt," said the voice in my toilet.

"What district are you from?" I said.

"Lichtenberg."

We went on a minute or two more until we figured out that we knew each other! This was Birgitt from my class at school—she was one of the six who hadn't been Stasi kids. You couldn't tell anything from voices because they were so echoey and distorted by the pipe.

"Hey, Ingo!"

"Hey, Birgitt."

And then the pipes filled up with water again, but after much work with our brushes we reestablished our lines of communication.

Birgitt was sitting in protective custody with another girl named Uta. "Hello, Uta!"

"Hello, Ingo! Birgitt says you're okay. It sucks here, doesn't it?"

Uta had murdered a Stasi man. Or rather, she'd pushed him down a staircase and he'd died as a result. He'd tried to rape her, she said. Now they were interrogating her about it and she was getting lots of physical and psychological abuse from them.

"What are you here for, Birgitt?"

"I tried to leave—to Czechoslovakia. What did you do, Ingo?"

"I yelled, 'The Wall must fall!' in the middle of a crowd of Stasi men and Russian soldiers."

"You always were an idiot!"

I explained to her that crazy Freddy was here with me, too, and through the toilet we talked about school, society, our lives. We laughed about some of our old teachers, and Birgitt hooted when I told her that big-eared Stasi-suck Frank had just brought me to my cell. He had always been a real asshole, we agreed. We talked about Lichtenberg, about Birgitt's job as a clerk at a drugstore, and about what our other friends were doing. And we talked about what would become of us. Birgitt had just been sentenced—three years, six months for "attempted republic flight"—and she was worried she'd wind up in Hoheneck, a terrible women's prison.

UNTIL NOW I'D always kind of enjoyed my cat-and-mouse game with the Stasi. It was also a game with my own emotions, I suppose, playing around with my own rage and fear. I tested how far I could go, but I never really considered what would happen if I crossed the line. They'd said, "Someday we'll get you." And now, in January 1987, they had me. And the games were over.

There were many interrogations conducted by different Stasi people. There were more smoke-filled basement rooms and more fat men like my stepfather sitting under pictures of Honecker.

In one room I was interrogated by four people at once, my hands cuffed behind my back. A woman came in, and she was one of the most frightening-looking people I'd ever seen. She made the cops and Stasi men look like Young Pioneers. With her tightly pulled back blond hair and her tight-fitting black suit, she could have been an SS officer. She put her briefcase down on the table, spun around, and yelled into my face, "You pig, you want to ruin the State? You're a low-down, weak swine! You're a traitor to the Fatherland! A vermin who needs to be sterilized for the health of the body of the people!"

She went on and on like that for about fifteen minutes as the four Stasi men looked on with what seemed like awe. Finally I asked one of them—they felt like my friends now—"Hey, what's going on? Who is this lady?"

The woman spun around and snapped at me, "I'm your prosecuting attorney, you fool!"

She was also Freddy Meisel's prosecuting attorney, and we each got a prison sentence of one year, which was the maximum allowable because we'd been given a "quick trial." A quick trial was less bureaucratic, and there was no audience present. It was like a plea bargain, only they took the time to get up and insult and harangue you in front of the judge, and it turned out to be simply a more public version of my interrogation at the hands of the blond prosecutor.

Freddy and I were both charged with Paragraph 220 concerning *Rowdytum,* which stated, "Whoever makes *Rowdytum* can be sentenced to a prison term of up to five years." This was a so-called "rubber paragraph" because you could easily twist and bend it to encompass almost everything. *Rowdytum* was literally when you destroyed something. I had only said, "The Wall must fall." But they said that it applied under the paragraph because my statement was "an attack on the Anti-Fascist Protection Wall." I didn't believe they could put me in jail for this absurd charge. I thought, No, for this you're sure to get probation.

It became clear when we made our appeal, in which you were always given a defense attorney, that it probably wouldn't have helped us if we'd had a lawyer at the trial. In the appeal, our lawyer asked that the twelve months in prison be commuted to ten months, with two months' parole. Freddy and I complained that he hadn't even consulted us and that, for us, the two months wouldn't make much of a difference. The mild-mannered attorney told us, "Calm down, boys, or you'll just make everything worse." We were sentenced to the full twelve months anyway.

My mother only realized where I was after four weeks. The police hadn't told her anything so that she couldn't make a public protest.

When she was allowed to visit me, she said, "I'll get you a lawyer so you get a fair trial." And I had to tell her, "Sorry, Mommy, I've already been sentenced." She couldn't believe it and broke down crying. I'd also just married Christine, and I had to inform my new bride that I'd be in prison for the next year. She promised to be faithful and to visit me regularly.

PRISON

AFTER MY SENTENCING, I was transferred for the time being to another part of Keibelstrasse Prison, where I was put into a cell with a thin, wispy middle-aged man in a suit who looked a lot like Fred Astaire. But this Fred Astaire had hacked his wife to pieces and put the pieces into a suitcase. When I asked him why he'd killed his wife, he looked at me, laughing: "Because she didn't feel anything." He'd kept the corpse in the suitcase in his house for two weeks. When I asked why he hadn't disposed of it, he said, "I didn't have any time—and my daughter came to visit."

Although I didn't want to hear any more about it, he was always saying "She didn't deserve any better!" In fact, his wife had spent twenty years waiting for him while he was serving a previous sentence for murder. His first murder, as he described it, had resulted from an argument that had escalated into a fight until finally he had smashed the other guy over the head and killed him. Fred Astaire had a deadly temper. It was probably "losing his temper" that had caused him to murder his wife, for I can only imagine that such a temper had become even more explosive over twenty years in prison. Six months after he had got out for his first murder, he killed her. He was now serving a life term.

Putting me, a nineteen-year-old in for the first time, into a cell with this murderer was a kind of joke for the guards, an extra punishment for yelling "The Wall must fall!"

Fred Astaire was very polite. Every morning he got up and shook my hand. Of all the prisoners I was to meet, he was the only one who always wore a suit. He talked to me about his family. He was always getting excited about his two daughters: "The women don't find it necessary anymore to visit their old father, even though I was always there for them. I would so love to meet my grandchildren."

He was not stupid, and, when he wasn't talking about his family, he went on about politics and economics or reminisced about Berlin in days gone by. He'd been in prison for much of his life in the GDR, and he was very nostalgic for his life in Berlin before the city was divided, in his youth in the late 1940s. He had a ready supply of quotes from many authors and was particularly fond of Brecht; he kept a collection of Brecht's poems with him in the cell.

Though he wasn't stupid or irrational on the surface, there was obviously some serious strangeness going on inside, and I slept badly with him in my cell. I was always a little worried he might confuse me with his wife. He's a murderer, I would think, looking him in his pale eyes, but he's actually nuts and belongs in an asylum or a hospital.

When they took me away about a week later to transfer me to a different prison, Fred Astaire gave me his hand and said, very politely, "Do well, my son, perhaps we'll see each other again. You know, the world is but a village."

"I hope we will never see each other again in this life," I said as the guard was closing the door from the outside. "The chances for that, thank God, are not so bad."

I was transferred to a prison called Rummelsburg. It had originally been built in the early nineteenth century as a cloister. During the Third Reich it had been used to house "foreign workers" and then as a prison. The GDR had continued to use it as a prison.

My hatred of "anti-fascism" grew exponentially in this prison, where the German "anti-Fascist" state carried on with the methods and trappings of the German Fascist state. I'd seen enough pictures of Nazis in museums and schoolbooks to recognize that, when I got to prison, the GDR guards were dressed in a way that was reminiscent of the Nazi guards. As they had under the Nazis, the normal police on the outside wore green, while the state security police and prison guards wore black, just like Gestapo men: black uniforms, peaked hats, boots, and riding pants. The hypocrisy of it bothered me more than anything: If you're going to worship power, why not admit it? At least the Nazis had been straightforward in their brutality. These people insisted they were beating you and locking you up for your own edification and for the sake of universal brotherhood.

You really thought about this when you entered what the prisoners called "the Green Hell" and what was officially called the "giving-over station"—the transfer point from green to black. When you were brought in from the outside world into the world of prison, the green police would take you to a cell where they'd leave you sitting for hours until the black guards came for you. In the meantime, you were fair game. The giving-over station was a kind of no-man's-land—while you were there, nobody was responsible for you, so both green and black could do what they wanted with you. You always got beat up here. The green cops would beat you when they dropped you off, then the black cops would beat you when they took you away. You felt a clear message in the Green Hell: "Now we've really got you."

The prisoners wore old police uniforms. The cops had taken off the badges and labels and replaced them with wide, bright yellow stripes on the shoulders and back and legs. Those stripes made it easy to shoot you from a distance. And they were sewn on in a special way—the material underneath was torn out and they were sewn over holes. So if you escaped you couldn't simply cut off the stripes. Your entire uniform would fall apart.

I was Prisoner Number 430064, though everyone would address me as "Prisoner Hasselbach." When you wanted to speak with the warden or a guard, you had to knock and say, "Prisoner Hasselbach would like to speak with you, sir." It was a violation to ever use your name normally. Even when I wrote a letter home to someone—my wife or my mother—I had to sign it "Prisoner Hasselbach."

Inside the prison, you wore normal handcuffs whenever you were out of your cell. But for out-of-compound visits, they put an elaborate get-up on you that made you feel like a serial killer: a chain around your waist that attached to a chain around your arms and another chain down to your feet.

What I really hated was that there was a school opposite the prison gate, and when the kids saw me walking in these chains they laughed.

They found it hilarious that men were chained up like tigers. Their laughing and pointing removed whatever mild enjoyment there was in being briefly outside the prison gates.

IN RUMMELSBURG I was put into a cell with Stefan, a frail, weedy sort of fellow with eyes that had no color somehow but simply looked cloudy. Stefan talked very quietly and in bursts. He'd say two sentences, then be totally quiet for five minutes, and then would come another sentence that apparently had some connection to the previous ones, though it was hard to fathom how. I asked him, for example, why he was here. He shrugged and looked around and didn't say anything for a few minutes. Then he suddenly said, "Yes, I had a cow."

"What?" I said.

"I had a cow."

"You mean you stole a cow?" I said.

Then he didn't say anything for a while, until he blurted, "I—I—*did* something with a cow."

"What did you do with the cow?"

Silence.

"Did you steal milk or what?"

"No, no, I *took* the cow."

"Yeah, you stole it."

"No, no . . ."

We went on like this with no progress for another ten minutes, getting closer to the truth, painfully slowly, until finally I realized where it all was leading. And I said, "So did you fuck the cow or what, Stefan?"

"Yes," he said relieved of a great weight. "Yes, exactly!" Then this young man from the country confessed to me how he'd had sex many times with a cow, until he was caught in the act. Almost lovingly, he described to me his special relationship with animals.

After he'd unburdened himself, I asked him, "What did they give you?"

"They punished me for hurting the People's Economy," he said, sadly puzzled at the idea. He could barely get out "People's Economy," and he clearly didn't understand what it had to do with him. "They punished me because I damaged the State," he said, attempting to make it clearer.

Finally, Stefan gave me the paper on which his sentence was typed. It was every normal criminal's right to receive a copy of his verdict, but political prisoners like me weren't allowed to. In the judgment against him, it was recorded that the cow he had raped had thereafter produced less milk and thus he had committed a crime against the People's Economy. He'd gotten one year in prison.

Stefan was illiterate, so even though he'd been carrying his verdict around in his pocket, he hadn't been able to read it. I read it out loud to him and then took an hour trying to explain it to him, as he got more and more upset. I had to explain every big word to him, and he didn't know the most basic things about his fate, not even how long he had been sentenced for.

"How long do I have to stay here?" he asked urgently.

"Ten months," I said, reading his verdict.

"Ah, ten months," he repeated, as though I might as well have said ten days or ten years.

I think I was the first person since Stefan had been imprisoned who'd really exchanged more than two words with him. The other prisoners and the guards didn't say a word to him because he was considered, along with the child rapists, to be the lowest of the low. During the free hour in the yard, all the other prisoners avoided him, and I was like a big brother for him. That garnered me a bad reputation at first. Other prisoners would come up and ask me if I knew what he'd done. "Yeah, I know," I'd say, "but I also know that he's not all there in the head, so you should have a bit of sympathy. He shouldn't be here, he should be in a hospital."

I wrote to my family on Sunday, and Stefan asked, "Can you write one to my family too?"

"Okay, no problem," I said. "What should I write?"

"Write that I'm here," he said.

"Look, they already know that, eh, Stefan?"

"Write it anyway, that I'm here."

"Okay, Stefan, I'll say, 'I'm still here in Rummelsburg Prison.' And I'll tell a little about it and tell your family that things are going fine and that you're looking forward to seeing them and much love to everyone." I wrote a whole page, and most of it I didn't bother to read to him because he would have had so much trouble understanding it anyway. I wrote letters to his mother and sisters.

Stefan asked me what I'd done to get here, but when I tried to explain that I'd yelled that the Wall must fall, he asked, "What Wall?" It became clear that he knew that there was a Berlin Wall and that it had something to do with the border, but he couldn't understand at all why I would want it to fall or go away. He had no concept that there was anything on the other side of it.

ONE DAY, PERHAPS because I was getting along too well with this sex degenerate they'd hoped would bother me, I was moved into solitary confinement. After all, it was very important to isolate political prisoners from the others, for I might be having a "negative political influence" on Stefan. He cried when I left his cell.

I was put in a subbasement. There was no more noise, except for when the guard brought the food in the morning, afternoon, and evening and pushed it under the door. I had ten minutes of free walking each day, during which I could leave the cell and walk in a fifty-square-foot yard with handcuffs on. When the guard didn't have any desire to let me out of solitary, he simply said it was raining.

If you "misbehaved" in solitary, you were taken to a more serious cell, an "arrest" cell, where there was a wall of bars between you and the toilet, so you had to ring the bell every time you wanted to go. They'd come and enter your cell, open your inner door, wait while you went to the toilet, and then lock you back inside your cage within a cage. It was always dark. There was very little daylight, and there was electric light but they didn't turn it on, except for at night, when they often turned it on to wake you up, to control you. So you lived in semidarkness all the time.

There were prisoners who'd sing in solitary—Freddy, for example, always sang the "Deutschlandlied"—and they put them into an empty cell with a concrete bed in the middle that was called the chain bed. They'd chain you to it and leave you there for up to twenty-one days. The guard would come three times a day to feed you and allow you to go to the bathroom. It was like the Middle Ages.

I passed many days in my ten-by-ten-foot cell, running in circles like a caged animal. I tried hard to distract myself. At first I tried, by knocking, to make contact with some of the other prisoners, but the walls were too thick. Only after I was let out of jail did I realize that Freddy had been imprisoned in the cell directly across from mine.

After a couple of days of solitary I was pretty close to insanity. I would have freaked out, but it wouldn't have made any difference. Nobody was interested in what I did, and no one reacted to me. For days I could hardly put together a clear thought. Finally my nerves were so frayed that I could only cry.

After a few days, though, this horrible state seemed to pass. I could retain my composure and think relatively clearly again. I wasn't swinging on a star or anything, but I didn't feel like I was at the bottom of the world's deepest pit, either. One morning the guard put my meal under the door like every morning. "Thank you very much, Herr Obermeister, and a wonderful good morning, how is the guard's health today?" The guard had no idea how he should react to my exaggeratedly friendly greeting, because I had been totally apathetic until then, depressed and not talkative.

I found myself then on the way to getting better, although it seemed as though all the feelings in me had died. This lack of feeling—a strange detachment—is an awful condition I still fight against today.

After each daily walk in the garden, when the guard took me back to my cell, I would say, "And again, locking up, better lock twice, because you never know—sure is sure!" I would grin at him because I noticed that it got him all excited. Each time I found this an unusually important experience: for a moment, I had proved that I still existed.

I passed most of my time in solitary confinement counting the bricks, the bars, and the rivets in my cell door. Sometimes I did push-ups and knee bends or simply ran from one wall to another a hundred times. When I felt a rush of depression, I'd shake the bars like crazy. I didn't want to cry, because then they would have chained me to the bed.

During the solitary confinement I got my first visit from Christine. In her letters she had written me that she would, whatever happened, stay true to me and wait for me. I looked forward to her visit for days.

At two in the afternoon the guard came and led me out of the cell to an anteroom. There I had to wait with the other prisoners until I was allowed to go in and see her. I was trembling, excited like a little boy at Christmas. An hour later I was led into the visiting room. Christine was waiting for me behind the separating wall. She was wearing a white T-shirt and short cutoff jeans. She looked more beautiful than I'd ever seen her. I sat down across from her.

Solitary confinement tends to ratchet up the importance of your human relationships outside to almost cosmic levels. I'd grown very fond of Christine, but after all we had got married mostly as a lark and out of convenience. But now I really thought I loved this woman, that she was the one woman in the universe who was waiting for me and my universe was only to wait for her.

All I could manage was a toneless "Hello." Then we didn't say anything for a few minutes as I looked at her. It was so hard to say anything, just seeing her was so powerful. Finally I knew I had to begin, for we had only twenty-five minutes left.

"So what's up . . . how are you?" I said.

"I'm probably better than you," she said, oddly distant. "It's nice weather outside."

I looked at her tanned face. "I can't judge that."

"One can see that," she said.

I must have looked terrible, pale as chalk and starved. I didn't know what to say.

Then Christine's tone changed somehow. It got clipped and businesslike, like there was some problem or other that needed to be discussed. I suddenly got stomach pains and looked at her face, trying to search it for signs of what was wrong. She avoided my glance and said hesitantly, "I've met someone, Ingo, with whom I now live."

I wondered for a moment if I was having a bad dream. Then I saw I wasn't, and it seemed like perhaps the saddest moment of my life until then. Everything I'd been waiting for, every hope, had been directed toward this one person. Now they were all being thrown back in my face. It was no dream. I was wide awake, and so was she.

Then Christine looked me in the eyes for the first time and seemed to notice all the emotion that was going on inside of me. I raised my hands high, showing her my handcuffs, as though to show her that I was a prisoner, in case she'd forgotten where we were.

She repeated, "I've met somebody with whom I now live."

Then I was consumed with anger. She's really lucky she's sitting behind that glass wall, I thought. The guard, who was sitting next to me and writing all this down, looked up and laid his hand on my knee. I looked back at him and said, "I want to end this now, because otherwise something might happen. . . . I'll just explode. Please take me away." The guard nodded.

Leaving, I turned around and threw my wife a contemptuous look. I think I had loved her a few minutes before, but now I could really have hurt her. It was a violent feeling inside me—a feeling far more normal in prison than love.

Christine looked back astounded and began crying.

The guard took me back to my cell. Normally after you had a visit in Rummelsburg, you were taken to a gathering cell and from there with the other prisoners to your own cell. The guard had noticed what was up with me and spared me this. As we went by the ante-room, I could hear that many of the prisoners had obviously had more fun on their visits than I'd had on mine. A guard the prisoners called "Good-natured One" took me to the entry of the solitary wing, where the lockup guard took over. He greeted me: "Back from the excursion, Hasselbach?"

I took a deep breath and said, "First, please take off these damned handcuffs very quickly, and, second, if I may give you a valuable suggestion, please stay out of my way today, or something could happen that we'd both regret."

"Don't be fresh," said the guard, but he hurried just the same in taking me back. Back in my cell I thought, I only need a rope to bring this story to an end once and for all. Now everything had happened that could happen. It couldn't get any worse. For some reason I started to whistle happy tunes and talked to myself for hours.

After four weeks I was taken out of solitary and transferred to a section where they did housework. In the meantime I'd become malnourished. I was quickly named a bucket carrier and was responsible for the care of the prisoners in custody awaiting trial. There was no cafeteria, so I would take buckets full of potatoes and meat around to them. After my solitary confinement, the next two months were the purest rest and relaxation.

IN AUGUST 1987 I was moved to Rüdersdorf Prison outside Berlin. Rüdersdorf was built like a concentration camp, with the same long barracks. It was a work camp: reeducation through work. There was a huge concrete fence, watchtowers, searchlights, hounds, machine-gun posts. You'd never even get to the wall because before that there was an electrified fence, then a ditch with a dog run.

In Rüdersdorf you could mingle more with other prisoners. We talked about escape at first, but it was unrealistic. Where would you escape to? You'd escape from the small prison into the big one. If you really wanted to escape, you had to find a way out of the GDR.

Besides, you'd never get out. As in Rummelsburg, the bars were made of a special steel—Swedish steel—that's almost impossible to cut through. The bars had thinner bars within them, and if you cut through one, the others would just roll, so it was impossible to cut through them completely.

Once a month all the prisoners were allowed to see a film. It was always a documentary about economic plans in the GDR or honorary work brigades or some bullshit like that. You had to go to these. If you didn't go to the film, you had to do cleanup duty in the kitchen or the latrine while it was playing. In addition, together with eight other political prisoners I regularly had to attend special ideological schooling so that I would finally grasp the merits of socialism. For Erich Honecker's seventy-fifth birthday and his approaching trip to the Federal Republic, for example, I was assigned to write him a letter showing how I appreciated everything he was doing for me. I wrote Honecker a letter, in which I gave him the heartiest birthday greetings and stressed the complete achievement of socialism; however, I also suggested that he should finally arrange a couple of things that would lighten the load of the people here, such as freedom to travel, freedom of expression, the end of spying through the Stasi, and the freedom to start a business. I signed the letter "With best greetings, your Prisoner from the State Penitentiary at Rüdersdorf." Hardly had I put it into the letter box than I was called in by the prison officials, who read and censored our mail. I was given a violent lecture and forbidden to take part in any more political education.

IN RÜDERSDORF ONE had to work together with about two hundred other prisoners making cement. After a couple of weeks I got so-called cement itch; my skin was covered with pimples. "You need a lot of sun and sea air," the prison doctor said, grinning at his joke.

Each cell in Rüdersdorf held nine beds, a table, and two chairs; the toilet was outside. Though you were with others, you didn't talk much: you were always working so hard that you were tired out. We made large concrete slabs for apartment buildings like the one my mother and stepfather lived in. I found out that all the enormous housing projects in Lichtenberg and Marzahn, including the Stasi Hauptquartier, had been built of materials supplied by prison labor.

The daily routine in Rüdersdorf was very monotonous. We were woken up at 2:30 A.M., and one hour later was roll call. At four we went to work. In the afternoon, at three o'clock, we were brought back. After that we had to do small cleaning tasks until six. We cleaned the cells, passed out food, cleaned the kitchen, the toilets. At seven there was another roll call, and then bed. This weird daily rhythm, without an evening, was hard on all the prisoners.

The GDR needed to keep people in prison for long periods, because without them the economy would never have lasted as long as it did. Even discounting the bizarre ransom received for political prisoners sold to West Germany, the prisoners were a boon to the economy. As in China, they were used as a source of labor. We produced most of the products the GDR exported to the West. We made lamps, tape recorders, stereos. Some products sold under West German brand names were actually produced in GDR prisons.

Everything in Rüdersdorf was about labor. We had a higher rate of production than normal factories. We had to produce twice as much per shift as regular workers, and we were always watched by the guards so we couldn't slack off. There were no pauses. It was not as harsh as the Nazi slave-labor system, of course, but it was in the same spirit. It was supposed to train you to be a better citizen.

One of my main jobs was putting cement into sacks for shipment to France. I also poured concrete slabs. Then I smashed apart old engines from trucks and trains with a big hammer for junk. I also worked in a chemical factory. When I was thrown back into solitary confinement, I worked screwing tiny screws into tiny lampshade clamps. I was given a mountain of screws and a mountain of clamps and I had to do two kilos of them per day. Evening, afternoon, and morning shifts—we rotated every week, in three-week periods.

Freddy's job in solitary was as the final checker on an assembly line that manufactured toy frogs. He had to sit in his cell with a mountain of frogs and check that they all functioned, that they jumped. He did this for two years, and when he came out of jail, he tended to jump a bit whenever he stood or sat in place.

IN RÜDERSDORF NO one used names anymore. Here I got used to my number—430064. Even though there was much more company, there weren't any friendships here. In my nine-man cell everyone tried to use everyone else. I kept aloof because I had seen more than once how young prisoners, after they had gotten close to older inmates, were sexually abused by them. Feelings were an invitation to abuse. Only the hard and the cold were left alone. I think that this attitude acquired in prison was ideal for my later life in the neo-Nazi scene. For many young men prison was a kind of school that prepared them for a life in a community without scruples. The harsh way the prisoners treat one another, the way prison wardens treat prisoners, how your mind works on you in solitary confinement, these are things I still can't completely shake off.

Prison was also the ideal environment for acquiring the rudiments of Nazism. During my stay in various East German prisons, I met several old Nazi war criminals who were more than happy to explain their "glorious cause" to me. Although they were called "war criminals," sentencing was so arbitrary in the GDR that I took that designation to simply be another injustice of the "anti-Fascist" state. I was looking for a new oppositional ideology and was eager to listen to them.

The two old Nazi prisoners whom I got closest to were Heinz Barth, known as "the butcher of Oradour," because he had led the SS extermination of the town of that name in France, and the former Gestapo chief of Dresden, Henri Schmidt, who worked in the machine shop.

Both Barth and Schmidt had been taken into custody in 1987. After the war they had changed their biographies, and both had been living in the GDR for years. Not only had they both lived there for many years unrecognized, they had even risen to fairly high positions in the Leadership Circle of the Communist Party. Barth and Schmidt weren't the only old Nazis who'd found the best refuge was a high post in the Communist Party. It was the best place to hide out if you didn't want to be punished. They had partially changed their identities. For instance, Barth had changed the spelling of his name to Bart and so had slipped through all the screenings. The Stasi had caught them, with the assistance of the KGB, which in the late 1980s had been redoing old background checks on individuals from the Second World War. You'd think it would have been a big embarrassment for the GDR when these people were exposed—and with the help of the Russians, no less—but on the contrary the authorities considered it a mark of their exemplary intelligence work that they'd caught them after all these years.

Heinz Barth, who had received the death sentence in absentia, was, by the time they caught him, a convinced Communist, or rather a convinced Stalinist. He'd gone from one totalitarian system to the other. He had found it proper that they had convicted him. There has to be order, he said. Hitler had imposed one kind of order on Germany, he said, but when that had failed, another kind of order had had to be imposed from the outside, by Stalin. In June 1944, when Barth still believed in Hitler's order, he had participated in what, until the concentration camps were discovered, was considered one of the most notorious deeds of Nazi Germany: the total elimination of the town of Oradour-sur-Glane and its people as a reprisal for the actions of the French Resistance. An SS Obersturmbannführer, Barth had given orders and helped massacre 642 men, women, and children and burn the town to the ground.

Henri Schmidt, the Gestapo chief, was, by contrast, still as much of a Nazi as he'd been in 1945. In a GDR court he had been accused of having said to some kids, *"Heil Euch Werwölfe!"* ("Hail, you Were-wolves!"—a reference to a postwar right-wing group). And then in court, he said "This is not correct. I actually said, '*Heil Hitler Wer-wölfe.*' " He was a real Nazi.

I talked with Henri Schmidt about what he had done during the Nazi years, and he told me why he considered it to have been a great time for Germany: the economy had improved, Germany had been freed from the criminal Versailles Treaty, through which the Jews had brought us to ruin; personally he had felt fulfilled, with an important position in the Gestapo, a job he liked and had performed outstandingly. All the Jews of Dresden had been deported under his orders, and he said he was still proud of this work and found it justified. Germany had had to win the war against the Jews, to protect the population from Jewish infestation and attack.

We had not learned much about the "war against the Jews" in school in the GDR, and during this, my first conversation about the subject with an old Nazi, I didn't really know what to think. I had never met a Jew in my life—at least if I had, I hadn't realized it. There were fewer than a thousand Jews in the East German Jewish community, so they were even more a rarity than in West Germany. Henri explained it mostly in terms of economics: first the Jews had squeezed the German people so they had lost World War I, then they had caused the economy to crash in the 1920s, and finally they had wanted to destroy the German economy after the Nazis came to power.

This old war criminal gave me some of my first ideas about the Nazi period beyond the rote formulas of "anti-fascism" that explained it all as part of the continuous capitalist assault on socialism. He had a strong influence on my future politics. It sounded as though what he had done had been justified: if the Jews had declared war against Germany, Germany had had to defend itself. The way Henri explained it to me, it had been these economic questions that had motivated him and others to act. Racial considerations had come only later. The Jewish bankers and the Jewish Bolsheviks had put Germany into a double stranglehold that—despite all the efforts of good Nazis like himself to break it—had eventually choked the lifeblood out of the Fatherland and left it divided, occupied by Communists in the East and capitalists in the West, with events in both halves controlled solely by Jews.

Of course, Henri also believed the Jews were an inferior, poisonous race. He had been taught this first by his parents and then by the Nazi state, and for him the racial question was settled. Henri was an atheist and had grown up without religion. I liked to listen to him, and I actually found him very likable. It didn't occur to me that perhaps somebody who had been a chief of the Gestapo in the Third Reich was similar to a chief of the Stasi in the GDR.

Henri Schmidt always told me that he had never killed anybody. He had been convicted not because he was a murderer, he said, but because he had been responsible for the *deportation* of thousands of people. Now I see that it was the same thing: he was just as much of a murderer as if he'd shot them all himself because he sent those people to concentration camps and death camps. But at the time, I thought, Okay, Henri hasn't killed anyone. He only deported the people, and he always said he didn't know what had happened to the Jews when they got to the camps. He said he'd just done his job of cleaning them out of Dresden, and what happened to the vermin afterward didn't concern him.

APRIL 20 WAS always a special day in this prison. It was Adolf Hitler's birthday, and the old Nazis painted swastikas on toilet paper that they made into armbands. It may sound pathetic, but it was an incredible provocation. Some of these old prisoners had been beaten by the Communists until they were crippled, and they turned up in their wheelchairs for this macabre ceremony.

Here were the oldest political prisoners in the GDR—some imprisoned since the war—who still hadn't given up their resistance to the
anti-Fascist state. Many of them didn't know anymore how long
they'd been in. They wore their toilet-paper armbands proudly and
proclaimed their continuing faith in national socialism. They hadn't
changed their beliefs at all. We younger political prisoners didn't
know much about their ideology, but we admired their resistance and
saw it as a parallel to our own efforts as punks and skins. They had
held firm, never allowing themselves to be influenced in another direction.

6

EX-CONS, NEW NAZIS

I WAS RELEASED from prison on October 19, 1987, and allowed to go home. But where was my home? I tried to contact my wife, Christine, but she still wanted to stay with her new boyfriend, so I went to my mother's. There I ate lunch and bathed, and in the afternoon I went to report to the police. When you got out of prison you were given a "letting-free certificate," which you had to take to your local police station. If you didn't do this the same day, they could throw you back into prison. At the police station I met Freddy, who had been let out on the same day. Freddy and I went straight away to have a couple of beers, and in the evening the cops arrested us for public drunkenness at a U-Bahn station. We were put into a sobering-up cell, where we spent the night.

We spent the next few days with an acquaintance who was being sought by the Stasi. He was one of the ringleaders of the skinheads who had attacked visitors at the Zion Church earlier that month. The punks had been attending a concert and a meeting of the "Church from Below," a human rights organization, at the church. Churches in Germany are often very tolerant and like to attract young people by putting on things like rock concerts. A troop of about twenty skins had attacked the church and beat up these young people, who were loosely involved in the left-oriented protest movement. Many had been seriously injured, and one minister had suffered a severe concussion.

Now the Stasi really came down hard. Even though the Ministry for State Security lost no love on the Church from Below, it was a great opportunity to crack down on the skins. Everyone involved got long jail sentences, and the GDR newspapers carried daily reports about the first skinhead trials in East Berlin. (Less than two years later many of the participants joined my neo-Nazi commune and became members of my neo-Nazi political party.)

By this point, the protest culture had split between Right and Left, with the Stasi and the State exercising clear favoritism in which side got disciplined most. As the West German state would later favor neo-Nazis over left-wing anarchists, the East German state now favored leftist punks over right-wing skinheads. Both groups were still considered—rightly so—to be enemies of the State, but the skinheads were seen as by far the greater threat. The skins had gotten more radical and brutal, and people who at first had been shocked by an orange mohawk now welcomed it as civilized compared with the new, raw, and vicious bald heads.

Even though most of us had been punks not long before, by 1988 or '89 we saw punks as leftist pawns of the State. We were too afraid to attack the Stasi or the police, so we defined a group of our peers to attack. The State had produced a protest culture, and now this culture had turned on itself in the most vicious way possible. We saw that skins were thrown into jail more quickly and given stiffer sentences than punks for breaking the same laws. The swastika was more provoking to the socialist state than the anarchist "A," so we resented anyone who wore the milder symbol. Once I had spray-painted "A"s and worn a mohawk myself. Some of my own friends were still punks, but it didn't matter to me. And we didn't care if they were in a church or not, it was important to attack them because they were now part of the big Socialist Problem—the leftist hegemony that needed to be slammed, kicked, scared, and brutalized to make room for us to breathe.

After a couple of days the guy we were staying with was nabbed by the Stasi, and Freddy and me along with him. It came out pretty quickly, though, that both of us had the perfect alibi for October 17: on that day we had still been in prison. The Stasi let us go.

We didn't see at first how hard the State would come down on the skins for that attack. But suddenly the Stasi was all over us, and the press was playing us up as the ultimate enemies of the people. As real Nazis.

This was the birth of the neo-Nazis in East Germany. The official papers wrote that neo-Nazis had attacked a church—the State was looking for a sensational excuse to arrest young people and to justify crackdowns. The skins who had attacked the Zion Church were violent and "right wing," but they weren't actually neo-Nazis. But the Stasi wanted a truly worthy enemy: neo-Nazis—real postmodern Fascists. They couldn't find them so they made them up, and in the process they helped create the Nazi problem that still plagues Germany today. Often the logic went like this: "Okay, the State says I'm a Nazi and arrests me as a Nazi. Then I will be a Nazi." That was really how a lot of it got started.

Really harsh sentences against young people were being handed down, often just for yelling "Oi, oi, oi," the skinhead battle cry. The guy we had been staying with got two years and six months for yelling that.

It was an exciting time in general in the GDR. Practically every day something unexpected and radical was happening. In late May 1989 there was a communal election in Berlin. People protested that they weren't going to accept another bullshit Communist election, and the day before the vote they threw stones through the election offices and sprayed protest slogans on them. Many people didn't vote.

For me, protest became ever more associated with the forbidden Nazi past. By the fall of 1987, I'd begun spraying swastikas instead of anarchist "A"s. I'd reached a point where I thought, I've always rejected communism and the idea of the GDR as an anti-Fascist State, therefore I can no longer make any protest from the Left. The only alternative was to orient myself completely to the Right.

NEEDING MONEY, I reported to my old company and started working again. My father-in-law, who also worked in the company, brought me into contact with my wife. Christine and I began an effort to save our marriage.

Freddy, meanwhile, was again in his favorite prison, Rummelsburg: he'd forgotten to report to the police and had failed to show up at work. He had also been given Paragraph 48, which meant he had to obey various control measures of the State. The paragraph was made up of six regulations, including the following: Point 1. Duty to report to the ABV of the People's Police (two times weekly). Point 2. Being tied to your place of work. This second point meant that you could never again change your place of work or your job; normally in the GDR, while you had to work, you were allowed to put in to change your place of work, to go to another factory or a different city. And then there was Point 5, which required the reporting of every private visitor to the police. Even if you'd met a woman, it was illegal to have her over unless you went and reported it in advance and got permission from the police. They had total control of your personal life, and, as they had a second key to your apartment, they could come and break in on you whenever they wanted, generally while you were reporting to them according to Point 1.

Overall, Paragraph 48 was a surefire return ticket to prison. It was a way for the State to get total control of you. It was usually an indefinite sentence, and with many people, once they'd gotten Paragraph 48, the State would keep extending it. In my case and Freddy's, if the Wall had never fallen, we could have stayed on under Paragraph 48 until we went to our graves. A week after being set free from prison, Freddy Meisel was again sentenced to a year's imprisonment. In the following months I visited my old friend in Rummelsburg many times.

While Freddy sat in prison, I was working on living a "normal" life. I went to work regularly, and I started working on getting a divorce. On the day my divorce finally came through, I met at the courthouse none other than Freddy Meisel, who followed me like a shadow. He'd just been let out of jail again, and this time he said he planned to report regularly to the police.

After the divorce decision Freddy and I went for the obligatory glass of beer. I spent an hour with him at a bar, where I confessed to him that during his time in jail, I'd slept with his girlfriend, Mareike, a couple of times. Freddy didn't get pissed off at me: "Better you than some guy I don't know," he said. We parted on friendly terms and arranged to meet over the weekend.

A couple of hours later, I ran into Mareike on the street. She had a black eye. "Freddy has already talked to you?" I said.

She looked angrily at me. "You must be crazy."

I grinned at her. "You certainly deserved it."

She grinned back. "You know damned well why I have a black eye."

We both knew I was the reason for Mareike's black eye. Freddy had all his things in Mareike's apartment and figured she was his alone. He slept with other women, but for every one of *her* flings, he decided she deserved a good little beating.

Some weeks later Freddy was imprisoned again. He'd been in a real fight and had done something to violate Paragraph 48. The court sentenced him to four years, eight months, plus a three-year ban from Berlin. He had to spend the three years after his imprisonment on an island called Hiddensee in the Ostsee. It was a very small island with very few inhabitants. He had nothing to do there but work. At the sentencing he insulted the prosecuting attorney and the judge. He always did so whenever he was given a chance to speak publicly or in front of anyone with any authority. He called them lying swine, hypocrites, perverts. He said he would sooner believe in the innocence of a whore than in justice in the German Democratic Republic. It was brave in a way, but not really, because he'd lost everything anyway, including his mind. By that point he was crazy. He was still a good friend, and it hurt to see what was happening to him—but it was clear that he would never get out again.

WHILE FREDDY WAS whisked back into the bowels of the East German prison system, I rekindled my friendship with Frank Lutz, the little Stasi boy from my class at school. I'd lost sight of the chairman of the Lichtenberg Young Pioneers during my late teenage years. I thought he might have followed in his parents' footsteps and become an officer of the Ministry of State Security. I was therefore surprised when I learned through the grapevine that Lutz was sitting in prison, sentenced to ten months for beating up a deaf-mute.

Apparently they'd exchanged angry looks over something mundane in a bar. But when I ran into Frank later, after he'd done his time, and asked him about it, he explained that, as the Third Reich had argued, he didn't approve of handicapped people—they harm the nation because they cost money "only to exist." It was an economic matter, much as Henri Schmidt had explained the deportation of the Jews. Bad genes also spoiled the Germans' biological heritage.

Frank Lutz, the son of Stasi officers, had become a Nazi.

But the hatred that was to make him into one of the cruelest and most unscrupulous neo-Nazi street fighters in Berlin hadn't come only from an ideological rebellion. It was compounded by his all-too-physical experiences at the hands of the Communist state. Soon after he'd become a skinhead, Frank had been arrested and beaten by the police and had sustained permanent damage to his kidneys and left eye.

Lutz couldn't be let out of custody in this condition, for it would reveal police brutality, so the district attorney issued a warrant for his arrest on the same day. After two days he began peeing blood, and though he kept asking for help no doctor ever treated him; as a result his kidneys were permanently damaged. After a half a year of custody pending trial, Lutz was put on trial. He had to be brought into the courtroom in a wheelchair because he was not able to walk anymore; he was black and blue all over and had swollen legs. This didn't help him, though, for the policemen said they'd beaten him in self-defense and the court believed them. Frank was sentenced to two and a half years in prison for resisting arrest.

Lutz was taken to Neu Brandenburg, the most modern prison in the GDR, where he spent two years in solitary confinement. Neu Brandenburg was a Stasi prison—since Frank was a child of "secret bearers," he couldn't be put into a regular lockup. You might think he'd have gotten better treatment because of his parents, but he got worse treatment. In fact, his parents were involved in this grotesque punishment. They thought that by allowing the State to unleash its full fury on him they could teach him a lesson. His father visited him in prison and said he approved of what they were doing to him because he was an antisocial parasite. His parents were monsters—real swine.

I've always been sure that that manhandling and the two years of torture were part of what made Frank into such an animal after he got out. I knew what one year in less horrible East German prisons had done to me.

One night soon after Frank finished this sentence, I went into another club with him and some of my other friends and I was pretty drunk. At one point I took out my pistol and started cleaning it. The bouncer came over and said, "Are you nuts? You can't do that here! Get out." He then tried to round up all the people I'd come in with and throw us out. I put away my pistol and started walking out with Frank, but then the guy grabbed Frank to push him along. Like so many big guys, the bouncer had a habit of pushing people around and an overestimation of his own physical abilities.

Frank pounced on him the minute he touched him, and they went at it then for almost half an hour, by which point they were both practically about to fall over from exhaustion. It seemed like a perfectly matched fight: the bouncer was bigger but Frank was tougher, and it looked like they'd worn each other out. I thought they'd probably both just collapse and call it a tie. But then Frank did something unexpected. He reached up, grabbed the bouncer by the ears, and bit him on the temple—so hard that blood started spurting out of the guy's head. The bouncer was completely stunned, and Frank used that instant of surprise to summon a final wind and push the bouncer over the railing of the outside terrace and down onto the concrete below. The bouncer was wasted; he didn't even cry out when he hit the ground. Frank started laughing then, strutting around like a victorious gladiator.

We left the club then and did something that reflected our perverse sense of humor at the time: all cars in the GDR were required to have a first aid kit. We broke into a car, stole the first aid kit out of the back, and took it back to the club, where the bouncer lay on the pavement. We then began bandaging the bouncer's head. He opened his eyes, looked at us, and said, "You always rip people apart and then bandage them up?" When we finished our gag, we slapped him and said, "It's okay, you can go home now."

Another time we were sitting in a bar, talking about our school days. A black man, an Angolan, came over to our table and asked Frank, patting him friendlily on the shoulder, if there was a free seat here. Without saying a word, Frank reached into his pocket, pulled out a razor blade, and slashed the black across the face twice. Blood spurted. Frank jumped up and ran. I followed him in order not to be involved in the incident. I didn't think he'd done it because the guy was black or a foreigner—I'd figured there must have been some reason, some fight about a girl or something—but I found out I was wrong. Frank simply couldn't stand the thought of a man with black skin touching him.

In East Germany foreigners had never been the focus of far-right violence. It was always punks or hippies. Foreigners practically didn't exist for us, and when they did they were often untouchable, like the Cubans or the Russians. All foreigners were "honorary guests from a Socialist Brother Country," even if they were just cheap labor like the Vietnamese and the Poles. There was resentment against them because they were thought to have special privileges (even though that was mostly not true). They were hated because the State told us to respect them, but they weren't hated as foreigners per se.

We East Berlin neo-Nazis only became real racists after we came into contact with West German Nazis after the fall of the Wall in 1989 and were indoctrinated with SS books about the "foreigner problem." But Frank Lutz was precocious in his run-ins with the Stasi, and during his time in prison some kind of monster inside him had developed, always waiting for an excuse to come flying out and go on the attack. In some ways he and Freddy had the same disease— a twisting, explosive hatred that, when they were with their friends, lay low and almost seemed not to exist.

THE FASTEST WAY from the Lichtenberg S-Bahn station to Pfarrstrasse was a street called Schwarzeweg—Black Way—which ran along the border of Lichtenberg and Friedrichshain, alongside a stretch of train track. True to its name, Schwarzeweg was a dark little road and a dangerous one, not a place to walk alone. My friends and I often walked there, and we were the main reason why it was best to take another path.

One night I was walking down Schwarzeweg with Frank Lutz, on our way back from a disco. We saw two punks in front of us, and, without exchanging a word, our assessment of the situation was clear: two potential victims.

When we got close enough that it seemed like we'd just walk by them, Frank asked one of the punks if he had the time. An old trick. As the poor guy looked down at his watch, Frank's rock-hard fist smashed into his side.

The other looked at me questioningly, and I thought it over for a minute: Could I take him? With me it was not really ever a pure question of size—almost nobody I met was bigger than I was—but I liked to assess how they were built, if their bodies suggested the strength and agility of street fighters. Looking at this guy, I knew instantly that his didn't. It was officially a "fair fight"—two to two—but it would be anything but fair. He was reedy and flaccid looking, with a pathetic, cornered look in his eyes and in his entire body stance. I was in especially tough shape at the time from working construction, both in and out of prison; after working with stones ten hours a day, grabbing and pounding this punk would feel like playing with a pile of soft clay. The guy wouldn't stand a chance against me, and that was exactly how I liked it. While I was becoming one of Berlin's toughest street fighters, I was in this sense a pure coward: I only began fights I knew I could win.

I'd learned my lesson a couple years back, before prison, when I was drunk and walking home from our local pub, FAS, alone one night. We were having a lot of trouble with a bunch we called the Grufties—an offshoot of the punks who were into Satanism and listened to bootlegged Cure albums and liked to hang around in cemeteries lighting candles. One night I saw a couple of Grufties walking near our hangout, and I thought, "Shit, I'll take both these guys and have a great war story to tell." Not in the mood for subtlety, I walked up to one of them and spat on him. It was really disgusting because the wad of spit caught on his shaggy, electrified mane of black hair and hung there, dripping down slowly. Well, the guy beat me up worse than I've ever been beaten before or after. What was worse, he didn't need help from his friend, who just watched. The next thing I knew, I was woken up by a streetcar conductor; he said he'd seen me lying unconscious on the tracks and had stopped just short of running over my arm. Lying in the hospital with a number of broken bones, I swore this would never happen to me again, and afterward I made a habit of carefully checking out my prey before I struck.

The easiest way to grab a punk is by his elaborate hairdo, and I grabbed this guy's mohawk and ripped his head down, slamming his nose across my knee. I was careful never to knee them in the chin or jaw area because I wanted the excruciating, blinding effect of a hard blow to the nose, which I'd learned back when I was eleven and had had my own nose broken for the first time. When I pulled his head up, his face was streaked with blood and tears, and I could see he couldn't see at all. He raised his hands to protect his face, and I hit him in the stomach. When he lowered his hand, I hit his face, and then he went down.

The other guy was also on the ground, groaning in probably much worse pain than my victim. Frank always hit harder and nastier than I did. As strange as it sounds, even when I was at my most violent, I always had scruples, which is to say that I was always slightly scared something would happen to the guys I was beating up—that they'd die or be paralyzed or crippled by a blow or a kick. Frank had no such scruples, he didn't give a shit. I'd seen him many times deliberately punch and kick people in places you knew could be deadly, such as the solar plexus. When you hit without holding back, it's a liberating feeling. You feel all-powerful. A street fighter with scruples is like a race car that is always being driven with the brakes on. Later, there were situations where—with the right combination of anger and ideology—I too would lose all scruples and try to do the most damage possible. But it never came naturally to me, which is probably why, unlike some of my Kamerads, I never killed anyone.

FRANK AND I hung out a lot in FAS, and we gradually met most of the people in the right-wing scene from all over the city, who were making it their unofficial headquarters.

One of them was a seventeen-year-old named Mike Prötzke. His friends called him Auschwitz because he was always so skinny and unhealthy looking. He was one of the most intelligent of the young right-wingers I met there, and also one of the farthest along in his study of Nazism. His grandfather had been in the SS, and he was very influenced by him. Auschwitz fit in with our set pretty quick and was soon one of the most respected members of the group.

His parents were divorced. His mother worked at a car repair shop; his father was an engineer. She was not political, and he was a purely opportunistic Communist Party member, not out of belief but for the career advantages. Auschwitz would tell me about his grandparents, I don't remember which side, who were both convinced Nazis. His grandmother was as much of a Nazi as his grandfather, he always said. She hadn't been in the SS but had been very active in the National Socialist Party and had told Auschwitz all about it as the best time of her life.

He became a real friend. He invited me to live with him and his mother. As I had no place to live after my divorce, I accepted the offer thankfully. Auschwitz's parents had split up early on, and he had grown up as a spoiled only child with his mother. Just as I had been first a punk, then a skin, that's how he'd grown into an enthusiastic neo-Nazi.

In 1988 Auschwitz was sentenced for the first time for "publicly belittling the crimes of the National Socialist state." The GDR had a

fairly broad interpretation of this statute, which could mean anything from outright Holocaust denial to reminiscing about how the
food had been good during the occupation of Paris. Mike had sent a
postcard with the return address as "Reichshauptstadt Berlin," a
term by which the capital had not been known since Hitler's time.
The verdict read "One year probation."

THE NEXT TIME I was arrested was in June 1988. I was sitting in a bar
with a friend, drinking, when a man came up and wanted to have a
beer with us. We let him buy us a couple of rounds, and then he
began to say that the GDR was a great country and weren't we all
happy to toast Mielke and Honecker. I looked him in the eye and
said, "You're a Stasi man." And he said, "No, I'm not." And I was
arrested for that the next morning. So obviously he was a Stasi man.
The crime was *"offentliche Herabwürdigung"* (public insult). I spent
two months in investigative custody before I was let out; then I was
tried in September and given ten months' probation. I had to report
to the Stasi twice a week. Of course, probation in the GDR was all
relative—you were under permanent watch anyway.

So my friends and I entered our twenties, always in and out of
prison for some offense or other. In January 1988 those of us who
weren't in jail at the time founded the first real neo-Nazi party in
East Germany. Until then the Stasi had simply found Nazis where
there were actually only right-wing skins protesting the State with
symbols that they—and we—didn't really understand. Now we figured it was time to start understanding them. We called it the
"Movement of the 30th of January," named for the date of the original Nazi seizure of power in 1933. We didn't think of it as a party
but as a *Kameradschaft,* the old Nazi term for "brotherhood," and
we called one another "Kamerad."

The seven original members, including Frank Lutz, Auschwitz, and
me, held training sessions in National Socialist thought, read forbidden Nazi books, watched illegally obtained videos of old Nazi propaganda films, and made plans for the future. But in the GDR it was
hard to get accurate information about the Third Reich. Everyone in
the group had either had experiences with old Nazis like I'd had in
jail, had been told about Nazism by a grandparent or relative, or had
stumbled onto some reading material. Frank Lutz had gotten books

about the Second World War and the Third Reich, but all in Russian; luckily he was fluent.

The Movement met in Lichtenberg, in Frank Lutz's apartment. He no longer lived with his parents, the Stasi agents, for after he got out of prison the second time, the State gave him his own place. In the GDR you only got an apartment when you got out of prison or got married—otherwise you had to wait ten or twelve years. It was an odd dual-incentive system. You got it after prison as a kind of resocialization. But not everyone got one. I, for instance, never did.

In the Movement we'd read whatever accounts we could get of the Nazi era—which were very few—and critique them and read between the lines, and Auschwitz would tell us what his grandfather and his grandmother said about those times. It was really a kind of reading circle at first—to bring us all to the same level of understanding about Nazism and how it was the solution to our problems of taking on socialism now.

Auschwitz was very important for our budding neo-Nazi group. Most of us were still just learning the basics of Nazi ideology, while he already knew all about it. He'd gotten a lot of books from his grandparents, and he'd read *Mein Kampf* a number of times. He'd done this all alone. It was great for him to have us to back him up and have our respect. We were his first friends.

THE WEIRDEST PERSON to join our group was a guy whose nickname was "Bendix." He had short, oily, dirty hair. He always wore army clothes, boots, old camouflage jackets, and a gray American Civil War cap from the rebel side. Bendix Wendt did not wash, and he always smelled of corpses—for good reason.

He had old maps from the war and had found Halbe, a battlefield outside Berlin. We decided we'd go there to look around. After the Wall fell, on weekends there were lots of collectors there—you'd meet anarchists, neo-Nazis, war buffs, and antique arms collectors, all scavenging around for weapons, many with metal detectors. But back at the time Bendix discovered it, we were more or less alone among the World War II dead.

When we first went to the Halbe woods it was a strange feeling, because Auschwitz and Bendix had explained the heavy fighting that had happened there at the end of the war. You had the feeling you were walking on a piece of history. It was a feeling of closeness to these dead. It was also a feeling of *Deutschtum,* of being close to a Germany that had existed before the GDR. Another Germany, a better one.

We found a number of skeletons, sometimes with their steel helmets on. Bendix spent more time there than the rest of us. He was always in this area, even before the Movement started. He'd discovered it in 1986. He had a sleeping bag and slept in the woods. For him it was a kick to be near the dead soldiers. It gave him a warm feeling. He was always digging and finding soldiers. He would play with the corpses when he was by himself. I don't think any of the other guys could relate to that. Auschwitz dug enthusiastically, but that was about it.

Bendix placed little value on outward appearances and washed a maximum of once a month. "In war one couldn't wash regularly either!" was one of his mottoes. If Bendix happened to wash, he made it a real ceremony. Like so much of what he used, he'd dug up his case and many of his toilet supplies from the woods at Halbe. Bendix preferred to use things that belonged to dead people.

We all said Bendix was crazy. But he was amusing and very useful because he knew a lot about weapons and explosives. He was a weapons fanatic, truly gifted with them. He could repair almost any weapon, having had the most experience with those that had been buried underground for fifty years. Bendix almost always kept some kind of weapon hidden beneath his military clothes.

IN MARCH 1989 our *Kameradschaft* was broken up by the Stasi. Several of our apartments had been bugged, and arrest warrants had been issued for Frank Lutz and Mike Prötzke. Based on his previous record, Frank Lutz got a jail sentence of more than two years. In the search of Auschwitz's apartment, the Stasi found a photo of me with my arm outstretched in a Hitler salute. For that I got probation of ten months and Paragraph 48, the restrictive measures that virtually ensured I'd get caught for something and sent to jail.

Bendix got three years for illegal possession of weapons. What was amusing was that, while he had worse weapons, he was sentenced for having the rusty barrel of an old Wehrmacht rifle he'd dug up. The ballistics experts in court said that Bendix could have gotten the rifle ready to shoot again, though he hadn't done it yet.

When the judge asked Bendix during the trial who his greatest role model was, he answered without hesitation, "Heinrich Himmler, chief of the SS." He got Paragraph 15, which declared him mentally incompetent.

During his time in prison, his father hanged himself. His father had had some high position in the Communist Party and could not come to terms with the fact that his son was in prison because of Nazism and weapons possession. As far as anyone could tell, Bendix had no reaction to his father's death. Occasionally he made jokes about it. His father was nothing more than "a red sock," he always said, and when asked how his father was by someone who didn't know, Bendix simply said, "He's kicked the bucket." But he used the word the Nazis always used when saying the Jews should die—*verrecke,* as in *"Jude verrecke!"* For him his father was only one step up from a Jew, because he was a Red.

Bendix was an ice-cold type.

7

ESCAPE

BACK IN 1986 I'd filed what in East German bureaucraticspeak was known as an *Ausreiseantrag,* a request to leave the country. Even though it was legal, in some ways this was the worst crime you could commit. By filing an *Ausreiseantrag,* you were openly declaring that you rejected the State. It often took many years to process one of these things, but eventually they'd let you go. The West German government was paying more and more to buy refugees, and the East German government, like the rest of the Soviet bloc, was getting more and more desperate for any source of hard currency. Especially in the 1980s, you were simply worth more "to socialism" as a cash payment than you were rotting in an East German jail cell, even considering the value of your labor.

But the authorities did not like to let go of you easily, even if they got a pile of money for it. To them, people who wanted to leave for the West were the ultimate asocials—worse than child molesters or robbers, who at least always had the hope of Socialist Rehabilitation. As someone filing to leave the country, you had to do a lot to prove that you couldn't stand to stay here anymore, and in the process of having you prove this the authorities would make damned sure it was true—that life truly was impossible for you.

Stasi men interrogated me about my exit petition many times: Why did I want to leave the GDR? I said because the State was shit and the youth had no freedom. But was it not my own emotional problem? they asked. After all, everything here was wonderful, it was a model system for human life. Had not my own parents struggled and gone to jail in the West for socialism? Why was I now going into the capitalist hell that my father had so bravely forsaken?

These polyester-suited agents were always trying to be avuncular when talking about the exit petition: Sit down, young man. Would you like a coffee? Some cigarettes? Something to eat? I always told them, "No, I don't want to smoke your cigarettes, I want my own cigarettes. I don't want to drink your coffee. And I'd rather starve than eat your food." You had to show them that you wouldn't have anything to do with them, for if they saw the slightest glimmer of hope of turning you into one of them, they'd never let you go. They were always looking for new double agents, and rebellious, antisocial types made by far the best double agents.

Three years later, at the end of August 1989, I got sick of waiting for my petition to get processed, if it ever would be. The Movement of the 30th of January had been broken up, Frank and Bendix were in jail, and I just didn't see the point of it anymore. I wanted out. By then it seemed like half the young people in East Germany were trying to flee the country, and this mass exodus became one of the main causes of the quick collapse of the GDR. Young people hated the system and wanted out. (The people who are now nostalgic for the GDR were either informants or opportunists or have very short memories.)

I caught a train at the Lichtenberg station that would take me to Dresden; from there I could go on to Prague or Budapest. When I arrived in Dresden, I was immediately stopped by a plainclothes cop asking to see my papers. At the time I only had one of the so-called PM12 passes, which read "Document in place of confiscated personal ID." With a PM12 I wasn't even allowed to travel outside Berlin, not to mention south to Dresden, near the Czech border.

The plainclothes man took one look at my substitute pass and said, as though it was some great revelation, "You obviously want to leave the GDR illegally." I didn't bother trying to bluff my way out, for I knew they didn't need to prove anything beyond their suspicion and, if they thought I was resisting further, they might make things even worse for me. I held out one last hope in the back of my mind: one was more likely to be "bought West" from prison. I was getting pretty desperate.

I was given over to the Stasi, who took me into pretrial detention in their underground complex on the Elbe River, and during two days of interrogation they asked me the same old questions about why I wanted to leave the GDR. It was somewhat ridiculous when I answered freedom of movement, freedom of opinion, democracy, and so on, when I was already a known neo-Nazi. But then the whole exercise was absurd. We were having an argument about the merits of the East German system in August 1989. When they got word back from Berlin on my record, they wanted to know all about what the neo-Nazis were planning and where our secret store of arms and materials and "Western contacts" were. As my Kamerads were mostly in jail and our stuff had been confiscated, I told them all sorts of horseshit just to pass the time. As always they wrote it down, producing reams and reams of documents. They also had detailed records about my family and asked me at length about my stepfather, my father, my mother, and my ex-wife.

It was a few sleepless nights and the usual psychological back-and-forth. You wondered how they could spend days on end asking questions that had such obvious, unrevealing answers, but the Stasi had infinite time and patience and a limited population upon which to work. This was actually a lightning-fast interrogation, for I've known people who've spent eight months with Stasi people talking about even less. They concluded by telling me at some length why I was a class enemy and should be ruthlessly punished. Go ahead, I said wearily. It seemed all over for me anyway. If they convicted me, with my record, I expected at least four to five years.

Eventually, they issued an arrest warrant for me for attempting to cross the border illegally. Fourteen days of detention in Dresden were followed by a month-long tour of the finest prisons in East Germany: Bautzen, Cottbus, Brandenburg, and, finally, back to good old Rummelsburg.

The day I arrived at my old prison happened to be the historic night of October 7, 1989, the fortieth anniversary of the founding of the German Democratic Republic. Soviet premier Mikhail Gorbachev was in town to kick off the festivities, and Honecker gave a speech praising the massacre in Tiananmen Square and said the Berlin Wall would stand for another thousand years.

There were unprecedented mass protests and riots in East Berlin that night. The first we knew of it, the front gates of Rummelsburg swung open and hundreds of human rights protesters, mostly from the Church from Below and other leftist groups, were escorted in at gunpoint. The Stasi had arrested them on grounds of "open incitement," the same charge used against Mike Prötzke.

Inside the courtyard the Stasi started beating the protesters bloody, swinging clubs at them without any cause or provocation. We prisoners looked down from our cell windows, and you could see the blood running down their faces. The protesters were utterly nonviolent, only standing there trying to cover their heads. The other prisoners and I observed this completely one-sided fight, and you could feel anger spreading through the prison air.

Suddenly, out of one barred window, somebody started singing the national anthem of the Federal Republic, the other Germany—which had also been the national anthem of the Third Reich: *"Deutschland, Deutschland über alles, über alles in der Welt . . ."*

As this one voice sang, the Stasi men continued walking up and down the rows of captured demonstrators with nightsticks, beating them. Then suddenly more and more voices in the prison windows started joining in with this one voice, singing the anthem we all acknowledged as the real one.

The chorus from the prisoners seemed to shock the Stasi, who stopped beating the inmates, stopped doing anything, just looked up, dead quiet, listening, astonished. Then the battered leftists in the yard started singing. And suddenly everyone in the prison who was not a guard or a Stasi officer was singing the "Deutschlandlied."

Chaos broke loose inside the prison. The guards and plainclothes Stasi men started running around everywhere. You heard handcuffs clicking, doors opening, and men shouting "Quiet, quiet! Stop singing, you! Quiet, or it's the chain bed!" The roaring of the guards running through the prison, trying unsuccessfully to calm the prisoners, competed with the singing.

It was an incredible moment for everyone—a moment when even the most right-wing prisoners felt a closeness to the leftist protesters because we were united against the universal oppressor, our State, and we sang and sang.

Then there was the sound of cells being opened and prisoners being taken away from the windows and silenced, one by one. The

protesters, however, remained in a large group downstairs and continued to sing. And many of the prisoners, even the ones being
dragged away from the windows, who were being thrown onto their
beds and smothered with blankets and pillows and beaten, continued
singing. Short of mowing everyone down with machine guns, I don't
think the guards could have stopped it.

THREE WEEKS LATER, on October 30, I was let out of prison. Honecker had been impeached, and his successor, President Egon Krenz,
formerly of the Stasi, had issued an amnesty for all those imprisoned
for "attempted republic flight." Still, the Wall was still standing and
an East German citizen could not legally go West.

On November 6 I was able, with the help of a borrowed passport
from my younger brother, Jens, to flee successfully to the Federal Republic via Czechoslovakia. I took the train to Prague, where I intended to go to the West German Embassy. On board I met a man I
knew slightly from Lichtenberg, a rather bourgeois type named
Stemp, who was also fleeing and intending to go to the West German
Embassy to get asylum. But in Prague I noticed on the big blackboard
that a train would be departing for Munich, and I said to Stemp, "Forget the embassy. This is our train." We got on, the train started at once
to pull out, but we knew there was one more checkpoint where we
could trip up, at the Czech border with the Federal Republic.

Things looked ominous at the border, which was being guarded by
the Czech Army—it was very unusual for them to be there. The soldiers acted stern as they checked everybody's identity papers and
stamped them, and I was shaking with fear because I had the wrong
papers with me. I had Jens's papers. I was wearing Jens's eyeglasses
to look more like him, and I could hardly see at all. It was a comic situation, for when the soldier came up to me and said, "Passport," I
could hardly find his hand to put it in. I was holding the passport in
the air, shaking it like an idiot, and the soldier said, *"In Ordnung"*—
"In order" to me in German. The soldiers didn't detain anyone, and
I think by this point they didn't know anymore what they should do.
The border was essentially open.

After the Czech military, we traveled through no-man's-land and
into the Federal Republic of Germany—the West! The German federal eagle was on the signs, and the buildings suddenly seemed in
much better repair, with satellite dishes strewn about between them

and Mercedeses instead of little Trabants and Ladas. "You made it!" I thought, biting my lip. "You finally made it!"

The landscape out my window was all grand forests and beautiful mountains, though I had to strain somewhat because of the eyeglasses; I still didn't dare to take them off. We were riding through the Bavarian part of the triangle where East Germany, Czechoslovakia, and West Germany meet. And from far off, I thought I heard the music of a brass band. First I thought, I'm hallucinating; then I thought, There's a celebration somewhere near here. As we approached the train station, I saw there was a real brass band playing in front of the station . . . for us! They knew the train was filled with refugees from East Germany.

I was looking out the window at the band when I heard awful noises behind me. I turned to see that one of the East Germans was so overcome by joy that he'd gone into an epileptic seizure. He was lying on the floor, shaking and twisting like a madman, his eyeglasses having fallen about ten feet away from him. I had to laugh at the sheer exuberant absurdity of the moment: the brass-band music was getting louder, the train was pulling into the station, and one of my countrymen was having a fit. It seemed typical, somehow. I ran outside as the train stopped and told the first uniformed man I saw that someone needed immediate medical attention. "He's the sixth one today to have a fit," said the officer, shaking his head.

We were allowed off the train only briefly and given free coffee by the West German border patrol, who kept saying "Hearty welcome, hearty welcome to Germany." It was all very quaint and petit bourgeois. The Federal German border patrol then informed us that we must go on to Hannover, where we would be accepted officially and given papers. We did this, and within twenty-four hours I had a West German passport in my own name. I had escaped.

THAT NIGHT, IN Hannover, my traveling companion, Stemp, and I went to a restaurant, and during the meal we started talking with a party of Greeks. They spoke German rather well. Some of them were already second generation. It was clear that these Greeks valued the chance to talk to Germans, and we must have seemed somehow more accessible, because, though we were Germans, we were also foreigners here ourselves.

They invited us to join them. This restaurant was empty except for us, the Greeks, and, a few tables away, three conservative-looking types. These respectable, racist West Germans got very excited about all the foreigners in the restaurant and shouted over to the Greeks that they should go home to their own country and stop using German money. They also shouted that we Germans shouldn't be sitting and encouraging these foreigners. But we ignored them and kept talking with the Greeks. When they found out where we had come from and how we had escaped, they insisted on taking us to a party.

The party turned out to be a wedding in a large Greek restaurant. Some of the guests came from Athens, others from little island villages. They told us about Greek culture and food, and then they told us how bad the economy was back home. It was all new to me. I don't think I'd ever given two seconds' thought to Greece, except as some cliché of ancient civilization and pagan gods. In the GDR I'd sometimes spoken with foreigners at work—Vietnamese or Cubans—but this was really the first time I'd ever had a social encounter with non-Germans. I was thoroughly enjoying myself and learning a lot in the bargain.

Despite my neo-Nnazism, I didn't have any problem talking with a bunch of foreigners. Only three months later, this friendly encounter would have been impossible.

When we left they gave us food and even took up a collection for us. We told them we had money—the federal government had given us 400 marks along with our passports, not that it was enough to live on long. We said we wanted to continue on to West Berlin and find a place to live there. They told us we had to accept the money—a gift to immigrants from immigrants. The German government does not dish out many presents, they said, and we'd soon be happy to have the money. It could be the last time you get money from anyone here, they said.

I didn't think about this experience again until much later, when I saw how ironic it was that the first experience of East Germany's neo-Nazi leader in West Germany had been to get money and presents from dark-haired foreigners.

The next day, I took a bus from Hannover to Berlin. As we had to cross East German territory to get there, we were checked by the Communist border patrol. I was shaking as the familiar uniforms with their arrogant, shiny black boots strode into view. But I reminded myself that the new West German passport in my pocket gave me immunity. The guards took away my passport for the longest time, and when they came back they told me I could go no further into GDR territory. They had me on file as a political troublemaker and said they were glad to be rid of me. So the bus went on with all the other passengers, including Stemp, and I stayed at the border station; after protracted negotiations, the West German border patrol drove me back to the airport in Hannover and gave me free plane fare to Berlin.

I was back in my hometown, but it seemed like another planet. I found Stemp again, and we stayed in a hotel on a side street near the Kurfürstendamm. It was actually on Fasanenstrasse, in a neighborhood that I now know is very popular with Jews who return to Germany, near a bookstore called Literaturhaus that specializes in literature about Jews and the Holocaust, and the West Berlin Jewish community center. It's just another small irony that this was the first place we East German neo-Nazis stayed.

My traveling companion, Stemp, had tons of money because he had worked and saved in East Germany. He had also dealt in black-market goods on the side and acquired West money, which he was now finally able to spend. He went crazy because he'd seen so many West German TV commercials and now was actually able to buy all the products they advertised. I think he really only came West for the chance to buy more and better consumer goods. I didn't know why I was hanging around with Stemp, except that escaping the country together seemed to have established an unpleasantly close bond between us. It was annoying.

While Stemp shopped, I fell ill and stayed in my hotel room. I had a high fever and slept on and off most of the time. During one of my waking spells, the TV was on with the daily news, and the announcer said the Wall in Berlin was open. I thought I was suffering from fever hallucinations. Then I went to sleep again, and when I woke up, Stemp was hovering, panic stricken, over me.

"Wake up, man!" he said. "The Wall is open!"

"What wall?"

"The fucking *Wall*, man! The Wall is open, and half of East Berlin is outside this window."

Dragging myself over to the hotel window, where I could see a swelling crowd on Ku'damm and hear honking horns, made me realize it was true. Every TV station was broadcasting a special report about how the Berlin Wall, after twenty-eight years, was now letting massive amounts of traffic through *in both directions.*

I felt like puking. For me, having finally made the journey over the border, it was like a slap in the face. I sank into a deep depression. It seemed history was laughing in my face: here I'd managed the nearly impossible—and three days later I could have done it all legally. I hardly wanted to speak with my fellow East Berliners, because they'd gone crazy; they'd gotten their welcome money, and, like Stemp, they were spending like maniacs.

After a couple of days in the hotel, Stemp and I realized that we were already half broke. He'd had ten times as much cash as I, but he'd spent it, mostly on a portable CD player and a whole stack of new CDs. But then, I'd gone to a café nearby and had a coffee and a glass of milk and the waitress had come with a check for 12 marks. I'd asked her whether she was crazy, but she'd just looked at me like I was delirious, which I half was. I hadn't eaten anything, and I'd figured the bill would be 3 marks, maybe 4 if it was expensive. But this was the West. It would be some time before I figured out that the prices varied greatly from shop to shop and neighborhood to neighborhood here, for in the East they were uniform. Even though our hotel was relatively inexpensive, I found myself with no choice but to check out and try to think what to do next.

For the next three nights I slept under the stairway of a high-rise building. I had only my jean jacket and a sweater to stay warm, and I got even sicker. I soon started wishing I was back home in my grandparents' apartment in Prenzlauer Berg, where it smelled of beeswax and delicious food. Even my stepfather's and mother's apartment across the street from the Ministry of State Security started to seem cozy and safe.

But I couldn't go to East Berlin. The authorities wouldn't let me in. I thought of calling my friend Silvio Baumann, the man who'd come to my father's apartment the day he went West, because I knew he had come to West Berlin, but he wasn't in the phone book, for he was living with other people. I tried to call my mother because I thought she might know where he was. All the East Berliners were in West Berlin and everybody wanted to call home, and there were ten people in line at every booth. When it was your turn, you never got through; the lines were all blocked, everywhere. Everyone around me seemed happy, but I was miserable and couldn't see that the repression of a lifetime was over. I could only see that I was lost in a crowd, tired, hungry, nervous, with no money, and I couldn't even call home.

Finally I got a connection and my mother told me that Silvio had been there—at her place! When the Wall had come down, he'd im-

mediately come east to look for me! Luckily he'd left her his telephone number in West Berlin. I called that number, and who should
answer the phone but my brother Jens, whose passport I was holding
in my pocket. I asked how he'd gotten over the border without it. He
told me that since yesterday they hadn't even been trying to look at
passports because all the checkpoints in Berlin were mobbed with
people, many carrying enormous boxes of stereos, hair dryers, and
vacuum cleaners they'd purchased in the West. Jens had simply come
through in one of the human streams and was now at Silvio's. When
I got through to Silvio, he invited me over to his place immediately. It
was a two-bedroom apartment in Tegel, near the airport in West
Berlin, and I stayed there on and off for the next four months.

I DRIFTED BACK and forth from Silvio's place in Berlin to a refugee
camp in Hannover and then another one in Hamburg. It was in the
camp in Hamburg that I first met West German neo-Nazis, or rather
they met me.

The West neo-Nazis came to the camp looking for contacts and
new recruits. They had no trouble finding potential subjects like me.
They took a look at my hairstyle and my army parachutist boots, and
they saw a potential Kamerad.

At first, like any political group or religious organization, they offered me literature. The first material I received was about what they
called "the Auschwitz lie." In the GDR we'd learned very little about
the concentration camps, though of course we'd already been contemptuous enough of them to nickname our pal Mike Prötzke
"Auschwitz." But it was not that we'd denied their existence, simply
that we'd resisted having them pushed down our throats as a reason
to be anti-Fascists. Now the West German neo-Nazis presented us
with a radical new idea. They said there were new scientific discov-
eries about Auschwitz that proved that no one had been gassed there.

The material described an American "gas chamber expert" named
Fred Leuchter from Boston, who had traveled to Auschwitz with the
latest measuring equipment and carried out scientific investigations
for Ernst Zündel, the Canadian engineer who'd emigrated from his
native Germany to preach Holocaust denial from the woods of
North America. By measuring the chemical residues in many places
where there had supposedly been gas chambers, the literature said,

and by examining the physical layout of the camp, Leuchter had conclusively proved that people could not have been gassed with Zyklon B at Auschwitz forty-five years ago. It was all a lie.

For us, this was a revelation beyond words. No gas chambers! No mass murder of the Jews! It had all been Communist lies, like so much else.

Auschwitz was the cornerstone of anti-fascism—it was a million Hilde Coppis and the ultimate crime against humanity—and now, in a moment, this American scientist had erased it from reality. The literature emphasized the fact that he had come from the United States, the one country in the world that still executed people with poison gas, and that he was an expert on the subject. The fact that he was American also seemed to make him more impartial.

"This is phenomenal!" we said. "This is wonderful!"

And in this moment of relief and joy for me and other new recruits, I think we passed from being simply rebels against the GDR to being true neo-Nazis. Even as citizens of the GDR, we'd grown up with German Guilt. We'd been told that millions of innocent people had been gassed by our grandparents, and even though we were always told that *our* Germany—the anti-Fascist Germany—had not been to blame, that it had itself been a victim, like the Jews, we still felt guilty. Somewhere in the back of our minds, unless we were real anti-Semites like Lutz and Auschwitz—but maybe even then, or especially then—there was this nagging guilt. This was not the legacy that belonged to a heroic *Volk*. Now this guilt was lifted.

Through these West neo-Nazis who came to the camp, we got the classic reading list of the Third Reich, things that would have gotten anyone twenty years' hard labor in the GDR. I read a lot in the camp: *Mein Kampf,* of course, and many of the modern neo-Nazi works such as the American Professor Arthur Butz's *The Hoax of the Twentieth Century, The Auschwitz Lie* by Thies Christophersen, and the Leuchter Report itself, with its long title: *Auschwitz: The End of the Line: The Leuchter Report—The First Forensic Examination of Auschwitz.* There was an enormous amount of stuff to wade through, and we studied and digested it as though we were learning a new language.

But I would soon meet a man who had far more influence on me than any of these books, a man who would inspire me to fight to destroy the Jew-controlled Federal Republic, restore the honor of national socialism, and establish a glorious Fourth Reich.

8

WALL-JUMPING NAZIS

IN MID-JANUARY 1990 one of the men who had been giving me propaganda material said to me, "Ingo, listen, I've met a few people from the Movement who would like to meet you. They're top people, leaders. It's very delicate. I have to be discreet, and you can't tell anyone."

The West neo-Nazis had focused in on me as more or less the "Führer figure" of the extreme right-wingers among the East German refugees. Although still pretty disoriented, I'd been making friends easily in the camp, though I hardly wanted any. Years of moving among hippies, punks, and convicted war criminals had taught me how to adapt to new surroundings and new people. And I had an immediate advantage among neo-Nazis: I was very tall and blond, exactly the "biological" type of the perfect German leader.

"If they're neo-Nazis, let's have a look at them," I said.

He arranged for us to meet at his apartment. The neo-Nazis would come at an unspecified time. We went by train to Hamburg-Bergedorf, a residential area on the outskirts of Hamburg. I didn't know that my friend's apartment was not even his but a gift to him from one of these "top" people in the Movement whom I was to meet that night.

We hung around the place and drank beer and played cards. We
waited most of the day, and around dusk I got impatient because I
thought someone was pulling our leg.

"Don't worry," he said. "They'll come."

Finally, around 7:30, the bell rang. I went to the door. I opened it
and stood face to face with Michael Kühnen, the founder of postwar
neo-Nazism in West Germany and the most notorious right-wing
leader in Europe.

"Good evening, Herr Hasselbach, my name is Michael Kühnen," he
said, just like that. There was an eerie but impressive calm about him.

"I realize that," I said, a bit taken aback.

He was a legend. I was always reading about him in leftist newspapers—how he was an embodiment of all that was wrong with West
Germany—and now he was standing before me.

Kühnen was much shorter than I was, but well proportioned and
fairly strong, and he had extremely fine, pointed features, like a
Greek statue or real pretty boy. He was in his mid-thirties, and his
skin was almost translucent and very white. He wore his black hair
cut close, shaved off on the sides, with a strong side part, reminiscent
of his idol, Adolf Hitler. And like the original Führer, Kühnen had
pure steel-blue eyes.

His clothes were all black. He wore German Federal Army pants,
a black shirt, a brown belt, a black leather jacket, and black boots.
From his appearance you might have guessed he was not your average businessman, but there was no way to tell he was a neo-Nazi. He
kept his trousers down over his boots. He looked like a rather elegant
man from Hamburg.

We sat down, had some coffee, and started to talk. Kühnen believed that we could actually found the Fourth Reich. While I was
convinced that we could have political influence, I didn't believe it
would happen through a coup. We agreed to disagree on this point,
and he wasn't the least bit arrogant or pushy about his side of things.

There was another man with him: Christian Worch, his deputy. I
had always heard that there was someone else in the background, but
I didn't know anything about him. Worch was taller than Kühnen.
He had a strangely shaped, round face, very pale and rather fleshy,
that seemed supported in midair by an expensive-looking silk ascot.
I later learned Christian Worch was probably the richest man I'd ever
been in a room with, for the neo-Nazi from Hamburg had inherited

millions and, somewhat on a whim, contributed lavish gifts and supplies to the Movement. Like Kühnen he had black hair, cut a bit longer, and his eyes were greenish brown. Worch made the impression of a calculating person, slightly false perhaps, but you had the impression that, whatever he did, he had a well-thought-out reason for doing it. And whereas Kühnen had charisma, Worch was merely cold. I didn't get a good feeling from him during the meeting. I didn't get a bad feeling, exactly, but I figured this was someone with whom I would not get along.

Kühnen wanted to know whether we were aware that they had a tougher orientation than the other right-wing parties in West Germany. He knew the Republikaner were making a big recruitment effort among the East Germans, and he wanted to warn us away from them in particular.

The Republikaner were the most successful racial-nationalist right-wing party in Germany since the war. They were a purely West German phenomenon, founded in 1984 by disgruntled far-right members of the ruling Christian Democratic coalition government who believed that Chancellor Helmut Kohl was moving too far to the center. Their name was an odd choice, for in Germany the terms "Christian," "socialist," "conservative," and "progressive" all had greater meaning and resonance than "republican." The words "German" and "national" were the ones traditionally used to describe a party like the Republikaner, and the name was part of a strategy to make the party's ideology difficult to pin down. The leader of the Republikaner, Franz Schönhuber, was a former SS officer, who, while claiming he was "no anti-Semite," regularly referred in his speeches to the Jews as "a fifth occupying force" in Germany, after the Allies.

"The leaders of the Republikaner and the other so-called far-right parties are money-grubbers," said Kühnen. "Bourgeois careerists who use German nationalism simply to find a political niche for themselves. They are no better than the mainstream parties."

Having already briefly flirted with membership in one of these parties—not the Republikaner but a similar party called the German People's Union—I was fully in agreement with him. These were not parties for young men. Their idea of action was glacial, and they dealt in innuendo and carping rather than all-out attack.

Kühnen knew exactly how to push our buttons; he guessed from the way we were dressed and the fact that we were from the East that we'd be particularly sensitive to bourgeois rightists. And I later found out that while Schönhuber and others like him were making money and gaining influence in German electoral politics with watered-down neo-Nazi ideology, Michael Kühnen remained an outcast and a pauper, though more famous—and feared—than any of them.

"What do you know about us?" Kühnen asked, and I told him.

I knew that Kühnen's political career had begun in high school—while we East Germans were getting smashed and dying our hair green. At fourteen he had joined the German National Party, the NPD. The NPD were the Republikaner of the 1960s: a "respectable" political party that did surprisingly well in local elections around Germany but whose aims were nationalistic in a way that attracted neo-Nazis and whose leadership included numerous former SS officers and Nazi officials. Unlike the Republikaner, the NPD had supported militant youth groups modeled on the Hitler Youth: the Viking Youth, the Young Storm Troopers, and the Ring of Youth. Many of these groups followed an overtly *"völkisch"* philosophy, harking back to that unique version of nationalism—developed before Nazism but eventually absorbed by it—that saw the entire universe as a struggle between cosmic racial-cultural forces culminating in a final clash between the forces of Nordic light and Jewish darkness.

These early organizations had probably reached more young people than any other neo-Nazi organizations before ours in the 1990s. Members dressed up in costumes very similar to those of the original Nazi Brownshirts—black pants and peaked hats, with badges as close to the original swastika as they could get without being illegal. They played march music at their meetings, trained with the Hitler Youth book *The Steel Hat Handbook,* and generally inspired a new generation with a sense of the "glorious German past" under Hitler's rule. Kühnen would later teach us how to use this network of Hitler Youth–style groups, especially the Viking Youth: when members were too young for us, we'd send them on to one of these groups, and they would in turn provide us with mature recruits who had had neo-Nazi indoctrination often from the time they were six or seven years old.

After his graduation from high school, Kühnen had joined the West German Army. He had served from 1974 to 1977, rising to the rank of lieutenant before he was kicked out for his extremist politics. During this time, he had swung briefly to the other side of extremism and became interested in Maoist-influenced West German communism. He was an admirer of the tactics of the Red Army Faction, or RAF, which at the time was terrorizing West Germany with a string of assassinations, hijackings, and bank robberies. While the RAF had nothing to do with far-right sentiments, Kühnen had seen a possibility for a symbiotic relationship. He had believed that if only the violent revolutionary currents from the right and left united, the bourgeois Zionist forces that ruled in Bonn would have collapsed. He maintained this belief later in life, but his youthful flirtation with Maoism had been brief, and like his then idol, Benito Mussolini, he had done an about-face back to the right.

After he left the army, Kühnen had gone public as a neo-Nazi. He had allowed himself to be photographed by an English journalist in black knee-high boots, black shirt, and swastika armband in a room decorated with Nazi flags and pictures of Hitler. This picture had been reprinted around the world and had caused the first public discussion of neo-Nazism in West Germany. It had been an important gesture for the simple reason that it sent the message that there were Germans who weren't just unapologetic about Hitler and the Third Reich but who openly embraced Hitler and his party as the greatest accomplishment of the twentieth century and dedicated themselves to rehabilitating and resurrecting this legacy. Even the hardest right-wingers in Germany had never dared exhibit their views so boldly, and Kühnen had instantly gained a reputation as the leader of a new and far more radical generation of neo-Nazis.

In an accompanying interview, Kühnen had said that the army would be a field of recruitment, that many old Nazis and neo-Nazis were there waiting for their moment; the young officers were behind him but could not reveal themselves because their careers would be in jeopardy. These and other hints of an imminent coup were a pure publicity stunt, to go with the costume and symbols. Yet the basic sentiments he described were certainly real; like the police, the West German Army—and, as I later learned, even more so the Austrian Army—was a hotbed of sympathy and support for neo-Nazis, especially among junior officers.

The spring Kühnen had been kicked out of the army, he had founded the Hansa Free-Time Group, his first neo-Nazi organization. At the same time he had also founded the SA-Storm 8th May, the fighting branch of the Hansa Free-Time Group. From the beginning, his main strategy had been to constantly found new groups to confuse the authorities; also, neo-Nazi organizations could always be banned under the German Constitution, but, by setting up practically duplicate organizations, when one was banned he could simply move the membership to another. The following year Kühnen had founded the organization that was to become synonymous with right-wing violence until its banning in 1983 and that was to make his name as a far-right terrorist: the Action Front of National Socialists, or ANS.

At the beginning of 1979 Kühnen was taken before the Hamburg State Court for the first time for demagoguery and spreading Fascist hate material. His group was accused of having written graffiti on and thrown rocks at the Israeli Embassy and the East German Embassy. And he was suspected of complicity in a much more serious crime: an attack on a NATO post at the Dutch border during which two Dutch soldiers had been murdered. They had been shot from behind, execution style.

Kühnen had never been sentenced for the killing because his involvement couldn't be proved; he had been found guilty only of distributing hate material. (Two others got life sentences, and they are still in prison.)

Then, later that year, he had confessed before another court to possession of explosives. He had planned attacks on a union-owned bank, a newspaper in Hannover, and truck traffic from East Germany. He had let it be understood that if he was sentenced it could lead to new terrorist acts by neo-Nazis, and he had warned the judge, "Think of the Kamerads who stand behind me." He had gotten four years.

By the time Kühnen got out of jail in 1983 the ANS had been banned, so he simply continued his tactic of starting new organizations. In the mid-1980s he had gone to Paris, where he had worked to arrange contacts with French Fascists and build up a propaganda network. When the French authorities had caught up with him with the help of a German investigative journalist, he had been deported; in 1985 a Frankfurt court had sentenced him for dissemination of Nazi propaganda. He had gotten out of prison again in 1988.

KÜHNEN AND I talked for more than twelve hours. I had many questions about various things I'd read over the years, and Kühnen was very patient and polite about answering them all and never pompous.

Finally he got down to what he wanted from me: Did I know any people in East Berlin who would be in a position to found a legal political party—the first neo-Nazi party ever in East Germany? I did, and within an hour we had chosen its name: the National Alternative, or NA.

That night it became clear to me for the first time that now was the time for real political work in the GDR. He also got us excited about opposing the "Jew-controlled Bonn Republic," as he referred to West Germany. Kühnen anticipated sooner than most that East and West Germany would be united within the year, and he convinced us to stop thinking in terms of two separate governments and to realize that German communism was finished.

In one night we set it all up. Kühnen gave us party programs, statutes, everything we needed. The guy in whose apartment we were staying pulled out a typewriter and acted as secretary. With Kühnen's help—he had done this many times before—we wrote out a legal application for approval as a political party. He had everything prepared.

Now we only needed to get to East Berlin to have the National Alternative registered as a party. Under Hans Modrow, the new East German president, all new political parties were being authorized. You could found the German Beer Drinkers' Union there now or the National Party of German Assholes, if you wanted to.

In the meantime, Kühnen kept saying he needed to drive to Holland by morning. He was quite compulsive. But it finally got too late, so he slept on the couch. One thing I found odd about him was that he never ate anything. He had easily had about forty cups of coffee in twelve hours, and he chain-smoked menthol Marlboros—unlike many neo-Nazis, he had no problem smoking American cigarettes. Worch, for example, smoked only German cigarettes and drove only German cars.

OUR TRIP TO East Berlin to register the National Alternative was my first over the border since escaping. But when I ran into trouble with the border control, it made me realize just how much the tables had turned in less than two months.

A Kamerad and I were driving through the customs checkpoint between West and East with a carload of neo-Nazi propaganda material from Kühnen. We had cases filled with swastika flags, stickers, and leaflets.

A customs officer approached the car. "Please show what you have there," he said, pointing to the cases, and my heart skipped a beat. East Germany still existed, and—despite the amazing citizens' storming of the Stasi central headquarters that month—the People's Police was still functioning and could still arrest me. I had a flashback to prison.

Then I recognized the customs official asking the question—he had once been one of my many Stasi interrogators!

I thought quickly and decided to take a gamble: "Say, when did you get a job in customs?" I said loudly. "And why this job? You had such a high position with the Stasi last time I saw you—we last met in Stasi Headquarters!"

The bastard could have turned three shades of green. My gambit had worked. This man was now at my mercy, far more terrified of me revealing his background than I was that he'd look in the cases. He'd obviously just succeeded in switching jobs—probably in the last few weeks—and in making sure that his "files" were conveniently lost. Everyone knew that a past with the Stasi was about to become as damning as one with the SS had been, and no one knew this better than members of the Ministry of State Security themselves.

"Please proceed," he said curtly and looked away, mumbling, "You're lucky," as he waved us through.

"*You're* lucky, you asshole," I said, savoring the air of a new political universe as I drove away from the checkpoint. It was one in which I was no longer under the bootheels of guys like him.

WHEN WE WENT to the Volkskammer to register, the officials there saw us in our boots and wanted to turn us away. We wish to register a party, we said. They looked at us and realized they had to let us. Then we went upstairs to the registration office, and someone shouted at us that we must be in the wrong place. But then Auschwitz said to him, "You can pack up your desk." (He was being ironic, but four weeks later we heard the man really had had to clean out his desk.)

It was an ordinary office of the Communist bureaucracy, like hundreds I'd entered throughout my life, only there was no picture of Honecker—just a gray spot on the wall where the picture had been hanging. They hadn't replaced it with a picture of Modrow. Maybe they knew that this was all temporary, or maybe they thought it would be bad to have anyone's picture up. It now could have been the office of any bureaucrat in the West, only some volumes of Marx were still lying around.

It was such a high, suddenly, to be back in the old system. The big prison. Only now I was a citizen of the Federal Republic, so none of this could touch me. At that moment I stood completely above these people. I did not have to say good morning. They could not do anything to me anymore. The reverse was true: now they were the ones at risk for their past, as the encounter with the Stasi man at the border had shown.

The NA's official registration as a party was approved on January 30. We made the application on January 21, and on January 30 we got the stamp. It was quite a coincidence, considering the date's significance in the Nazi calendar: the day the original NSDAP had taken power in 1933 and the reason I had called my first party the Movement of the 30th of January.

ON THE DAY of its founding, the National Alternative had all of seven members. Frank Lutz, my old partner and the cofounder of the Movement, was not one of them, for he was still in prison. (Auschwitz was there, as were some other old friends, like Silvio Baumann.)

But just two weeks later, Frank was let out of prison. When he got out, he was scared and disoriented by the new situation. He didn't know what was happening in the GDR, and he was shocked that he'd gotten amnesty from the new government. I took him home from jail, and he was completely exhausted; he had become very thin, and he was happy to see us.

We went to an expensive restaurant that night, and he said, "We'll never be able to pay for this." He looked like he was going to have a heart attack when I pulled out wads of bills from my pocket. "Where did you get all that money?" he gasped. "You're a millionaire!"

I explained that I had a West German passport and was already receiving unemployment benefits in West Berlin. I received 800 marks a month in unemployment compensation, which I changed into East money at an exchange rate of 1 to 20. I really was loaded.

Then we took a taxi to a bar, and he kept shaking his head and saying "We should be walking." We got completely drunk, and I told him he could stay the night. He asked, "Where do you live now?" I said in West Berlin, and when we had to pass through the border, he became very pale. He panicked, begging us to turn back, he couldn't face more cops tonight, not so soon. There were a few customs officials and some border patrols, but they did not check anymore. Finally, when we passed the border, Frank calmed down.

The next morning I took him shopping at the supermarket and he went crazy buying all the West products. It was funny. We took a long walk in a park, where I told him about the NA and the events of the last few weeks.

"We've met Michael Kühnen."

"You've met Michael Kühnen!" he repeated, stunned. The world was becoming stranger and stranger since his release.

"He's the godfather behind it all," I said, and we started to talk nonstop about our plans for the Movement.

IN LATE JANUARY a large group of neo-Nazis from West Germany, including Kühnen, came to Berlin to meet with me and Frank and the others. It was a sort of get-acquainted meeting between East and West. We agreed that we were all working toward the reestablishment of the NSDAP, the original Nazi Party, as a legal political party in Germany. The National Alternative was to be our legal method of working toward this goal.

We worked on the NA's platform, planning in principle—the same way Hitler and the original Nazis had—to gain votes from people who wouldn't otherwise be anti-Semitic or far right by pretending to care about traditional "quality-of-life" issues, the family, and national patriotism. Kühnen was brilliant at this. He had drawn up a list of demands to put to the government: first was the immediate merger of the two German states into one; then there were environmental themes, about how dangerous chemical plants had to be closed down; then there was the need to sustain social benefits for the unemployed and elderly and maintain subsidies so the people would not be too "shocked" by the change. Hell, we sounded like the PDS, the newly renamed Communist Party! The whole program was designed to play to an East German audience.

After the meeting Frank and I took the S-Bahn home and were attacked by foreigners! It was probably the only time I can remember when we were attacked by foreigners rather than vice versa. It wasn't because we looked like neo-Nazis either, because both Frank and I were dressed quite normally that night. I'd left my boots at home and was wearing sneakers.

"You asshole, get up!" said a young Turk to me a number of times.

We tried ignoring him, but then more Turks came into the compartment and said, "You German assholes, you heard him, get up!"

The S-Bahn car was completely empty except for us and this little gang of Turkish thugs. Finally, when the young man realized I would not react to him, he said, "You want to offend me, you asshole?"

Oh, shit, I thought, if I say anything now, it will surely prove to be what most "offends" him. He's not going to let me get out of a fight.

The boy then took out a stiletto. I got up because it usually makes an impression, since I'm so much taller than anybody else. But it didn't make an impression on him. He punched me in the ribs. It was a punch like I'd never experienced, some sort of martial arts thing. Then I realized it had been a kick. He had been standing there and suddenly had spun around and kicked me in the ribs, cracking one of them. But he didn't use the knife, because I fell down on top of it. It was on the floor, and I held on to it, so he wouldn't push it into my stomach.

They all kicked the shit out of Frank and me and took our money. Then they said, "We'll throw them out of the S-Bahn." You can force S-Bahn doors open while the train is moving because they don't lock in place. Shit, I thought, this is an elevated train, we can't jump. I struggled to get away and yelled out to Frank, but it was hopeless.

At that moment some people from the next compartment came in and shouted for them to leave us alone. The Turks then backed off and sat down, grinning at us. At the next station they got out with our IDs and about 500 marks, and later we went to the hospital to get patched up.

The incident seems almost funny now, because those Turks didn't have any idea that purely by accident they'd hit the right targets— they were beating up the neo-Nazi leadership of Berlin. They only wanted money and a chance to kick the shit out of some Germans.

One practical effect of the attack, however, was to reinforce my feelings against foreigners. Another irony, I suppose, was that the Greeks had helped me while their enemies, the Turks, had attacked me. Never in my life had I been beaten up by foreigners. It wounded my pride more than anything and was perfectly timed to fit in with all the neo-Nazi ideology I was reading and hearing.

Soon after the attack, I talked it over with Kühnen and he laughed. "It's something that happens quite often, that foreigners attack Germans," he said. "Now you know how they do it. It was good indoctrination for you, because now you know what you're talking about."

From then on, based on this one experience, I became convinced that foreigners should leave Germany. I became an "ideological arsonist," even as the homes of Turks and other foreigners were being set on fire by those I influenced.

The other concrete result was that Frank and I did not want to stay in West Berlin anymore. It was too far from our base of operations and it was too dangerous taking the S-Bahn, which was often filled with Turks. If we had been dressed more obviously, we'd have been even bigger targets. Over the next few weeks we recruited more than three hundred young men into the NA, but now we had no place to meet. This was becoming a real problem. East was our turf. We'd feel at home only if we established ourselves there once again.

9

THE NAZI HOUSE

"LET'S OCCUPY A house," I said to Frank Lutz one evening in February 1990. "The leftists can do it, why can't we?"

And that was that. Within a week, we had done it—we had broken into one of the abandoned buildings near the center of East Berlin and moved in. Just three months later, it became a criminal offense to live in abandoned houses anywhere in Germany. The law was not applied retroactively, though. Any occupation that took place by May 30, the date the law took effect, would be legalized; any place occupied afterward would be forcibly vacated. We had gotten in just in time to be legal, and it would be very hard for the Berlin city government to throw us out.

Michael Kühnen came to visit us the first week, even though he was officially not allowed to enter the GDR. He saw himself as the patron saint of our house and wanted to keep an eye on it. For my part, I considered the visit of the Führer of West Germany to be a great honor.

He arrived in his beat-up old Ford Granada. He had everything he owned in this car. Unlike most of the other West German and Austrian neo-Nazi leaders I was to get to know, Kühnen was dirt poor.

He didn't care about material things. While many neo-Nazis drove only BMWs and Mercedeses, Kühnen's cars were neither fancy nor German. This one was American, and later he drove a Lada, a Russian car—both from the "occupation" powers.

The arrival of Kühnen's car was like the arrival of the Nazi public library. In the trunk of the Ford, in cardboard boxes, were books he'd read in prison over the years. He also had what seemed like the entire transcripts of the Nuremberg trials, as well as files pertaining to his own many court appearances and volumes and volumes of National Socialist literature.

Kühnen sometimes held class, so to speak, around the trunk, offering us various things to broaden our minds: race ideologist Alfred Rosenberg's *The Myth of the Twentieth Century,* if we wanted some classic Third Reich philosophy, or *The Auschwitz Lie* by Thies Christophersen, for the "truth" about the camp where he had been a guard. Lots of other Holocaust denial material. Books of Nazi art, to teach us how to appreciate ideal forms, and a book on degenerate art, to show us how Jews and subversives depicted people and things, part of the all-important understanding of our enemy's psyche.

Kühnen always instructed us to read a lot of books about the Jews—about their history and about how and where they lived. He even recommended the Talmud. He said it was important to learn about the Jew both as individuals and as a race.

As a child Kühnen had been a bookworm, and he had always been interested in history. When I knew him, he was always reading, and he emphasized reading—books, magazines, pamphlets—as a way of spreading the Cause. I never saw him with a novel, though he once told me he liked science fiction. He was interested only in politics. For fun he probably read the Nuremberg trials transcripts. He didn't like fast cars, booze, or women, and he wasn't even as much into explosives and weapons anymore as he had been in the early 1980s.

He was also always writing, and he had published six or seven pamphlets and books, as well as an encyclopedia of national socialism. This was a big, heavy tome published by the NSDAP/AO in Lincoln, Nebraska. They also published all his pamphlets, of course, such as "Forward to the Second Revolution" and "If I Were the Government." He also offered these from the trunk.

* * *

THE AUSTERE FÜHRER from Hamburg could spend only so long help-ing us in our occupied house before duties in other parts of the Reich called. When he wasn't in jail, Kühnen was always on the move. Be-fore he left, however, he installed, more or less formally, some old pros to make sure we East neo-Nazis didn't screw up what was to be a historical milestone for the Movement.

He invited Gottfried Küssel and Günther Reinthaler, the two lead-ers of the Austrian neo-Nazis, to Berlin to oversee our organization of the party and the occupied house.

Gottfried Küssel was a huge, beefy type, with the manner of an Austrian farmer and the booming voice of a rabble-rouser. His deputy, Günther Reinthaler, was shorter and not quite as plump or powerfully built as Küssel. Both had inherited a great deal of money and lived in luxury—Küssel in Vienna, Reinthaler in Salzburg—and they arrived in Berlin in Reinthaler's new black BMW.

Though we thought they would be staying briefly, they made themselves at home and stayed for nearly all of 1990. Reinthaler was constantly driving his BMW back to Salzburg to take care of busi-ness—managing neo-Nazi affairs as well as a number of apartment buildings he owned. Küssel, however, was usually with us; though he stuck out as a flamboyant Viennese, he loved our northern city, which he still considered the capital of the glorious Nazi Reich, of which Austria was rightfully and historically a part.

His job was to oversee my work and make sure everything was running smoothly. Kühnen had known Küssel for more than ten years, and he knew he had more experience than any of us. Obvi-ously, Kühnen felt the operation was too important to leave in the hands of amateurs. The other East Germans and I resented this lack of confidence, but we accepted Kühnen's decision. Also, it was plain that we could learn a lot from the two Austrians, who ran perhaps the most militant and closely disciplined neo-Nazi organization in Europe. Over the next few months, Reinthaler and Küssel did a great deal to lay the ideological and practical foundations of the new united German neo-Nazism.

IN MARCH 1990 our house in Lichtenberg was declared a historic landmark. Apparently, its façade, built around 1910, was unique in Berlin.

The housing authority suggested a deal: they would offer us one of twelve other properties in exchange for it. They gave us an enormous set of keys, and Küssel and I drove around looking at real estate.

We decided on a small apartment building at Weitlingstrasse 122. The building was big enough for our purposes—it had about a dozen two- and three-bedroom apartments—and was in good, livable condition. Most important, its location was strategic. It was five stories tall, had a flat roof you could walk on, and was on a corner. You had good views of the neighborhood. The building also had a big courtyard, and at the rear was a wall, which we topped off with barbed wire. Besides the twelve apartments, it had an enormous attic where we could hold meetings and parties.

We established the WOSAN e.V., which stood for Weitlingstrasse Wohnraumsanierung e.V.—Weitlingstrasse Building Renovation. The letters "e.V." after an organization denote nonprofit status: *eingetragen Verein,* which literally means "registered organization." With this status, we were able to deduct contributions and material costs. The costs of our racist posters and pamphlets about the "foreigner problem" were thus tax deductible over the next year because they had to do with issues of renovation and real estate: we were trying to improve our neighborhood by kicking all non-Aryans out of it. We had the same status as the German Red Cross.

As PARTY CHAIRMAN, I now devoted myself to the NA. In the following months we had a huge influx of new members, so that we soon became one of the strongest right-wing radical parties, in terms of membership, in all of Germany; by late 1990 we had about eight hundred members.

We had no problems recruiting. Every day new kids showed up whom we either took into the National Alternative or sent on to one of the many other parties under Michael Kühnen's umbrella: German Alternative (DA), the National List (NL), the National Offensive (NO), or, if they seemed especially immature or the type who'd like Aryan campfire rituals, into the oldest neo-Nazi organization, the Viking Youth.

In some cases, we made more or less extreme accommodation for personal style. The best example of this was a twenty-two-year-old skinhead whom everyone called "Stinki." Oddly enough, Stinki had trained as a hairdresser. He showed up at our door one day with anarchist tattoos mixed in with his swastikas. He had zero idea about and even less interest in joining a "political" party. But he'd heard about the house on TV and wanted to move in. And Stinki was a guy who did not easily take no for an answer.

Ideology didn't interest him at all, and he often embarrassed us by making ridiculous statements to the press. One time a French television team was shooting in the Lichtenberg train station. The journalists interviewed me and Stinki as we walked across the station, and three Vietnamese cigarette peddlers coming toward us greeted him. Along with the other skins, he ran an extortion operation in the station, and all foreign peddlers had to pay him a percentage of the take. He was simply a little Mafia boss to them, and if they weren't polite, they'd find themselves and their wares in shambles. But Stinki returned the greeting warmly and said to the bewildered journalists, "See, this is all nonsense about hostility toward foreigners. We here in Lichtenberg all help one another." They reported his weird humor as news and broadcast it in a French television spot about the troubles in Germany.

Practically everyone in the house loved Stinki, so his antics were tolerated. Even Michael Kühnen had to learn to tolerate the chaotic little bald hairdresser. When Stinki got word of Kühnen's rumored sexual preference, he started ostentatiously standing with his back to the wall whenever Kühnen was in the vicinity and saying "Always keep your ass to the wall when the Führer comes!"

You may wonder why Kühnen didn't use his authority to have Stinki kicked out of the house for this. But he'd simply smile and say something like "Oh, you've really got some crazy guys in the house. But they'll come around. Be patient, give them time to adjust."

Küssel, on the other hand, always wanted to get rid of him. One time Stinki got into a big fight with the Austrian and posted a sign on the door of his room that said FOREIGNER OUT! Küssel chased Stinki through the house, but most of the residents sided with him, sick of Küssel's constant bossing. Unlike Kühnen, Küssel was always acting as though he had no confidence in any of us in Berlin. He always checked everything three times, while Kühnen would say, "Let's see how they do it—if they don't succeed, they'll learn from their mistakes."

Like many skins, Stinki got a certain satisfaction from tormenting people. He found violence amusing. He once tied up an anarchist

woman in his room and interrogated her for four hours. He terror-
ized the Vietnamese vendors at the Lichtenberg train station almost
daily. He once brought a middle-aged businessman into his room and
handcuffed him to the bed for a supposed failure to settle a gambling
debt for which he owed Stinki his Mercedes. Another time, he broke
into the apartment of a fellow skin, started to take his television, and,
when the surprised pal walked in, hit him over the head with a baseball bat. Stinki was also unpredictable. He went through a phase
after he'd heard something about pacifism where he went around the
neighborhood chewing out people who were violent; that lasted
awhile, then he started bashing heads in again.

Sometimes, when it got too boring for him at the house, he would
dress up as an anarchist and go over to Mainzer Strasse, where they
all hung out. There, masked in black, with a Palestinian scarf
wrapped around his face like a bandit, he'd join the Anarchist Anti-
Fas throwing stones at the police. He probably threw stones at us
once or twice. He simply didn't give a shit.

BUT THE NEO-NAZIS didn't attract only people like Stinki. Every
group was represented. Most of our members had decent jobs. They
were bakers, shoemakers, roofers, or whatever; some of the better
educated were economists, engineers, physicians, lawyers, academics. We accepted members from age eighteen, the legal age to join a
political party.

While the backbone of our organization was young men in their
teens and twenties, we also got many visits from older people (our
oldest member was seventy, an old Nazi, now, of course, retired).
They often provided us with propaganda from the Third Reich that
they'd carefully saved at home. These old Nazis—some from the SS,
others from the Wehrmacht—would speak about the principles of
national socialism in a way that made the concepts seem real and immediate. They could convey an enthusiasm for the SS, Hitler, and the
Cause that simply could not be duplicated by someone who had not
lived through the time.

These were not "important" Nazis, by and large, but that didn't
matter. They were the living embodiment of not only Nazi glory but
German glory. I came to realize then how fully Hitler had succeeded
in merging the concepts of nationalism and Nazism in Germany and

what a benefit that was to us. It had occurred to an extent that has no parallel in any other country. Both Spanish nationalism and Italian nationalism continued to exist in those countries as robust entities, distinct from fascism. They didn't die at the end of the Fascist dictatorships. But in Germany the Nazis totally merged the concept of the German nation into their ideology, and the two have never been successfully separated.

The result was that many, if not most, Germans denied themselves any national pride, and many young Germans still prefer not to be identified as such, because to be German still has Nazi associations. But the other young Germans—the kind who came to us—wanted to be nationalistic, and in Germany, alone of all countries, this instantly pushed them into the right-wing extremist and neo-Nazi camp. This bizarre situation was exemplified by the fact that the phrase "I'm proud to be a German," on a T-shirt or bumper sticker, was considered a neo-Nazi slogan.

One man who came to us had belonged to the SS Leibstandarte, the elite SS bodyguards who were always around Adolf Hitler. This man educated us about race, about the system of national socialism and its entire program, about everything. He was still completely fixated on Hitler.

His name was Joachim Modrack. He came to our organization through the West Berlin neo-Nazis, and he was probably about eighty years old. But then the Leibstandarte had mostly accepted men who had either fought in the First World War or were pioneers for national socialism. And they had to meet specific criteria. They had to be tall and slim and have blue eyes. Modrack incorporated all this. Everything one thinks a Nazi or Aryan should be, he was. In my eyes there is a bit of green, but his were perfect. I couldn't help but stare into his eyes when he talked.

He always used me as an example. He liked to say that I was the ideal Aryan. I'd never really given much thought to my "race" before, except to think that I wasn't black.

Modrack began our race education by making us aware of the racial characteristics of others. We started to pay attention to the size of everyone's head, the shades of color in their eyes, the shape of their hands. We learned to recognize the typical features of a Jew. For example, Modrack taught us that a short back of the hand is typical for Jews and that a Jew will never have a straight body. Such things.

For the neo-Nazis, the Jew was still the main enemy. There was more violence against foreigners simply because Jews were harder to find. You would not see any recognizable Jews nowadays in the street. I thought I'd met a few people who were Jews—I wondered about it and tried to check the signs—but I couldn't be sure. There were hardly any Jews left in Germany, so we got little chance to practice our knowledge. But our Movement was always about the past and the future more than the present. It was important to learn about the racial characteristics of Jews in order to be able to understand the original Nazism, the history of our Movement, and it was also important for the future, when we might need to spot and segregate Jews again. The present was merely a stepping-stone between the Third and Fourth Reichs.

Anti-Semitism had never been a theme in the GDR—I'd never heard the term before I met Kühnen. Even though we East Germans called ourselves Nazis, this cornerstone of Nazi ideology had been completely unknown to us. In order to bring us up to date on racial questions and our invisible enemy, the Jew, Kühnen had left another resident "adviser" in Weitlingstrasse: Arnulf Priem.

Priem was a stocky guy in his forties who wore his hair shoulder length and greasy; he had a mustache and sunglasses and a headband with an SS skull-and-crossbones pin in the middle of it. He looked like a Nazi rocker, but he was actually a graduate in business administration and the chief of an organization called Wotan's Volk, after the Norse god. Priem was the Movement's leading expert on Germanic lore and the history and customs of the SS.

Priem's group was mostly made up of men twenty years younger than he, though they all dressed like little clones, with the same headband and death's-head pin. He trained them to think of themselves as a sort of SS troop who happened to look like bikers. Along with their death's heads they had buttons that said "I love it, I burn it," "I'm proud to be German," and so on.

Like us, Priem was from the former GDR. He had spent four years in prison for trying to flee before the Federal Republic had bought his freedom in the early 1970s. But in the West the authorities had quickly realized their mistake when Priem raised a huge swastika flag on the Victory Column in the middle of Berlin. This was typical of him, climbing probably the most famous monument in West Berlin after the Brandenburg Gate and hoisting a Nazi flag. And it was a big flag—the old classic red flag with a black swastika, fluttering above Berlin until the authorities took it down and arrested him. For that he got just over a year in prison.

He had an enormous collection of old SS race education books that he brought to the house for us all to use. He bought them every Sunday morning at a flea market in Berlin in front of the Victory Column. You found them by looking for the tables that were selling original editions of *Mein Kampf* (legal to buy and sell only as an antique).

Priem rode his big bike all over the place, toting a saddlebag full of Holocaust denial material, SS race handbooks, and Nordic folklore. He looked to me like a modern, sleazy-looking version of the Pied Piper of Hamelin. In addition to carrying a wealth of printed propaganda with him, Priem was Germany's leading source of old Nazi movies, available nowhere else.

I first really grasped the power of our work, in fact, when I saw the face of a sixteen-year-old new recruit, eyes riveted to the screen as he watched one of Priem's films—*The Eternal Jew*—for the first time. It shows the Jew as a rat that destroys the *Volk* from below. The film is filled with the faces of Jews, and, as he watched it, entranced, Priem—or I or one of the other leaders—would pat him on his shoulder and say, "Look, look at the face of your enemy."

Priem also wrote pamphlets on such topics as "Race Mixing" and "Race Defilement"—he actually didn't write badly—and he made up a calendar with all National Socialist and Teutonic holidays. He called it "The German Year."

Priem used all this material to educate his own children. I got my first taste of what a neo-Nazi family looked like when I visited Priem at his apartment one day; this wild-looking guy was one of the only neo-Nazi leaders with a family. When I rang the bell, the door was answered by his youngest daughter, an adorable little girl, who raised her right arm in a Hitler salute and said earnestly, *"Heil dir!"* ("Hail you!"). Priem regularly took his children on National Socialist excursions to former concentration camps, where he taught them his own version of history. He warned them not to believe in the Holocaust, this "swindle of mass murder."

Among Priem's other most effective "teaching tools" that he used both for his children and for our new members in Weitlingstrasse was a neo-Nazi version of the popular comic strip "Asterix." It was created by Küssel in Austria and was called "Asterix and the Final Solution." The story was an ironic version of postwar German history with the Allied occupiers as the Romans. Asterix was still the hero and the Romans were the occupiers, but Asterix was German and the Romans were the Americans and the Jews, together.

Another way we introduced the subject of race was through concern for the environment. We had an official "ecology platform." Of course, we weren't the Greens and our commitment wasn't very deep; basically we used these issues only to attract other people to us—people who already had right-wing sympathies but also wanted to do something for the environment.

I planned excursions into the woods for party members. We'd clean up certain areas and hike alongside tourists, like we were Boy Scouts. Lots of other right-wing organizations did the same. When I think it over, these were the only positive things we ever did. But it was schizophrenic: during the week we attacked people and put up hate propaganda; then on weekends we took care of the woods.

Küssel always told us that national socialism was a "natural science" that had to do with love of the *Heimat* and the landscape of the Fatherland. It was no coincidence that we incited against whole races of people and at the same time made a show of "protecting nature." It was a way of avoiding feeling guilty for causing destruction all the time. But, more important, it was a central part of the original Nazi ideology: that cosmopolitan and internationalist forces were destroying the very biological foundations of life for the German people— through the degradation of the German blood on the one hand and the degradation of the German landscape and ecosystem on the other. Thus, even our race hatred was connected to ecology, for we believed that foreigners and Jews were destroying the environment and taking too many of our limited resources. Aryan nature had to be preserved for the Aryan people.

There was a small women's organization within the Movement, the Deutsche Frauenfront, which was modeled loosely on the female equivalent of the Hitler Youth, the Union of German Girls, and, as its precursor in the Third Reich had done, it worked on so-called "family" matters. The most important was antiabortion campaigning. Like environmentalism, antiabortion campaigning provided a basis for gaining broader support outside the Movement. But concern for the unborn was more seriously tied to the Nazi and neo-Nazi ethic than was concern for the environment. Opposition to abortion had been one of the most consistent planks in the Nazi platform since the Movement's beginnings in the 1920s, and for a simple reason: abortion was race murder. While permissible, even desirable, among the colored women and Jews of the world, among Aryans it was the ultimate sin.

One day, leafing through one of the bigger German newsmagazines, I saw my old friend and partner in crime Freddy Meisel in a photograph holding a sign that said "Prisoners of Socialism" in front of his chest. It made me happy as a kid to see my old friend again. I'd figured he was dead by now—or had killed somebody else and gotten life for it, which would have amounted to the same thing.

A few days after I saw the picture, Freddy showed up at the door of Weitlingstrasse 122 on a prison furlough. He'd seen our little Nazi house on television and wanted to join. The West German skinhead who was acting as our door guard didn't want to let the odd-looking convict in at first. Freddy was covered from head to foot with tattoos. He was clearly a Nazi, because out of the 200 tattoos on his body, at least 150 were various versions of the swastika—small, big, modern designs, some without the connecting bars, some that had round corners and looked like sun wheels from Germanic myths. On his right shoulder Freddy wore a big "D" for "Deutschland." It was forbidden to get tattoos in prison, but there were many who did it professionally in there; Freddy himself is practically a professional tattoo artist. When Freddy showed up at the funeral for the chairman of Germany's Jewish community, Heinz Galinski, he didn't need to make any "Heil Hitler" signs or carry any flags. He was a giant living swastika.

But the skinhead was just a little overwhelmed by this guy in front of him. He insisted on going to check before letting him in. Freddy punched him in the side of the head and pushed him aside. Then he ran up the stairs and cried, "Hey, Hasselbach, where are you hiding? Hey, Ingo, you old Nazi robber!"

We greeted each other and went right away to a bar to get drunk, as was our old tradition. He told me stories about his endless "jail career." Freddy had spent practically his whole young adulthood in the prisons of the GDR—and, talking to him, I began to see that it had taken a toll.

He told me that during one of his many stays in Rummelsburg he had been supposed to take the position of bucket carrier. This job, which I'd once gladly done after getting out of solitary, was considered highly desirable, for it guaranteed extra food and offered the chance to wash daily. In anticipation of Freddy's eager agreement a prison administrator announced the news of his promotion. Freddy stared silently at him for a moment, then screamed, "A German officer carries no bucket!," grabbed the soup-filled bucket, and poured it over the head of the astonished bureaucrat.

He said that in another prison he had written a note to the prison director suggesting a new way of operating the watchtowers, hydraulically, so as to better observe the prisoners. The result was that the director ordered Freddy himself to be more carefully guarded in future.

Then, in Brandenburg, perhaps the toughest prison in the GDR, he was locked in a cell under a staircase—you could only stand up in one corner of the cell, which was about two yards long and one yard wide—for ten months. During those days in his cell under the stairs, Freddy told me, he thought continually of the Communists who'd dogged us our entire lives. Then he'd thought of the Jews. "We need to gas them all, Hasselbach," he told me. "The only evil of Auschwitz was that it didn't last long enough to kill most of the Jews. Millions escaped to Israel and the United States and Russia. We neo-Nazis will finish the job."

He spoke ever more violently about his neo-Nazism, which had mostly developed during his final year in prison. He'd had much more time to spend with Heinz Barth, Henri Schmidt, and the other old Nazis, and they'd come to have a relationship I could hardly guess at—a bond of true and deep hatred for the "race enemy . . . the eternal Jew."

I could see that Freddy had become much more anti-Semitic than I or any of the other GDR Nazis. Even after all Kühnen and Priem were teaching us now about the Jews, I knew that Freddy's feelings went beyond anything I could ever learn to feel. The Jews occupied the center of his mind, like some all-present, all-powerful army, against which his every action was a rebellion.

Freddy told me with relish the story of what he'd done to a prison inmate he'd suspected of being a Jew. Freddy had ambushed this guy, dragged him into a cell, tied him to the bed, then tattooed a Star of David on the prisoner's forehead. "It's actually easier to tattoo on the forehead because the skin is so firm there," he said, swigging his beer.

The story repulsed me, but it was a sign of my own hardness and the race hate that was taking root in me that I just took a gulp of beer and said, "At least you didn't kill the Jew, Freddy, that would have gotten you another ten years."

"The Yid still got me another year," he said. "I should find him and kill him for that."

After a couple of days with us, Freddy went to visit his mother, whom he hadn't seen in four years. She nearly didn't recognize her son, and I don't think it was only the physical change, though that was extreme. I'd known Frau Meisel for almost ten years, and I knew that Freddy's troubles had really been a blow to her. She was a member of a committee that tried to help the political prisoners of the GDR. She was completely physically and psychologically finished by the time he got out of jail, and then, after years of pointlessly challenging the system for her son, seeing him covered with swastikas with that look of hatred in his eyes was too much for her.

She died a week after he was let out of prison, completely unexpectedly. She saw at once, I think, what we shortly came to realize: that prison had pushed Freddy much farther than me or even Frank Lutz. It had made him into a monster.

We accepted him in our house, but even for neo-Nazis he was a bit extreme. He was a pure sadist. While the rest of us did things with an elaborate sense of political hierarchy and often with a sort of cruel irony, Freddy was a pure animal. He was like a skinhead in that he enjoyed nothing so much as beating people up. During a street fight, the unlucky ones who'd run into Freddy Meisel would scream in pain and horror at some unimaginably cruel thing he'd done to them.

When I looked at Freddy, I still felt affection—he was still perfectly friendly when he was around his Kamerads—but I was also disturbed, for I think in him I could see the rawest version of what we all were becoming. Frieder Meisel was obviously someone who lived to exercise hatred.

10

ANARCHISTS

WHILE WE WERE setting up our neo-Nazi headquarters in Weitling-strasse, a few blocks away, in Kreuziger Strasse, the anarchists—also known as "Autonomen"—had occupied a row of houses.

There had been a violent anarchist scene in many West German cities, but especially Berlin, since the early 1970s. The modern anarchist movement was one of the outgrowths of the 1968 Revolution, which had produced more violent subcultures in West Germany than almost any other country. Germany's unique history had made the stakes of the '60s rebellion higher. Taking on the "pigs" and "Fascist establishment" had taken on a new dimension when every third policeman had been not only "Fascist" in a vague way but had actually once worn a swastika on his uniform, when court officials and judges and bureaucrats had once sentenced people under Nazi laws to labor camps and to death. And the fact that Dad had been a company drone who'd done what he'd been told without blinking had taken on a somewhat more sinister light if the company he'd been working for was I. G. Farben, which had employed slave labor and supplied chemicals to gas people.

The anarchists had loose ties to a jumble of leftist causes and traditions. The Anarchist Anti-Fa and the Autonomen, for instance,

were both staunch supporters of the Palestinians against the Israelis—and in this they were odd bedfellows with their enemies, for
we neo-Nazis also supported the Palestinians. Thus, one of the ironic
sights of the early '90s in united Berlin was that of left- and right-
wing German gangs going at each other, each masked, robber style,
by Palestinian scarves.

The rise of violent neo-Nazism in the 1980s under Kühnen and
then even more so in the '90s under the reign of our house in
Weitlingstrasse reinjected a sense of political direction into the anarchists. They had evolved certain traditions—for example, until the
mid-1980s, one day a year nearly all the anarchists in West Germany
would pick a number of cities to "sack." They would do millions of
dollars worth of damage and generally upset the bourgeois citizenry
of the Federal Republic.

The rise of the neo-Nazis as the main enemy, replacing the bourgeois state, renewed the waning anarchist movement. Anarchists in
the '90s saw themselves as the main defenders of the Republic against
the forces of fascism, and many announced themselves as the inheri-
tors of the romantic fighting tradition of the Edelweiss Pirates, spray-
painting the name of this historical youth gang all over Berlin.

During the Nazi era, the Edelweiss Pirates had been a loosely organized working-class youth movement that had been formed to
fight the Hitler Youth. They liked to take American names for their
local gangs; in 1944, the branch of the Pirates called the "Navajos"
had assassinated the chief of the Cologne Gestapo. Now the struggle
between the neo-Nazis and the anarchists was causing the youth of
Germany, left and right, to connect to the past in a way they hadn't
done since the war.

So in the streets of the capital that had been a calm Communist in-
ternment camp until just three months ago, next to a blitz of American
cigarette ads—like the Marlboro signs that told wide-eyed East Berliners of "A timeless land. Where horses still run free. Where some men
do what others only dream about"—a sort of war of political nostalgia
began to be fought. Next to their ordinary slogans—ANARCHIST ZONE,
ONLY HARD CORE, NAZIS DIE—we began to see the words EDELWEISS
PIRATES AGAINST NAZIS!! Often with a skull and crossbones.

To which we'd respond with a swastika and the words HORST WES-
SEL LIVES!—referring to the martyred Nazi storm trooper who had
been shot by a Communist in 1932.

By 1990, just as there were a million and one neo-Nazi groups,
there was now also a cacophony of anarchist, anti-Fascist—or Anti-
Fa, as everyone called them—groups, though the two main official
organizations were the Anti-Fa Youth Front and the Anti-Fa Edelweiss Pirates. Both groups of Anarchist Anti-Fas dressed like punks,
with green hair and rings everywhere. They tended to wear Dr.
Martens boots with red laces or, as I did, Bundeswehr parachutist
boots, which were better for kicking heads in. As fighters they were
often just as tough and unscrupulous as most of the neo-Nazis.
Their standard symbol was a fist breaking a swastika, and they all
wore this somewhere on their clothes. The Anti-Fa Edelweiss Pirates
also wore a picture of a pirate with a skull and crossbones on their
shoulder.

Günther Reinthaler got furious the first time the anarchists blew
up his BMW. But this became standard practice for both sides. The
anarchists would blow up our cars and we'd go into Friedrichshain,
the left-wing district on the border of Lichtenberg, and return the
favor. Both sides usually struck late at night—around three in the
morning.

The anarchists tended to use hand grenades, chucking them into
the front seat. Grenades were plentiful that year. Soviet soldiers still
stationed in East Berlin were selling bags of them for two bottles of
vodka and a few cartons of cigarettes. Even so, we usually blew up
anarchists' cars with Molotov cocktails. It was not so much the cost,
a Moli was just more satisfying. But it took more time. First the seats
would catch fire, then the gas tank would explode, and finally the car
would burn out completely. When the tank exploded it made a huge
sound, like a cannon. Then it was too late to save the car. But you
had to wait around with a Moli because, if only the seats were burning when the owner showed up to put the fire out, the car could still
be saved. You could tell someone working with grenades was in a
hurry, and the anarchists really didn't like to get caught around our
neighborhood. Both sides were always blowing up each other's cars,
and sometimes at night all the explosions made it sound like Berlin
was under siege by heavy artillery.

The anarchists also staged demonstrations in front of our house to
try to get us kicked out of the neighborhood. We talked for some
weeks about how to take action against them. It would be difficult
because, like our house, the anarchists' houses were well defended.

They had stockpiles of Molotov cocktails and bricks and other weapons around. Kreuziger Strasse was very narrow, and whenever one of our vehicles pulled into the street, the anarchists would sound an alarm that would alert everyone in all the occupied houses.

We decided we would have to go at night and take them by surprise. In mid-March, Bendix and I devised a plan. Over the course of a week, we gradually stashed everything we needed in an abandoned building nearby. We went in one man at a time, never parking our vehicles on the street so as to provoke the alarm. Among other things, we stashed nightsticks, baseball bats, flare sticks, a few tear gas pistols, black hoods, and a ladder.

On the agreed day, at four in the morning, thirty men accompanied Bendix and me to Kreuziger Strasse. After picking up our equipment and donning our hoods, we approached the anarchist house we'd targeted in groups of three. As luck would have it, there was an open window on the second floor and our ladder was more than long enough. Very quietly we leaned it against the house, and Bendix and I silently crept up it and stepped inside. All the anarchists were sleeping on their futons and mattresses. We managed to get downstairs without disturbing a soul, and then we let in all the other Kamerads.

The anarchists' house was similar to ours on the inside—like us, they had practically no cupboards or drawers, and papers were lying all over the floor. The pictures on the walls were different, of course: they had Che Guevara posters, we had Rudolf Hess; they had Chinese flags and pirate skull-and-crossbones, we had Reich battle flags and the occasional swastika.

Once we were all in, we moved quickly. We methodically cleaned out the house from top to bottom, room by room. We encountered practically no resistance from the groggy anarchists. It was hilarious to see our normally tough and violent enemies, some of them as big as the biggest of our men, tough and tattooed and battle scarred, marching nervously through their own house with pistols shoved into their necks. They were taken completely by surprise, and most of them looked ready to shit in their pants. I think some of them thought we were going to kill them, and we didn't exactly rush to disabuse them of the notion. We must have cut an ominous figure: thirty neo-Nazis carrying bats and pistols, with black masks over our faces.

Bendix and I had decided beforehand upon a strict rule of silence during the entire action. This was partly to keep the anarchists from recognizing us but at least as much to add to the eerie efficiency and terror of it. It went off perfectly. During the entire raid, not a single neo-Nazi uttered a sound. We only gestured and pushed them with the butts of our weapons. The entire raid was silent except for the sounds of the anarchists screaming, being beaten or punched if they resisted, and the occasional pistol going off for effect.

Anarchists in Berlin are known for their dogs, and I had antici-pated some trouble from them. We had brought a bag of meat along to pacify them with if we needed to. As it turned out, we found all the dogs, mostly German shepherd and collie mongrels, in one room. They were docile and sleepy and seemed hardly interested that their masters had visitors.

With very little trouble, we managed to assemble the majority of the anarchists and locked them up in one of the large rooms on the first floor. Two of them resisted violently. Bendix broke the ribs of one with a baseball bat. Some other hooded neo-Nazis—I couldn't keep track of who was who on our side—beat up the other one and tied them both up in a closet. A few others escaped out the windows, but we'd stationed five men in the yard to take care of them.

Bendix strolled through the room inspecting the rest, mimicking the inspection walk of an SS officer in a concentration camp. We had made them all line up, and now he walked down the rows, poking them and occasionally looking at their teeth, as though deciding who should be allowed to live. Of course, we'd planned it all out in ad-vance and we had no intention of doing any permanent harm to any of them. Frank Lutz and I stood guard at the doors while other hooded neo-Nazis walked up and down the rows of anarchists, hu-miliating them.

"Leave us alone, we didn't do anything to you!" said an anarchist woman. One of the hooded neo-Nazis promptly kicked her in the stomach. There were many women among the anarchists, but while you might think such war games would involve raping or abusing them, we didn't go in for that. This was, after all, an argument be-tween political opponents, and we considered rape to be against our entire program and ideals. Neo-Nazis, at least in my experience, were always extremely strict about not allowing rape as part of their actions.

But we were perfectly amenable to plunder. We stole their Molotov cocktails, boots, and bits of cash. And then we simply laid waste: we burned their banners, demolished their windows, destroyed their doors, and threw all the dishes in their kitchen out the window. It made a giant ruckus, of course, and from other houses on the block we heard a few angry neighbors, perhaps some of them anarchist squatters themselves, shouting "Quiet in there!" or "We're trying to sleep" or "It's four in the morning!"

After we had smashed up or stolen everything in the house, Bendix and Frank Lutz went into the room where all the anarchists were standing, closed the windows tightly, and sprayed tear gas everywhere. Then they ran out, locking the door behind them. I'm sure Bendix was thinking of another kind of gas when he sprayed it in and locked the door on the room full of screaming anarchists.

On the way out, we stole our grand trophy: the black-and-red anarchist flag hanging on the outside of the house, one of their favorite symbols. Then, as we were leaving, we saw the strangest thing: a car full of East Berlin police parked directly across the street. They had been just sitting there as we raged through the house. We wondered if they were going to arrest us—after all, we'd walked out of the building in black hoods, carrying bats and pistols and assorted plunder—but they simply sat there. This naturally emboldened us and made us feel that the whole city, the nation, suddenly stood on our side.

BACK IN WEITLINGSTRASSE, there was a feeling of total victory and supremacy. We had succeeded in conquering an anarchist house, an unprecedented coup, and we'd humiliated hundreds of usually nail-tough opponents. We were surprised that it had gone so well, that it had been so simple. And we were proud of ourselves.

There was lots of drinking and singing in Weitlingstrasse that night. We didn't go in for skinhead bands like Bad Uncles or Destructive Force; we preferred marches and folk music. So Gottfried Küssel pulled out his guitar and struck up some nationalistic German folk songs, including many of his own compositions. They all had pleasant melodies and Küssel had a sweet tenor and played well, but what came out in his Viennese accent had a harder edge.

One refrain was a series of questions:

"Do you see his nose, no? Do you know his nose? His nose you do not know? Is it crooked and ugly? Then hit him in the face. He is a Jew, a damned Jew, bloodsucker of the European race."

I didn't bother to reflect on the peculiarity of it then: we'd just attacked a bunch of left-wing Germans who were surely as Aryan as we were, but all we sang about was the Jews.

"A Jew is hooked and ugly, he deserves the worst we can do," went another ditty. "He's a subhuman vermin, but his earthly days are through. Get down to Hell, Jew—but even the Devil doesn't want you!"

In one of the songs, Küssel related the tale of a Jew on a trip to Auschwitz, which ends with the singer in the gas chamber. It may seem an odd contradiction of our dogma that there had been no gas chambers in the concentration camps—that Auschwitz had had swimming pools for the prisoners instead of crematoria—but our response was always "If the Jews can invent something like that, they have to count on ending up in it."

Küssel had also made up little songs of praise about the Movement. He sang a song that I don't recall exactly now, but the sense was "A man is standing at a train station with a suitcase filled with explosives and he travels to Vienna to blow up Simon Wiesenthal's, that fat Jew's, villa." I didn't know then that I would soon be on intimate terms with this particular folk hero. It had an especially nice tune, very catchy.

THE NEXT DAY, we hung the anarchist flag out our window in Weitlingstrasse, but we'd added new lettering across the front, something like NATIONAL OPPOSITIONAL POLITICS, some bullshit. The important thing was the color scheme: our lettering was white, so it was now a red, white, and black flag—the colors of the German Reich. Nobody could prove where we'd taken it from, but it was a provocation to every anarchist in Berlin: their flag had been stolen and transformed by the neo-Nazis.

The result was that even more trouble from leftists rained down on Weitlingstrasse. There were continuous revenge attacks on our house. We could no longer just relax and watch TV, for stones would start flying in through the windows, along with Molotov cocktails.

The anarchists had developed a new system for throwing Molis with catapults—any rock or Moli delivered with one had an enormous punch. We'd find holes all over the walls of the building, and sometimes the projectiles would actually go through the walls. These catapults were sold in the 1980s as sports weapons in Germany, and if you were hit by a rock or bottle launched by one of them, you could forget it. We had to cover all the windows with garbage can lids and boards.

The street battles, on the other hand, went fairly evenly, but I did notice that we had an advantage when it came to being arrested. The cops tended to favor us short-haired racists over the long-haired anarchists. There was one particular incident that drove this feeling home to me—this feeling that the law was on our side.

We'd had a street fight, and the cops had attacked and arrested a lot of fighters from both sides. As we were driving to the station in the police van—eight policemen, two neo-Nazis, and two anarchists—I found out to my amazement that I hadn't been arrested. Rather, I was to serve as a *witness* against the anarchists, to show that they had attacked us and caused lots of damage. Of course we'd claimed this and of course it wasn't true—you always said that about the other side when the cops busted you in these battles—but the cops had simply chosen to take our side. We were the clean-cut blond boys, and the anarchists were long-haired and didn't bathe; our jeans were fresh, theirs were ripped. In the van, looking out the side of his eye at one of the anarchists, one of the cops held forth: "Yeah, this guy really makes us want to puke, him and this whole left-wing pack. You guys are a lot better for us, you don't attack us, you attack the foreigners, who are a load of trouble anyway." The anarchist sat there, terrified, looking like he didn't know who he was going to get it from first—us or the cops.

THROUGHOUT THE SPRING, the combat between us and the Anarchist Anti-Fa groups escalated. There were continual street fights in front of our house. Sometimes more than two hundred people would beat one another up right in the middle of the street. The police never moved in, and I'm sure some were happy when we bashed one another's skulls in. There was a special unit that was trained to handle soccer hooligans and brawlers, and occasionally they moved in. They were enormous guys who, for camouflage, dressed more or less like the anarchists, in jeans and often wearing patches with a fist smashing a swastika. Gradually, we all got to know who these plainclothes guys were, and I even got to be good friends with two of them. Later they would become the only officers to ever help me change my life.

But in general the cops gave us free rein—both sides, really, even though they favored the neo-Nazis. And this, more than anything, was how we knew that East Germany was really over. Every big shot in the country was scrambling to hide his Stasi past and suck up to his new Western landlord. The way we saw it, we neo-Nazis were the only untainted group here: we clearly hadn't been Stasi agents, while often other protesters had been. In GDR times, we hadn't had street battles—the power of the State had been too omnipresent. This was partly what now made it such a trip. We were all of us cutting loose in a way that was wilder than anything we'd ever imagined. It was an incredible feeling of freedom, roaming the streets, blowing up cars, and guarding our fortress against anarchists, even if it did distract from the political work at hand.

We had gradually occupied three buildings to the right and left of ours, so that there were now four neo-Nazi houses on Weitling-strasse. This allowed us to form a complex, extending around the corner. It was strategically brilliant. It was a self-enclosed fortress, protected by NATO barbed wire—the kind that was double bladed so that if an unlucky intruder got caught in it, he'd get sliced up pretty good before he got himself out.

We now had maybe three hundred people living in the houses. The buildings had four stories, and there was an enormous attic that con-nected all of them. I was responsible for creating this single attic. The masonry skills my socialist state had taught me finally came in handy. I broke holes in the stone walls with a hammer, put in beams above the holes, put in door frames with concrete, and hung doors.

We always kept lots of Molotov cocktails around our houses, pre-made. They were off in a basement in a separate room, so there was no danger that someone would come in drunk and accidentally set them off. It was our little wine cellar: four hundred bottles of vintage explosives. We also kept piles of cobblestones lying in strategic places around the house waiting to be distributed in case of attack.

One time, though, I was happy when the East Berlin cops inter-vened to stop one of our "defense" actions. Günther Reinthaler, the Gauleiter of Salzburg, had gotten particularly worked up one day—maybe he was down looking at the charred remains of his BMW—and we knew there was a virtual army of anarchists on the way over to attack us. We got everyone on the roof armed with Molis, and Reinthaler had the bright idea that we should tip four hundred liters of gasoline from canisters onto the leftists in the street. It would be something medieval. Then we'd throw down Molis to make the whole thing ignite. If the police hadn't been so energetic that day, there would have been a conflagration. They busted the anarchists and confiscated about 150 liters of our gas that was already prepared as Molotov cocktails. They left us the rest.

Something happened a few weeks later that reminded us that throwing enough Molotov cocktails could result in somebody getting hurt. We were attacking the Anarchist Anti-Fa central headquarters on Oranienburger Strasse—a massive wreck of a building—when a mass of soccer hooligans at the Stadium of World Youth, one of the biggest soccer stadiums in East Berlin, heard that something was up, and ran over to Oranienburger Strasse in order to mix in on our side. (The soccer hooligans were mostly apolitical, but they were always looking for a good fight, and they tended to side with the right wing.) The attack was a total success, but later we learned, through the newspapers, that one anarchist woman had been blinded during it. It was never clear whether she'd been hit in the face by one of our Molis or had been crippled by "friendly fire."

I got to know only one anarchist well. He was my biggest enemy in Lichtenberg, and today we've become good friends. His name is Olaf Arnwalt. He was a West anarchist, but the first time I ran across him was on Weitlingstrasse, where he'd come to harass the neo-Nazis. We glimpsed each other from a distance, and I know now that we were both thinking the same thing: "Hey, he's huge, this kid."

Arnwalt was about my size, with a broader build, and he had long black hair. But otherwise it was amusing that we were so diametrically opposed in terms of looks, like good and bad guys in a Western—one with short blond hair, the other with long dark hair. I've since seen Arnwalt's picture in the window of a fashion boutique on Ku'damm. He had posed for an ad for some very expensive black jeans.

But at the time I first met him in Lichtenberg, in 1990, he was always masked and usually wore leather pants, which were hard to grab on to and also to slice through. And he was really tough—a true street fighter. You could see it immediately.

I encountered him again a couple of months later, when we were both on a talk show in Munich to discuss the big riots over house occupation in Berlin. I was the featured guest, and he was there to respond to me. By this point neo-Nazism was such a hot issue in

Germany that we were getting regular invitations to appear on talk shows. Before the show, when we were putting on our makeup, we had a friendly chat about Berlin.

But as soon as the program started, Arnwalt went crazy on me. He got really furious at one point and shouted, "In Hasselbach's name, people are being killed in Lichtenberg!" I thought he was about to leap up and attack me. Then I got pissed off because he knew damned well that nobody had been killed in Lichtenberg, and certainly not in my name. Things had gone pretty far but not that far. But he wouldn't lay off. And while I'd noticed him in the street before, he knew a lot more about me at the time than I knew about him. It was hard to do much but rebut his accusations.

He was a member of the Anarchist Anti-Fa Youth Front, but he really had no idea what anarchism meant. He was just a street fighter at heart and someone who hated right-wingers. When I asked him to define anarchism, he said that true anarchism for him meant when all Nazis would be shot.

The program had an appropriate title: *Live from the Slaughterhouse*. The studio was in a converted old slaughterhouse for pigs and cows.

THE STREET WAR between right- and left-wing youth got so bad that it was the subject of many city council meetings, talk shows, and political speeches by the major parties. Among other things, the war between the anarchists and the neo-Nazis was costing Berlin, which wanted to become Europe's new cultural and business capital, its much-needed reputation as a safe city. The fate of the 2000 Olympic Games, for which Berlin was competing, hung in the balance.

To this end, an event was sponsored in a theater on neutral territory, a so-called "roundtable" discussion to find an answer to the question: How can we stop the escalation of violence? The entire leadership of the National Alternative was invited to this roundtable, as were representatives of all the Anarchist Anti-Fa groups.

We drove to the meeting in a jeep: Reinthaler and myself in the back seat, and two other neo-Nazis in front, one as bodyguard and one as a driver. We felt like soldiers driving through enemy territory on the way to peace talks. It was a nice day, around 5:00 P.M., and it was fun to be driving into the grand center of Berlin, which only recently had been the stomping grounds of the East German elite—the Party, the Stasi, the military.

But when we turned our jeep into Schumannstrasse, near the theater, we saw that the "peace talks" would not be what we'd expected. The street was packed with people in black masks carrying boards and Molotov cocktails. The Anarchist Anti-Fas were waiting for us.

"Turn around, man!" shouted Reinthaler.

The guy driving the jeep tried, but it was impossible. The street was too narrow.

An instant later, we were surrounded by left-wing radicals.

"Brown scum, die!"

"Nazi swine!"

They were screaming all around us and pushing the jeep. They were also hitting us. We hit back. But our bodyguard was hit hard with a baseball bat and slumped forward, groaning.

I freaked out, but I didn't have time to be afraid. I was calculating what we'd do if the driver was stopped and they dragged us out of the car. It was four people against a hundred, but we'd fought street battles with equally absurd odds before. No matter what the difference in numbers, you can manage. The situation was not exactly winnable— we'd get slaughtered either way—but any street fighter knows that there are better and worse ways of getting the shit kicked out of you.

Suddenly the driver of our jeep panicked and, without thinking, hit the gas. We drove straight into the crowd. There were screams all around us. The anarchists were running and they were falling, to the side or—

The street was very bumpy, but suddenly I felt a much bigger bump. As we were driving away to safety, in the rearview mirror I saw one man lying on the ground, screaming. He had trousers on, but they were all bloody and I could see that his legs looked broken. Shit, we must have run over him. I couldn't see much more, for people were running toward him and it was hard to tell exactly what was going on. We hadn't had much choice: if they'd stopped us, they would have kidnapped us or torn us apart. It was a shit-shit situation.

The anarchist survived, though his legs were broken. The neo-Nazi who ran over him got two years' probation and a sizeable fine as compensation for the anarchist's pain and suffering. There were no more attempts to bring the violent Right and the violent Left in Berlin to the table to talk.

11

FÜHRER FIGURES

KÜHNEN FELT THAT, while the battles with the anarchists were spectacular and generated great publicity, they weren't quite "hard core" enough for Germany's first official neo-Nazi-occupied house. He was also worried that our politics were being identified purely with the street war against leftists, when there were "other issues" to deal with. When I asked what he had in mind, he explained that painting neo-Nazi graffiti in Jewish cemeteries, destroying socialist monuments, and attacking refugee shelters would get us headlines of "the right sort."

Around this time a little man arrived at the house who had great experience in generating headlines of "the right sort."

It was Arnulf Priem who brought the little man with him. I asked Priem, the head of Wotan's Volk, who this little man was. He answered unusually gravely with another question: "Have I ever brought anyone along who wasn't in order?" Küssel told me that evening that the man was none other than the most infamous of all German right-wing terrorists, Ekkehard Weil.

Weil often carried explosives in his briefcase—a gram or two of TNT. He had been born in Berlin in 1949 and had done his West German Army service in the late 1960s, when he had gotten his basic grounding in the "art of explosions," which he pursued gleefully for the rest of his life.

Weil seemed so gentle that you wouldn't think he could hurt a fly. Yet he had once shot a Red Army soldier guarding the Honor Monument for the Soviets near the Brandenburg Gate, as a way of attacking the presence of the Allies in Berlin. As the Soviet soldier had lain on the ground, dying, a West Berlin woman had run over to help the soldier; Weil had shot her in the leg. For this ruthless act he had become the first West German citizen ever sentenced before an Allied court for an attack on the occupation powers.

Then, in 1979, when he had been put on trial for firebombing the offices of the Socialist Unity Party of West Berlin, he had also been prosecuted for attempted murder in an entirely unrelated incident. Apparently someone had observed him trying to run over someone he had hit with his car—trying to kill the guy so he couldn't identify him as a reckless driver. During this trial Weil had caused riots among the bystanders and at one point had got up from the bench and punched a journalist; using one of the many fighting tricks he knew, he had broken the fellow's nose.

Weil didn't talk about his past "accomplishments" at all, but everyone knew about them. He preferred to make pleasant conversation about the weather or the Jews or whatever. But he was really nuts—fanatical about Jews and explosives. He spray-painted Brecht's grave, for example, with "Sow Jew," the traditional German anti-Semitic curse. But it was ridiculous—Brecht wasn't even Jewish. "He had a Jewish way," said Weil, grinning. "Brecht was a Sow Jew at heart."

For Weil everything was Sow Jew or Swine Priest—the latter were Communists or lefties. When reading about desecrations of monuments or graves in the paper, I could always recognize Weil's work because of the language used, the giveaway expressions *Sau-Jude* (Sow Jew) and *Schweinepriester* (Swine Priest). He always had a spray-paint can in his attaché case.

Weil was notorious not only for his terrorist attacks and desecrations but for his antics in prison. When he was in the Tegel Prison in West Berlin, the guards came one morning to open his cell and found it empty. The headlines in all the Berlin papers shrieked WHO ORGANIZED EKKEHARD WEIL'S ESCAPE? What had happened was less sensational but much funnier, and typical of him.

In each cell there was an air vent, just wide enough for a person to fit into. There were bars over it, but they weren't very strong because the air vent didn't lead outside. One day Weil, who was small and wiry, climbed inside the vent and put the bars back very carefully so you couldn't tell they had been disturbed. He'd first written a letter, saying he'd run away and that the prison needn't bother trying to catch him.

When the guards found the letter, they put out an alert. For two or three days the police searched for Weil throughout the city. Finally, when he got too uncomfortable, he simply climbed out back into his cell and laughed himself half to death. No one would have thought a prisoner would be weird enough to do something like that, and indeed no other had been. The story became a legend in Berlin.

I gave Weil an apartment in the house, next to that of Stinki the skinhead. Weil immediately set up a chemical experimentation laboratory in his apartment, and Stinki complained to me, "Who knows what the hell he's tinkering around with in there? In the end we'll all go up."

Certainly Weil's most famous exploit involved blowing up a house. And it had been enough to make the quiet little man a household name among neo-Nazis and anti-Semites everywhere, for the house he had blown up belonged to Nazi hunter Simon Wiesenthal in Vienna—it was this action that was celebrated in one of Gottfried Küssel's folk songs. Weil got five years in jail from the Austrian authorities. He had done a total of fourteen years' time in German and Austrian jails, and it showed on him. He had permanent rings around his eyes. But he laughed a lot, he was a happy guy.

One of the few people he got really close to was Küssel. They desecrated Jewish shops together, harassed prominent Jews in Austria, and enjoyed discussing political developments in the Middle East. When Priem first brought Weil over, Küssel and Weil hadn't seen each other for almost ten years, since they had been sentenced together in Vienna for anti-Semitic violence.

A couple of days after Weil's arrival in Weitlingstrasse, Christian Worch, Kühnen's right-hand man, called from Hamburg. He was furious and told me urgently to get Weil out of the house: "Wherever Weil puts up, the State Security Service and the Jewish secret service can't be far away."

In the meantime, however, I'd befriended Weil and couldn't simply throw him out of the house. But Worch was right, for we were now being watched by both the State Security Service and the Mossad, the Israeli secret service. Some State Security Service agents told us. They wanted us to realize what a serious situation we were in.

LIKE MOST PEOPLE who worked with explosives, Ekkehard Weil was a man who lived by the clock, and he made the mistake of demanding the same from everyone else in the house. In this way he made himself unpopular with most of the skins, who were not known for their discipline or early hours. Most of them were doing their best to become good neo-Nazis, but obeying Weil's orders was another matter.

Every morning punctually at a quarter to seven Weil would get up and try to wake the others. One morning he wanted to wake up one of the skins: "Kamerad, Kamerad, everyone in the house is already working!"

Half asleep, the skin didn't understand what the feeble-looking Weil wanted from him. After a few minutes the legendary terrorist came back into the room to shake him awake. The volatile young man got very upset: "Tell me, old man, are you off your rocker?" Weil didn't understand him: "But Kamerad!" The skin had had enough. He smashed Weil one on the head, and Weil staggered back down the stairs, speechless.

In general, the house fell in behind Weil, though, not because we believed in his clockwork efficiency but because we had a deadline for fixing the place up. Part of the contract we had signed with the city said that we agreed to renovate the building we were occupying. During the week, if nothing political was going on, most of us would get up at eight and go to work. We renovated the kitchens, laid new electric wire, put in windows and doors, and replaced pipes. We tackled everything from top to bottom.

The difference was that Weil got upset when other people didn't fall into line behind him, while I couldn't care less nor could most of the other people. We pretty much believed that neo-Nazism was something you did out of conviction, not routine.

THAT SPRING I was named house leader and house "speaker." Frank Lutz was the official leader of the National Alternative, but he didn't make a good house leader. His approach was more like Weil's—he got angry if people didn't do things exactly as he wanted them, and he lost his temper easily. I got along with everyone in the house, from Weil and Lutz to Stinki.

No one appointed me, and there was no election. There are no "elections" in an undemocratic organization. Things just crystallize. This was very important to us—what we called the "Führer princi- ple." Leaders in various fields just developed. It made the whole thing seem predestined somehow—no debate or election could ever be as important as the biological mandate by which we would rule others and ourselves.

I was a natural leader in the Movement because people liked me; I could give orders without alienating anyone or seeming like only a boss, rather than a Kamerad. I fit the type of the ideal Nazi: with my height and coloring, I superficially resembled the idol of the neo-Nazi movement, Reinhard Heydrich, leader of the SS security forces, who himself had looked like the cliché of a Germanic hero. We were al- ways reading Third Reich race theory books, and Heydrich was men- tioned in every single one of them. The funny thing was, if you looked at the neo-Nazi scene in Germany, I was one of the few truly "Aryan" types; if they regulated the scene by who had the right fea- tures, there would be practically no neo-Nazis at all. Most were dark haired and distinctly lacking a lean Nordic body type, much as Hitler and Goebbels and the original Nazi leadership had been.

Ironically, even for obsessive admirers of the SS like Bendix and Priem, SS leader Heinrich Himmler never played a big role. Part of the reason was surely the fact that he had been short and bald and nearsighted. Later I decided there was another reason: he had never played a big part in the politics of the Third Reich except in his con- trol of the mass murder of the Jews, but since we denied that had happened, we also denied his importance. Heydrich, on the other hand, had been big and blond and athletic, and the fact that he had been killed by assassins in 1941 made him a martyr. Like Rudolf Hess, Hitler's deputy and the other great idol in our pantheon, Hey- drich was someone who could not directly be blamed for anything that had happened from 1942 to 1945.

ON THE MORNING of April 20, 1990, Günther Reinthaler, our house- guest from Salzburg, came to me, very excited. "Have you prepared everything?"

"No, what do you mean?"

"What do I mean? Today is the Führer Adolf Hitler's birthday."

I suggested he check around the house to see if someone wanted to organize something.

"This can't be true! Where are we then? Is this a neo-Nazi headquarters or Communist Party Central?"

I tried to explain to Reinthaler that most of the house residents actually weren't big followers of Hitler and were instead "Strasserites"—followers of the Strasser brothers, Gregor and Otto, who had been left-wing opponents of Hitler within the Nazi movement during the 1920s and early 1930s. They had dubbed Hitler the "Pope of Munich" for his hobnobbing with the wealthy and fashionable elite of that city. We also admired Ernst Roehm, the leader of the original storm troopers, whom Hitler had murdered along with Gregor Strasser in 1934. These were the more "revolutionary" of the original Nazis, whom Hitler had killed in order to appease the moneyed interests, big business, and the army.

Strasserism denies that national socialism ever failed—it was simply betrayed by Hitler. The trick would be to do it again but do it right this time. But for Küssel and Reinthaler, it was heresy to see any flaws in Hitler. They agreed with their Führer that the German nation in 1945 had been a nation of traitors and deserved what it got. To me this reflected an obvious self-interest on their part: First, they were Austrians, which meant that Hitler was their countryman and that they resented having been detached from the German Reich after the war. Second, and more important, both Küssel and Reinthaler were fabulously rich and lived in a style much more suited to the "Pope of Munich" than to the Strassers' revolutionary austerity. National socialism would hardly appeal to them.

Anyway he tried, in a forced way, to organize a celebration in the house. He read poems in front of five or six people, and afterward they sang a couple of songs, during which everyone else either slept or listened to completely different music. Reinthaler called Küssel, furious, to complain about our attitude. Küssel later gave me a long speech on the meaning of Hitler, but I told him that despite all that I was still more oriented toward Strasser.

The argument finally came down to whether you were a fan of the SA, the brown-shirted storm troopers who had fought in the streets to bring the Nazis to power, or the elite force that had replaced them and executed their leaders, the black-shirted SS. The

SS—until late in the war—had been a smaller, more regimented group selected in terms of "racial" qualifications; they tended to contain more middle-class and even aristocratic members than the SA, which had been a proletarian army. The rivalry between the SS faction and the SA faction was about the question of whether the neo-Nazis should be an elite or a mass organization—and the Jewish Question. Whereas the SA suggested the broader meaning of Nazism, the SS focused in on the ideas of racial superiority and anti-Semitism. It was no coincidence that the most anti-Semitic and ruthless neo-Nazis became obsessed with the SS, while most of us preferred the romantic street-fighting tradition of the Brownshirts.

Michael Kühnen, the ultimate authority, came down on both sides of the issue. He was a pauper who identified with the socialist, Brownshirt tradition of Strasser and Roehm, but he was also part of the personal cult of Hitler and found the Führer infallible, if bourgeois. While he wouldn't go so far as to reject Hitler, however, Kühnen was clearly an SA man. He liked to be referred to as "Chef," like his hero, SA founder Ernst Roehm. But the argument about Hitler and the Brownshirts was more than historical, as we were soon to find, and, like the original SA leaders, our Chef had something in his closet that many neo-Nazis would not tolerate.

BENDIX, OUR GRAVE-ROBBER friend and World War II fetishist, loved the SS and wanted to found a black-shirted troop in Weitlingstrasse. In this he clashed with most of the people in the house. One West Berlin SA fan, Oliver Schweigert, was particularly adamant about keeping SS cults out of the house. Schweigert and Bendix were always getting into fights about this.

One day Bendix went into Schweigert's room and painted a red heart around the portraits of Ernst Roehm and Michael Kühnen that Schweigert kept above his bed. Then Bendix put a big red kiss with lipstick on the portrait with his own lips.

"Do you know why the SA wore brown shirts?" Bendix said to Schweigert, when confronted by him.

"Why?" said Schweigert.

"Because they were a bunch of ass-fucking homos, like Michael Kühnen!" said Bendix with glee.

Schweigert lost his temper and threw Bendix into the street. "Nobody talks that way about the Führer in this house," he said.

"I'll get you!" shouted Bendix, as he left. A couple of weeks later he was back, but he didn't sleep at the house anymore. He also didn't kill Schweigert, but that couldn't have made Oliver entirely comfortable. Bendix always carried a sawed-off shotgun under his long SS field coat and often had a grenade or two in his pockets—and besides, anyone who slept with the remains of dead soldiers and used their fifty-year-old toiletries to groom himself was not entirely predictable.

Most of the people in the house supported Schweigert and congratulated him for having stopped an SS-faction coup d'état. Actually, I think they were just happy not to have somebody around calling them brown-assed Jew homos, as Bendix had taken to doing, and probably equally glad to be rid of the smell. Still, Michael Kühnen's sexuality was hardly a problem that affected only these two men.

Since the late 1980s there had been rumors that Kühnen was gay and was infected with the AIDS virus. A journalist with whom I've since become friends first broke the story—his name was Warner Poelschau. Kühnen was in jail at the time, and Poelschau went to get an interview. It was a strange story, for this journalist had been responsible for getting Kühnen extradited from Paris in 1985 and sentenced to jail in Germany. He had a dogged interest in seeing him brought to justice, since he had shadowed some people in the Parisian Fascist scene and found him living underground in Paris; he had shadowed him, taken notes and photos, and turned Kühnen over to the authorities.

Then Kühnen gave Poelschau an interview. This was remarkable, but the interview was for *Stern,* one of Germany's biggest magazines, and Kühnen could never pass up good publicity. He was afraid of passing out of the limelight after being in prison so long. Kühnen reminded Poelschau that he was still his enemy and that he would have him killed as soon as he decided he had no further use for him. But he said that in the meantime he'd give him an interview.

But Poelschau had set up the interview because he had a trump card: he already knew that Kühnen was HIV positive. He had a friend who was a doctor in the prison who had told him; Kühnen, he said, had been moved to a ward for prisoners with infectious diseases. Poelschau wanted to confront him.

So he did the interview, and when he asked Kühnen whether he was homosexual, Kühnen lost it. He panicked and said there was a smear campaign of leftist propaganda out to destroy him. "Be careful, my friend, you're HIV positive, you're infected with AIDS," said Poelschau. And Kühnen broke down, saying it was all foul lies and that he was obviously being blackmailed. Actually, Poelschau kind of liked him—he just hated his politics—and he offered to help him. But Kühnen just responded with threats. Poelschau told me later that he had had doubts about publishing the interview in *Stern*, but he went ahead.

As a result of these revelations a group of former Kühnen followers formed an antigay faction and wrote a manifesto that stated that homosexuals were "traitors to the people" and "corrupters" who spread AIDS, "a disease designed for wiping out a healthy *Volk*." At the end it said, "No gay can ever be a true National Socialist."

I had heard that Kühnen had answered with a sixty-seven-page manifesto entitled "National Socialism and Homosexuality," in which he recalled the homosexual tradition of the brown-shirted SA. He suggested to his former Kamerads that they stop being influenced by the "Jewish-Christian petit bourgeois morals" but rather acknowledge the biological reality of nature, in which homosexuality has its place.

We started to hear rumors about Kühnen and Michel Faci, the French Fascist mercenary, together at orgies in Paris. A video of Kühnen with Faci at an S & M party in Paris supposedly later turned up in the hands of another apparently gay neo-Nazi, the blond Führer of Munich, Ewald Althans. It was filmed by a friend of Kühnen's in Paris (who was found shot to death with half his face burned off by acid not much later). The French secret police are rumored to have played the dirty tape of Kühnen for the German secret police before deporting him. Then somehow Althans got hold of it, or claimed he had. Althans also said he had a video of Faci running around the Croatian front in a pair of leopard-skin underpants, holding a machine gun. Althans was always unusually interested in homosexuality among neo-Nazis, without necessarily being critical of it.

But the main force of the attack against Kühnen came from the only significant group of German neo-Nazis not in his orbit: the Free

German Workers' Party, or FAP, which was under the control of sixty-five-year-old Friedhelm Busse. The silver-haired, potbellied Busse had always been an archrival of Kühnen's, and this gave him extra ammunition. He took to calling Kühnen a "nest dirtier" in interviews and accusing him of trying to poison the whole neo-Nazi scene with AIDS.

So IT WAS hardly a revelation to us when Bendix painted the heart around the pictures of Kühnen and Roehm in Schweigert's room. But after the Wall fell Kühnen had been recognized by practically all the neo-Nazis in the GDR as their new Führer, largely with my help, and the fact of his homosexuality and the suspicion that he was HIV positive had been taken as "left-wing propaganda." We treated them like rumors. The charge that Kühnen was HIV positive had come out three years before, but he was still alive and apparently healthy. We took his skinniness and lack of appetite for nervousness and overwork.

For much of the West German neo-Nazi scene, and of course for Busse and the FAP, Kühnen's homosexuality was a fact. But for all of us who were part of Kühnen's orbit—which included all the most important and ideologically firm neo-Nazis with the exception of Bendix—Kühnen's homosexuality was simply an "un-fact." As Busse had had a long-term rivalry with Kühnen, it was easy to view him as a jealous competitor spreading evil lies. We basically dealt with Kühnen's homosexuality much as we dealt with the Holocaust: we denied it. For most of us, neither carried any weight.

Kühnen's manifesto was not available anywhere. Certainly he wasn't passing it out. We treated it as a "rumor" that the pamphlet had ever existed. Then one day I saw that Schweigert had it, but the fanatical follower of Kühnen would not let me borrow it or even examine it for long. He would accept no challenge to the truth about his Führer, for his idea of national socialism was built around this unconditional loyalty. Kühnen had been naïve to write the pamphlet thinking he could change any minds, for even his staunchest supporters simply had to deny his homosexuality to themselves, as it would not fit into their ideological universe.

Of course, Kühnen never admitted in the pamphlet that he was gay—he only said neo-Nazis should stop preaching this Christian petit bourgeois moral that gays cannot fight alongside the rest of us.

And he argued that gays are in the end better Kamerads because they do not start families, they are freer and more independent, and they integrate better into men's associations; the SA, he pointed out, had been a purely homosexual men's fraternal order. I really don't know how somebody could have lived with such massive contradictions, when after all, he knew that gays had been murdered in the camps along with Jews and anyone with different opinions. But then again, we denied that anyone had been killed for anything.

But Worch and Kühnen always planned to establish their own concentration camps for political opponents, homosexuals, AIDS patients, and Jews—after the inevitable birth of a Fourth Reich—so it was impossible to know what they really thought about homosexuality.

ALONG WITH BENDIX, Auschwitz became one of the first strong opponents of Kühnen. Though still very young, Auschwitz had great influence and was well respected; he was among the smartest of the people in the house, and his knowledge went deep. But I stuck by Kühnen to the end. My point of view was simple: I didn't know for a fact that he was homosexual, and even if he was, he could still be an important leader and enlightening to all neo-Nazis everywhere.

Auschwitz replied that a rumor was good enough and that a homosexual had no place in the Movement.

"But after all, you're one of the greatest supporters of Roehm and Gregor Strasser," I said, "and there have always been rumors about their homosexuality, especially Roehm."

"That's not the same!" he barked back.

And it wasn't. In the scene you didn't seriously attack historical idols like Strasser and Roehm, because that was like attacking the foundation of the ideology. These people embodied our ideology for us, and as such they were untouchable. They were the Founding Fathers. Kühnen, for all his charisma, gall, and popularity, was just a living idol, waiting to be torn down.

I STUCK BY Kühnen for personal as well as political reasons. I often spoke with him not only about the Movement but about completely unrelated things. He was a wonderful debater and always displayed a kind of enthusiastic openness. But when you spoke at length with him, you realized that he had no real friends. He always spoke of Kamerads, and sometimes I had the impression that he really liked it when he could talk with me about something personal. I've never met anyone who was lonelier than Kühnen. He had no family, no friends. He had only Kamerads.

BUSTED

On April 27, 1990, I visited my ex-wife, Christine, for coffee. We'd become friends, more or less, and the wounds of our breakup had healed. She lived near Weitlingstrasse, and I went over late in the morning, had a good conversation with her, and stayed longer than I expected. Around two I finally left her place and walked home. I stopped to do a little shopping on the way, and, as I rounded the corner into Weitlingstrasse, I thought, That's funny, half the street is closed off. There were some construction sawhorses, and buses were being diverted onto another street. Then I looked up and saw someone standing on my balcony. That's really funny, I thought, I know I locked my door.

I squinted and thought I saw a rifle in the man's hand. And then I saw that all along the roofs of Weitlingstrasse there were men with rifles and machine guns. I clutched my bags of groceries tighter against my chest and thought, This can't be happening. I'm hallucinating.

I turned to walk back around the corner—half thinking that, if I simply did an instant replay and rounded the corner again, things would be back to normal—and before I could move I was surrounded by men in green uniforms and black masks. They ripped the groceries out of my hands, threw me to the ground, and handcuffed my hands behind my back. They didn't say anything. It was a beautiful, sunny day, but these guys were acting like we were in the middle of a war.

Suddenly I glimpsed a familiar face beneath one of these masks, and I couldn't help laughing: it was an ABV guy, a neighborhood sheriff, from my old neighborhood in Lichtenberg. Meyer was the lousiest ABVer I ever met. Once, I had been roaming around late at night with Auschwitz and we had bumped into Meyer. *"Ja, Herr Hasselbach,"* he had said, grinning. "Papers!" He'd known I was under Paragraph 48 curfew at the time. "You can forget it, Meyer," I'd said, and when I'd turned my back to him, the coward had bashed me over the head with his billy club as a bunch of other ABV types had jumped out of the bushes and arrested us.

Now it dawned on me who these masked clowns were.

Meyer had obviously joined the Stasi and managed to get into the one division that wasn't being disbanded now that communism had collapsed. This was the Stasi elite unit for fighting terrorism.

"Now, Meyer, what are you doing here?" I said with mock cordiality. "Just as we've got our asses up against the wall!" His masked colleagues seemed to look at him askance, and Meyer himself didn't know for a minute what to do.

"We've got your bunch, Hasselbach," he said. "You're antisocial."

"And you're in the Stasi, Meyer."

I had a sticker on my coat with a Germanic coat of arms that said "I'm proud to be a neo-Nazi." Meyer ripped it off, rather theatrically; later, the Stasi tried to use the sticker as evidence against me but found that it didn't violate the law in the "new" Germany, or at least they couldn't figure out exactly how.

Another masked man with a machine gun slung over his back and a checklist in his hands came over and asked Meyer who I was. "Hasselbach," said the man, checking me off. "Good, he's one we needed."

The scene in the street was wild. It seemed that everyone, even the most innocent bystander, was suddenly a cop. In the little shops, both customers and employees were also pointing weapons and arresting people.

Other people were wandering around with video cameras on their shoulders, filming everything. Someone shoved a camera into my face as I lay on the street in handcuffs, but he didn't seem like a reporter. And nobody asked me for my opinion or a statement.

As I later learned from Frank Lutz, he and Freddy Meisel had been in the attic of our building playing cards. They had heard some odd noises on the street, and Frank had said to Freddy, rather casually, "What's going on down there? Check it out, will you?"

Then Freddy had gone and looked out the window and said, "Hey, man, there's some kind of antiterror unit storming the building."

"Over the roofs," Frank had said, and he had climbed up a ladder and opened the skylight. A dozen machine-pistol barrels pointed back at him. Frank had closed the skylight and said, "The roof's closed, Kamerad."

Then Freddy had run to the window that looked out on the courtyard and poked his head out. Machine-gun fire had strafed the wall.

"Shit! They're here to kill us!" Freddy had shouted.

"We have to go out downstairs and surrender," Frank had said. "Otherwise they'll shoot us trying to escape."

But on the way downstairs, they had heard explosions, followed by more bursts of machine-gun fire, and Freddy had said, "Fuck this! If they're executing us, I'm not going to make it easy on them."

They had tried to run back upstairs then, but the masked men had already been on them. "Hands up or we shoot!" they'd shouted. Two minutes later they had been led out of the house, one by one, handcuffed and with a pistol to their necks, like everybody else in the house. It was especially ironic for Freddy, who was still on prison furlough and had just told Frank that he wasn't planning to return to jail; he figured in all the confusion of the government collapsing, they'd forget to come after him. Now here an elite Stasi troop had come, and at four o'clock sharp he was escorted back to jail.

When I heard all the commotion from below, I also wondered if they weren't just shooting all the guys in the house. I lay there on the ground and stayed calm when a bunch of the brawny masked guys lifted me into the police van. If I make a move, I thought, who knows what they might get away with saying happened?

The Stasi really shot up our building. Actually, they sabotaged our efforts to renovate it according to our contract with the city. You can still see bullet holes on all the inside walls of the courtyard where they shot at Frank and the others who looked out the windows. They opened all the locked doors with hand grenades, and in the basement they blew open our safe with plastic explosives.

Though we'd never figured on something as dramatic as this, the raid wasn't a total surprise to us. A couple of days before, a cop had come by the house, supposedly wanting to deliver a summons to me to appear as a witness or something. But this cop had looked around so curiously that it had made me jittery, and when he had left, I'd wondered if something wasn't up, but I'd had no idea what. Then the next night one of our guys who'd been in custody said that he'd heard something funny at the police station. He thought he had heard something about an operation against the house. That together with the subpoena had been enough to send up the alert. I'd begun to clear out the heavy weaponry, as well as the most inflammatory propaganda material, moving it to safe apartments and into the trunks of cars parked around the city. (After the raid, we made this a regular practice.) But I'd only done that for a few hours that night and hadn't expected the raid to happen the next day, so the Stasi still managed to confiscate thirty boxes of propaganda and hate literature, as well as explosives and other incriminating stuff.

However, partly as a result of our precautions, I later heard that the raid had disappointed them. They'd expected more weapons and "foreign" Nazi material from Lincoln, Nebraska, and the NSDAP/AO—the stuff we had moved first. Also, purely by chance, Weil and other "wanted" Nazis were far away at the time of the raid. The Stasi took nineteen people into custody, but most were allowed to go home that evening. The prosecutor asked for arrest warrants against Frank Lutz and two others. Freddy Meisel, who hadn't committed any crimes yet, was simply returned to prison to continue serving his time. They got Frank and me for distributing Fascist ideological material, which in the GDR could get you a heavy sentence.

I found out later that the interior minister of East Germany had ordered the raid personally. He was a young, brash guy and wanted to establish himself in the new unified system. Later, his intimate connections to the Stasi came out and spoiled any chances he might have had of doing that. It was clear at the time: he'd only been able to bring the attack off so smoothly because he was tight with the Stasi elite, which was looking for a chance to show that it had a purpose in the new era.

The raid played on the GDR state evening news—a special report about the breakup of the first neo-Nazi fortress ever established in Germany, a center of a massive conspiracy plot to overthrow the country. The footage was pretty effective, especially the shots of the disciplined masked men with their submachine guns. The Stasi had clearly choreographed the raid and filmed it for maximum effect. It was like an advertisement for their services. It was then picked up as a special report on all the stations in the West.

They took us to the jail at night, under heavy guard with double handcuffs, and we could hear the prisoners whispering as they looked down at us, "They're from Weitlingstrasse. They're the neo-Nazi terrorists." I was in the lockup with all these old, hardened murderers and robbers, and they were scared to death of me because I was a "terrorist" who'd been brought in by special forces under su-perstrict guard.

That night I heard a voice outside my window: "Ingo!" I went to the window and heard the voice again. It was Frank. We started talk-ing—I was on one of the lower floors and Frank was somewhere higher up, quite far away. But we could hear each other. We made an arrangement: we would string the interrogators along telling them nonsense about the scene, but very intricate nonsense. The govern-ment was collapsing anyway—the East German authorities were en-gaged in a hopeless struggle to keep their state together in a post-Communist form—and we figured that by the time we'd spun out our bullshit to them, there wouldn't be a prosecutor's office left to come looking for us.

Eventually the guards heard us talking and I was transferred to the other side so we couldn't communicate anymore, but they either hadn't heard or didn't care enough to pass along what we'd said to our interrogators. Or maybe the interrogators knew and were play-ing some sort of triple psych-out game with us. At this point, who knew?

We were taken around to a number of our familiar old stomping grounds, including Rummelsburg and Keibelstrasse. The prisons were much more relaxed during this transitional time. We were the only ones who were actually under strict lock and key. We were kept under special guard and sequestered in separate areas so that we wouldn't come into contact with one another. The only time we were taken out of our cells was for interrogations.

I learned a lot during these: for example, that our local bar in Licht-enberg where the waiters had always been so drunk had been watched every second by the Stasi, which had had cameras all over the place. My interrogators would show me pictures and ask, "Do you know him? What about him?" I saw that all these had been taken at our hangout and photographed from below—from the angle it was clear

that the camera had to have been concealed in the table itself somehow. Had the completely fucked-up management of the place—the
Wirt who'd sold me his cigarettes and the drunken waiters—had they
all been Stasi? No, we'd raised too much hell in the place.

I learned only later, reading my Stasi files—after they were stored
in the Gauck Archive and the new united German government
passed a law allowing everyone access to his own file—that there
had been a parked car in front of my apartment building in 1988,
rigged with a remote-controlled camera. Every time the front door
of the house opened, the camera had taken pictures. Also, from
1987 on the Stasi had, once a month, secretly entered my apartment
when I wasn't there. I hadn't noticed a thing—not a trace, they had
done it all so perfectly. When I read it, I thought, No way, they're
making this up. But then I saw pages from my appointment book
and address book from 1987, perfectly photographed on my desk.
The Stasi had simply slipped in once a month and then left, making
sure everything was in exactly the same place. They had done these
monthly searches practically until the Wall fell, with a pause for the
time I was in prison. (When I looked through my Stasi files, inci-
dentally, three of the most important ones were missing—about
when I was beginning to work as a neo-Nazi in the GDR—and
I'm sure the Stasi gave them to the West German authorities as a
present.)

Anyway, Frank and I made our statements to our interrogators
without endangering anyone in the scene but still making the Stasi
feel they were getting a big return on their investment. We were in jail
for six weeks, and, as expected, by the time we were all free again,
our tormentors were practically out of a job. It was now June 1990,
and the GDR had just had its first democratic election in more than
forty years. It had decided to abolish the state by September and
merge with the West.

The main downside to our weeks in prison, in fact, was that we'd
missed the elections, which meant that no neo-Nazi party was able to
run in the first free GDR vote. Worch suggested that we sue the State
for hindering our participation and committing fraud by arresting
the entire leadership of the party the month before the elections. But
we decided not to, counting ourselves somewhat lucky that, while the
government that had arrested us was about to be sent into oblivion,
the NA was still legal.

Frank Lutz went on a spree of trying to "put his life in order"; he got a regular job, and his girlfriend got pregnant. When he moved out of Weitlingstrasse to live with her, I took over the official first chairmanship of the National Alternative. I had already been its Führer in practice for some time.

MONEY

THE STORMING OF our house by the antiterror unit had one conse-
quence the State couldn't have been too pleased about: it made the
National Alternative famous. Within a few weeks our bank account
increased fivefold, as money from new members and the press—
which we charged for interviews—rolled in. Suddenly, we were able
to pay the attorneys for our endless court cases.

Journalists from all over the world wanted to do reports about the
house in Weitlingstrasse, and I was giving up to four interviews a day,
as well as staging press conferences in the lobby of our building. The
fee for one-on-one interviews was 200 to 1,000 marks. If they
wanted Hitler salutes or Nazi songs, that was extra.

We discovered that Americans were more reluctant to pay than
the others were. For simple interviews, we allowed them to buy us
meals and bottles of whisky to assuage their consciences. One time,
an American journalist tried to get an interview without paying
anything. He argued that even the president of the United States
didn't take money for interviews. "The American president can do
whatever he thinks is right," I said. "We take cash." The American
paid up.

The best thing was to get a good Japanese or South American news team. Then you were sure to make major additions to the operating budget. A Japanese TV team offered us 10,000 marks to let them film us with heavy weapons during an exercise at one of our paramilitary camps—we were beginning to stage war games at various sites throughout Germany and Austria—but I decided that was too dangerous. They insisted we use live weapons and explosives, which simply carried too high a penalty if the German authorities got hold of the film.

Most of the money flowed into the party coffers of the National Alternative, but *how* much was at my discretion. During this time I had more money than I'd ever had in my life, I could buy what I wanted, and of course I didn't have to go to work anymore.

STILL, WE NEEDED more funds, since the party was growing, and I started paying visits to a group called the German Cultural Community about once a month. Recommended by Michael Kühnen, it turned out to be one of our best sources of support, since it offered a way to meet West Berlin's Nazi professional elite.

The Community was a sort of salon run by an elderly woman named Dr. Valeria Krebs. She gathered only the "best" people around her—academics, attorneys, doctors—people who had grown up during the Nazi period, many of whom had been children of high-ranking Nazis; not famous or absolutely top people but the ruling elite of SS and Wehrmacht officers, lawyers, judges, and upper-echelon Party bureaucrats who had kept the Third Reich going. It was like a very particular sort of clique where the parents had all eaten at the same restaurants, played at the same clubs, and summered at the same places—only these places had all been in the Third Reich.

The members met in restaurants, always in a special room in the back. They were mostly between fifty and seventy-five years of age, and they all had good jobs and respectable positions and had to be discreet about their involvement with the Movement.

Usually there would be an event—a presentation, say, about the economic pressures caused by foreigners in the Federal Republic or discussions about NATO and the nonalignment of Germany. I often gave a little talk about all the good work we were doing at

Weitlingstrasse, and I collected gobs of money. They were very interested in the "younger generation," and they had high hopes for us, hopes that they'd never lost that a Fourth Reich would come.

In general people who gave large sums preferred to be anonymous. At one meeting, a man came up to me and said, "Hey, young man, tell me your bank account number. You're the right sort of party, you're on the right path. Tell me your bank account number." I told him the number and later saw that a large sum had been deposited.

Members rarely talked about themselves. One well-known attorney from West Berlin told us how his parents had been Nazis and he'd gotten a Nazi education in the Hitler Youth. Usually the others just said, Yes, my parents were there and they knew each other all very well, Germans treated one another better back then, things were better and fairer.

They'd pat you on the shoulder and say, "You're doing the right thing." They always said that. "You're doing the right thing, young Kamerad."

I was usually the only one who went to these meetings, but someone who occasionally came with me was the head of Wotan's Volk, Arnulf Priem. Oddly enough, despite his rough appearance—he showed up at these meetings dressed the way he always was, in a jean jacket with Nazi badges, his long, unwashed hair hanging down from the bandanna with the death's-head pin, usually in sunglasses— Priem made an excellent impression on these people, and they all respected him. He was exactly between their age and mine, and though he looked like a rocker he could talk about Nazi race ideology like no one else who was born after 1945. He also came from a "good" Nazi family, and many of these old people had known his parents. His father had been a high officer in the SS and was now the head of a large shipping company in the GDR. The senior Priem occasionally donated sizable sums of money to our party and dropped by the Weitlingstrasse house.

Not only did these old bourgeois types seem to have no problem with Priem's biker image, they actually seemed to like it that he was such a wild man. In a way he was living out their fantasy, for they all pretended to be good citizens of democratic West Germany, when in fact they wanted to throw off their suits and put on SS garb and live like Nazis. Whatever else you could say about Priem, he didn't pretend to fit in. He was not afraid to say openly that he was a Teuton

and wanted a strict Aryan state, with a reinstatement of the Nuremberg Race Laws and new concentration camps.

If these people liked Priem because he could speak their language
even while looking so different, I had the opposite appeal. I looked
like the stereotype of a good Hitler Youth boy. The old ladies would
come up to me and compliment me on my perfect features and racial
background. They all liked me, and I felt pretty comfortable. But of
course we didn't have anything in common—my father was a radical
Communist, and my grandparents had all been fairly anti-Nazi. I
preferred to listen at their meetings.

I did like the fact that even though everyone in the group was
wealthy, they never seemed to look down on me because I was poor
and from the East. The East-West difference did not exist for them.
Only your beliefs counted. And your genes.

WITHIN A SHORT time, with the help of the German Cultural Community, the NA and the Weitlingstrasse project had at its disposal an
excellent circle of donors, for the most part made up of academics,
lawyers, and physicians from West Berlin.

If we really needed money badly, a telephone call to a well-to-do
"friend" was all it took. One time there was a transport problem: one
call, and the next day I had 5,000 marks in hand to buy a car.

This money was the gift of an elderly woman whose husband had
been very influential in the National Socialists but had died during
the war. These Nazi widows were usually well off because they got
pensions from the State; in the case of the more fervent ones, their
husbands had usually been rather high-ranking Nazis, and, as pensions were based on rank, this made them very rich indeed. It is an
irony of the West German system that the widows of resistance fighters often didn't get any pension at all, while the widows of SS gener-
als lived in luxury.

These old ladies all treated Michael Kühnen with great respect.
He'd stop by their meetings, which would take place in individual
homes or rented rooms, where they'd always serve coffee and lots of
sweet cakes; the atmosphere was dainty compared to the meetings of
the establishment professionals in the German Cultural Community.

Kühnen would stop by to shake the old ladies' hands and to gossip
with them about their health and the Jews. And they would gawk like

a movie star was in their presence, for they knew Kühnen was the Führer of the Movement, even if he wasn't their Führer, because that title would forever remain in the hands of their girlhood passion—Adolf Hitler, the *Führer!* In return, Kühnen had a deep respect for these militant Nazi widows. Partly because of this, he founded an organization called the HNG—the Help Organization for National Prisoners—to give old Nazi widows something useful to do: take care of young neo-Nazis sitting in prison.

THE HNG WAS explicitly devoted to the rights and comforts of imprisoned neo-Nazis. It remains one of the most important features of the neo-Nazi landscape in Europe because it is constant. Because these old ladies are supposedly engaged in "humanitarian" work—and because they are old ladies—it is difficult for the government to crack down on them as it does on other organizations. Like our organization on Weitlingstrasse, the HNG is a legal nonprofit, so its official name is HNG e.V.

These Nazi widows send prisoners food and cigarettes and keep them supplied with propaganda material. In dark moments, they encourage them to hang on so they can fight the Jew another day. The HNG also publishes a monthly newsletter, the *HNG News,* which is distributed to all "political prisoners"—only neo-Nazis, not Communists, of course—to keep them abreast of all the goings-on in the scene.

The organization was a remarkably good idea. Not only did it give the old women and the prisoners something to do, it made sure that imprisoned neo-Nazis wouldn't turn bitter against the Movement but only against the State. When they got out, they would be eager to get involved again.

Moreover, all the different neo-Nazi groups and parties helped support and finance the HNG—both the Busse and the Kühnen factions—because they knew that when a member was in trouble, the HNG would not care what party he came from.

It might sound odd that all these parties led by militant young men would compete with one another but learn to behave under a group of old women who invited them to coffee klatches. But these old ladies were actually ideologically harder and more ruthless than most neo-Nazis of my generation.

In their youth, they had been hard-core Nazis, and they held stubbornly to this ideology. Bitterness and old age had only further hardened their love of the Führer and hatred of the Jews. A meeting with them was no ordinary coffee klatch. When these women began to gossip, they would talk about Auschwitz—or rather, the "Auschwitz lie"—and about the Jews and foreign pigs and Communists who should all be kicked out of Germany.

But first and always, they talked about Jews. Hatred of Jews was their deepest conviction, and Jews were their favorite topic of conversation. I don't think I ever talked about Jews as much as with these venomous little old ladies.

But they didn't just talk. They distributed propaganda and Holocaust denial literature—and they had a distinct advantage in that they were inconspicuous. They also worked as secret agents and spies for the Movement. They did come under surveillance, and about once a year some action was taken against the HNG. But usually the authorities would simply take the propaganda material away from an HNG member and tell her to stop passing it out in the future. It was a tough call for the cops because one couldn't very well put old ladies behind bars, though many of them really belonged there.

For one thing, they also held big meetings in which they would give speeches not *directly* calling for arson. But they might say, "It's about time something is done against foreigners, something our cowardly, corrupt democratic government in Bonn has neither the will nor the morality to do. . . ." Officially they would oppose the bombings and fires, while praising the young men who set foreigners' shelters on fire as being brave and patriotic in a land of cowardly democrats and multicultural mongrels.

And eventually they would express regret that they had to fight foreigners instead of the Jews. They'd say, "Nowadays there are only the foreigners, it is important to fight them . . . but we should not forget the Jews! We should not forget the Jews," they would always add, hopefully.

And many of the active young neo-Nazis, twenty or twenty-five years old, who did not have a deeply ingrained anti-Semitism, were affected by all this. Personally, I always had the opposite reaction. I took the ladies' money because I never looked a gift horse in the mouth. But I didn't like their way of speaking or the look in their eyes. It was unsettling to see old people so full of hate. It made me think of my grandma and grandpa, who were so humane, and here were these old people sitting there and talking about the annihilation of an entire portion of the human race—men, women, and children—with glee.

Somehow, it seemed more natural for young people to have these beliefs. I know that sounds crazy. But it is a uniquely sinister sensation to be sitting next to an eighty-year-old woman who is eating a piece of cake and dribbling coffee onto her blouse, and saying, "We absolutely should desecrate more Jewish cemeteries this month." And somehow I hated them for trying to incite a young person like me to do such things.

TALK

THROUGHOUT THE EARLY 1990s, the media, especially the German media, continued to present us in a surprisingly helpful way, for they never presented us as anything less than a serious political danger. They didn't exaggerate the threat we posed so much as dignify it.

They'd interview me or Christian Worch and give us five minutes' uninterrupted time to express our views. I can remember a talk show that gave one of our more articulate leaders almost half an hour to express his views. Rebuttal or correction of any false or misleading statements was left till the end. For any young people watching, this might be enough to get them interested, and they no doubt wouldn't wait until the end of the show to listen to the sober commentary telling them to disregard what they'd just heard.

Later in the 1990s, for example, when we participated in the Berlin elections, a big German network came and did an interview with me on *Heute Journal,* the German version of the *Today* show, which runs during prime time. Since I was one of the NA's candidates in Lichtenberg, they gave me ten minutes uninterrupted. I spoke about the foreigner problem, of course, and about how our party was offering a radical solution that was necessary to preserve German jobs and culture. And while we didn't win that election, my talking head on TV commenting on the issues of the day conferred legitimacy on the party and got us a lot of new members.

But Christian Worch was really the best at manipulating television for our benefit. One time Danish TV staged a meeting between him and the most famous left-wing investigative journalist in Germany, Günther Wallraff. Worch made Wallraff look stubborn and dogmatic, while he, the Fascist and Nazi, looked pretty liberal and rational by comparison. Wallraff started out with the moderator on his side as well as perhaps the entire Danish audience, and he ended the encounter flustered and practically speechless. You might have expected Worch to have berated and violently attacked him—that was the old Nazi style—but Worch, carefully dressed and with neatly cut hair, is the quintessential new Nazi, and his style is to always give the impression of reasonableness.

The whole point of our public appearances was to try to confuse people about the nature of Nazism and hence neo-Nazism. The goal was to make our opponents look like knee-jerk lefties and multiculturalists, while making the neo-Nazi look like a practical man responding to the grumblings of the average German. Although he is in fact an eccentric millionaire, Worch's appearance on TV conformed to the cliché of a German *Biedermann,* the sort of hardworking, taxpaying German the country loves so well.

For many years a notary's assistant (a sort of paralegal), Worch had completed much of his legal studies, and it showed. But he never received his law degree because he got a profession ban shortly before he would have finished school. The same measure that had been applied to my father in West Germany for being a Communist, the profession ban was really a strange—and effective—law designed to lower the economic and social status of political troublemakers and in effect to kick them out of society. (In Worch's case, its effect was muted by the fact that he was independently wealthy.) It was a part of the West German Constitution.

Worch even managed to make the concept of "Aryan"—the basis of all Nazi race theory—sound somewhat reasonable. The original Aryans had come from India and moved across the Asian landmass to Europe. The term was actually coined by philologists in the nineteenth century in their description of the world's language groups—hence, the Indo-Aryan language group. It was actually an entirely misleading and false description when taken as a "racial" definition, but the Nazis used it to say that Jews were alien to the European people, who were all, no matter what country they were from, "Aryans."

When the Danish interviewer asked gravely whether he thought he was "Aryan," as if this would prove that he still embraced the most evil and intolerant race theories that made him hate all non-Europeans, Worch chuckled and related an anecdote about his brother, who had married an Indian woman. When some of the more simply bigoted people in his family had objected, he had said to them, "Please, I beg of you, she's more Aryan than any of us." Thus the Nazi taught a little *tolerance* to some unenlightened, conservative Germans.

Worch was also careful never to endorse violence against foreigners, though he would say he could understand the anger that caused it. Meanwhile, in their face-off, Wallraff tried to convince Worch, on camera, not to be a Nazi and asked him questions like "Have you ever been to Africa? Have you ever seen one of their cities? The wealth of culture there?" Worch would politely point out that none of that was really to the point, for he didn't live in Africa, his concern was Germany. And so on.

While Worch was brilliant at a debate format like the one he entered into with Wallraff, his many speeches to outdoor crowds of neo-Nazis left something to be desired. There was a certain quality that got in the way of his ability to inspire an audience—he was the opposite of enthusiastic, a combination of morose and disdainful. Worch would say in a speech something like "and so, my Kamerads, we will forge Germany and Austria once again together into one Holy German Reich"—speaking about one of the grandest political goals of the Movement—and his tone would be so abstract and monotonous, he might have been reading a train schedule.

But one of our "star" speakers avoided these pitfalls and was considered the ultimate neo-Nazi for a crowd. This was Heinz Reisz. You didn't count on him for insight, but when it came to parties or conventions or leadership meetings—or, as Priem taught everyone to call them, from old Teutonic, "Things"—Reisz was your man. I went to see him once at a Thing in Langen, near Frankfurt, where he was from.

Heinz Reisz—"Nero," we called him—was fifty or sixty years old and an alcoholic. He claimed to have been a member of the SRP, the Socialist Reich Party, the first attempt to reconstitute the original

Nazi Party under a new name after the war, though it had been banned in 1952, when he was still a teenager. He had been a member of many other far-right parties in the 1960s and '70s, however, before joining Michael Kühnen's ANS.

Nero was a flamboyant speaker, and we let him talk at all our events. He had the old nationalist way of giving speeches that mostly died out after the war. It's an art, actually—an exaggerated speaking style with a lot of shouting and emotion. It is not only a Nazi style but an old Germanic style. If you ever saw Kurt Schumacher, the great Social Democrat, on TV, you've seen a bit of this now mostly bygone style of German speechmaking. It was the Germanic idea of inspiration and idealism in politics that became generally discredited by Hitler. If you ever saw Konrad Adenauer, Germany's first postwar chancellor, speaking, you've seen the opposite style: completely bland and factual. Our East German politicians were somewhere in the middle, trying to sound passionate but always having a bit of trouble when the subject was ball-bearing production quotas. The old speaking style can be very powerful—it is about the emotions one feels for a nation, a people, an idea.

Though a drunkard and an egomaniacal braggart, Reisz was always a hit. He would let out everything and exhaust himself completely. It's funny, he could look like an idiot if you only saw him sitting, but you only had to see him give a speech once. Reisz was not one of the most serious leaders in the Movement by any means, but he was among the most reliable people to invite to an event. He may have been more talk than action—but what talk!

In his closing speech one night in Langen, he shook with righteous fury, his enormous hook nose pointing down at the crowd like a weapon as he spat words through his huge walrus mustache, talking about the filthy Jewish vermin robbing the German people of every bit of their heroic grandeur, just like the left-wing unions. "The unions are a Jewish swindle!" he shouted. "And I would fully understand it if some honest worker would rise up against his slimy Communist union boss and smash his mushy brain in with a brick!"

But Reisz nevertheless had the charm of a Hessian—a man from the middle German state we were in that night. The Hessians drink a lot, and they make no secret of it. Reisz would drink three liters of beer before he started to speak—something that was quite customary with the neo-Nazis anyway. They wouldn't get totally drunk but much more unpleasant, half drunk. You can imagine that race ideology sounds much more reasonable after having a couple of liters of beer—your head gets a bit "mushy," as Reisz might put it. The speakers and the listeners were all a bit drunk. Actually, the whole ideology stinks of too much beer.

IT IS WORTH reflecting on the speaking and debating styles of the Movement's leaders because, in the final analysis, this was a large part of our appeal. Like its original model, neo-Nazism was built on the twin political platforms of public speaking and street fighting. Sixty years ago, during the last years of the Weimar Republic, Communist and Nazi street gangs had battled it out on the streets of Lichtenberg. Josef Goebbels, then the Gauleiter of Berlin—the post I now held—had stood on the street corners where we now fought, in his black leather trench coat, haranguing the workers about the virtues of *national* socialism. The tools the Communists and the Nazis used were the same as the ones they use today: the voice and the fist.

I actually thought of myself as one of the weakest speakers among the leaders of the Movement, and I was very self-conscious about it. I was good one on one and in small groups—I could convince almost anyone to follow me into danger. But my ideal platform was a group the size of a football huddle, where I could incite the team to aim for a specific goal. In front of a large group, I was hopeless.

I found this out in June 1990, when I realized what made Michael Kühnen such an effective speaker, even if he did not always sound as clever as Worch or as inspired as Reisz. He knew how to work his audience into a frenzy.

We went to Cottbus, a drab city near the Polish border, for the first official rally for a new party, the German Alternative (DA). I was officially the deputy chairman. The German Alternative was one of Kühnen's many "reserve" parties in West Germany—the kind he kept functioning on paper—and he'd simply found some local right-wing guy in Cottbus to serve as chairman. (The latter has since become an important politician in a slightly more mainstream right-wing party.) This was useful for extending the Movement's reach east, where there was a great deal of unemployment and local hatred of the Poles who came over the border.

Over the next few months, Kühnen, Gottfried Küssel, and I often visited the grimy little border city, where we could always be sure of large, enthusiastic crowds. Kühnen had especially high hopes for the youths there. He was excited in general about people from the East because he said they were less materialistic and more trained to accept the power of ideology. The West neo-Nazis were all infected with consumerism to some degree, and this was a stumbling block for us: they were not willing to sacrifice comfort for the Cause.

Yet there were hardly ever any problems between neo-Nazis from East and West, and considering how fast Easterners and Westerners in other parties and walks of life were learning to hate each other, that was quite a difference in our Movement. Of course, common hatred of the outsider and the Jew was an easy antidote to inter-German, East-West antagonisms.

As I was the deputy chairman of the DA and supposedly the meeting organizer—the logistics of the event itself had been taken care of by Küssel—I was expected to give the speech introducing Kühnen. Just the prospect of getting up in front of an audience made me queasy. Kühnen's health was beginning to fail noticeably by this time, though I still didn't realize that his illness was fatal. He looked pasty, but then he so often looked unhealthy. He'd probably just driven five hundred miles to get there and smoked two hundred cigarettes on the way. He was nevertheless marching around with his sardonic little grin, shaking hands and nodding his paternal nod at the throngs of people who'd come to hear him speak.

We had rented a sort of hall with a bar. The ceilings were very high, and there was a stage and a podium already set up for us. On the stage there was a big table in front, draped in an old imperial striped black, white, and red flag, the original flag of the German Reich from 1870. (That was the way to tell a skin meeting from a neo-Nazi official meeting. We always used the official Reich flag, whereas the skins would always display the Reich battle flag, with the eagle and the iron cross.)

About four hundred people showed up, mostly from the area. The audience was a mixed group of men and women from twenty to forty or fifty; there were no skinheads. Most were so regular looking that you couldn't tell they were neo-Nazis. They didn't wear any neo-

Nazi symbols because in Germany it's illegal to wear any symbols or uniforms at public gatherings. The whole hall could be arrested for it.

There were also a lot of press people in the crowd. Just before the start of the ceremonies and speeches, I told them to clear out. They left. Journalists were always willing to submit to almost any of our conditions in order to get their story.

After I'd dealt with the press, I began to think about my speech again, and I imagined myself turning green and throwing up all over our glorious Reich's colors.

I found Küssel and said, "Hey, Kamerad, I've really got cold feet about speaking in front of so many people. Couldn't we get someone else to introduce you?" The Austrian shook his head.

I began feeling sicker and sicker; my stomach got pains in it, and I became as pale as chalk.

The people in the hall had begun to sing the "Deutschlandlied." We'd sometimes sing Nazi songs, but we never yelled *"Sieg heil!"* or "Heil Hitler!" ever. Anyone in the audience who did was disciplined or thrown out immediately. This was a legal party, and any obvious Nazi rituals would have gotten us banned immediately. At these events there were always spies from the Office for the Protection of the Constitution.

Then it got quiet in the hall. The main event was about to start. I think I was actually shaking from fear; I wished so many people hadn't shown up. I wanted to be anywhere rather than there—better to be surrounded by three hundred angry anarchists, I thought, than speak to three hundred expectant potential Kamerads.

Küssel saw my anxiety, came over to me, and said, "Just start speaking, Kamerad, the rest will come of its own accord!"

I stood to deliver my opening remarks and was clearing my throat, slowly, when something happened to take me off the hook.

There was a disturbance by the door, where two beefy DA guards were talking with an older man who'd come in. "Could the person in charge of this rally please come outside for a moment," he said. "There is a question about the hall permit." He was very mild mannered, some sort of local cop or bureaucrat, and as soon as he'd said his piece he went back outside.

There was murmuring in the hall. But I was happy to get out of speaking for a minute more. I left the stage and walked up the aisle, expecting some sort of complaint from the local authorities that we'd have to argue about. But when I opened the door, I found myself face to face with a group of masked men, all aiming guns at me.

Looking down these twenty barrels somehow made me less nervous than I'd just been waiting to give the speech. I could tell this was some kind of special unit—the bulletproof vests under the cops' bomber jackets tipped me off—and their top-quality jeans and sneakers were a tip-off that they were some kind of *West* outfit, not Stasi.

I soon made out that the street behind them was clogged with police vans and cars, as well as a platoon of regular cops, all with weapons drawn.

The leader of the special unit stepped forward and asked me to identify myself. I told him my name and confirmed that I was the leader of the meeting. Then he explained what all the fuss was about.

"We're here to arrest Michael Kühnen."

"Then go ahead and get him," I said defiantly. I wondered if there was going to be a riot.

"No, no," he said. "Here, this is the warrant. You go back and bring us Herr Kühnen."

I took the paper, went back into the room, and gave it to Kühnen. He read the warrant out loud with elaborate emphasis, so that the crowd could hear him. The audience began to cheer. Kühnen laughed and said calmly, "Please go out again and bring all the press people in."

And just as the dozens of waiting journalists streamed into the room, the people in the audience were reaching an absolute frenzy, shouting "Küh-nen! Küh-nen!" and raising their arms in all sorts of legal, half-legal, and illegal salutes.

Michael Kühnen marched through the raving throng, as cameras flashed all around him, and went outside to be arrested.

Kühnen had gotten what he wanted—he had managed to turn his arrest into an effective media event. And I was happy I didn't have to make a speech.

15

BUSINESS TRIPS

One day Gottfried Küssel called me at my apartment in Wotanstrasse. I'd managed to acquire the place as a sort of private retreat for when I didn't want to deal with the scene over at Weitlingstrasse. I allowed Kamerads to call me there only in emergencies. Küssel very mysteriously said that somebody from overseas was coming to visit. He didn't want to tell me the guy's name in order to avoid spreading any rumors, but he said I could guess that it was somebody very important to the Cause.

"So, Kamerad, could we use your apartment to entertain this distinguished foreign guest?" said the Viennese Führer. "We urgently need a place for this person to shoot a film and also spend the night. Weitlingstrasse is too hot. The *Verfassungsschmutz*"—he was making the pun neo-Nazis often did, combining the German words for "constitutional protection" and "dirt"—"the Jews and God knows who else is watching us. We need somewhere private."

My apartment in Wotanstrasse was especially "safe." I had sublet it through a series of people and kept it secret from all but the most trusted Kamerads. We'd used it before for top secret leadership meetings.

"Sure," I said. "You can use my house to entertain your guest."

"We'll be there in twenty minutes," said Küssel. "Heil Hitler!"

I didn't return the compliment.

Having been brought up in a world where the Stasi tapped every tenth phone, I was uncomfortable using an illegal greeting over the phone. And of course, unlike Küssel, I had never been such a Hitler fan.

Exactly twenty minutes later Küssel appeared at the door of my apartment with a scruffy-looking director from London, his TV film crew, and a little, bespectacled man with a neatly trimmed mustache who raised his hand in a Hitler greeting.

"Heil Hitler! Hello! My name is Gerhard Lauck," he said in excellent German.

I was standing face to face with the chief of the NSDAP/AO, Gary Rex (Gerhard) Lauck from Lincoln, Nebraska. To say that the international neo-Nazi scene would collapse without Lauck was an understatement. He was the source of practically all the neo-Nazi propaganda pasted up on walls and windows from Berlin to São Paulo, as well as the center of a worldwide organization of which practically every serious neo-Nazi was a member.

The first part of NSDAP/AO stands for "National Socialist German Workers' Party," while the "A" is an abbreviation for both *Aufbau* (building up) and *Auslands* (abroad) and "O" is for "Organization." During the Third Reich, the original NSDAP had had its own "AO" in every foreign country where there were Nazis. Now Lauck's organization was the only true heir to Hitler's party, and by remaining a purely umbrella organization, exercising no direct control over local parties, it maintained order in an otherwise chaotic subculture.

As each member of every other neo-Nazi group was a member of the NSDAP/AO, Lauck's membership lists were huge and a lot of money circulated through the organization. And Lauck had great relations with old Nazis in South America, whom he would visit and who would occasionally make large donations. Actually, this is one of the main sources of significant Nazi donations—South America, and also South Africa, in both of which places war criminals own businesses and ranches. Lauck is especially good friends with Goebbels's former press secretary, Wilfred von Oven, who still gives speeches in the scene even though he is close to ninety.

Meeting Gary Lauck face to face was almost as great a shock as my first encounter with Michael Kühnen in Hamburg. My first thought was that he made a pretty subdued impression for the leader of a worldwide radical network. In a way, he conjured up for me what a middle-aged NSDAP member in the old days must have looked like: a respectable citizen doing the Führer's work.

But he fit the part of a neo-Nazi much less than Kühnen did. While the German leader always wore army pants and black boots, this guy, who was in his early forties though he looked ten years older, was dressed in a blue suit with a white shirt and tie. Even our middle-aged mad bomber Ekkehard Weil didn't wear a tie.

"Heil Hitler, Kamerad Hasselbach," said Küssel in a perfunctory greeting. Then Küssel started talking and I practically forgot about Lauck for the next few minutes as the Austrian dealt frantically with setting up everything just right for a film crew.

"Show me where all the electrical outlets are, Kamerad," he said. "The TV team needs curtains, a backdrop—we cannot shoot the leader of the NSDAP/AO in an empty room."

The damned Austrian was being pretty demanding about the whole thing, I thought, considering I'd let them use my apartment. But I suppose it was pretty sparse. They put up a blanket on the wall as a backdrop.

Küssel and Kühnen were both very tight with Lauck, but Christian Worch was warier, at least in public, because he knew that messing around with an organization like Lauck's could eventually get him thrown back into jail. Every time he was in Germany, Lauck was a fugitive from justice, like now, in my apartment, and the sentence for violating the ban on reestablishment of the NSDAP would be harsh—after all, the difference between "NSDAP/AO" and "NSDAP" was just a couple of initials.

During the filming, Lauck kept making little jokes, mostly about Jews. He'd be talking about Jews and comparing them to rats. Then he'd act as though he were terribly chagrined and say, "No, please excuse my rudeness to the rats."

LAUCK SAID HE had been born in Germany but had grown up in the United States. He even claimed that his family had had something to do with Frederick the Great, which was why he used Rex as a middle name. His real name was simply Gerhard Lauck. He ran his own publishing company, which distributed Nazi propaganda materials around the world.

He was also the publisher of the journal *National Socialist Battle Cry* (*NS-Kampfruf*), which appeared in six languages. I'd already been getting *NS-Kampfruf* automatically, because Lauck kept perfect track of every neo-Nazi organization in the world and put its leaders on his mailing list. *NS-Kampfruf* covered any current news regarding neo-Nazis, Jews in Germany and Europe, Holocaust denial conferences, Israel, and terrorist attacks. The content was often historical, with a lot about the life and struggle of the SA men in Germany, as well as serializations of classic Movement books such as *Mein Kampf* and *Protocols of the Elders of Zion*. Then there were contemporary features on neo-Nazis in prison, and on the last page of every issue there was a complete list of all such prisoners in Germany, the United States, and Austria.

Of course, there was also a membership application and a form to order things such as swastika flags, bumper stickers, Nazi marching records, Nazi books, Nazi videos. A lot of things that cost a fortune or were unavailable or illegal in Germany could be gotten from Lauck; for instance, he was the leading source of copies of *Mein Kampf,* which was banned in Germany.

I'd actually had quite a lot of contact with Lauck before this meeting, because I'd ordered stickers and propaganda material from him for the occupied house. And afterward, from time to time, he would write letters encouraging us in our struggle and asking for news from Berlin. He never tried to tell us what to do, but he offered connections to American Nazi groups; through Lauck, I later became a pen pal of Tom Metzger, leader of WAR, the White Aryan Resistance, in southern California, as well as Dennis Mahon of the Ku Klux Klan. Lauck always asked me how things were going with the Allies, and though he was an American by citizenship, he hated his own country like the plague. To him, Germany was the only Fatherland, and the "Jew-nited" States was useful only because it had no restrictions on weapons and political speech.

In Germany he could not have possibly run the NSDAP/AO. There were always a dozen arrest warrants out for him in several Federal German states. But from abroad Lauck concentrated his efforts here, because Germany was the "holy home soil" from which national socialism had arisen.

Almost all the propaganda materials he printed in Lincoln, Nebraska, were in German. Lauck's standard offering was little books of stickers featuring Nazi sayings from the 1930s, like *"Kauf nicht bei Juden!"* ("Don't buy from Jews!"), *"Jude verrecke!"* ("Die, Jew!"), and of course the neo-Nazi favorite, *"Wir sind wieder da!"* ("We're back!"). The idea was that those who were on our side should be learning just enough German to understand Jew-hating slogans in the mother tongue and that our enemies, especially the Jews, would have fear struck into their hearts by the resonance of these signs. Lauck relished the thought that concentration camp survivors would see his stickers.

We were constantly ordering all this stuff from Lauck, who himself largely subsidized the cost, which must have been substantial, considering he couldn't do bulk mailings. The German authorities checked the airmail and sea mail for this kind of material much as they checked it for drugs. Lauck had many tricks for sending letters and small packages.

For example, he often put as a sender "Alfred Silberstein" or some other Jewish name. It was a nasty little joke, but he'd actually found that packages with Jewish names as return addresses got opened less often by customs. And then he'd never mail anything from Lincoln but always from larger cities, usually Chicago, Los Angeles, Houston, or New York; he'd ship things to members of his organization there who would remail them. The material usually came via a third country and was repackaged many times.

But while you could send letters and small packages with false names, large packages were more problematic, especially if they were sent to me or to the Weitlingstrasse house; the authorities were not blind. So most of the mailings were done via Germany's bordering countries, from which they could be brought in by truck. The most popular route was over the northern border with Denmark, with the help of the organization of Thies Christophersen, the former death camp guard and author of the book *The Auschwitz Lie,* who leads the neo-Nazi movement there.

Christophersen is a former German citizen, and the German authorities have been trying to have him extradited from Denmark for years. But as in the United States, free speech is protected and Holocaust denial is legal. This was why Christophersen chose to base his Holocaust denial organization in Denmark and why he could so eas-

ily receive Lauck's mail there. It was ironic, considering the Danes
had one of the best European records of opposing the Nazi occupation—the king and queen of Denmark said, "We are Jews," when the
order came from the SS to make Jews wear yellow stars.

Now there was a political party in Denmark called the DNSP, the
Danish National Socialist Party, and its legal status made it a beacon
of the entire European neo-Nazi system. And the central computer
mailbox for all neo-Nazis in Europe was based in the city of Randers,
Denmark. We considered this famous anti-Nazi country to be one of
our safest bases of operation.

Via the mailbox in Randers, Lauck sent us lots of anti-Semitic
computer games, such as "Concentration Camp Manager"; these
were useful because they taught the user to treat human beings from
a certain group, with certain recognizable features, as simple cartoon
creations to be gassed and murdered. On the more realistic side, we
also got a lot of terror programs from Lauck: there was one program
called "A Movement in Arms," an instruction manual for terrorists
that taught effective techniques of robbery, silent killing, and bomb
planting; the best weapons to take on what kind of mission; and
things you might forget when planning a terrorist operation.

Another safe base was Holland, which was the home of an organization that was essentially the European equivalent of Lauck's: the
GdNF, or Like-thinking Community of the New Front.

Most serious neo-Nazis in Europe were members of this group,
and if you were a member of the NSDAP/AO, membership was automatic, and vice versa. Traditionally there hadn't been any membership requirement except to be accepted by the leadership, but in 1988
Kühnen began forcing members to take the SA oath, in which one
swore allegiance to the Führer. For that reason, I never officially
joined, though they may have considered me a member anyway.

I was a true believer, but I never liked oaths. If you had a genuine
conviction, you didn't need to take an oath. The oath did its job
only when your conviction wavered, but then it was keeping you
tied to something you didn't necessarily believe in. I was never again
going to be part of a political system that I couldn't leave of my own
free will.

The GdNF meetings took place in Groningen, Holland, perhaps
sixty miles from the German border, and I went to at least two that
spring. Our objective was mainly to discuss the organization of the

new people from the GDR, as well as the annual Rudolf Hess Memorial March coming up in Wunsiedel, Germany, in July.

In Groningen we stayed with Eite Homan, a very young and militant Dutch neo-Nazi. All the major players stayed at Homan's house during those meetings, signifying to me just how important a center this was: Christophersen, Lauck, Kühnen, Küssel—the most wanted neo-Nazis in the world were all gathered under one roof of an unassuming, rambling old house.

Homan spoke a mixture of Dutch and German, and he also spoke fluent English. He and the other neo-Nazis in Holland were all a fit bunch. It was amusing: they were much more "Aryan" looking than our crowd from Germany, except me. They were all blond and tall and strong. There had been a very large SS division from the Netherlands, and many of these young men were the grandchildren of men who'd volunteered for that.

Homan himself was very close to an old man whom I met at his house, a Dutchman who told me about his days in the SS Division Brandenburg. He was a horrible person, actually, with pale, watery eyes that seemed to look through you. He talked of his glorious fighting days, and I later learned that the SS Division Brandenburg had been a special division that consisted solely of professional murderers, chosen because they would relish mass shootings of civilians.

One of the oddest people at those meetings was an old Dutch Nazi widow named Flory Rost von Toningen. Her husband had been some sort of high Nazi Party man here, and she hated her fellow Dutch people for "what they'd done to him after the war." She had been convicted a number of times in Holland for what in Germany is called "incitement of the population." She must have been quite good looking at one time, blond and with a delicate face. She was very thin. She gave fiery speeches about Holland's glorious Nazi tradition, about how the Jews had poisoned the climate there so people supported the little Jewess Anne Frank rather than her poor dead husband. Her life was "dedicated to persecuting the Jews" as a moral obligation to him. She reminded me of our own murderous little old ladies back in Berlin.

OUR INTERNATIONAL CONTACTS took us far and wide. A few weeks later, I went together with a Kamerad from Hamburg on a business trip to Barcelona to speak with Pedro Varela, the chief of the Spanish Fascist organization Cedade. Our purpose was to make arrangements for the Spanish Fascists to attend the Rudolf Hess Memorial March in Wunsiedel.

It was my first trip outside northern Europe, but I hardly got to see much of Latin culture. They called themselves "nationalist Europeans," but as far as I could see, these neo-Fascist Spaniards hardly had much national pride. They seemed to wish that they were Germans, and all their propaganda showed big, Germanic-looking types, obviously cribbed from old Nazi posters of the 1930s. The Cedade ran a store where you could buy every manner of neo-Nazi propaganda, including Lauck's materials. Also the classics like *Mein Kampf* and little portraits of Hitler.

The Cedade believed that someday there would be a general National Socialist uprising in Europe. The whole concept was a bit vague, but of course the Jews were at the core of it. It was all about the common fight against their worldwide influence, which could be felt in Europe through the colonization of Coca-Cola and McDonald's and also through the North African immigration (an absurd notion, since of course North Africans were usually Muslims and enemies of the Jews).

These neo-Nazis envisioned Europe as a big community that would fence itself off from Jews, Americans, Communists, Japanese, and the Third World. Though it would gain strength from the individual nationalism of each country, the point was, in the end, Europe as a racial and cultural ideal.

The irony was that while Michael Kühnen took great care of such foreign contacts, encouraging us to pay the greatest respect to the Cedade leaders and invite them to the Hess March, our main cultural event of the year, he had utter contempt for them. He believed that "international nationalism" could accelerate the establishment of a Nazi dictatorship in Germany, and he agreed with the Cedade that all European states would one day have Nazi regimes, whose model would be the Germans. But Kühnen also said that Pedro Varela, leader of the Cedade, was not really an Aryan and that after the seizure of power he'd have to be kicked out of the Movement. The southern countries were always full of non-Aryans, according to Kühnen's interpretation, and while they were cofighters, they were never really Kamerads. This was especially true of Spain and Italy, where so many people looked like Semites. "Europe" was all relative—Denmark was not Spain, and only Nordics could be Nazis.

"Fascism is for underdeveloped peoples," Kühnen always said. Only a real German was worthy of national socialism. During the time of struggle, he said, we must use our friends abroad, but after the seizure of power, we would have to make a careful racial selection. From the Aryan point of view, these inferior peoples might be allowed to continue to embrace fascism, as the Spanish had after the war, but no dark foreigner could ever be a real National Socialist.

Kühnen always said that national socialism was a "natural science." It was about biological facts and hierarchies, while fascism was a purely political and social concept. The Spanish Fascists could fit into the neo-Nazi scheme of the world better than democrats could, but they would never be National Socialists. Our doctrine predetermined all place by race, so they could never be anything but the helpers of our race. In this sense, national socialism was much more precise than fascism, which was about uniting the nation. We were trying to unite the nation behind us only so that we could then divide it up according to our notions of "biological" order and cleanliness.

16

FOREIGNERS

THE LICHTENBERG TRAIN station was exactly at the other end of Weitlingstrasse from our house, and in the spring of 1990 it was the makeshift home for hundreds of Gypsies who, in the chaos of the collapse of the Communist bloc, were arriving daily to try to make a go of it in the West. Some had been driven out of their homes in Eastern Europe, others were trying to grab their share of the German social service budget by claiming to be political refugees. Doubtless many came for both reasons. They arrived by train, mostly from Romania, with no idea where to go. They slept in the train station with their children and everything they owned in the world spread out around them.

The station was attacked daily by people from our house, both skinheads and neo-Nazis. But even with our daily beatings of the refugees, we were hardly the most militant antiforeign group in East Germany. All around the country, neo-Nazis and even ordinary teenagers were starting to bomb refugee shelters and attack Gypsies on weekends. In many East German cities foreigners were becoming too terrified to go to discos they'd once frequented—and with good reason. In places like Cottbus and other towns near the Polish border—an area that was acquiring the nickname "the Nazi Belt" for the appeal we had among the residents there—beginning sundown on Friday night, no foreigner was safe. The favorite targets were Vietnamese, Africans, and anyone who looked suspiciously dark, who could be a Gypsy or Jew. But Poles were also favorite game. Young Germans had learned to make foreigner bashing part of their nightlife, and a little shelter bonfire was considered a good way to kick off the weekend.

But I never got a kick out of attacking foreigners, and, even if I had, foreign refugees were not nearly as abundant in Berlin as in other German cities. As for Berlin's large Turkish population, they had their own neighborhoods and their own extremely tough street gangs. Anyway, I had a different strategy. For me the foreigner problem had to be solved politically, with appropriate legislation, so that the state could more carefully control who would apply for asylum in Germany. (Actually, our demands on this score were more than met by the legislation Chancellor Helmut Kohl forced through Parliament in 1993 in the wake of the Solingen bombing. We knew then that our tactics had worked to pressure the government.)

I thought one could work against foreigners without attacking them, simply by informing German taxpayers what a foreigner costs the State per month, about 6,500 marks, calculating social services and so forth. Germans care about nothing so much as their precious deutsche marks, and I thought they could be turned more quickly against foreigners by pointing out what foreigners cost rather than by setting them on fire. Germans have never liked disorder. The Reich's Kristallnacht pogrom of 1938 had been a public relations disaster because the German people, while they would tolerate prejudicial laws against the Jews, would not support such violence, looting, and chaotic destruction.

The only violence I considered legitimate was the violence against the Anarchist Anti-Fas, who attacked us with equal fervor. But Gottfried Küssel and Günther Reinthaler, the Austrians, greeted the arson attacks against foreigners with relish and believed they were the only way to force a political solution. They wanted to put pressure on the government via firebombings, and they wanted to launch one from our house. They said it was sad but the government couldn't be made to understand any other way. I still believed that, from a political perspective, this strategy was fatal.

"We have to take some concerted antiforeign action," said Küssel. "We are the first neo-Nazi-occupied house, the beginning of the Nazi wave of the future, the symbol of the new day for all Germany! We cannot afford to be left behind on this issue."

I wasn't sure what Michael Kühnen thought about the whole thing, for, though he was in favor of violence against foreigners, he was also very interested in building up the neo-Nazis as a political force and thus moving away from the terrorism of the early 1980s. But he wrote us after the attack on the anarchist center—the one where a woman was blinded—that he was especially pleased with this action, which had "contributed to sweeping the Red mob from the streets once and for all." In the same letter, he warned the house that, despite this success, "we shouldn't neglect our foreign fellow citizens." Oliver Schweigert copied the letter and hung it on a bulletin board, like a manifesto or call to arms.

So I went along with the rest of the leadership, and we began to plan. We chose a refugee shelter that lay not far away in the Hans-Loch quarter in Lichtenberg, a little over a mile from Weitlingstrasse. We debated for a long time what would be more effective—a poster action or an attack—and it caused a rift.

I said that if we attacked with stones and Molotov cocktails, we would only reinforce the negative picture of us in the press. We were participating in elections at the time, and many voters would be turned off by the violence. It would be pointless and idiotic to commit a violent attack in Lichtenberg, I argued, the very place where we were campaigning and trying to show that we could bring stability and order.

But many others, led by Reinthaler and Küssel, were in favor of an attack. They said that the foreigners wouldn't understand anything else and that we would get lots of sympathy from the *Volk*. After a violent action, they claimed, most of the foreigners would simply leave.

It became an argument between some of the most militant neo-Nazis and us, the founders of the NA, who still thought more of being a normal party. On Reinthaler and Küssel's side were the skins who regularly beat up the Gypsies in the Lichtenberg train station. The skins were our storm troopers—the idiots who cleared the streets for us and intimidated our enemies—and enjoyed a bit of violence anytime.

Finally, we compromised: some of the people, including myself, would go armed with posters and stickers and paste up the refugee shelter with political propaganda, the others would bring gasoline.

In June we attacked with about 150 people. We began between nine and ten in the evening, and the whole action lasted about an hour and a half, until about eleven.

We had arranged to meet at a spot near the shelter. Reinthaler came in a new BMW he'd just driven up from Salzburg. He was carrying Molis and sundry weapons in the trunk. Meanwhile, I went with Frank Lutz and about thirty or forty others armed with stickers and signs. We all agreed to park on streets a little away from the shelter so as not to alert the refugees, mostly Romanian Gypsies.

The poster party arrived at the shelter about ten minutes before Küssel and Reinthaler's men. We set about methodically covering every wall with stickers and signs: "German workplaces were taken by foreign workers." "Foreigners are social parasites." Stuff like that. Some had a slogan printed underneath: "Vote National Alternative." There were no Nazi symbols or sayings because these were "anticonstitutional," and, despite the violence that was about to go on next to us, putting up posters was a legal political activity. We were a registered political party doing legal campaign postering, and we didn't want to compromise that status.

When we arrived, we could hear music inside—some sort of non-European music. I found it a rather pleasant accompaniment to putting up the posters.

We could tell Küssel and the others had arrived when we started to hear the familiar chant: *"Ausländer raus!"* ("Foreigners out!").

As SOON AS the first shouts of "Foreigners out!" rose up from the street, the music and talking stopped and all the lights in the shelter went out. It became completely dark. Now it was impossible to tell there was anyone inside.

From the other side of the building, where Reinthaler and Küssel were, I heard a new sound mix in with the chanting: Molotov cocktails hitting the concrete walls and stones smashing some of the windowpanes.

Reinthaler and Küssel had a lot more people than we did, including at least seventy or eighty skins from Lichtenberg. We were on one side of the building putting up stickers and posters, and exactly on the other side Küssel and the skins were throwing Molotov cocktails. I knew Küssel was moving in a circle. It was an effective tactic.

It was entirely calculated violence—meant only to scare and do damage, not to seriously hurt people or set the house on fire. No one threw Molis through the windows. Still, they look terrifying. A single Moli creates a huge tongue of flame that burns about ten minutes.

As Küssel said, the bomb action was done as a warning. It was no accident that they threw their Molis only at the concrete walls, not through the windows. When you throw a Moli against a wall, it smashes and everything immediately goes on fire. It actually looks much worse than it is.

Our Molis were always two-thirds gasoline, one-third oil—the best is motor oil—and a piece of cloth down the middle. You can make them with gasoline only, but it's a much riskier weapon to use, because gasoline lights immediately. With only gasoline, just the fumes can ignite. But if you use about one-third oil, it works per-fectly; in midair the oil and the gas begin to mix, so when the Moli hits, the mixture ignites. The Anarchist Anti-Fas had tested this out to perfection, and we'd gotten copies of their instruction pamphlets and distributed them among ourselves. If you built the Molis this way, you had about ten seconds to throw them.

You don't actually target people, because the bottle doesn't break. Instead, you throw it in front of their feet. This is much more effec-tive; it sets their trousers ablaze.

At the refugee shelter, however, the linoleum staircase inside was in flames. The people inside hadn't had time to lock the door, and you could see the flames licking up the stairs. Küssel also had some skins busy hurling smoke bombs through the windows.

I don't think there were many children in the house. Otherwise there would have been more screams. But even if they had been cry-ing, one would hardly have heard them what with the hellish noise we were making outside, where Küssel, strutting around in his bomber jacket and black boots, was barking orders into a mega-phone:

"Don't throw any Molis in there. . . . Enough with that side—you men there around to the next row of windows! . . . There's a man missing here. . . ."

Küssel had a powerful effect on skins. They liked to be bossed around, and he spoke their language.

Küssel was the only one in the whole street one could actually hear clearly, shouting into his megaphone in his melodious Viennese accent. Otherwise there was only the sound of glass shattering and the whooshing and crackling of flames. Then the cries of the skins: "Foreigners out! Foreigners out!" *"Sieg Heil!"* "Red Front die!"

It didn't matter that there were no Reds inside, only refugees; they just threw all the phrases together. Küssel led them in the chants on the megaphone, but he never said *"Sieg heil,"* because this was a criminal offense. If he had, the authorities could have arrested him. As it was, they couldn't, for as far as the law was concerned, he hadn't done anything wrong. What did he do? He'd simply shouted from the street "Foreigners out!" And that was his right. He'd perhaps been a bit too noisy, but nothing else. You couldn't prove that he'd led the attack. He was simply a "concerned citizen" with a megaphone.

TWO REFUGEES CAME home during the attack and tried to get into the house, but they were beaten up by skins. I didn't see it, but there was a report about it the next day in the paper. I didn't hear or see any foreigners during the entire attack. It was like a ghost house.

When police sirens came screaming down the street, we retreated a bit. But then we saw the police post themselves and simply watch, like spectators at a Roman arena. They didn't attack. They didn't try to stop it. They didn't say anything.

An hour and a half later, no fire trucks had come. After another few minutes, though, different vans started to drive up, each holding perhaps ten cops. Some cops with helmets and shields got out. They had just started to close in when Küssel's group, which had made a full circle of the house, started to pull back.

One of the cops, who apparently recognized me though I didn't recognize him, came up to me and said jovially, "What are you up to this time, Hasselbach? You really never learn!"

"You can see what I'm doing," I said, holding up the pile of posters. "I'm a politician." Then I continued my work.

Shortly afterwards, we "politicals" decided it was time to pack it in. It looked as if the police were now forming a chain and might block off the street.

Actually, they didn't do anything. They moved in only when Küssel was finished. Then they started to close off the street, but the people who'd been participating were able to get to their cars and get away quickly.

As we were leaving I heard one or two of the refugees in the house finally say something. "Pigs!" they screamed. "Leave us in peace! We didn't do anything to you!"

DURING THIS ACTION I never thought about the safety or well-being of the people in the house—people who could have been hurt by the stones we were throwing or the flames. The people in the house didn't exist for me. Only my friends and I existed. And the Cause, the Party. The foreigners were far away from me somehow, even though I was acting as though they were so much in my way and pasting things on the walls of their house.

It wasn't that I hated the refugees or particularly wanted them to get hurt. I was indifferent to them. For me it was a pure political action, and the consequences of it as such still worried me as we left the burning building of fearful people behind and went off to our local pub to tell stories and sing songs and get trashed.

But Reinthaler had been right, because a few days later the house was cleaned out by the politicians. It wasn't used as a refugee shelter anymore. The action had been a success.

AFTERWARD, I COMPLAINED to Küssel that he had sent us "politicals" in as a pretext and cover for his violence. And that he had actually risked *our* safety by putting us in the line of fire while we were simply postering. Now I recall this with particular shame. I realize that you can't separate what I was doing with the posters from what Küssel was doing with the Molis. I may not have been as ready to embrace racial violence as he was, but I was just as responsible for it.

THE FINAL IRONY was that I didn't even particularly dislike foreigners, and, if I'd had more opportunity, I probably would have made some foreign friends. Foreign women, at least, were completely fine with me, though most Nazis would have flipped out at this thought.

Shortly after we attacked the refugee shelter, I had my first sexual encounter with a foreign woman, and I liked it a lot.

She was from Thailand. I met her on a trip with Auschwitz to see Christian Worch in Hamburg. After talking politics for a few hours, Auschwitz and I went to the Reeperbahn, the famous red-light district of Hamburg, and that's where I met her. I suppose she was a prostitute, but that wasn't what our encounter was about. I think she just liked the way I looked.

It happened like this. I was walking around with Auschwitz, and in front of an Asian restaurant we saw this very good looking woman. She was standing there with her girlfriend and was sort of winking. Auschwitz walked up to her because he thought she was winking at him, and she shook her head. "No, no . . . him," she said, and pointed at me.

I went over and she said, "Come with me."

"Where?" I said.

"Please come."

"I have no money," I said, because I thought she wanted money.

"You no money," she said.

So we went to her apartment, not far away, which was quite nice. We had sex, and she didn't want any money for it. It was a lot of fun. I didn't think it was strange that she was foreign or Asian at all. I liked her, and I gave her my telephone number in Berlin, not thinking I'd ever hear from her again.

But then she kept calling there. I got the idea that she'd fallen in love with me. She'd get the answering machine at Wotanstrasse, but at the time I had a couple of other neo-Nazis staying with me there. She would leave messages on the machine. A voice in broken German would say, "Hallo, here Nikko."

Then the guys got all excited. "What's going on here?" they asked. "You're friends with a foreign woman? An Asian?" This would have been *Rassenschande*—"race disgrace," the word that used to be used to refer to relationships between Jews and non-Jewish Germans.

I kept getting the messages. "This is Nikko, calling for Ingo. I want to come to Berlin to be near you. I want to see you."

I never spoke to her again.

17

REMEMBERING RUDOLF HESS

RUDOLF HESS WAS always an idol and a martyr for the neo-Nazis. He sat in Spandau Prison for forty-one years for the crime of being Hitler's deputy during the Third Reich. When he was found dead in 1987 in his cell, hanging from an electrical cord he'd supposedly tied around his own neck, the ninety-three-year-old Hess was the sole prisoner serving time for the sins of a nation, years after all the other Nazis had been let out. (Almost all the others were freed within five to ten years, after the Allies ceded jurisdiction over the Nazi crimes to the new West German state.) This suggested to many that there was something fishy about the Hess case. At the Nuremberg trials, the only prisoner who'd been in Allied custody for more than four years—in the Tower of London, on Winston Churchill's orders—he'd sat silent, his stonelike square face with its famous sunken eyes looking dead and vacant. His last words before being sentenced to life imprisonment were *"Ich bereue nichts!"* ("I regret nothing!").

You see these words now, emblazoned over Rudolf Hess's picture, on countless T-shirts worn by right-wing youths across Germany. Like his mysterious flight to England in May 1941, they have many possible meanings. They could, of course, mean what many skinheads and neo-Nazis take them to mean, that Hess had known about the mass murder of the Jews and didn't regret it. But it could also mean, I was in England before Auschwitz was built and therefore I have nothing to regret. Or it could even mean, I came offering Churchill a separate peace and was locked up instead, silenced so that the world could suffer four more years of war, so I have nothing to regret.

For me and the rest of the SA faction, Rudolf Hess was the greatest hero among the leaders of the Third Reich both because he had not been part of the disastrous war years and, more important, because he was a symbol of the heroic pre-1933 "years of struggle." Hess had been a cofounder of the SA and one of the earliest Nazi leaders. I believed that Hess had seen that the war with England, which Hitler wanted to carry on, made no sense and had tried to stop it, a bold act for which I admired him. Other neo-Nazis, for much the same reason, saw him as a traitor. But everyone used him as a martyr and a symbol around which to rally.

When Rudolf Hess died on August 17, 1987, at age ninety-three, he provided the Movement with an event far more effective than Hitler's birthday—and certainly more than Hitler's dying day, since the Führer had committed suicide with his mistress. Hess was buried in his birthplace, a little Bavarian town called Wunsiedel, and when the neo-Nazis first organized a demonstration and march there to commemorate him, it was surely the biggest thing that had happened to the town since the Third Reich, when their hometown boy had been vice Führer of the whole country. Now Wunsiedel has become the neo-Nazi Mecca. The march is always quite a spectacle, attended by neo-Nazis of all ages and walks of life—British Fascists, Italians, Spanish, Americans, Scandinavians. The expenses of the march are usually paid largely by the Movement's millionaire, Christian Worch, though funds arrive from other deep pockets as well.

IN AUGUST 1990 I took part in the fourth annual Hess March with a group from Weitlingstrasse as well as another group I'd convinced to come along for the ride.

The previous month Germany had won the World Cup soccer championship, and in each big city there'd been huge celebrations. For many Germans this was the first great chance after unification to celebrate their feeling of new national power. But in Weitlingstrasse there was no celebration. It was nice that Germany had won, but it was the wrong Germany—the democratic Federal Republic we hated.

The hooligans went nuts, of course, using the event as an excuse to go on a looting binge. I'd known some of the hooligans toward the end of the GDR, when the disorder had been imported, like everything else, from the West. They'd done pretty much the same as they were doing now—fight at soccer games with the police and other hooligans—but the fall of the Wall had meant one huge new possibility for them: plunder. In the GDR they'd gotten arrested for banging heads, but if they'd tried to steal and destroy property, they'd have gotten sent so deep into the bowels of Brandenburg prison that their next soccer game would have been in Hell. All property in the GDR belonged to the State, so an attack on property was an attack on the State. Now, in the transitional period between GDR and united Germany, no one really knew who owned anything in East Germany. These were honeymoon days for the German hooligans.

All summer, I had been making overtures to them, trying to get to know their leaders and to use them as soldiers in our cause. There was a fairly wide cultural gap: just as we didn't care for professional sports, the hooligans didn't like organized neo-Nazism. They didn't give a shit about ideology, and they found people like Küssel uptight, boring, and bossy. But that year, in the wake of the soccer victory, the hooligans were one of the fastest-growing groups of right-wing youth in Berlin—and I wanted them on our side.

After much effort, some hools confided to me that I was the one neo-Nazi leader who could communicate with them, and I felt like I'd embarked on an important development in the scene: a long-term pact between us. The hooligans would not only add to our numbers at events, they'd also greatly enhance our ability to intimidate leftists and the police. I became friends with one of the most important hool leaders, a tough, brutal type named Johnny. A real ladies' man, Johnny was quite intelligent, though he used this intelligence . . . selectively. He was a leader in the hooligans' scene to the extent they have leaders, which meant he yelled the loudest at their riots and led them on to plunder.

I considered it a coup for the Movement when I convinced Johnny to get his boys together to come to the Rudolf Hess Memorial

March, the biggest neo-Nazi pilgrimage of the year. Their motive would be a road trip with the chance to conquer fresh territory. No matter: their numbers and strength could be very helpful.

So on August 16, at 11:00 P.M., a couple hundred hooligans showed up at our meeting point.

Johnny and the hooligans were all drunk. He came up and slapped his hand on my back. "Hey, Kamerad! Heil Hitler!" he said, kidding.

My younger brother, Jens, was with me, looking pretty tough except for his glasses, which always made him look kind of bookish. These were the glasses that had helped me escape to the West. Jens couldn't see a thing without them. We hadn't really hung around together much until the last few months; after all, I'd usually been in jail or avoiding the house while he was still living with my stepfather and my mother. But after the Wall fell, I had taken more interest in him. I had convinced him to come over to the neo-Nazis, and he was now living with us in Weitlingstrasse. Jens looked like a classic skin, with his bald head, bomber jacket, and black, steel-toed Dr. Martens boots. You could tell he was a neo-Nazi skin because of his white laces.

Back in the GDR, if you had Dr. Martens on, you were a neo-Nazi. You often weren't served in restaurants if you were wearing them. But now everyone in all the youth scenes in Berlin wore Dr. Martens boots. More violent types had the steel-toed kind, but that wasn't evident at first glance. So the color of the laces had become the only real way to tell them apart: white meant white power and foreigner hate; red meant anarchy and leftism. Black laces could pretty much mean anything, and these were what I wore.

I didn't wear Dr. Martens, though. I didn't like the fact that they were "radical youth" footwear, and I also didn't think they were the best boots for running or fighting. I wore Bundeswehr parachutist's boots, which I'd bought in a secondhand shop. They looked totally brutal, with harder, thicker soles than Docs. I don't care what kind of toe caps you put into your Dr. Martens, with Bundeswehr boots you could do a lot more damage—they were simply weapons. The parachutists were trained to kill with a stomp of their boots.

And while many of my Kamerads wore nylon bomber jackets or jean jackets—and Küssel and Kühnen wore black leather—I had another unusual piece of clothing from our "democratic occupiers": a NATO field parka. I always loved this coat and still have it today, even though I've thrown away almost everything else that reminds me of the Movement.

But nothing in the neo-Nazi or skinhead wardrobe could compare with the fashion statement made by the two hundred hools standing before me. Their clothes—garish sweaters, polo shirts, and silk jackets, cost what most Berliners earned in a month. They all wore only the most expensive brands. Next to our skins with their pea green bomber jackets, the hooligans looked like peacocks in their silk windbreakers and Italian leather. Of course, by tomorrow morning, these thousand-mark sweaters and silk jackets would be torn to pieces, and by tomorrow night, they'd have new ones. It didn't matter to them—hooligans never paid for their own clothes. They stole them, like they did everything else.

I was so pleased to have my pack of well-dressed barbarians assembled on time that I almost didn't notice that, even before we were all in the bus, a brawl was about to break out between some hools and Oliver Schweigert, who was attempting to search everyone getting on for weapons. He was just following customary procedure: before a trip people were checked for weapons because there might be problems with the police and if they found weapons they could confiscate the whole bus. But in this case it was a bad idea.

Johnny took me aside and made it clear that there wasn't a single hooligan who was ready to freely hand over his flare rocket. "You stop him, Ingo, or one of my guys will lay him out," he warned me.

The flare rocket was the hooligans' standard weapon: it suited their personality—frivolous, festive, crude, and dangerous. You pressed a flare down onto the base and then hit a button to make it go off. At a distance it dispersed and disappeared, so mostly we used it as a "scare" weapon—the flashes made every hooligan brawl look like New Year's. But at fifty feet, a flare could be deadly. First the force would knock you down. Then, if your clothing caught on fire, you would get a big burn spot and the magnesium in the flare would eat into your skin. What's worse, you couldn't get rid of it; the stuff would run down your body like burning soup.

Flares were legal to buy because they were the same kind used on boats and for emergencies: magnesium mixed with phosphorus. It wasn't legal to carry them around, however. If you got stopped with one, you pretty much had to prove that you owned a boat. The advantage of a flare rocket was that it was so small you could easily hide it in your pants or boots; there was a pin you could push up and then it was secured, nothing could happen. I had a flare rocket on me at the time, one I'd use later in the trip.

I calmed Johnny down and was able to dissuade him from laying Schweigert out flat. "Plunder, Johnny," I reminded him. "There will soon be lots of plunder."

So we boarded the buses, a big double-decker and several Volkswagen microbuses. Everyone had chipped in about 20 marks toward the cost, and Johnny handed me the hooligans' cash. I thanked him again for keeping his hands off the members of the leadership committee of the NA, namely Schweigert, and we finally got on our way.

We had flags with us, but we didn't hang them outside the bus. We didn't want to draw any attention on the autobahn because of the anarchists, who were headed to Wunsiedel for a counterdemonstration. Not long after we left Berlin, we spotted several travel buses one after the other with skull-and-crossbones flags waving out of the windows. (Oddly, the death's-head symbol—which had come to stand for the SS death's-head divisions of concentration camp guards and professional murderers—was also the symbol of the anarchists.) Fortunately, they didn't notice us.

After about twenty-five miles, at the request of the hooligans, we stopped at a highway rest stop. As we were getting out of the bus, one of them cried, "Germans, let us plunder!"

A couple hundred hools stormed the late-night convenience store at the rest stop. The salespeople seemed to have made the acquaintance of hooligans before, for all of them immediately ran from the room in panic. The place was a sort of supermarket, but it also sold other things, like CD players.

The hooligans began helping themselves. The store was full of them. They didn't demolish many things, they only took them away. They cleaned out the food, alcohol, and cigarettes, as well as stereos and CD players from the shelves in cartons.

The driver sat, stunned, as the hooligans brought all the stolen goods back to the bus. One of the youths scolded the driver: "Don't stare, you bum, get going!"

There was a police car parked about a hundred yards away from our buses. The cops sat and watched. To be fair, what could they have done? Two policemen against two hundred hooligans. But they had radioed for assistance, so that after about fifteen minutes on the highway, three other police cars overtook us, their blue lights flashing. We pulled off, and the cops informed us that we would have to return to the rest area.

So we turned around and, accompanied by the police cars, went back to confront the people we'd just looted. The consequences could have been pretty serious. "Looting"—stealing en masse and rampaging the way the hooligans did—was a more serious offense than individual stealing.

A cop asked one of the still-terrified saleswomen, "Can you recognize any of the perpetrators here?"

She shook her head vigorously and answered, "No, no, they looked different. None of them is here."

"Please look at these men again carefully—otherwise we'll have to let them all go."

The saleswoman and her colleagues insisted. There was nothing else the police could do but to let us all go. For some reason, it never occurred to them simply to look in our bus.

The drive continued without further incident. In the meantime, most of the travelers, hooligans as well as neo-Nazis, got totally drunk. At six in the morning we got to the meeting point in a small village outside Wunsiedel, where we were gathering with all the West German and foreign neo-Nazis.

We lay down in a nearby field and slept off our drunk. A few hours later, when the first supermarket in the area opened, we stopped in for breakfast. Now I was starting to get into the spirit of things. Everyone ran through the market, grabbing whatever he liked to eat. Some hooligans even went to the checkout clerks and asked for bags when the cookies, bread, sausages, jam, and butter they were gathering started to fall out of their arms. It was odd rampaging in the morning, because you had a different feeling when you'd just gotten up. Here is this small, tranquil town, just getting ready to start the day. And in rolls the barbarian army, bringing ruin.

All of the neo-Nazis participated in these rampages except Schweigert, who had moral—or, as we'd say, "ideological"—scruples about plundering German stores. I might have had scruples if I'd thought about it, but I'd gotten into the hooligan frame of mind and was enjoying it: I was hungry, why should I pay? There was some shiny object I wanted, why shouldn't I take it? It was thrilling just to

take things without paying. Later I felt sorry for some of the people
who were being robbed by the hooligans and realized I couldn't really be one myself. I just couldn't be that callous, at least not for reasons of pure selfish self-satisfaction. But for the moment I was along
for the ride.

We got back into the bus, drove to the meadow, and ate our breakfast. Then we set off for the cemetery, but the cops had sealed it off.
Here it was nine in the morning, and already hundreds of cops with
shields and helmets and nightsticks were blocking every possible way
of slipping in. They wanted to keep away the neo-Nazis and, perhaps
more important, the anarchists, who might have destroyed the cemetery just to get at Hess's grave and destroy it.

At the entrance one of the cops asked me brusquely what I wanted.

"There lies a friend of mine," I said in a friendly way.

The cop grinned at me. "Come on, get lost, Herr Hess won't be
visited today."

We went back to the car. An old lady, clearly the type who sent
cakes covered with inspirational quotes from *Mein Kampf* in frosting
to imprisoned neo-Nazis, approached us and said, "You've come all
the way here specially, and now they won't let you in. You must come
again tomorrow, when the pigs are gone!"

In the meantime, roughly three thousand neo-Nazis had arrived
from all over Germany, and the street in front of the cemetery took
on the look of a neo-Nazi fashion show. No one was wearing overtly
Nazi symbols that could get him arrested, but the runway abounded
with the latest modifications of old Nazi signs and symbols that met
the fashion sense and legal modesty of today's neo-Nazi. The words
"Blood and Honor," either belted or worn as a patch, were popular
this year, as was the Celtic cross—a cross inside a circle, symbol of
Küssel and Reinthaler's Austrian party.

As always, the best uniforms and paraphernalia belonged to the
FAP, the organization led by the beer-bellied, white-haired old Friedhelm Busse, the only serious competitor in the German neo-Nazi
scene to our myriad of Kühnen parties. Busse's men wore getups as
close to the edge of legality as you could get, and from a distance they
looked exactly like a group of original Brownshirts. Their armbands
were ingeniously close to the real thing: all red with a white circle,
within which was their party's symbol: a black wheel like a sort of
machine gear with the letters FAP inside.

Probably the most cryptic neo-Nazi symbol—one therefore of great symbolic use within the Movement—was a little triangular patch we called a *Gaueck,* or "*Gau* corner." The "*Gau* corner" referred to the system of regional administrative units—or *Gaue*—into which Germany had been divided under the Third Reich. I had one sewn into my NATO parka on my right shoulder, and by its color any neo-Nazi could tell I was from Gau Brandenburg, which contained Berlin.

Each *Gau* had been administered by a sort of governor called a "Gauleiter," or "*Gau* leader." Goebbels, for example, had been the Gauleiter of Berlin/Brandenburg, the title I now had. While the rest of their countrymen had moved on to new forms of government administration, as far as several thousand people in Germany and Austria were concerned, they were still governed by the old Nazi system. The original Nazis had operated just such "shadow" administrations during the 1920s, often with *Gaue* as tiny as ours were today, while 95 percent of Germans and Austrians knew only about their democratic institutions. When Hitler came to power in 1933, the *Gau* system, which had been functioning within the Movement, simply replaced the democratic local administrations—governors were fired, Gauleiters took over their offices and budgets. The years as a sort of play government had helped them prepare for the seizure of power, and we followed the same logic today. Thus, the Gauleiter system was taken dead seriously, even if it seemed ridiculous.

As it happened, *Gauecke* were legally prosecutable anticonstitutional symbols, since they represented the Nazi administrative system. But conveniently for us, hardly any policemen knew what they were. *Gauecke* were useful because they let someone know instantly where you came from. It was also somehow satisfying to know that we understood an entire bureaucratic system—an entire government—that these slow-witted democrats didn't even realize was there.

ABOUT SIX THOUSAND policemen and more than five thousand Anarchist Anti-Fas had come to greet the three thousand representatives of the many *Gaue* of Austria and Germany, as well as our distinguished foreign guests. Television cameras from around the world were also on hand to record the turmoil. We were happy to oblige.

The police chief requested that we give up the memorial march—he was determined to stop an outbreak of violence and maintain order. But Worch, who'd organized and paid for this thing, was so thrilled that so many Nazis had come that he wouldn't cancel any of the events. He did take me aside and complain about the rampage at the rest stop, however. Embellished reports about the events of the previous night had spread like wildfire, and most of the neo-Nazis found the attack on the convenience store rather funny. But Worch was annoyed. I told him that everyone had been hungry and he should be happy that so many had come along. He told me that if they couldn't be made to act like real neo-Nazis, perhaps we weren't so lucky to have them.

In the end Küssel recruited me and a group of my Berliners for the job of keeping order. Punctually at three o'clock the announced demonstration and march began, led by Michael Kühnen. We marched down the little main street of Wunsiedel. Everywhere there were police cars, motorcycles, even helicopters hovering overhead. Worch had arranged it with the cops, in order to keep the anarchists from attacking us and starting a riot. The anarchists stood by the roadside and shouted "Nazis out!" and "Brown swine!"

It was the same as any other demo by radical rightists, only this was our first one of this size, and in a town as small as Wunsiedel it felt impressive. We marched through town with our banners: "Rudolf Hess Martyr," "Foreigners out," "I don't regret anything." Then there was a rally with speeches by Kühnen, Worch, and Pedro Varela of the Cedade, whom we'd recruited to come from Barcelona. He spoke in good German and talked about how much Hess and Hitler and the German Nazis had done for Europe.

Then, on the march out of town, the anarchists tried to attack us from the side streets. I fired a flare stick in their direction and ran toward them together with other marshals, half of whom were Johnny's hooligans. We were armed with fence slats and posts. We hadn't brought any baseball bats to the Wunsiedel demo because they would have been incriminating and bad publicity in front of the press cameras; the slats had to be carried slung in people's belts, like swords. Of course, now we had an arsenal of loose cobblestones beneath our feet, and we made good use of these as well. We beat back the first anarchists we ran up against, and the others turned around and ran head over heels into the arms of a police unit. The police attacked with their rubber truncheons. As darkness began to fall, the whole street was lit up by a flare fight—red, green, yellow.

Many Anarchist Anti-Fas were taken into custody; few neo-Nazis were arrested. The cops got Küssel for openly wearing his chain with the golden swastika—it would have been legal inside his shirt. They came up to him, looked at his pendant, and said, "Please come with us." They put his arms behind his back and handcuffed him. Some in the group got all excited about it, but I thought, if he's so stupid as to run around with a swastika chain, he deserves to get arrested. Küssel was always showing it off. He'd had the golden swastika made at a jeweler's in fourteen-karat gold: a sun wheel with a swastika in the middle.

But we bailed him out in about two hours—for 4,000 marks—and had a big laugh about it. Then we went to eat at a local restaurant— Worch, Kühnen, Küssel, Schweigert, and some others from Berlin. We were in high spirits. Kühnen said he hadn't imagined so many people would come and wouldn't the march look great on TV. Also how holy it was to be in the town of Hess's grave, and surely the English had had him murdered in prison. When we came out of the restaurant an hour later, we found a big fight going on between some anarchists and hooligans right in front. We joined in a bit. "Bashing a couple of leftists is good for the digestion!" said Küssel. Kühnen looked on approvingly. Then we drove off.

On the road back to Berlin, a few miles out of the city, we stopped the buses. At some distance from the caravan several small groups of skins, hooligans, and neo-Nazis had posted themselves in the ditch along the street. It was getting dark, but you could still make out people passing in cars. If they were anarchists, they were bombarded with cobblestones. Some stopped or skidded into the ditch, and our people would then run over and work the cars and the passengers over with fence slats. It was like they were playing highwaymen or stagecoach bandits.

But while the skins concentrated on destroying the cars and hurting the people, most of the hooligans simply were interested, as always, in what they could get—and at this hour what they wanted was to get high. Most hooligans were alcoholics, as well as taking whatever drugs they could get their hands on—Ecstasy, coke, marijuana. The hooligans would bash up the car and the driver for a few minutes, then Johnny would ask the shocked driver the same question: "Do you have coke? Where's it stashed? You can't tell us you're driving around here without coke, we know better, we know for sure."

Johnny's search yielded only modest results, but enough so that on the ride back he and his hooligans seemed convinced that old Rudolf Hess had been a pretty cool guy after all and that it had indeed been worth coming to pay their respects.

18

DEADLY GAME

Over the next couple of months, I often invited the hooligans to our parties at Weitlingstrasse, and I also went out with them. For me it was a welcome change to be able to hang out with people who weren't obsessed with the Movement. It was like being on vacation. Of course, I justified it by saying that I was recruiting them as storm troopers, but for the time being it was more like they were recruiting me. I'd found the plundering at Wunsiedel amusing and pleasantly anarchic. So in October, shortly after the formal reunification of Germany, when the hools invited me on one of their trips—the big Leipzig-versus-Berlin game—I accepted.

The Berlin hooligans were good at what they did, you had to give them that. Their models had always been the English hools. There was a "hit list" or "chart" of the most ferocious hooligans in the world, and until this year the English hools had been in first place. (Hooligans kept up with this sort of thing in their fanzines; the whole hooligan scene stayed in touch that way.) But the top position had now shifted to BFC Dynamo Berlin—the Berlin soccer club. They were unbeatable, which, for the hooligans, meant they destroyed and stole the most stuff.

Most of my fellow neo-Nazis looked down on the hooligans—and askance at me for my new ties. In general they distanced themselves from wholesale property destruction. The other leaders in the house thought that if hools couldn't be strictly ideologically disciplined—and they couldn't—they weren't worth associating with.

We met on Alexanderplatz. There were ten rented travel buses waiting for six hundred of us. About an hour outside the city, they made their apparently traditional pause at a rest area; this time I joined in as they rampaged through the convenience store and brought everything that wasn't nailed down back to the bus. To speed things up, we formed a chain and passed the stolen goods down the line. Three security guards tried to stop this conveyer belt; some hools beat them up and threw them down an embankment.

When the supplies were stowed in the buses, we got back onto the highway. In the meantime, whoever wasn't drunk got drunk. And soon everyone was hungry.

Three of our buses pulled up in front of a tiny wurst and burger stand. Hundreds of hools poured out of the buses and up to the counter and ordered bratwurst from the proprietor. They were very polite and friendly, saying, "Could I please have bread with that" and "We'll just pay when we're through, if that's okay." It was eerie, because I could feel the dam waiting to burst.

The little owner of the stand brought his whole stock of sausages out, laid them on a tray with a pile of rolls and mustard and beer, and said, "Hopefully they will be enough to satisfy all you young men."

He wrote everything down on his little pad, adding up the sausages, rolls, and beers. He didn't even have a cash register. You could tell he was a typical new "East capitalist"—a man who'd lived his whole life under communism and had now borrowed and mort-gaged everything he had for a chance to become a capitalist. Such a person generally opened up one of two types of businesses in East Germany in 1990: a used-car dealership or a bratwurst and burger stand. This guy was so thrilled to have so many customers, he couldn't stop grinning as he rushed around filling the orders and writing it all down. He probably thought he'd make enough to retire on in the next fifteen minutes.

I sympathized with the poor chump, for when it came time to pay, Johnny's friendly manner suddenly disappeared.

"Nobody could eat this dreck you serve!" he cried, and, raising his hand like Geronimo leading the charge, he let out a battle whoop that spelled the end of the small-business man's hopes for riches.

Before the little man could protest, we pushed over his entire wurst and burger stand, with him inside it. The stand had a heavy base, and it took forty or fifty people to push it over. But the hools organized the operation with exactly the right allocation of manpower, as though they'd performed hundreds of similar tasks. We cheered as it hit the ground. I was feeling a little guilty but joined in the cheering anyway.

"Stop it! Stop it!" shouted the man in the tipped-over stand. "Leave me in peace!"

We obliged him. Sated by the tray of sausages he had prepared, we ran back to the bus, leaving the seller under the ruins of his stand.

At a parking lot near the town of Bitterfeld, about five hundred West German hooligans were waiting for us. Together we drove on toward Leipzig. Once at the stadium, we all waited on line outside to buy our tickets. It was all very orderly, though of course it took a long time to sell tickets to eleven hundred hooligans. But suddenly the word began to filter down the line that they were letting us buy tickets but then not allowing us into the stadium.

A couple of hools and I went to check out the situation, and, sure enough, they were letting the old people and kids and normal people in but turning the hooligans back. I asked a cop what was going on. He replied flatly, "There will be no hooliganism at today's game."

A mass of hooligans had begun to build up at the gate where they weren't letting any of us through. I wondered if they would charge into the stadium and start a riot. But then, from out of nowhere, more cops started arriving. A lot more cops. They were marching in front of the stadium in riot gear, in lines. Shit, they're serious, I thought. They're really going to try to keep us out.

The rows of armored cops got thicker and thicker. The mass of hooligans built up too, as everyone had given up buying tickets. There was no communication between the sides yet. We didn't try to break through their chain or even sneak through. We were waiting to see what the cops wanted. Then we found out.

Without warning, the cops shot tear gas into our midst. They started to shoot rubber bullets as well: hard rubber bullets that could cause serious damage, tear out pieces of skin, not to mention the danger to your eyes and ears.

You could feel the rage spreading through our lines like a rumor—a rumor of impending disaster—of violence to answer violence. We had been waiting in an orderly line to get into the game. These bastards had attacked us. They wanted war? They'd get it!

About a thousand hooligans went at about half as many policemen. Behind their shields and helmets, these were ordinary Vopos—People's Police—nothing we couldn't handle in close combat. A mass brawl erupted. It was about 2:30 in the afternoon.

After our initial attack—punching and kicking and getting ourselves clubbed in return—we retreated down the road from the parking lot in the direction of the train station. About ten blocks away, we came to a major street crossing and the word went around that we should stop and prepare a barricade, something to defend against the pursuing cops. There was a strong mood not to run but to hit them again, right in their stupid, cowardly, helmeted heads. But what would be our barricade?

Opportunity arrived in the form of a lone police truck. It was a big army-green truck of the kind that could hold fifty Vopos easily in its covered rear bay; there was chicken wire over the windshield for combat situations. The truck was driving down one of the cross streets, probably in response to the alarm from the stadium, very likely carrying fifty more cops to add to the fight against us.

But when the driver saw us, rather than stop, he skidded into a turn, doing everything he could to hightail it down the street. That was it. We charged. The vehicle wasn't nearly fast enough. It was also empty. We had him trapped.

The driver didn't bother to shoot or even pull his weapon. In the face of hundreds of angry hooligans, he just jumped out and ran.

One of the hooligans took his place and drove the truck straight into the crowd of cops coming up the street. The cops panicked and ran in every direction, clearing the street.

It was incredible. I'd grown up in a place where the police had always used every truck, every car, and every building against us with utter impunity. Now we were attacking the People's Police with their own truck! And they were running like rabbits. The cops' organization was shattered, and they were humiliated. The hool drove around honking the police truck's horn, and everyone shot up flare rockets and cheered. It felt like a revolution.

Then we got lucky again. This time a regular city bus was passing by and the hools had an idea. Charge! They attacked the bus and threw out the driver.

A couple of minutes later, a tiny Trabant came down the street and met a similar fate. Charge!

And then, as if acting on some primal unspoken agreement—they didn't need Küssel with a megaphone to tell them what to do—the hools pushed the bus into the middle of the intersection, parked the police truck next to it, and rolled the little Trabi, which with its plastic body weighed far less than the wurst stand, on top of it. We had our barricades. Long live the Revolution! But not for long.

What the hools did next surprised me, even considering they were hools. They methodically removed the fuel from the bus and the Trabant and splashed it all over the canvas top of the truck and around the other vehicles. After this, most everyone retreated to the edge of the intersection, to a safe distance. Then a number of flares were fired simultaneously into the canvas of the truck.

Whoosh—boom—roar! The street was an inferno. And the hools shouted in victory. *This* was the revolution, 1990 style. It had been accomplished by an almost equal mix of West and East hools working together—the spirit of reunification and cooperation Chancellor Kohl and all the big politicians were always trying to encourage. The hooligans were model new Germans.

Hundreds of outnumbered, outmaneuvered policemen stood at some distance and watched the proceedings, aghast. Eventually fire trucks showed up and put out the blaze. We withdrew from our fiery barricade, shooting off flare rockets as we went, and made for the train station.

BY THE TIME I got to the train station, it seemed as though most of the hools were already there, and a kind of pensive mood had set in. Everyone was milling about on the gravel beside the tracks. The cops began to line up on the embankment, facing us and watching for signs of what we would do next. They seemed to think they had us cornered here at the station and were deciding what to do with us. They didn't realize that we were deciding what to do with them.

But in the middle of this calm, I had such a strange feeling. A feeling of sudden seriousness. As though I knew it was going to be very serious here in a minute. I suddenly wanted to get out, I didn't feel comfortable here in this scene. These guys didn't know what they were doing, and they didn't care. It was amazing, the balls they'd had to attack the cops. We'd paid those Vopos back for firing at us without provocation. And it had been thrilling to watch the fire. But half the crowd had forgotten it already. They had no planning or strategy. They acted on mass impulse. This made them tremendous brawlers and street fighters, for there was no time to really communicate in such situations anyway. But it didn't make them good strategists.

The cops wouldn't forget or forgive what we'd just done. They couldn't let themselves be made fools of. They'll hit back hard, I thought, and now's the time to beat it while we still can. That's what we neo-Nazis would have done. But the hools weren't doing anything of the kind. Confrontation was their game. Barbarians on the rampage. Into the blades of the legionnaires' swords, screaming "Germans, let us plunder!" You can't just keep acting like this, I thought, there's force and then there's force. When a hole opens up in the State's armor, it makes sense to charge through. But holes don't last forever, and you have to be smart enough to get out before they close up, leaving you trapped on the wrong side.

Suddenly one of the hool leaders shouted, "Forward! Attack!" Their orders never got more complicated than that. But then the crowd began chanting, an eerie sound like a cave full of animals all growling in unison:

"WAH . . . WAAHH . . . Take the cops! WAH . . . WAAHH . . . Attack the cops!"

There was almost something musical to it—you might think we were on a giant gravel stage, putting on some sort of weird modern opera. Our audience, the cops, didn't know what to think, and so they did what cops sometimes do when they don't know what to think. They drew their weapons and began firing into the mass of growling hools.

"Shit, I wish I were shorter," I thought as the bullets whizzed by my ears. At six foot six, I was an easier target, even crouching down, and, unlike in a street fight, my long limbs couldn't help me. I tried to pull everything in as close as possible.

While I was worrying about my anatomy, out of the corner of my eye I saw someone get hit and fall to the ground. I figured the impact of a rubber bullet had knocked him down. He was about thirty feet to my left.

Just after I saw him fall, however, someone saw me and called out, a voice I recognized.

"Hey, Ingo, it's me, Heinisch!"

It was Michael Heinisch, a twenty-seven-year-old do-gooder who'd taken my brother Jens into his Christian Youth Project before I won Jens over to the neo-Nazis. I had known Heinisch for a long time—he was always working with the punks and leftish asocial kids back then, on a permanent mission to convert all East Berlin's violent "scene kids." We'd actually always got along pretty well, even when I had pulled Jens away from his project and competed for its other members as well. I wasn't surprised to see him here, either. He was always right in the thick of it, wherever kids were getting into trouble. Heinisch would never have thrown a stone himself—he was always standing in the middle of the riot, trying to set a good example and defuse the violence.

I called back a greeting to Heinisch and gestured to the fallen kid.

"Let's see what happened to him!" shouted Heinisch.

We both ducked low and ran over to the boy. It was Mike Poley, a seventeen-year-old hooligan well known around East Berlin. Not a bad kid at all, a pretty ordinary teenager. His head lay to one side, and the thinnest stream of blood was trickling out of his mouth. Heinisch felt his pulse.

"He's dead," said Heinisch.

"How can he be?" I said. "They're using rubber bullets. Did he have a heart attack?"

Heinisch shrugged, and we examined the body for some sign of a wound. I tried to lift the boy, but he was too heavy because he was dead. Heinisch put his hand on my shoulder to stop me. Instead, we ducked lower over the body as the bullets flew around us.

That's when we noticed the wound, a tiny hole in his chest. We rolled him over on his stomach and saw the larger hole where the bullet had emerged. Of course, I thought, it always enters small and exits big. Where had I learned that? Mike had gotten a clean shot through the heart.

We were both lost in thought for a moment. When we looked around us again, we saw several other wounded, bleeding hooligans on the ground.

We laid Mike's body on the tracks. A hool near me was shouting at the police in a frenzy. Suddenly I couldn't stand to hear it any more, these bravura insults.

"Oh, shut up, you asshole!" I said. "Mike Poley's dead."

The word got around immediately. It spread even faster than the chanting "Attack the cops" had. And a hush began to spread over the hools until, what seemed like quite suddenly, all thousand of us were silent. Dead silent. The only sound was of bullets whizzing and policemen shouting and some wounded hools rolling around in the gravel and some others screaming in pain.

A hooligan took a photo of Heinisch and me bending over the body. The hooligans always had expensive cameras with them, and they grabbed any opportunity to use them.

"We should go to the police and tell them there's a dead boy here," said Heinisch.

"Stay with him, I'll look for an ambulance or a doctor," I said and crept off. Almost as soon I was away from the body, though, I realized how absurd that idea was. One always reacts to these things by rote, I thought, ordinary responses to an extraordinary situation. It was absurd. How could we go report this to the authorities who were firing on us? The only thing we could do was surrender, and that was less likely now than ever. What good would a doctor do a dead boy, anyway?

The police were firing less frequently now, and I suppose they were discussing how to move in and arrest us. I didn't see Heinisch again that night.

Various things around us were still on fire, and the fire trucks were spraying water as the cops were shooting. But the overwhelming noise here was the silence from the hools. Now I knew what the end of a battle feels like, the horrible calm that settles over the losing side. All memory of our earlier victories had disappeared. Mike Poley, barely seventeen, was dead.

Hard as we thought we all were, hooligans did not play with real guns. Neither were the cops supposed to. I don't think anybody could believe that the cops had done this. It wasn't part of the game: the game was that you did as much damage as you could and eventually they subdued you and arrested you.

AFTER THE LULL, the hooligans' shock and depression began to turn into rage. Then they seemed to deliberate, en masse and with very little verbal communication, what to destroy, weighing their options for the future: near term, the next ten minutes; long term, the next two hours. The idea began to circulate that it was time to hit the shopping district.

A number of the hools had managed to escape from the field of fire
out the back part of the train bed, over a steep embankment, and up
onto the street. It was completely dark on the embankment, so it was
easy to scramble up without getting shot. More and more hools took
off, and I followed them.

On top, we found ourselves on a road with a tram stop in front of
us. Of course, we stopped and stormed the next passing tram car. The
passengers all got out and ran away. The fat tram driver didn't rush
from his seat. He just sat there looking at us in his gray uniform and
hat. Then he lifted his hands from the wheel and said, "Take it."

We did. The fat driver got off and, rather than running, walked
about thirty feet to a bench and sat down and watched. One of the
hools took his spot and started us off, full throttle, toward the center
of town, no scheduled stops.

I was surprised to see how easy it was to drive a tram. There was
basically only this little wheel—not for turning but only to make it go
forward and backward.

The police didn't follow us. I suppose they were still in a standoff
with the hools down in the train bed, or maybe they were dealing
with the wounded or Mike Poley's body.

The tram was full to bursting with hooligans. The mood lacked the
usual sense of celebration that would have been there after conquering a city vehicle, but the memory of Mike's shooting was also clearly
fading, as everyone got psyched for the rampage to come. I was trou-
bled by this, but I didn't know what else I should be doing. I sat there
smoking and looking out the window. It's shit to continue with the
violence that's just killed someone, I thought. On the other hand, an
urge for vengeance was growing in me. An urge to revenge ourselves
on the city and the public order. To lay waste to what they were trying to protect.

At one point I looked up and recognized my old friend and fellow
neo-Nazi Silvio Baumann, whose place I'd stayed at after first escaping from East Germany. Silvio was wounded but basically in one
piece. He always got injured when something like this happened.

Silvio had gotten a fractured skull at the celebration after the
World Cup game in July, and they'd had to remove a piece of bone
from his head. He had been hit by a paving stone. I couldn't understand how he could be at it again so soon after being healed, but I
think that part of it was that this whack on the skull, rather than

knocking some sense into him, had only knocked more out. Six weeks after getting out of the hospital, he was supposed to go back to get a plate put into his skull. But he never went back to get it. We had an ongoing quarrel about this. "What kind of an idiot are you?" I would say. "Go and get the damn plate put in your soft head." It made me really mad that he wouldn't bother going back for his treatment, when he obviously had a serious condition. Sometimes he'd suddenly faint on the subway or in the street.

Over the past few months, at events where there was violence, I often found myself watching out for two people: Jens—because he was my younger brother but also because he depended so much on his eyeglasses that, if they were smashed, the anarchists could easily have killed him—and Silvio, because of his head, which I suppose without that plate had about as much protection as an egg. Luckily Jens wasn't here, and now I'd found Silvio.

Silvio was taking lots of medication and wasn't supposed to drink, but as usual, he was trashed, with blood dripping down the side of his neck, a fence post in his hand. He was barely coherent but managed to say "Hello, Ingo, we're going to the center of town to fuck it up . . ." Silvio was an example of why not to start hanging around with the hooligans; around them, he just kept taking his pills and getting smashed.

Silvio was an intelligent guy, but, like so many of us, he had deep, deep wells of anger inside him. The knock on his skull hadn't actually made him lose any of his faculties; he had simply become more extreme. It was like he kept no distance at all from death anymore. He was always in front in dangerous situations. And yet with only one more good whack on his head, he'd be dead. I knew that with Silvio there might be a specific reason for his self-destructive rage, because Silvio Baumann, this hard-boiled neo-Nazi, had a Jewish grandfather.

He never spoke about it. I assumed it was too embarrassing for him that he on the one hand wanted desperately to belong to the scene and on the other hand had this in his family. We knew it from his mother. On occasions when something about the neo-Nazis came up, she'd say, "But how can he be a neo-Nazi? After all, Silvio's grandfather is a Jew." Silvio always got angry and said his mother was crazy. And indeed she may just have been making it up to get him to reconsider what he was doing. But you don't usually make up that sort of thing.

Many people in the neo-Nazi scene had rejected him after that rumor got started. Then, with his head injury, he was really out. So he had gone over to the hooligans, though he continued to live in our house. Later I invited him to live with me. I felt sorry for Silvio, but I didn't know what to do to help him. The best you could do was keep him from throwing himself directly under a truck or into the arms of a club-wielding cop.

THE CENTER OF town, which had been deserted, was suddenly populated by hundreds of hooligans, who stormed out of the streetcar shouting. The first person we ran into was another man in a wurst and hamburger stand. This one wasn't fooled for a second that we were customers. He grabbed for his tear gas bottle and began spraying us excitedly. I broke in through the side door and he momentarily blinded me, but then some other hools were easily able to get the can away from him. The disarmed vendor fled in panic, and we methodically destroyed his stand, ending by tipping it over. I don't even think anyone was hungry this time. The man was lucky—skins would have followed him and beat the hell out of him, but hooligans at such moments tended to forget about the people and focus purely on property. When hooligans attacked people deliberately, it was usually other hooligans.

In the melee, I lost track of Silvio. Shit, I thought, I hope he doesn't get killed tonight too. I followed the group onto a shopping street, where I bumped into Stinki, who'd come with another group of hooligans. Stinki had three cameras around his neck and looked like a professional reporter. He handed me a camera with a friendly gesture: "This is for you, Kamerad—come on, it's Christmas, Hasselbach!"

I grinned back at him. "No thanks, photography isn't really my thing."

"It's your own fault if you don't take advantage of a day like this," said the happy skin. Seeing Stinki always put me in a good mood, somehow. Unlike Silvio, he seemed indestructible. I'd heard that if there was a nuclear war, the only species that would survive would be insects. Insects and Stinki, I thought. Like them, he could adapt to anything.

I walked on a couple of streets farther. All around me windows were being smashed, walls sprayed, cars demolished.

In front of one store, I watched a determined-looking hool throw a giant cobblestone through the plate-glass window. What a crash! Shards of glass sprayed like ice in all directions. It reminded me of the iceman who used to come down my grandma's street in Prenzlauer Berg as I was growing up and pull his wagon up in front of the house—a real wagon with a horse—and chop a block of ice for the house with his ax. He'd shave it with the ax until it was the right size, and little crystals would fall all over the cobblestones, just like the glass here. The stone thrower looked pleased and stared for a moment at all the groceries lying in front of him, there for the taking. Then he reached in and took out a candy bar. That was all. One candy bar. And then he moved on.

Passing by one store, I saw a cash register suddenly come flying through the window. The hools looting the store hadn't opened it, they'd just picked it up to use as a missile. It hit the cobblestones, and bills went flying everywhere. Only some of the hools took notice and stuffed their pockets. I got five fifty-mark notes—West fifties, nothing to scoff at.

Someone slapped me on the shoulder from behind. "Hey, Hasselbach, you old Nazi, how's it going?"

It was Raider, one of the best-known hools in Berlin. Raider was even better known than Johnny. He was almost thirty and had been participating in the scene for almost ten years—a senior hooligan.

I had to laugh to myself when I caught a whiff of him. He must have just smashed a bottle of hundred-mark cologne over his head. He was also wearing a few gold chains, not to mention the four video cameras he had strung around his neck.

Raider was in his element. "You know, Hasselbach, Nazism is fine. But politics isn't really my world. Plundering—that's it!"

Everywhere hools were running around with stolen video cameras, CD players, televisions, VCRs, and . . . vacuum cleaners! These tough guys who an hour before had been battling five hundred cops and dodging bullets and tear gas were now running through the streets of Leipzig with top-of-the-line vacuum cleaners in their arms. They were thinking ahead to Christmas, when they would need something to give their mothers. This was very important because, despite everything, most of these well-dressed little boys still lived at home, where they kept their treasure chests full of jackets, sweaters, perfume, and more electronics than they knew what to do with.

The whole thing was beginning to disgust me. I couldn't get into the spirit of plundering anymore. Mike Poley was dead. And besides, these were small stores into which people had poured their whole life savings, like the poor sausage seller. These weren't big chains, like the convenience stores on the highway. This wasn't a political action, it didn't hurt the State, it didn't accomplish anything at all except give people a chance to vent raw aggression and cop a vacuum cleaner.

On the drive home we took the back roads through villages. It was dusk at the end of a long day. At one point, we stopped our VW van at a light. Just before the light changed, one of the hooligans opened the sliding door and grabbed a purse from the hands of a stunned pedestrian. The driver floored it, and we sped down the street, with the purse waving out of the window like a flag. A few blocks later, having emptied the purse, he let it fly out into the night and closed the door again.

WAR GAMES

AUSCHWITZ WAS A weapons fanatic. Like Bendix, he got most of his weapons in the woods in Halbe, where the last battle for Berlin had taken place in the spring of 1945. In their flight from the Russians, the Wehrmacht and the SS had thrown down their weapons in the woods.

We would go there with a metal detector and the thing would go crazy, beeping all over the place. We found still-loaded weapons with full magazines. We found the Russians' AK-44s, so well preserved by the earth that they'd work as soon as you dug them up. It was an amazing feeling, digging up a weapon half a century old and drilling a tree to pieces with it.

We also found heavier weapons, a lot of bazookas and of course mines. Luckily, most of the mines weren't as functional as the other weapons; they were rusted through, for they were made of very thin material. We'd dig them up and remove the explosive material.

When you were lucky you found pistols, but mostly it was machine guns. We'd clean all the guns, use them a bit, and then bury them in oiled paper in designated places. We couldn't keep them in our apartments because, as known neo-Nazis, we always had to reckon with surprise searches.

There must be thousands of weapons still out there. The Halbe woods alone is as big as Berlin.

ANOTHER MAIN SOURCE of weapons for us—actually a more important one—was the Soviet soldiers stationed in Berlin.

During the summer of 1990 the Russians were clearing out their barracks and dumping everything in garbage heaps. They'd dump completely full magazines for Kalashnikovs; they also threw away antitank mines, explosives, uniforms, everything imaginable that they didn't feel like carrying and couldn't sell. We'd go there with knapsacks and fill them up with ammunition.

The Kalashnikovs themselves we had to buy from the Russians. The price of one was a bottle of vodka. We'd get into our jeep, pack up a few bottles of vodka and a few cartons of cigarettes, and go weapons shopping. We'd drive into villages where the Russian barracks were. We always met some soldiers cleaning the streets or outside walking around. They didn't speak German, and I could only manage a few words of Russian. But our old Stasi pal Frank Lutz could speak perfect Russian, and he became our main weapons buyer. For two bottles of vodka you could get a bazooka. They then sold us bags of tank grenades—which were fired from a bazooka— for 100 marks. After all, they were getting practically no salary anymore, so 100 marks would make them rich back home. And who knew when we might need to blow up a tank?

Bendix always needed lots of regular hand grenades, because he fished with them. He'd go to the lakes outside Berlin, chuck a grenade in, and next thing you knew five hundred fish would be floating there on the surface of the lake. You'd think they wouldn't look too good on the plate, but actually only about half the catch would get messed up. The others would be fine. I often ate fish with Bendix.

As far as the rest of us were concerned, though, Bendix went a little over the top with his weapons. He always carried a bazooka under the seat of his jeep. One time he was driving along with Reinthaler and Küssel and, in broad daylight, pulled out a Russian-made bazooka and pointed it at one of the buildings occupied by the Anarchist Anti-Fas. The other two practically had to tie him up to keep him from firing. Bendix just became more and more impulsive.

Much as he hadn't cared when his father had killed himself while he was in prison, he now seemed to care less and less about anyone else, even himself. He told us how he attacked a pregnant woman on the street with a field spade. He took her for a leftist and totally beat her up with the thing. I don't know what happened to the woman's child, but I know she wandered around looking really crazed for quite some time after that. The cops looked for the perpetrator for a long time, but they never were sure it was Bendix who had done it. Bendix told us the story over breakfast, laughing about it.

Aside from fishing with Bendix, we wasted hand grenades on all sorts of other pranks. While we didn't favor them for blowing up cars, like the anarchists did, we enjoyed blowing up empty Russian barracks and occasional Lenin monuments, as we found them. The barracks were ghost towns by then, so no one could get hurt. I only knew grenades from films, so it was interesting to see how they worked.

At first I was worried about blowing myself up, but then I realized that the little egglike objects really are not so fragile. You pull the pin out, and you hold down a lever on the side. When you throw the grenade, the lever falls off and then you have between ten and twenty seconds before it explodes. You just have to be sure the lever doesn't come off before you throw it, but that isn't hard. You run maybe fifteen feet and get behind something.

We also got barbed wire from the abandoned Soviet barracks. It was easy to take with us because it hadn't been used, so it was lying around in rolls. They'd gotten this expensive, first-class barbed wire and then left it sitting around the base in rolls. They just didn't give a shit, the Russians.

The Russian barracks were a total horror. It must have looked like that in the gulag, I thought. The groundwater around the barracks was contaminated from all the chemicals they'd just tipped out of barrels onto the ground. The toilets looked like World War II.

After one particularly good search through a Russian barracks, we went to a nearby field and played badminton. It was in an area with barbed wire all around and signs that said WEAPONS TESTING. ATTENTION MORTAL DANGER. As we hit the birdie around, I remembered playing a bit of soccer in the Stasi complex so many years ago. But now the wooden towers and gray buildings around us were all empty. No soldier or agent would ever come out of them again.

* * *

IT WAS REALLY something to have access to Russian weapons, because in Germany it was incredibly hard to get a permit for anything.
You had to prove that you were in danger, and you were checked
over by every authority, every institution, everyone up to the highest
court, to see if it was true. There were just a handful of weapons permits given out in Berlin last year. One was to a jeweler who'd been attacked six times. Then he was finally given a weapons permit.

The Office for the Protection of the Constitution and the State Security of Berlin realized only much later the dimensions of the Russians' garage sale of weapons. There are now secret caches of
weapons stashed all over Germany, which were mostly purchased
from the Russians in 1990. And the weapons weren't registered, so it
was impossible to tell exactly where they ended up. In the GDR,
when you got a weapon, its serial number had been registered along
with your ID number, and they kept perfect track of it.

GARY REX LAUCK, head of the NSDAP/AO, always found the
weapons situation in the Fatherland rather ridiculous. He was always
laughing about it and then trying to get us to lobby for change. I
imagined that in Lincoln, Nebraska, Lauck had more arms than a
barracks of the Bundeswehr in Germany. He always got excited that
in our neo-Nazi platforms we didn't demand the legalization of
firearms.

But most Germans were happy that they could walk in the street
without being afraid that a fourteen-year-old would put a pistol to
their head. Unlike in America, where almost everyone on the Right
seems to be for private weapons ownership, in Germany the right
wing is actually the most in favor of strict control. There are some
hard-core rightists who would be in favor of a U.S.-type system, but
they are few and far between.

While Americans always like the idea that citizens can rise up
against the state, in the United States you've never experienced it; citizens kill only themselves or their neighbors. In Germany, in just
thirty years, we've had extreme examples of radical groups taking up
deadly arms against the government. The Federal Republic lived
twenty years with the problem of Red Army Faction terrorism, for

example, because individuals had turned their arms against the state. (And if in Germany possession of arms was legal, I'm convinced I would not be alive now. Some eager young neo-Nazi would have shot me to death for my "treason.")

In Germany, mostly when you hear about weapons, they involve foreigners. For instance, there are many armed Turkish street gangs and a lot of Russian mafia, too. The criminal element in these communities, of course, has little to do with most ordinary foreigners, and they hardly use their weapons to defend themselves against racist Germans. Rather the opposite: the foreign communities are preyed on by racist neo-Nazis on the one side and their own criminal cousins on the other. We even built up contacts with right-wing Turkish groups and bought arms from them.

ACQUIRING MILITARY WEAPONS was fun, but we didn't really need them to attack refugee shelters or fight anarchists. If we used them in Berlin, we'd find ourselves behind bars before we could reload. For these weapons to be really put to use, we needed some sort of war. Our chance came when Iraq invaded Kuwait in August and the United States responded by sending troops to Saudi Arabia.

As international preparations for the war progressed that fall, many neo-Nazis saw it as their great chance to get involved in a fight against Israel. Michael Kühnen and Michel Faci, the French Fascist, founded an "Anti-Zionist Legion" of German neo-Nazis to fight in the Gulf on the Iraqi side. Faci was well known for getting himself involved in all kinds of conflicts. In the early 1980s he had "seen action" in South America when he was hired as a mercenary. For Faci, war was like a kind of pornography—an endless snuff film in which he got to play soldier with real weapons and real bodies.

Faci went to Baghdad at Saddam Hussein's invitation to set things up. They signed a contract to provide German volunteers for Saddam Hussein to support Iraq against "the present aggression of Zionist and U.S.-imperialist forces," specifying that every neo-Nazi officer was to be guaranteed 5,000 deutsche marks, every legionnaire 3,000.

But while the Gulf War was a bit of a disappointment—its speed and scale made it inappropriate for much mercenary involvement— on its heels came a war that provided far better opportunities for neo-Nazi intervention.

*   *   *

IN THE SPRING of 1991, the civil war in Croatia began. The Movement saw it as the perfect chance to give those who wanted it real experience killing people. Moreover, there was a historical tie: during World War II Nazi Germany had played an active role in Yugoslav ethnic politics; the Nazis had supported a puppet dictatorship in Croatia, the Ustashe, that had built concentration camps in which mostly Serbs but also Jews were killed.

The current government in Croatia was reviving the tradition of the Ustashe and in many other ways honoring the former Fascists. Units of the Croatian Army were flying swastika flags, and many more were flying the old Croatian Fascist symbol. Croatia had become the first European government since World War II to openly embrace these symbols. Meanwhile, the Serbs were instituting policies of "ethnic cleansing" and racial warfare. It was a neo-Nazi dream come true.

All of the West German neo-Nazis saw it as a wonderful opportunity, but Nero Reisz, the barking anti-Semite from Hesse, was particularly pleased. The problem for him was that there weren't enough Jews being killed. But Serbs would do.

A system was set up whereby potential recruits for Croatia were first trained in paramilitary camps in Germany, then passed on to middlemen who were responsible for arranging their transport, clothing, and food on the way to the front.

The way it worked was first through a word-of-mouth network. We had to be careful about doing any advertising because hiring mercenaries was strictly illegal in the Federal Republic. It was simply known in the scene that you could go to Croatia, if fighting was your trip, and that in Berlin I was one of the contacts. The other main contact people in Berlin were Arnulf Priem and Oliver Schweigert. Once we'd checked out recruits to make sure they weren't spies, we took them to a paramilitary camp to get tested and trained. We were mainly interested in whether they were physically fit to go down there. Mental fitness didn't interest us much.

I knew one guy from the GDR who'd been loosely involved in the Movement for about a year and then went down to Croatia because it was a chance to kill Communists, i.e., the Serbs. He wasn't even much of a neo-Nazi, really. He simply hated the Stasi, who'd tortured him in jail, and was half crazy to get some revenge on anyone for his suffering. He had shoulder-length hair, like a hippie, and hardly any sense of purpose at all. He just wanted a chance to kill Communists, and he got it in Croatia. In a documentary some television team made at the front, he was interviewed and he talked about how many Serbs he'd killed and how much he'd learned about weapons. Less than a year later, he was killed himself.

But the more sane and careful ones came back after a few months or a year with valuable training in weapons and explosives. They'd of course also learned what it was like to kill people. (Many stayed down there, living in the hills, constantly involved in skirmishes no one ever heard about, and are only now coming back into Germany and Austria and forming the basis of the most militant and dangerous neo-Nazi cells.)

The effort to organize young German neo-Nazis and send them to Croatia to fight and kill for the Ustashe—as the SS had once done—was organized largely by the Movement representatives in Hesse, Bavaria, and—for logistical reasons, as it was directly on the border with Yugoslavia—Austria. The main man in charge in Germany was Nero Reisz. He organized transport and took care that everyone got uniforms and weapons. Then Michel Faci and his right-hand man, Nikolas, organized most of the Croatian neo-Nazi units, training both young Croatians and Germans who'd come down for the ride. Faci trained Croatians as young as ten years old to kill "Communists" while teaching them the basics of Nazism. With his childish antics, he is good at making murder seem like a game.

The neo-Nazis mostly fought independently from other units, as a legionnaire corps. But they received arms and ammunition, even tanks, from the Croatians. From what I heard from men who came back, they fought against Serbs but also against Bosnian Muslims, even though the Muslims had been in the SS during World War II. They simply fought against whomever they could get an excuse to kill. They kept track of how many Serbs they killed and tried to collect per-body pay from the Croatians, but they actually got hardly anything, apart from invaluable experience.

I NEVER WENT down there. Personally, I wouldn't have gone to Croatia for anything in the world. I saw no reason to risk my neck for another nation. I was only interested in the potential of getting battle-hardened recruits back from the front. The actual fight in Yu-goslavia didn't interest me.

So I organized paramilitary camps and helped provide training. We tested the recruits with the help of a few sympathetic people from the Bundeswehr. There was a lot of physical training—jogging, crawling, scaling. Recruits learned how to use firearms and how to dismantle, clean, and reassemble them. There was explosives training and prac-tice in throwing grenades and using bazookas. We modeled our course on Bundeswehr training exercises and what we could piece to-gether about the old Waffen SS training with the help of training manuals and the memories of our retired SS supporters. But the basic source for our training was the West German Federal Army.

We set up the camps mostly on the island of Rügen or in the woods around Berlin. There were big forests in the direction of Frankfurt an der Oder, near the Polish border, where there was no danger of dis-covery. We almost never ran into anyone out there, but I remember once we met a forester. The old man was driving a Trabant jeep, ba-sically the standard East German plastic-framed matchbox car with its top lopped off. It looked particularly silly to us in our West Ger-man army jeep. He saw that we were armed to the teeth. He stopped, got out, and asked what we were doing here. He explained that it was now "rutting season" and we weren't allowed to go through the woods.

Bendix went toward him a few steps and shouted, "Stay very calm, my friend! You find yourself here in a prohibited military area!"

"I don't have the feeling that you belong to any military unit," replied the forester with a firm voice.

"And I don't have the feeling that you, as a civilian, can judge that! I suggest you get lost quick!" shouted Bendix back.

The forester got into his car and drove away.

Bendix could be very authoritarian.

One of our most amusing war games during the summer of 1990 took place when we were invited by Jürgen Rieger, a neo-Nazi lawyer from Hamburg, to a Federal Army camp outside Hamburg, where a club of "enthusiasts of military-historical vehicles" was meeting. Rieger was the head of this association, which was entirely legal and ostensibly not political. He was also the leader of a nonprofit organization called the "Association for Biological Anthropology, Eugenics and Behavioral Ethnology," a group that did research in the old Nazi tradition on "problems" within the races. I'd met Rieger at a protest march with Kühnen and Worch in Hamburg earlier that summer. Rieger defended practically only Holocaust deniers and neo-Nazis; he was the defense attorney at all important neo-Nazi trials and openly admitted that he was a National Socialist. He made a slimy impression, but he was a very good attorney. For example, there was a case in Stuttgart against twelve leading neo-Nazis and Rieger stalled the proceedings for more than two years, costing the taxpayers more than 11 million marks before the case was finally dismissed on a technicality. He knew all the tricks, like a Mafia lawyer.

All the people visiting Rieger at the Federal Army camp showed up in camouflage uniforms—mostly Austrian Army uniforms because their brown-and-white pattern looked almost exactly like the old Waffen SS uniforms. Austria was not part of NATO, so they didn't yet have the familiar blotchy red-and-green "NATO camouflage" clothing that the German Army used.

Rieger divided the approximately sixty people into two groups. Each drove off in an opposite direction, planning to meet again at a prearranged place. We set off in restored World War II vehicles: an Opel Blitz truck, a motorcycle with passenger sidecar, and an old VW jeep. It was an odd feeling playing invasion, with so many people dressed in what looked like SS uniforms. The drive took us across fields, through mud, over stones, and across riverbeds. "Now, Kamerads, we're invading Russia!" someone shouted. "The Bolsheviks and the Jews will never survive our war of conquest!"

During our maneuvers we encountered regular Federal Army vehicles, and it was like two historical stages of the German Army greeting each other, crossing paths in some weird forest time warp. Even more odd was encountering an American jeep from the Normandy landing force with a Nazi soldier's helmet mounted on the hood.

This weekend, several people had come along who collected historical vehicles from the Allied forces. After all, the "enthusiasts of military-historical vehicles" was not a neo-Nazi group. But when we encountered the other vehicles in the woods, as we passed by we shouted, "Heil Hitler, Jew!"

And now encountering a jeep "from Normandy" was just too much. The guy driving it was dressed up like GI Joe, with an American helmet and a pack of Lucky Strikes. The German helmet on his hood had one bullet hole through the front of it, probably original. There was also a white-lettered inscription that read 1944 LANDING NORMANDY.

"Hey you shit *ami*, you Jew," we yelled at him. "Want us to blow you up? Hey, Bendix, get the bazooka!"

We pretended to be about to blow him up, as we continued to insult him. He'd obviously found his way to the wrong group. After a bunch more provocations, he fled.

When we stopped driving around and harassing the other troops, we got out of our vehicles and began weapons practice. First we blew up some tree stumps and practiced slitting one another's throats. Then five soldiers from the Federal Army joined us and participated in target shooting. They sponsored a target-shooting contest and the winner got an old but functioning carbine from the German Federal Army. It was legal because this was officially a "shooting festival." The man could hang it on his wall at home, but he was not normally allowed to use it. I wondered if the soldiers realized they were awarding this rifle to a hard-core neo-Nazi who was determined to bring down the state they were defending.

In the evening we were invited to a barbecue with free beer. Then we spent the night in the barracks with the soldiers. It was illegal for us to sleep there, but a few officers came by and nobody seemed to mind. The next morning we were awakened like soldiers with reveille.

FOR A TIME we also practiced war games with members of the Ku Klux Klan. In many German cities chapters of the group were being founded. Gary Rex Lauck often told us that he wanted to win a permanent place for the Klan in Germany. Lauck was always forging contacts between us and the KKK, which was looking for people in the Berlin area.

Dennis Mahon, a Grand Imperial Dragon of the Knights of the KKK who'd had a lot to do with neo-Nazis in the States, came to do a cross burning in the woods outside Berlin and met with us. I arranged the contact, but I had no interest whatever in working with the Klan. I found their carnival costumes and cross burnings silly. I was always skeptical that the KKK could really take root in Germany. It was simply too foreign a version of racism, when God knows we had enough of our own; it was too obsessed with the blacks rather than the Jews. The Klan's symbol—the Celtic cross inside a circle—was already being used by the VAPO, the Austrian neo-Nazi party, and various neo-Nazi groups. But otherwise, I didn't think much of the symbolism or content was transferable.

The Klan was biggest in West Germany. Those who were becoming involved in it did so mainly because they found it fun to run around in robes and burn crosses and preach American-style racism. And of course everyone in the scene loved the movie *Mississippi Burning,* it was a real cult classic.

Our biggest operation with the Klan members took place when we attacked a castle being occupied by anarchists not far from Berlin. It had once belonged to Gustaf Gründgens, an actor from the Nazi times, but had been abandoned for years under the Communists. The occupiers were Anarchist Anti-Fas from the Kreuzberg, district of western Berlin, and our assault was a coproduction of KKK members and neo-Nazis. We attacked several times, using it as a sort of extended war games exercise. It was odd running through the fields with these guys in white sheets carrying machine guns.

I didn't have a part in leading this assault, which was the KKK's big chance to show how they'd like to work with us, but it certainly didn't help convince me of their competence. I would never have led such an operation with Kalashnikovs and other heavy weapons, because it's crazy to use such weapons unless you really intend to kill people. War games when you're by yourself are one thing, but to combine war games and street fighting with the anarchists was foolish. I don't know why more people didn't get seriously hurt or killed during operations like this. The only serious injury was to a young house occupier from the Netherlands, who had most of the blood vessels in his shoulder shot apart by a bullet.

BY FAR THE most serious war games I observed were in Austria. They were organized by Küssel and trainers from the Austrian Federal Army, the Bundesheer. I went as an observer for the north German neo-Nazis. We took video cameras so we could film their camp for our own training exercises. What I saw in Austria made me realize that our exercises had all been childish games.

The exercises were run by Küssel and another Austrian neo-Nazi named Hans Jörg Schimanek. They were held in Langleuten, a town where the far-right Austrian Freedom Party was very strong. The Austrian trainees arrived on Friday evening and practiced until Sunday afternoon—without sleep. It was total round-the-clock paramilitary training. During the day they practiced target shooting, grenade attacks, and laying explosives.

At night more specialized training took place. Night marches were accompanied by hand-to-hand combat in the dark and training in the art of silent killing.

"The best method is to approach from behind, plunge your knife into the kidney, and then turn it high," said the stone-faced, deadly-looking instructor from the Austrian Army. "Then your opponent will bleed to death. There's nothing anyone can do for him. He's lost."

Needless to say, we German neo-Nazis took notes.

There were no silly KKK sheets or elaborate period costumes here. What was unusual were the straw dummies used for the killing exercises. These were all dressed as concentration camp inmates, with striped uniforms and yellow Jewish stars on their breasts.

The Austrians would line up a row of these macabre scarecrows, and by the end of the practice there'd be little left of them. They practiced shooting them, stabbing them, and then, when they were mostly destroyed, putting them into a pile and blowing them up with grenades or timed charges.

The sadistic nostalgia for concentration camp tortures could hardly have been lost on anyone, but everyone participated cheerfully, taking the costumes as an amusing joke.

"Jews die!" a row of troops would scream as they led a bayonet charge against the scarecrows or shot them. Before blowing them up, there was simply mechanical efficiency, because it was a purely "technical" operation and they were clocking one another. They seemed to have an infinite supply of these striped concentration camp uniforms. I have no idea where they got them.

Between the war games and killing practice, the Austrians did sprints, cross-country runs, push-ups, and every other conceivable exercise. They'd crawl over fields, through waist-high mud, until they were soaking; most came home from the weekend with terrible colds.

Gottfried Küssel, the leader of the Austrian neo-Nazis, participated in every exercise. He asked the others to do only what he did himself. Under these conditions I saw what a strong person Küssel was, both psychologically and physically. He would be hard to break in combat or in prison. It was odd to realize it was the same puffy fellow who'd harassed us about fixing up the Weitlingstrasse house and barked so ineffectually—the same guy who'd sung us anti-Semitic folk songs after we'd attacked the anarchist shelter. Küssel was much more a man of action than I'd given him credit for. I wasn't at all sure we had such a tough leader in our organization. And that would soon become an issue of the utmost importance for everyone.

20

FALLING HEROES

DURING THE FALL of 1990 things began to fall apart. The founder of modern neo-Nazism—whose appearance before the cameras in a full storm trooper uniform in the late 1970s had forever altered the boundaries of political rebellion in Germany—was dying of AIDS. During the months leading up to his death, Michael Kühnen spent most of his time obsessed with the looming war in Iraq. Working with his old friend from Paris, the gay mercenary Michel Faci, he was negotiating his contract with Saddam Hussein to supply an "Anti-Zionist Legion" of neo-Nazi mercenaries to fight in the Gulf. In his twilight moments, the man who'd spent his life playing with Nazi symbols and attacking all sorts of substitute targets was struggling desperately to seize the opportunity to kill some real Jews before it was too late.

While we heard less and less from Kühnen, we heard more from the second most senior leader in the Movement—Gottfried Küssel—and his deputy, Günther Reinthaler. Both these young men were extremely "old" fighters, as we called them, for they'd been following Kühnen for over a decade, and, though the organization they'd built up in Austria was relatively small, it was, as our experience in the war camp had showed us, ruthlessly anti-Semitic, determined, and loyal to its leaders.

Yet the stocky Austrian Führer himself seemed more and more ridiculous to us in Berlin, as he suddenly decided to bring everyone in the houses under iron discipline. He was always running around with a hammer and chisel, prodding people to get working: "Pick up that hammer, make yourself useful for national socialism!" Küssel was someone who couldn't stand not to have his way for a second, and he lacked Kühnen's ability to work with all sorts of people by employing different styles to deal with them.

Of course, he had a good justification for trying to put things quickly in shape. In their efforts to kick us out, the housing authority was increasing its demands that our buildings meet the building codes, and we were having trouble meeting its schedule. If we didn't rewire all the buildings, rebuild the plumbing, and replace the broken windows, not to mention making a thousand other small repairs by the deadline, there would soon be no more neo-Nazi house. The work was stretching our finances. The city was also objecting to the fact that we were running a political party out of the house, which, it said, violated the contract.

Küssel and I went to a city council meeting in Lichtenberg that September. We spoke as representatives of the houses on Weitlingstrasse, not as neo-Nazis or politicians, and tried to justify their continued existence. I spoke first. I explained our practical reasons for occupying these houses—simply that our people, mostly young Berliners, desperately needed apartments and work; by fixing them up, we were providing both and thus were a service to the community. Then Küssel explained the political side of things: these houses needed to be cleaned and occupied because the old Communists in the GDR needed to be kept down with a strong force of young rightists in the heart of East Berlin, otherwise communism would return.

While Küssel was becoming more and more fixated on the house, the other NA leaders and I were negotiating an arrangement with the housing authority that would allow us to exchange all the Weitlingstrasse buildings for nine large apartments elsewhere, which we would be allowed to pick out. It would be a big loss of space, but we thought it was a good move, because, if the authority simply took the house from us, as seemed likely, we would be left with nothing. In this case we would at least have apartments for a few people.

But when Küssel found out about the deal, he said it was out of the question. "Under no circumstances can we sell or trade this house!" he boomed. "It is the sacred property of the new National Socialists. It is an example for all Germany. And it is a reconstitution of the original Brown House that Hitler and the Nazi Party established in Munich and that was the ideological center of the struggle throughout the Third Reich. Money plays no role. There are enough people in Germany and Austria who will help us with money."

In fact, either Küssel or Günther Reinthaler, the Gauleiter of Salzburg, could have bought the house outright. Reinthaler owned property in Vienna, Salzburg, and Barcelona, and he had a fortune of 60 million Austrian shillings besides. But the Austrian neo-Nazi's wealth was a secret in the scene.

THE LAST IMPORTANT event that Kühnen attended during his career as a neo-Nazi was in October, when we all accompanied him to Dresden for a giant march whose ostensible purpose was to protest the city's new prostitution and drug-dealing problems in the wake of reunification. It was a good cause for us, not only because the Movement officially opposed drugs and prostitution but because many of the pushers and pimps who had descended on East German cities in the months since the Wall fell were foreigners—Poles, Russians, and Asians of every variety. Even as the NA and the house in Berlin were disintegrating, that march in Dresden seemed to represent the dawning of a new era of power and respectability for the Movement—and the rise of a leader who seemed to be challenging my position as Führer of the East.

Before he became known as "the sheriff of Dresden," Rainer Sonntag had built up a career as a neo-Nazi in the West. He was originally from Dresden, the easternmost city of the GDR, next to the Czech border, but he had settled in Frankfurt am Main, in the West, after he was bought out of an East German prison in the mid-1980s. It was later speculated that the Stasi had trained him as a spy before selling him to the West. He had met Michael Kühnen at the end of the 1980s and made it known that he saw himself as a potential political candidate for the extreme Right. Kühnen gave him a position within the National Coalition, one of the many parties under his umbrella. But even while he was working as a neo-Nazi leader in Frankfurt, Kühnen confided to me, Sonntag was best known in underworld circles as one of the city's up-and-coming pimps. When he was caught stealing money from the party coffers, Kühnen unceremoniously forced him out. But luckily for Sonntag, the fall of the Wall soon gave him a chance to have another go at neo-Nazi leadership, this time in his own city and on his own terms.

Returning to Dresden in early 1990, he quickly established an organization that was a loose combination of neo-Nazi political party and organized crime syndicate. His followers rampaged through Dresden's growing red-light district, attacking brothels and making pimps and whores cough up protection money. Sonntag was a tough, crude type, but he had a brilliant sense of how to present himself in the media. I'd been impressed that entire year, watching his work from afar, with how he'd been able to turn his obviously shady organization into the model of a "legitimate" neo-Nazi party. In television interviews, he claimed that the entire city stood behind him and that he was only doing what everyone wanted: cleansing the city of drug dealing, gambling, and prostitution.

With his German shepherd at his side, discoursing on subjects like safe streets, antidrug action, and keeping foreigners from stealing your lawn ornaments, he often sounded like the local school superintendent. His deep, slurring Saxon speech had the effect on me of a dozen sleeping pills. But he wasn't trying to appeal to a national audience, and his accent, like his themes, made him the darling of postreunification Dresden.

Kühnen once described Sonntag to me as an "unprincipled, characterless pig." It was one of the only times I recalled Kühnen using such strong language against someone in the Movement. And Sonntag didn't have a good relationship with the other leading neo-Nazis either.

But there was no denying that he knew how to run things in Dresden. His Saxon SS went so far as to put the numbers players—the ones who wouldn't pay off Sonntag anyway—in handcuffs and take them to the police. The local cops, rather than worrying about having their authority usurped by neo-Nazis, expressed their gratitude to Sonntag and thanked him for his initiative. One cop was so pleased that in his free time he drove Sonntag around the city in his patrol car. Sonntag became the first neo-Nazi leader to have a police chauffeur. (The Berlin police were happy to chauffeur me or the other Berlin neo-Nazis, but it was always to the same place.)

The day the NA joined Sonntag's party for the antidrug demonstration, we all marched from the city center to the famous Semper Opera House, where the rally was being staged. Sonntag had arranged total police cooperation, and they were taking all steps to see that the anarchists didn't disrupt our "wholesome" event. The officer in charge even came up to Kühnen and me and said—in a play on the neo-Nazi expression "We're back"—"*Wir sind wieder da!*"—"We're also back, Herr Kühnen!"

Then another obsequious cop came up to us and said, "*Guten Tag,* my name is Obermeister Lustig." Chief Inspector Funny—it was too much!

Kühnen laughed with delight.

"Michael Kühnen," he said, smiling one of his sly grins. "Pleased to meet you, Inspector Lustig."

They all treated Kühnen like a politician, and the appreciation went to his head so much that a pink glow seemed to briefly erase some of the gaunt paleness from his face. He kept looking at me and grinning with pleasure, as if to say, Maybe we've been too harsh about Sonntag.

The situation with the authorities got more and more unbelievable. When a journalist suggested to the police that they take action against a crowd of local neo-Nazis and onlookers who were raising their arms and shouting "Heil Hitler!," the policeman replied, "I don't see anyone shouting 'Heil Hitler.' "

The journalist stared at him, dumbfounded. "They're there!"

"I don't see them," said the cop and walked on.

The only time I spoke with Sonntag that day was to discuss a spy who'd infiltrated first the Dresden organization, then ours in Berlin, before we'd figured out that he was with the Anti-Fa. Then he'd fled to Vienna, and Küssel's organization there was looking for him—a skinhead named Elvis. We got into a discussion about traitors, then we talked a bit about the logistic problems of Berlin versus Dresden.

But the difference between the two cities was more than a matter of logistics. While Berlin remained a battlefield where the "Red" forces outnumbered us vastly, Sonntag seemed to be turning Dresden into the first truly "Brown" city in Germany. He had to be the only neo-Nazi leader who'd ever had the open support of so many public officials and been driven around by a police chief in broad daylight.

*　*　*

AFTER SONNTAG'S BIG demo, Kühnen became so sick that he hardly
ever even faxed us anymore. The man in the black leather jacket,
who'd seemed like such a powerful, mysterious, and driven figure
just six months ago, was now too weak to get out of bed. Worch, his
closest lieutenant, who worshipped him, gave us overly optimistic reports on Kühnen's health, but I think we all knew what was coming.

With the housing authority breathing down our necks and Kühnen
out of touch, I began to feel somewhat adrift. I divided my time between organizing for the coming elections in December, trying
against fate to fix up the house in time for the inspection, and getting
high. I also did my part in organizing the war games camps and mercenary volunteers for the Gulf. But I felt myself regressing to my old
ways as a punk and delinquent. Of course, where before I'd been rebelling against my parents and the Communist society—the mainstream—now I was rebelling against the established value system of
a fringe group. Every group, no matter how radical, has its authority
figures, and you can become an outsider even among those who are
outsiders themselves.

The incident that made me most aware of my alienation was the
so-called Heroes' Memorial Day in Halbe, which took place each
November. After the anniversary of the death of Rudolf Hess, it was
the most important date for the German neo-Nazi scene, and in
November 1990 more than two thousand neo-Nazis from the different groups met in Halbe, near the forest where Bendix and the gang
dug for weapons and corpses, to honor the troops who'd fallen in the
last battle for Berlin.

The event was naturally required for all the residents at Weitlingstrasse 122, and though I attended and took a group with me, my
attitude was hardly "suitable" to the somber tone adopted by the rest
of the gathered Kamerads.

Though it was not yet midday, the group of skinheads I was chap-
eroning arrived at the cemetery in a stolen bus, totally drunk and
stoned. As best I could, I tried to discipline the drunken heap piling
out of the bus, but I was almost as drunk as any of them. We had arrived late to boot, so, as the skinheads bawled out drinking songs, I
trudged out in front, holding the black, white, and red flag and trying to hide behind it.

It was a real insult to the dead Nazis. The skins with us were supposedly serious neo-Nazis who'd appreciate this somber event;

they were skins I'd reeducated, and I was bringing them partly to show off how serious they'd become. They'd collected signatures for NA candidates, distributed propaganda, and then had started to draft fliers and to think ideologically. There were also people who had completely changed their appearance; at my encouragement, they'd let their hair grow out so that people didn't immediately get frightened when they approached, and they'd started to dress and talk normally as well. But now, as the Weitlingstrasse house was unraveling along with my commitment, I'd let them get trashed before taking them to the most somber neo-Nazi event of the year.

About two thousand mourners had assembled in a semicircle around the monument. The memorial service was already in progress, but in our condition we hadn't noticed. We had to walk from the road onto the cemetery grass, but they could all see us from where they were holding the services. We were the last guests to arrive.

Everyone looked at us indignantly. I tried as best I could to disguise my drunkenness. But some of my pals had even walked into the cemetery carrying their beer cans. Arnulf Priem, who was standing nearby, immediately moved away; he obviously wanted to avoid any association with us.

I spotted my current girlfriend standing in a silly-looking traditional Bavarian peasant's dress with the German Women's Front (Deutsche Frauenfront). I always found dirndls so stupid. They were the ultimate uniform of the neo-Nazi petit bourgeoisie, the "proper" side of our radical Movement. When she caught my glance, she shook her head unappreciatively.

A member of the Viking Youth came up to me: "Kamerad, Kamerad, flag bearers all the way to the front by the monument!"

"Leave me alone, I'll stay here with my troop," I said drunkenly. He turned on his heel and walked away.

We staggered around and then stood by the Vandals, who were also drunk. The Vandals mostly looked like Priem. They wore long hair and jean jackets with patches. "I'm proud to be German" buttons. Stickers that said "I love Eva Braun." On the back of his jacket, every big Vandal had a disguised swastika, not easily recognizable but there in the design just the same: a hammer and an ax on top of each other and a sun wheel and, in the middle, a swastika.

Suddenly one of their women collapsed. Her friend standing next to her, a long-haired neo-Nazi rocker, didn't seem to notice. One of the leaders reprimanded him: "Hey, your dumb bitch has just fallen down!"

"What am I supposed to do about it?" the rocker replied.

"That's your old lady, isn't it?" the leader said sharply.

The woman was lying passed out on the ground. So the Vandal pulled her aside and leaned her against a tree. It turned out she was a whore whom they'd met in a pub the night before. The whole thing was really making all of us look terrible.

Many of those in attendance were incensed at what was going on before their eyes. The old Nazis had come to Halbe to remember their dead, and they didn't appreciate that many of the younger ones were there only to sober up. I was very happy that the gathered guests were finally paying more attention to the Vandals than to us. I felt slightly less conspicuous.

When the speeches began, everyone spoke about the heroic battle that had taken place in Halbe, where soldiers had fought to the last drop of blood, and said we had an obligation to remember these heroes. Old men, many of them missing arms and legs, went on euphorically about the battle. They talked about how they had lost their best comrades and how they had nevertheless remained true and loyal to them. Others reminded us that the battle had been not only for the defense of Berlin but for the defense of their Führer, Adolf Hitler.

After the ceremonies Arnulf Priem and the other neo-Nazis decked the graves with swastikas. Some people had brought wreaths with old Nazi Party and SS slogans like *Meine Ehre heißt Treue* ("My honor commands loyalty"), *Treue bis zum Tod* ("Loyalty unto death"), and *Führerbefehl wir folgen dir* ("Leader's orders, we obey") in gold lettering on the ribbons. A common one had on one side *Meine Ehre heißt Treue* and on the other a swastika and skull. They'd ordered them in the cemetery nursery. The nursery hadn't blinked: they'd been given the designs, they'd do whatever turned a buck.

In December we received an eviction notice at Weitlingstrasse. I was worried that it would be fatal to our organization, for it would be impossible to occupy another house like this, and, even with our rich donors, no one was offering to buy us an apartment building this size.

We were so furious that on New Year's Eve we all took hammers, chisels, pliers, and clubs and destroyed every bit of construction work we'd done. Then we demolished the furniture. The inside of the combined Weitlingstrasse houses was completely destroyed that night, and to this day it remains a wrecked shell. Nobody regretted destroying the work we'd done with such pride and purpose. Why should we leave this to somebody else, to our enemies? was our thinking. Let them start from the beginning, I thought as I smashed my masonry work to bits.

MARTYRS

AT THE BEGINNING of 1991 it seemed like we were all waking up from some wild, crazy dream. I let Frank Lutz and some of the other NA people stay with me at my apartment while we planned our next move. Küssel and Reinthaler had gone back to Vienna. The reunification year was over. The neo-Nazi house was gone. Nobody knew what to do next.

This was when Michael Heinisch, the do-gooder I'd run into over Mike Poley's dead body, told us that he was looking for people to work in a new social project he was establishing at Pfarrstrasse 108. The terms were simple: he had also acquired an abandoned house from the city of Berlin; it was in worse shape than the Weitlingstrasse house had been and needed to be rebuilt from the ground up. If we'd help, we'd get regular wages for our work, and when the house was fully renovated we'd get apartments there.

Heinisch made only one strict condition: we had to keep all politics out of the project. He was recruiting most of the young people for the house from outside the scene, and he didn't want to find them all suddenly members of the National Alternative. Aside from his opposition to our politics, there was the practical matter that on Pfarrstrasse there were already a number of buildings occupied by anarchists—both Anarchist Anti-Fas and their more hard-core brethren, the Anarchist Edelweiss Pirates. If it seemed like Heinisch was establishing a neo-Nazi house on the block, there'd be a bloodbath.

We were all unemployed and had financial problems—Auschwitz, Frank Lutz, Stinki, my brother Jens, and me—and we agreed to his terms without hesitation.

I couldn't join his project as long as I was the vice chairman of the NA. I solved that problem easily. I resigned my chairmanship and officially quit the party. This wasn't only a gesture to get into the Heinisch project; I really was disillusioned with the results of our political work. We hadn't won any elections, and our central headquarters was gone. I had decided that legal neo-Nazism was useless, but I left my options open for some other sort of work. I asked Kühnen about my decision and he said it was okay if I quit the party so long as I was still with the Movement; by this point he was so weakened by the symptoms of full-blown AIDS that I doubt he would have strenuously objected to much of anything. He had less than four months to live.

Michael Heinisch came from a very strict East German Protestant family and had grown up in a small village near Berlin. In the early 1980s he had come to Berlin and got involved with the Christian civil rights movement against the Communist state. He had started his first project then, with the support of the Protestant Church, developing a youth club for punks. I had met him around that time, when I was still more or less a punk. We were often not allowed in pubs or restaurants, so there was almost no place where we could hang out. But we could always go to visit Heinisch at the church on Tuesday, Wednesday, and Thursday for dinner and a few beers. His club became a meeting place for us, along with people from the radical Protestant Church and university students. Heinisch was always protesting against the GDR in some way, but as far as I know he was never put in jail.

I had lost sight of him for years and only heard of him again in 1990, when he started another project to help young people deal with the turmoil of reunification; it offered everything from a place to play billiard games to local excursions to the country outside Berlin and even trips abroad. My brother Jens went with the Heinisch group to the island of Majorca, sponsored and paid for by the Protestant Church; it was his first trip outside Germany. But Jens and I weren't talking much at the time, and when we did talk, all he wanted to tell me about was how great the Church project was. I told him my opinion of religion, which wasn't favorable, and predicted that Heinisch's project would collapse. Heinisch had been a good big brother to me as well once, and I knew he was all right. But with my new ideology, I couldn't stand my little brother having anything to do with the Church.

This was just before we occupied Weitlingstrasse the first time, in the 1910 landmark building, which happened to be just around the corner from the church where Heinisch had his club. My Kamerads and I began meeting his kids on the way back from the Church club and trying to convince them to come over to us. Heinisch responded like a good sport and started trying to steal our members. The competition was funny. And we actually shared something politically in common, for, unlike so many of our Anti-Fa rivals, Heinisch had come from the human rights movement of the GDR, which meant that we'd fought against the same system.

ON JANUARY 3, 1991, we began the work on the occupied house in Pfarrstrasse. Hooligans had, in the previous few months, regularly attacked the houses occupied by the anarchists on the street and blown up their cars. Even though we hadn't had anything to do with them and even though we were all officially "apolitical" now, the anarchists held us responsible for these attacks. So from the first week my Kamerads and I began working on the Heinisch project, the anarchists began attacking it regularly.

They threw rocks and Molis, jumped our people as they walked home from work, and blocked the street so we couldn't get to work in the morning. To them, it was a cardinal sin that Heinisch was mixing apolitical kids in with us. They didn't believe in our conversion—to them, you were either Right or Left, Nazi or Anti-Fa—and, as they saw it, Heinisch was simply protecting the leaders of the Berlin neo-Nazi movement and giving us a new base from which to recruit and rebuild in the wake of losing Weitlingstrasse.

When we kept cleaning up the damage from the rocks and Molis and kept coming to work despite the harassment, the anarchists began to attack with a new weapon: butter acid. When I first heard about butter acid, I thought it sounded like a little kid's weapon—

like neighborhood kids who all piss into a pot and then dump it onto someone's head—but, properly made, butter acid is really dangerous. The anarchists would pack butter into a container and leave it in a basement room for years. An acid formed that smelled like rotten eggs, and it was extremely corrosive. If you put strong butter acid on a table, it would eat a hole through the table. I saw it. And the smell was really unbearable. We would have used butter acid ourselves, but we weren't patient enough to wait around three years—our whole Movement was as old as the weapons they were throwing at us.

The butter acid began flying into our house through the windows in small bottles, like Molis. To clean it up, we had to scrape the floors and walls with rubber gloves on. Some of the people in the project, not the neo-Nazis but the ordinary kids, were seriously injured. The acid splashed onto them and ate into their skin, leaving scars. They had to be taken to the hospital.

Heinisch always reacted calmly to these attacks. He would go over to the anarchist houses and talk. But the anarchists saw Heinisch himself as a rightist. "If you work with the neo-Nazis, you are a neo-Nazi," they'd say to him. He'd reply patiently that he was no neo-Nazi and that we weren't either, that we were attempting to reform. Heinisch was a devout Christian, who believed in the good in people and in forgiveness and patience. But he wore his hair as short as a skinhead, which was another reason the anarchists saw him as a right-winger himself. The fact was that even when all his friends had been with the leftist human rights movement and had had long hair, he had always had short hair simply because he thought it looked good. Heinisch was by training a priest and social worker, and the anarchists scornfully nicknamed him the neighborhood's "National Socialist worker."

Heinisch took a lot of flak for us, and I could see that he was getting exasperated that every time we'd make some significant progress, an anarchist attack would mess the place up again. He worked with his own hands to clean things up and set a good example, and he kept talking with the anarchists after every attack and run-in. We offered to fight back and help protect the place. But he wasn't interested in establishing another fortress like Weitlingstrasse, and everything had to be strictly nonviolent, as well as nonpolitical.

I managed to keep myself and my men under control. We were all interested in a little quiet work, after a year in Weitlingstrasse, and I

honestly think we all wished the anarchists would just go find something useful to do with themselves besides attack us. But that was not
to be.

Heinisch was loved by most of us because he'd gotten us work.
Still, I had reservations about him, for I found his friendliness exaggerated in that way religious types have. He was always announcing
that one day he'd put us on the right track and we'd all be happy to
follow Christ's example. I let him talk to me because I was happy to
have found a job and I figured his gabbing was the least of my problems. But Heinisch noticed that I didn't take him very seriously, and,
to get my sympathy, he tried even harder to engage me in conversations. That got on my nerves, but I pulled myself together because I
didn't want to lose the job just yet.

But I could see that the project's chances were pretty slim. What we
built up during the day the anarchists smashed apart at night. When
we caught one of them somewhere, away from the project, we beat
them up. We didn't do it on Pfarrstrasse, because of our promise to
Heinisch, but these fights were going on on a daily basis. Heinisch
didn't seem to notice how bad things had gotten. He just responded
with Christian patience and perseverance and more positive talk. The
anarchists regularly shot at us with air guns and slingshots and threw
butter acid and rocks into the building. Heinisch helped us clean up
and warned us not to let our hearts fill with hate.

IN JANUARY 1991, just after we'd moved into the Pfarrstrasse Project,
I was walking with Frank Lutz down Schwarzeweg, almost exactly at
the point where we'd beaten up the two punks years before, when we
saw a lone black-clad figure walking toward us—an anarchist.

The train tracks running alongside the "Black Way" were now
covered in snow. It was a freezing January day, and Frank and I
wanted to get home as fast as possible. I don't even think we were in
the mood for a fight. But as this fool approached us, he said, "Hey,
you stupid Nazi pigs!" Maybe nothing would have happened if he'd
kept quiet, but what would happen now was clear and unavoidable.

He was physically pretty well developed, so we approached with
care. Frank went off to one side, while I walked up to the guy,
grabbed him by the jacket, and punched him in the nose. The instant
I did, Frank ran in from behind and kicked him in the middle of his

back. I gave him another one in the face. I was wearing a ring at the time with a raised iron cross, and it left a bloody bruise on his cheek in the shape of this old German war medal.

Then we really went at him. As he lay on the ground, Frank and I kicked him in the neck, in the stomach, in the face, in the skull. We were both wearing our Bundeswehr paratrooper boots, designed to be deadly weapons, and I was thinking, as I kicked, Sure, his bones are breaking beneath my feet, I want them to—he provoked us, he asked for this pain, he earned it. I didn't feel an ounce of guilt.

As the snow around him turned red, I kicked harder, enjoying his pain. The anger in me seemed infinite at that point, yet somehow releasing it was so wonderful that I found myself laughing hysterically at the fact that I was kicking this guy's guts in. My mind and my feet were released from all rules. I wasn't laughing out of some sadistic sense of humor; I was laughing for pure joy.

I knew it was cowardly to attack two on one and to keep kicking when he was on the ground, but here my "politics" came in to help me: this was my political enemy, and neo-Nazis were supposed to fight their enemies ruthlessly. In this way, ideology had "improved" my fighting more than any gain in physical strength ever could have by the fact that it justified my every move. It allowed me to fight without scruples, to truly let go and feel that everything I did was right—that every blow, no matter how dirty and what the consequences, was holy.

It was a special, surreal pleasure to be kicking someone who was on the ground and couldn't fight back, a pleasure entirely separate from that of a fight situation. The basic condition of a fight, whether fair or not, is that you must reckon with a response when you strike. Opposition exists, no matter how feeble. But when you have someone on the ground, utterly at your mercy, it's something entirely different. You feel like you have the power of life and death over this creature whose face you're stamping boot impressions into. Standing over him, you feel like a God—*his God*. It's a deeply intimate feeling. You are the most important person in the universe to him at this moment, the man who will decide whether he lives or dies. And when I said to Frank, "Okay, stop, enough," it was as though I said to him, "Okay, let him live, let's go"—as though I'd given the creature back his life after snatching it away from him and playing with it for a few minutes in the snow. As we walked away, our victim lay still, not moving at all, and he could have been dying, for all I knew or, frankly, cared.

When we got almost all the way home, near my house, I realized I didn't have my keys. I said to Frank, "Shit, man, I may have dropped them when we were fighting back there." We went back to the site and the guy was still there, lying exactly where we left him, even though it was at least twenty minutes later. I squatted down and rummaged around in the bloody snow, looking for my keys. At one point, our victim woke up slightly, lifted his head and opened his eyes to look at me. Frank, standing over us, kicked him in the back of the head and he fell back unconscious. No matter how hard I looked through the snow around him, I couldn't find the keys. Finally Frank rolled him over and, sure enough, we saw that our victim had been lying right on top of my keys all along. "You asshole, you stole my keys!" I shouted at him, though he probably couldn't hear, and we took off. At least he was alive, and I had my damned keys back.

A few days later the guy showed up at Heinisch's project. I was surprised and a little disappointed to see him walking, although he was walking with great difficulty and his whole face was black-and-blue and puffed up like a fruit basket. The most obvious damage was on his cheek, where he still bore the raised welts from my iron cross ring, like a brand. I had to restrain myself from laughing when I saw it. I'd left the ring at home since that fight, just in case he showed up with such a mark. "These two guys beat the crap out of me," he said, pointing me and Lutz out to Heinisch. We of course denied it all and said he was paranoid, on drugs, and had probably done it to himself. He couldn't prove anything, and, though Heinisch may have suspected us, he decided to officially believe that we hadn't attacked the guy.

MICHAEL KÜHNEN DIED on April 25, 1991.

I visited him the day before he died. Christian Worch was also there, along with his girlfriend and one other mourner. Kühnen could barely speak at all. Only his eyes seemed to have grown in size and power through his illness.

Kühnen could tolerate a lot of pain. I saw him spitting blood several times that day. His weight was down to about sixty-five pounds. He could hardly speak, and his body was completely dehydrated, the eyes, everything was inflamed. I had never seen anybody who looked like this.

At that moment politics didn't matter at all. He wasn't just the Führer but an incredibly close friend. But it was hard not to think about the implications for the Movement, all the same. Before Michael Kühnen there had always been right-wing radicals, but never anyone who so spectacularly professed to be a National Socialist. They had all had jobs they were afraid to lose, parties they were afraid might get banned if they went too far. Kühnen had had no apparent limits and had given himself totally and ruthlessly to the Cause. His brazenness combined with his youth had really made the difference.

He had started his first party in the late 1970s with the symbolic gesture of appearing before BBC news cameras in full Nazi regalia. It had been a slap in the face to all those who had worked so hard to perfect West Germany's new democratic image. And it had come at the point in time when youth rebellion from the Left in Germany was at its peak and neo-Nazism was represented by a waning crowd of middle-aged men. Kühnen combined the power of both, combined what he'd learned working for the German National Party and what he'd learned as a Maoist.

Of course, there had always been something missing in Kühnen that had kept him from becoming a new Hitler—the thing that created the need for leaders like me and Küssel. Kühnen was, in the final analysis, too intellectual, too removed. His influence on intelligent people was like a magician's—even well-known leftist intellectuals had become fascinated with Kühnen—but people who were not so intelligent often did not comprehend what he was up to. He was too far "above" them, the opposite of someone like the earthy Küssel or me, who talked to people on their own level.

So Kühnen was not the Führer the Movement is always looking for—the new Hitler, who could speak to peasants as well as intellectuals. If you look at Hitler's original power base, it was strongest among utterly uneducated peasants, on the one hand, and professionals and academics with more than a college education on the other. (The workers doubted him and stuck more with the socialists and Communists.) This broad appeal was what made him so unique and so dangerous. We had no one today to compare.

But then, I thought, that was *my* potential. I was as popular with intellectuals in the Movement—as well as journalists and other non-

Nazis—as I was with the basest skinheads and hooligans. I could communicate with everyone.

"Damn you," I cursed myself as I watched Kühnen die. "You've been letting yourself slide back into decadence, even though you're perfectly healthy and strong. You've let his death kill your zeal. But it's an insult to this man, you have the potential and you need to do something to advance his ideas—do it for his memory!"

So, oddly enough, even as the months of suffering leading up to his death had demoralized me, his imminent death now reawakened my resolve to work single-mindedly as a neo-Nazi. I would go back to Berlin and found a new party and a new Movement. I would carry on the work of the Führer.

At one point, Kühnen asked us softly if we would please leave him alone because he wanted to die. The doctors said he might have still perhaps ten, twelve hours.

WORCH AND I left the hospital and went to a coffee shop. Kühnen had been a good friend to both of us, we agreed, without ever losing touch with the goals of the Movement, which were, after all, the highest goals of each of us individually expressed through the Community of the *Volk* . . .

Our conversation took that sort of tack, meandering from the personal to the political to the personal again. We agreed that this had been Kühnen's most important quality as a leader: that he had always been able to separate the human aspect from the political aspect without forgetting the connection between them.

Worch had supported Kühnen financially as much as he would accept—paying for his car, for example, which was a traveling hotel and library. Worch was always trying to give Kühnen more money, but the spartan Führer had refused any charity and only took what he absolutely needed to work. Worch told me then that Kühnen had been suffering from pneumonia earlier that year and that he'd had horrible lung infections but couldn't afford medication for them. "This was practically the only time the Führer came to me for anything," said Worch. "He must have been in terrible pain."

We'd both been moved by the sight of our Führer dying, but Worch was even more devastated than I—more than anyone, I think, because he'd been by Kühnen's side all these years, more than half his life, and could hardly imagine life without the Führer. It would take him some time to recover.

BUT AS SOON as I got back to Berlin, I knew what to do. I went to my brother and a few other people who I knew had remained loyal to Kühnen to the end, despite the gay problem and AIDS, and I said, "Hey, let's build up a new organization. Something to make him proud."

We didn't give our group a name right away, but we decided it wouldn't be a political party but rather a *Kameradschaft,* a close-knit circle ready to take action for the Cause.

We began meeting for weekly "*Kameradschaft* evenings" on Thursdays at my apartment on Wotanstrasse. Aside from a handful of regulars, we invited Arnulf Priem, the SS fanatic and Teutonic scholar, and Worch, whenever he was in town.

In a way it was like starting again at the beginning, the way Lutz, Auschwitz, and I had worked in the final year of the GDR, when we'd established the Movement of the 30th of January. It was a kind of discussion group, dealing with everything having to do with national socialism.

Mostly we'd have some kind of ideological indoctrination for new members, usually on a theme—for example, "The Building of the Party Program of the NSDAP" or "The Duties of the SS, the SA, and the Wehrmacht"—or else someone would read from the great tome of Nazi philosophy, Rosenberg's *The Myth of the Twentieth Century.* We also sponsored evenings devoted to the works of Ernst Zündel and Fred Leuchter and other leading figures in the Holocaust denial movement. I led these evenings, but the speeches and readings were given by different people each week.

We also acquired a copy of Kühnen's massive *Lexicon of National Socialism,* which had been published by Gary Lauck in Nebraska, and read a little from it each week, as training but also as homage to the great man's work. There were one thousand key words in this lexicon, and each week we'd take one word and someone would give a brief speech or lecture about it: "The meaning of '*Lebensraum*' is that the moral and biological destiny of every people is irrevocably bound to geography and soil, and that history presents a challenge to the German people above all to fight for its space on the earth." "The meaning of 'Jew' is a cancer that eats at the biological and cultural heart of every society, sapping its essential strength and injecting a poison that must be rooted out if the social organism is to survive."

During the day we'd work on Heinisch's project. We hadn't yet taken active steps to recruit young people at the project—we didn't know what we would do with them, since we wanted the *Kamerad-schaft* to remain a small, exclusive group—but we'd begun to pull them subtly in our direction. Meanwhile, the anarchists continued to attack us with little or no provocation. A group of skinheads coming back from a disco smashed up the anarchist houses on Pfarrstrasse pretty good one night, and we of course got hit back even harder the next, even though we'd had nothing to do with the attack. We continued to take our hits and play it cool. Little did they know that when our *Kameradschaft* did move from talk to action, it would be something considerably more spectacular than a few stones through their windows.

THE LAZY PACE of work and indoctrination was broken at the beginning of June by some shocking news: Rainer Sonntag had been shot dead.

It was the sort of death we might have predicted for the neo-Nazi "sheriff of Dresden": he had been killed with his own weapon. With his speeches and marches against crime in the city, he hadn't reduced any of his demands for protection money from the pimps, gamblers, and pushers. When the bordello owners hadn't paid, Sonntag's men had threatened to "flatten" their establishments. With a certain Greek bordello owner and his partner, the burly leader of the Saxon SS had miscalculated. From a distance of six feet the foreign "businessmen" had shot him with a shotgun Sonntag himself had previously sold to them.

We called a special meeting, and all the important neo-Nazi leaders in Germany showed up to decide what to do about the murder. Coming on the heels of the Führer dying of AIDS, it seemed a bit embarrassing that the death of another major figure in our Movement would reveal such sordid involvements. But Christian Worch set things straight:

"It doesn't matter what exactly happened in Dresden. Who cares about the details of Sonntag's life? Now we have a new martyr on the right-wing side."

"I couldn't stand the guy anyway, he's of more use dead," said Nero Reisz, never one to mince words. "And he's a martyr to boot—that's not too bad for a little Saxon pimp. What more does he want?"

It was clear that we all thought Sonntag had been a small-time pimp, a freeloader, and an asshole. But that didn't stop us from taking a maniacal pleasure in rewriting his life and death. Sonntag would become the Horst Wessel of the 1990s. Wessel had been a storm trooper leader in Berlin in the years before Hitler took power who'd combined Nazism with petty crime; like Sonntag, Wessel had been killed in an argument in a whorehouse. Yet if you'd told anyone who called himself a Nazi or neo-Nazi that Horst Wessel had been a cheap pimp and his heroism was a propaganda invention, they would have said you were spreading Red or Jewish lies.

In fact, my own personal model of a Nazi fighter was none other than Horst Wessel. I'd read the Nazi biographies of him—they were popular in the scene—and I knew that in fighting the Communists in the streets, he had always been right out front. That he'd been shot by a Communist, who had done it in a cowardly way when he couldn't defend himself. I thought Wessel embodied the noblest principles of the Nazi struggle. Like me, he had not asked anything from people that he would not do himself, and he had always taken risks for the honor of the Movement.

But I once read in a more objective source that Horst Wessel was a pimp and never cared much about politics. I mentioned this to Gottfried Küssel, who got very upset and said that to even suggest such a thing was an indictment of the entire Movement and I should forget I'd even read it. Once you created a martyr myth and it flew, it would never come down.

Then I watched for myself how a "Horst Wessel" was created. At every Nazi event thereafter banners appeared saying "Rainer Sonntag—Martyr for the Reich." It was interesting that the death of Kühnen, even though he had been a thousand times more important than Sonntag, was entirely useless, because even with the most calculated fabrication, it was impossible to say that he'd been a martyr for the Cause.

WE ARRANGED A huge mourning march for Rainer Sonntag in Dresden. This event was to be one of the largest marches of neo-Nazis

ever. It would have much in common with the Wunsiedel marches for
Rudolf Hess, only here was our own martyr—a neo-Nazi who'd been
killed by underworld foreigners infiltrating the Federal Republic with
the collusion of the corrupt Jewish-run political machinery in Bonn.

Hundreds of young men marched through the streets of the ancient
city carrying signs that read "Foreigners out! Germany for Germans!" and "Germany awake! We are somebody again!" Some wore
shiny jackboots and black leather coats, others wore rubber-soled Dr.
Martens boots, jeans, and nylon bomber jackets embellished with
neo-Nazi patches and Celtic crosses. There were more than two
thousand people there. Actually our rivals, the anti-Kühnen FAP,
were the most impressive, with their Nazi-looking red armbands
with the FAP wheel and their huge medieval German drums with
painted flames running up the sides, beating out a slow, monotonous
march like something out of a thirteenth-century costume drama. We
marched through the center of Dresden in rows of four, chanting
"Rainer Sonntag, martyr" and "Foreigners out!" and *Sieg heil!"*

The police lined the streets to our left and right. The anarchists
didn't disturb us. They didn't dare. Not one could be seen. There
were more than a thousand policemen—you could almost imagine it
was a march for a fallen comrade—and there were Federal border
police as well. This wasn't so much brazen support for Sonntag, I
think, since his popularity as a crime fighter had waned a bit since we
had visited him last October. I think the overwhelming police presence was more a way of ensuring that no violence would erupt.

We marched to the old movie theater where Sonntag had been
shot. We placed a wreath there, then observed a minute of silence.
After that, though, many neo-Nazis began to shout, "Damned
pimps, they destroy us, they kill us all!" and from there ran shouting
through the streets to the banks of the Elbe River in the middle of
Dresden. There we held a final rally.

Nero Reisz, the two-faced bastard, made a grand speech about
Sonntag, what a great hero he was and martyr and honorable man.
Worch made a speech whose theme was "Rainer Sonntag looks down
on us from Valhalla." Then one of Sonntag's brothers made a speech.

Arnulf Priem was by my side the whole time, looking like he'd lost
a Norse god. He didn't offer to make a speech. Later at another
rally, though, speaking before hundreds of skinheads, he offered a
prize of 1,000 marks—about $700—for the heads of Sonntag's mur-

derers. It was nothing for him, but to the skinheads this was a huge amount of money, and I heard they actually made an effort at a nationwide manhunt.

Eventually Rainer Sonntag's murderers were arrested in Bangkok, Thailand, and they're sitting in prison now. But these pimps had done the Movement a huge favor, because Sonntag's death brought everyone together again, just as Kühnen's death caused me to get my group together for serious work. In fact, it was probably the combination of these two deaths, coming one on the heels of the other, that gave everyone such a powerful sense of injustice and purpose. Suddenly it seemed like the nationwide neo-Nazi movement was back on track.

Meanwhile, the general mood all over Germany in 1991 had shifted tremendously in our favor. There were four to five firebombings of foreign asylum shelters per week and thousands of racially motivated attacks. Almost all of these were committed by young people with only the loosest ties to our Movement, so we could only imagine what serious organizing could accomplish on such fertile ground.

22

INDOCTRINATION

My FACE WAS still well known in Germany, through the media, and young people were regularly approaching me on the street and asking how they could get involved with neo-Nazism. Some even inquired about the conditions of admission to the new *Kameradschaft*. It had gotten around through the grapevine that the most serious neo-Nazis in Berlin, the former followers of Kühnen, had formed an exclusive new group. Of course, I didn't want just anyone in the group, but I also didn't like to discourage people from becoming involved in the scene. I always wanted to get new members onto the rolls of some organization, to get them thinking in terms of race and Nazism. And I confess I also got a certain enjoyment from searching out people's psychological and intellectual weaknesses and exploiting them for the sake of political training.

While our work within the *Kameradschaft* was geared to building an extremely tight, exclusive faction—and to cementing further the ties between leaders—general ideological indoctrination of beginners played a big role in keeping the scene together; it was as important as war games or collective actions like fighting foreigners or anarchists. The very concept of indoctrination seems negative to a democratic way of thinking, but in our worldview it was a positive idea, much like the concept of propaganda. Both were a means of spreading national socialism, which we saw as the highest end. The goal was to produce as many people as possible who were ideologically "fit," which meant they identified 100 percent with the program of the Nazi Party and lived according to its goals. The effect was not necessarily to make them more violent but to take the violence that was in them already and channel it in a directed and politically useful manner.

I'd done indoctrination in the organized parties, but it was far more important now that we were no longer trying to work legally. The goal of a normal political party is to get more and more members, presumably people who may not truly identify with the cause but who can be persuaded to vote for you based on some issue or other. That's why we put in all sorts of environmental issues and prattle about economic conditions of reunification into our platforms. But what was liberating about putting aside regular politics and working illegally was that we could forgo such compromises and concentrate on training people whose minds were fully open to our cause.

The basic requirement for indoctrination was youth. We accepted older members, of course, but far fewer and treated them differently. It was assumed that if you joined an organization like ours when you were over, say, twenty-two, you were aware of what the Movement's history and implications were. You had at the very least the foundations of hatred and loyalty, a basic understanding of who the enemy was and why you wanted to fight him. This is not to say that older members weren't indoctrinated—in the Movement it was a permanent, ongoing process; you were never too old to indoctrinate or be indoctrinated—but we focused on indoctrinating teenagers.

We looked for people who were inclined not only to share our views but to join something exclusive and prohibited, something from which there was no easy turning back. When I introduced a new member to the scene, I usually gave him a task, any task involving the Movement; most often, I'd ask him to read some training material we'd worked up about race theory, just the basics about Aryans versus Jews, for instance. Much of this had been worked up by Priem, and we used Küssel's Aryan rewriting of "Asterix" as well. After he read what I'd given him, the new recruit had to make an oral presentation to a leadership group of usually about ten senior members. After his presentation, we asked him questions about the mate-

rial and how he related race theory to his own life. We could then assess what he had digested and whether it was clear to him. At the
same time, he could also ask us questions if he did not understand
something.

It was like a test, but one that the recruit couldn't fail, at least not
knowingly. Often normal education has the effect of making people
feel inadequate or stupid, especially in the German system. Our goal
was the opposite, to make the recruit feel as comfortable as possible
with the theory—to make him feel that the Nazi way of explaining
things was one he could master, one that would make him seem intelligent and win him a circle of approving friends. The last thing we
wanted him to think was that race theory might be difficult—at least
for him. He was to feel that it was easy for him because he was part
of the chosen group by birth, that he was biologically superior and
hence could grasp the concepts of biological superiority, while normal, confused people living under a blanket of Jewish and American
lies did not understand it.

We'd test people along these lines for the first six months or so that
they were with us. It's hard to remember any of these young men
now, because I never once became interested in them as people.
Somehow, it all remained a very abstract exercise to me, though to
them it was as personal as could be, all about their own fears and
friendships and sense of self-worth. To me and most of the other
leaders, the young recruits were nothing more than a faceless, pulpy
mass on which we worked.

Occasionally, if someone was really slow, we couldn't use him no
matter how loyal he was. For the NA we had recruited people who
were too thick to really do political work just for the sake of doing
"street cleaning" at demos and other such tasks. We'd needed storm
troopers. But the way we'd decided to work now—secretly and ultimately as terrorists—second-rate people could only be a hindrance
and a possible security leak. I remember one guy who couldn't make
a presentation at all. The extent of his conversation was "Foreigner
out!" or "Dirty Jews run everything" or "You have to hit the Fijis
[Vietnamese] one on the kisser." He had zeal and brutality but nothing else. Kühnen had always said that such people were our "useful
idiots." But in this case we sent the young man to the skins because
it would have been ludicrous to bring him into any of the politically
oriented groups. We were careful not to hurt his feelings in the pro-

cess, though; we said, "Kamerad, you are a manly type who can fight in the streets. Not everyone is up to that task, and it would be a waste of your talents to keep you away from the Nazi skinheads, who need your muscle."

I sometimes couldn't resist playing little games with my recruits when they seemed particularly dim-witted. One day, for instance, I was at an ice hockey game, and a hooligan named Johannes Hochstetter approached me. The pudgy little fellow wanted to know how to get involved with my new secret *Kameradschaft.* "Well, Johannes, it's a long and arduous procedure," I said and proceeded to make up all sorts of trials and tests he'd have to perform. I knew from the start that Hochstetter was barely bright enough to manage being a hooligan and certainly couldn't have become a serious neo-Nazi. Once Hochstetter had walked right up to a plainclothes cop—someone everyone knew—and said, "Hey, man, tonight we're going to attack the anarchists in the Pfarrstrasse." When his pals had confronted him later, he had said that, yes, he'd known the guy was a cop, but his attitude was so much like a hooligan's he'd figured it was okay. "Of course he acted like a hooligan, you idiot," his pals had explained. "That's what he was going undercover as."

I told Hochstetter that as his first test to see if he was fit to join the *Kameradschaft,* I would take him to a concert of the right-wing radical singer Frank Rennicke, and afterward he would have to prove to me that he had understood the meaning of the lyrics. Rennicke sings songs like "A German Girl," about how beautiful and honorable German girls are, and similar stuff about "the German family" and "German honor." On the more aggressive side, he sings songs like "When the Turks Move into Kreuzberg, I Get Sick." Nothing it takes a rocket scientist to get.

Rennicke was the most popular singer among the neo-Nazis. He sang in a style like Küssel but had a lot more talent. One of his most popular numbers was "Resistance Against the Enemy in Our Land," in which he sang about the Jews, the leftists, and the Allied forces all in one song. But he often left his meaning totally vague and suggestive, singing about "dark powers" without spelling out exactly what he meant. At a Frank Rennicke concert you always saw the broad spectrum of the serious neo-Nazi scene: elderly people with their grandchildren, teenagers in clean pressed shirts and Adolf Hitler haircuts. It was the scene minus the skinheads and other people who were more into bashing heads than true ideology; they preferred their hard-core racist rock. It was like going to a Joan Baez concert, if Joan Baez had been a blood-and-soil nationalist.

During the concert I noticed that Hochstetter had pulled out a little pad and was taking notes. Afterward, I asked him what he'd gotten out of it. He looked very worried and glanced at his notes. "Well, yes, Rudolf Hess is a hero . . . that's one thing . . . and it's important to have National Socialist convictions . . . the family is the first cell of society, of German society, which is based on the family, which is the root of society . . ."

I didn't laugh at him, but I corrected him when he said something ridiculous and otherwise nodded my head seriously. "Yes, that's very perceptive," I said. "More on that?" I let him feel successful, and that was the important thing. Like most young people who approached us, Hochstetter was frustrated with his stupid little life. He had probably acquired ten CD players and an excellent vacuum cleaner in his time as a hooligan, but it wasn't enough. He was envious of what seemed like a "higher mission."

I built Hochstetter up and praised him in order to give him a feeling of self-worth, and by the end of my work on him he would have cleaned my shoes if I had asked him to. Such recognition made a person like him completely dependent on the *Kameradschaft* and on me, his new Führer. The *Kameradschaft* became for many like a kind of drug they couldn't kick. Having gotten no recognition in their regular lives, they were isolated and had few social contacts. National socialism would become their only meaning in life.

The best subjects, however, were boys more intelligent than Hochstetter—and younger. I liked to approach fourteen- to sixteen-year-olds after school. We looked for kids wearing bomber jackets and Dr. Martens. Usually they didn't really have a political position, but for whatever reason they'd decided it was cool to be right wing. The first thing I did when I met one of these boys was to show that I wanted to be his friend, to hang out with him, which, coming from someone older, especially someone over twenty, was a real compliment. I'd act a lot like an older brother; we'd go into the woods together and do things like Boy Scout exercises, building forts and making trails. I'd always slip in a bit of ideology against foreigners along the way, saying some racist things like how there are such big differences between the white and black races, for example. But only casually at first.

We often didn't get into the Jewish question at first because it was too complex and explosive. Recruits had to build up to anti-Semitism. Often they'd start asking me questions based on what I'd said before. For example, if I'd made remarks about black people, the next time they'd ask me about whether the same things were true of Turks and other brown-skinned people. I'd explain that there wasn't much of a difference between them. Black and brown, they were both inferior races.

Then you could start with anti-Semitism, when you were sure that some basis for hating "inferior races" was there, which made it easier to absorb the idea of a person so inferior that his very existence threatened to negate your own: the ultimate *Untermensch* to our *Übermensch*.

At some point we'd suggest that recruits join one of the various youth parties—not the *Kameradschaft,* which was still an exclusive group—and begin formal schooling with the Party program of the original Nazi Party from 1921. It was more effective for new recruits to start at the beginning; they were usually fascinated with Germany's history. We taught them about Germany in their grandparents' era, Germany the last time it had been a great power in the world—and we gave them a map of Europe at the time.

Together we'd look at the map showing Germany in 1937 and Germany today, and I'd say, "Look at the Poles, they took this from us . . . the Czechs took this . . . and Austria too belonged to the German Reich. All this is gone. It was stolen, taken unlawfully from us Germans." You inflamed the recruit's feeling of injustice. And you began to draw all the strings connecting everything to the Jews. The land was gone because the Jews had stabbed Germany in the back in the First World War and then created the lie of the Holocaust in the Second. We'd begin to spend a lot of time on the *results* of the Holocaust lie, even before proving it was a lie. That way you first established Jewish guilt and made the idea suspect without having to confront the evidence. The Holocaust myth was simply a way to weaken Germans, as well as how the Jews had swindled Germany into financing the State of Israel.

And you could watch a fourteen-year-old quickly develop a total feeling of injustice. This could have been someone who'd never thought about the Jews before, and in a way that was even better, because he'd had no time to develop perspective or counterarguments.

What you wanted was a fresh tablet upon which to write. With the exception of someone whose grandparents had been concentration camp guards and who had been a ruthless Jew-hating Nazi from the cradle on, anyone who had thought much about the Holocaust before you got to him was basically disqualified from indoctrination. We didn't want to waste our time on him because he'd have too many questions in his head, too many doubts. But if you took a real blank slate and you worked on him, the result would often be someone who was soon filled with hate and prepared to either commit violent acts or at least express his anger in some other way.

With an eighteen-year-old, you might have to start on a somewhat different basis. You had to judge how much he already knew about the history. You couldn't tell him that everything had been stolen from Germany if he'd learned something different already. A fourteen-year-old you could tell, almost no matter what he'd learned in school, that it was shit, that the State had an interest in brainwashing him. As long as he hadn't been particularly deeply involved or interested in the subject before, he'd believe you. The best older people to work with were not exactly stupid but in some kind of way thick and had had problems either communicating with other people in school or learning in class. They were grateful for individual recognition, for praise, and for the communal feeling we could offer them. They got a feeling of power. Many young people don't know what to do after school, for example, and we gave them an answer. No matter how directionless they were, they suddenly had an important lifetime mission. Never again could anyone say they were wasting their time and just drifting.

They began to want to prove themselves, and you'd get them first to do a spraying action, which you'd applaud as a "hero's deed." That sort of praise would prepare them to do more, perhaps something violent, perhaps something deadly. After they had done a couple of things on your command and learned a great deal, they began to initiate actions themselves. They knew—or thought they knew—the basic principles of the struggle, so they felt quite free to act.

Sometimes, if a younger member did some risky act—graffiti spraying or some other kind of vandalism, like smashing some windows—you'd give him a prize—send him to an educational camp of the Viking Youth, say. You could get into the Viking Youth only by recommendation, usually from the leaders of a party like the NA or some other official neo-Nazi group, so our sending someone on one of the Viking Youth weekend trips was considered a great honor. It meant the fourteen- or fifteen-year-old got a chance to join an elite group. I'd also send kids on to the Viking Youth whenever they seemed too young to work with us. The point was to bring as many people into the fold as possible. Under these circumstances, the Viking Youth became more useful than ever as a "drop-off point" for young people who came to me looking to join the Movement.

The Viking Youth was the oldest existing neo-Nazi organization; it accepted children starting at age six. It had been founded by Walter Matthaei, a former official in the SS Ministry for the "Germanization of the Eastern Territories," in 1952. Later it was taken over by Wolfgang Nahrath, who forged its ties to the "establishment" neo-Nazi party, the NPD. Officially, the Youth looked like Boy Scouts. But they propagated total racism, stressing the evils of race mixing and things like that. They emphasized music, and most of the members played some instrument and got instruction in traditional German music.

The Viking Youth was a rich organization. It owned big farms and tracts of land on which members practiced their rituals and held their festivals. In many ways it was like a sect that cooperated with all the other neo-Nazi parties. Like most sects, it was hard to leave once you had joined. One family got threatening phone calls after they withdrew their son, and eventually their car was blown up.

SOME OF THE young men who came to us during this time were more than fit enough to join our *Kameradschaft,* perhaps even tougher than our oldest members. One of the best was an eighteen-year-old from West Berlin named Oliver W.

Oliver caught our attention from the moment he came to inquire about the Movement. An impish blond teenager with a reptilian gaze very much like SS security chief Heydrich's, he had no problem digesting any aspect of national socialism. He understood it all instinctively. He'd just passed his high school exams when he came to us; not only was he college material, he was street smart and had a cruel calculation about him that you saw immediately. He absorbed everything. Within a month he was thoroughly immersed in neo-Nazi ideology, and in two months he was talking like he'd been in Kühnen's inner circle for years.

Oliver had grown up in Kreuzberg, in the midst of West Berlin's most "multicultural" quarter, filled with Turks and Arabs. His mother was blind. It was a perfect background for producing either an extremely tolerant soul or an ultraviolent neo-Nazi: growing up surrounded by foreigners in a household headed by a handicapped person! Oliver was driven by contradictions. He believed handicapped people were inferior, but he loved his mother. His parents were divorced, and he was someone who needed a strong father figure, growing up around a blind woman whom he had to look after.

I became that father figure—but within the context of the Movement, which meant that, ultimately, our relationship didn't go very deep. It just meant that Oliver was able to get deeper into neo-Nazism faster. Michael Kühnen had played the same role for me. But while I had watched my father figure die of AIDS with great regret, Oliver would later plot to murder me.

23

KÜSSEL'S HOUSE OF HORRORS

GOTTFRIED KÜSSEL CLAIMED the mantle of successor immediately after Kühnen's death, even going so far as to maintain that Kühnen had named him as his legitimate follower on his deathbed. Christian Worch and I had also been with Kühnen when he was dying, and we doubted this was true. But Worch was not someone who wanted to inherit power. He remained a loyal right-hand man even when there was no longer any man to be the right hand of—a presence behind everything, not out front. If I had wanted to compete with Küssel, I suppose I could have; now that Sonntag was dead, I was the undisputed Führer of the East, the great new territory where the Movement was finding its most fertile ground. But I didn't care to become the godfather of neo-Nazidom, and I didn't care to get into a fight with someone as dangerous as Gottfried Küssel.

So Küssel took over. It seemed an apt transition. He'd been the Führer of Austria for more than ten years, and the organization he'd developed there, the VAPO, was one of the most tightly knit and ruthless in Europe. Besides, it seemed appropriate, for obvious reasons, that the Führer should come from Austria.

Küssel embodied the qualities of Hitler that Kühnen had lacked, namely an ability to appeal to and excite the common man. There was something of the brutal peasant about him, the beer hall rabble-rouser. Yet he was fiercely intelligent and a perfectionist in organizational matters. His charisma worked on all types of people, and, with his Austrian charm and melodious Viennese accent, he was the best speaker in the scene. As I'd witnessed at the Austrian war games camp, he also had great physical stamina, ferocity, and an ability to lead men in arduous conditions.

And, like Kühnen, Küssel had a fervent, unshakable belief in a Fourth Reich. But this would be his undoing, for while Kühnen had never set a time frame for his millennial reconquest of Europe—he'd always said that if we didn't make it, our grandchildren or their grandchildren would—Küssel was not one for patience.

Almost immediately after Kühnen's death, in May 1991, Küssel ordered a handpicked group of leading neo-Nazis to Vienna to form a new "cabinet." He wanted us to be prepared to take full control of the Austrian and German governments in the impending Fourth Reich, which, I discovered, he saw just around the corner.

When I got to Vienna, I realized that Küssel was planning to exclude many of the most important people in the Movement from his new Regime of National Awakening. Anyone who might cause a potential power struggle was out. Thus, he hadn't invited Worch, the most important strategist in the Movement. He also hadn't invited any of the important East Berlin people except me. I was supposed to be the Reich finance minister. I couldn't be too flattered with the post, considering that dim-witted Oliver Schweigert had been chosen to be the Reich defense minister. Arnulf Priem would be minister of culture. After all the ministerial posts were "given away," the only one that was left empty was that of Reich chancellor, the one Hitler had occupied, and you can imagine whom Küssel picked for that.

The whole thing took place in the dining room of Küssel's unusual apartment, which was nothing short of a museum to Nazism and racial hatred. I had never seen anything like it in my life. We all arrived there early in the morning. The special meeting on the subject of the putsch was to take place before we broke for lunch.

It was a vast apartment in the Seventeenth *Bezirk*, a rich district of Vienna. Küssel wasn't hiding his wealth anymore. First you went through a fancy lobby, along a carpeted stairway, and then down a long hallway. Inside, the first sign that it wasn't just another upper-crust Viennese home was the guest toilet, located at the end of the entrance foyer. Inside the toilet bowl, meticulously painted in yellow porcelain enamel with a black border, was a Star of David. To visit Gottfried Küssel your anti-Semitism had to be unquestioned, for when nature called you were forced to piss on a Jewish star.

The apartment abounded in images of demon Jews and Nazi soldiers. Wax figures of black-clad SS men in full uniform with steel helmets greeted you as you came in the front door. They were so perfectly done that at first sight they looked real, and you couldn't help forgetting they weren't sometimes, even when you'd been in the apartment for hours. Most of the figures wore the uniform of the death's-head concentration camp guards, but posted in the various rooms were also Waffen SS men in camouflage uniforms and military field officers. In addition to the SS wax figures, there were regular World War II–era German soldiers, these in cardboard, also life size. SS men were also guarding Küssel's bedroom, along with two brown-uniformed storm troopers.

Though the "personnel" must have cost a fortune, the furnishings were plain. The walls were plain white, not wallpapered as would be usual in such a place. The cupboards were made of simple, unfinished wood and looked old and worn. In the bedroom, there was an old wooden bed that was surely from the 1930s, and over it was an enormous blanket, also of an anachronistic, Nazi-era vintage. The apartment almost gave the impression of a military barracks. Küssel even had hanging in his closet six identical SS-style camouflage uniforms of the kind he liked to wear in public.

But then, on one of the worn old cupboards, sat the latest modern telephone/fax/answering machine, and next to that were a TV and shelves and shelves full of videos. Küssel had eclectic cinematic tastes. His favorite movie was *The Blues Brothers*. I'd seen it for the first time with him, in fact, in this apartment, and when I'd wondered about how he could so enjoy a Jewish Hollywood movie (it was a given in the scene that Hollywood was entirely Jewish), he'd said, "Sure, it's conceived of and created by Jews, but that doesn't mean we can't get a few laughs from it. You north Germans are so humorless about your anti-Semitism."

Küssel was the world's greatest anti-Semite, but, almost because of this, he was able to watch movies he knew were made by Jews and

enjoy them because he had no mixed feelings. The Jews were the
Devil. This was the Devil's entertainment, and I'm sure that in some
way by watching *The Blues Brothers* he managed to stoke his hatred
of the Jews even further.

Needless to say, Küssel was a vigorous Holocaust denier. For him,
the gassing of the Jews was a taboo subject. In his mind, there had
been no gas chambers. It hadn't happened. Yet his library was filled
with books about Auschwitz and the Holocaust, as well as a mass of
other materials about Jews. (The three biggest libraries in the scene
were Küssel's, Priem's, and, formerly, the trunk of Michael Kühnen's
car.) I'd estimate that almost half the books in Küssel's library were
written by Jews or had Jews as their subject: one has to read what the
enemy writes to be able to present an argument to him, he said.

Küssel was a total Aryan fanatic, and herein lay another irony
about his Holocaust denial: while denying that Jews had been killed
in Auschwitz, he was a great admirer of the SS doctor Josef Mengele,
whose work selecting Jews for gassing there had earned him the nickname "the Angel of Death." Küssel admired Mengele for his experiments, widely condemned as the most bestial in the history of
medicine, to "produce Aryan characteristics" in Jews.

"He tried to make something sensible out of useless, inferior
types," Küssel said, referring to how Mengele had tried giving Jews
injections in the eyes to see if he could change their eye color. Küssel
found this a worthy sort of research. He believed in racial alchemy,
that you could do such things to create a perfect race. Kühnen and
Worch surely also thought such things, but they weren't so vulgar as
to say them. Küssel was like a peasant; he said what he thought was
right at the moment. "Yes, Mengele had the formula down," he'd
say. "It was a great loss for humanity and science that Mengele could
not finish these experiments." Küssel didn't give a shit about what
had happened to the victims of these experiments; they would just
have been killed anyway, so why not get something useful out of
them? The research would have been used not to make blue-eyed
Jews but to take non-Jewish children who had black hair and green
eyes, say, and inject them to create "enhanced Aryans" out of them.
For Küssel, the bestial "medical" experiments in Auschwitz were not
about the Jews at all but about creating new and improved Aryans—
"a boon to humanity." In his mind, Mengele should have won the
Nobel Prize.

Küssel's anti-Semitism was something I never fully understood, since for me the Jews had never been a great theme. They were the central enemy in my belief system, but I hadn't really had any contact with them; I fused my vision of the socialist state, with which I'd had ample experience and which I hated, with my vision of Jews. But for Küssel the Jews were a separate entity that hovered over the entire world, with plans for apocalyptic mischief. Hollywood was always mentioned as the source of the conspiracy (as well as of entertaining movies like *The Blues Brothers*). Küssel could work himself up into a nervous sweat thinking about the influence the Jews supposedly had in the movie industry or in banking and business. For him America was a bigger danger than Israel. In fact, he was content that the Jews had their own country—he saw it as only a temporary solution, which would get them out of European society and occupy them with wars, weakening their thousand-year-old parasite culture.

But the Jews in America terrified him. He always said that there was a highly explosive mixture in the U.S. of Jews and decadent Americans. For him Americans were the epitome of imperialist war-mongers, and he saw this imperialism as an enormous danger to the German nation. America had succeeded in colonizing most of Europe since the war—Coca-Cola colonialism, corrupting all national cultures with the Judeo-American internationalist culture of junk food, Hollywood entertainment, and constant consumption. He saw World War II and the Holocaust as a war of the Jews against the Germans, with American help. In his view, it was the Jews who had declared war—economic war—against Germany, not vice versa.

It's much worse today, he said, since the Jews nowadays, forty, fifty years after the war, are everywhere again. One should look to Israel to see what torture and murders the Israelis commit in Palestine, he would say, and then look to Hollywood to see how well they brainwash the world.

Of course, his video library also contained Nazi propaganda films like *The Eternal Jew*, Leni Riefenstahl's *Nuremberg Party Day*, *Hitler Youth Quex*, and *Hans Westmar, Story of an SA Man* as well as speeches by Hitler and such things. But he also had Monty Python movies. His favorite was *The Life of Brian*. He loved humor. He was typically Viennese in this respect, the sort of person who, in any situation in life, had a joke about it. It didn't matter whether it was political or personal. He could go into a pub and sit there for six or

seven hours and talk to all kinds of people without any trouble. He
could become a regular anywhere immediately. While many of us
simply made contact with people via politics, Küssel would start talking with anyone, about general things—movies, current events, birds.
Küssel was an amateur ornithologist; he loved birds and occupied
himself with them whenever he wasn't studying the Jews or the
movements of the planets.

In a guest room he had another old-fashioned, simple bed, and a
big Nazi flag on the wall. Küssel had a number of cats; two of them
were sitting on a wooden table when I walked in. Against one wall
was another table on which he had laid out a remarkable assortment
of small figures made out of cardboard. The figures were meticulously painted renderings of historical figures who'd fought against
Germany: Winston Churchill, Franklin Roosevelt, Josef Stalin. Just
above this table was a mobile made of more of these cutout figures.
The ones flying around in the air included two prime ministers of Israel, Gorbachev and Honecker, some Jewish film producers, and Al-
bert Einstein. The figures were painted on both sides, back and front.

Finally, when you got to his dining room, you felt like you'd
emerged from the barracks into the general's headquarters. There
was a long, polished oak table surrounded by high-backed chairs and
a swastika flag on a pole in the corner. On one wall next to the table
was a caricatured image of a Jew—meticulously, elaborately painted
in the style of the old cartoons from the Third Reich—with the Star
of David on his forehead, like a bull's-eye. This enormous picture
covered the entire wall. It was so big, Küssel said, because the Jews
wanted to be bigger and more powerful than everyone else—to dom-
inate everybody and everything. "It is not larger than life size," Küssel corrected someone who asked. "It *is* life size—it is a purely
realistic portrait of the Jew." It was also convenient that his target,
the Jew's forehead, was large and therefore easy to hit. He used "the
Jew" for playing darts.

The new "cabinet" sat down at the long oak table with a VCR and
TV at the one end and a swastika flag and blackboard at the other.
Küssel spent the entire morning drawing frantic lines and pyramids
on the blackboard to show us exactly who was what and where and
under whom. After that we watched some old Nazi propaganda films
on the VCR. It was material none of us had seen before, propaganda
footage that had been used in the early 1930s to build up the structure of the original Nazi Party in preparation for the transition to

power. Then there was a film about the actual seizure of power in the spring of 1933. The videos were interesting, but about half the people in the room were rolling their eyes. He was showing us this footage of 1933 as though it could be a how-to guide for our present situation—as though we could just practice a few goose steps, put on our uniforms, and march into power. Still, nobody would have dared tell Küssel to his face that he was being an idiot.

We spoke then in detail about how to deal with our enemies after the putsch. Concentration camps would be our first order of business, just as they had been in 1933. It would be important to get the problem of subversives and Jews in hand before they undermined our regime.

"I think that Kamerad Priem is the most suitable one to deal with our degenerate friends," said Küssel, "and I believe we do not have to talk about what will need to be done."

Priem nodded seriously. The SS fanatic and Nordic enthusiast had long dreamed of getting to play Himmler. He would also probably take quite a sadistic pleasure in the day-to-day running of a concentration camp.

I tried to keep a straight face and take all this seriously. But I basically felt that Küssel was leading us through a kindergarten game. Plotting to establish neo-Nazi political parties or commit terrorism was one thing—they were extreme but possible. Plotting to take over the country and deciding who would run which concentration camps was something else—it was absurd. True, Austria's up-and-coming, far-right Freedom Party—which had been founded largely by former Austrian Nazis and was now led by the charismatic son of Austrian Nazis, a grinning yuppie who praised the "labor policies" of the Third Reich—had just risen to above 20 percent in the polls. Küssel had much sympathy for people in the Freedom Party, and we had sympathizers in their ranks. "It's not our politics," Küssel used to say of the mainstream far-right party, "but it's the legal possibility of doing something in politics. Even if they're conservatives, they're closer to us than any of the other parties in Austria."

The two main political parties in Austria were the People's Party and the Socialists, both of which had the reputation of being hopelessly corrupt. The Freedom Party had soared in popularity in the 1990s largely by playing up its oppositional, outsider status. But its antiforeigner rhetoric about the need to protect Austria's "cultural purity" didn't seem to hurt either, nor did its leaders' veiled praises of the Third Reich or their support for SS veterans groups.

The Freedom Party had old Nazis and neo-Nazis alike in its ranks, along with conservative nationalists and extreme free-market conservatives. Skinheads and prominent businessmen both cheered at Freedom Party rallies. In this way, it was the first party in Europe since the end of World War II to successfully bring Hitler's original constituency of disgruntled German workers, laissez-faire industrialists, and *völkisch* nationalists all under one tent. The existence of the Freedom Party in the mainstream spectrum in Austria allowed Küssel's VAPO to play a different role than it might have played in Germany. Here, a radical brown boy like our Gottfried didn't need to bother staking out the blander territory of Nazi sympathizer or apologist—the more mainstream people did it for him. Here, he could concentrate on planning the Fourth Reich.

But the Fourth Reich was not going to be a reality anytime soon. I was glad I was Reich finance minister, since they didn't seem too interested at the moment in how anything would be funded. If I'd been called on, I suppose I would have said, "I will nationalize the banks and the Wiener schnitzel manufacturers on the first day, so as to get all of Austria's wealth into our hands." I must say I also didn't much care for being in Austria in the first place. I had never been a fan of the South, whether Bavaria or Austria, and for all I cared they could leave it out of the Reich.

Before lunch, Küssel gave each of us an assignment to do at home—homework for a seizure of power. Most of the people had been taking notes during the meeting. I had brought along a microcassette recorder and taped the proceedings.

We toasted the Fourth Reich with some good Austrian schnapps, and then Küssel broke out the darts. "The Jew head is always there, waiting for us to cut into it, to puncture it," he said, gesturing welcomingly at his wall.

This was a regular feature of all indoctrination meetings at Küssel's place—the game of darts with the Jew's forehead as bull's-eye. It was played in a lighthearted, raucous mood, after all that forced seriousness during the putsch planning.

"Take that, you dirty Jew!" cried Priem with great feeling as he scored a perfect hit.

AFTER LUNCH THE program was pretty much free until the evening. With Küssel as a guide, Priem and I took a tour of Vienna. I think we were followed in our sightseeing by the Stapo, the Austrian political police, but I could never catch anyone. Küssel was an enthusiastic guide. He hardly mentioned Jews or Nazis all day, though he pointed out some relevant Third Reich sights when we happened to pass them. He took us to museums and coffeehouses, the old cathedral, and the Prater, Vienna's amusement park. Finally, as dusk was falling, we visited a *Heuriger,* one of the open-air bars on the outskirts of the city where *Heurig*—new wine—was served next to the vineyards where it was harvested. Except for the morning discussion, it was a real traditional day in Vienna.

Later in the evening, the whole gang that was to run the next Austro-German Reich met up with some more Austrian Kamerads at another *Heuriger,* where we ate dinner and Küssel gave us a speech about the connection among all the Germans of the South.

The *Heuriger* was filled with kitschy objects—stuffed animal heads and old weapons and signed portraits—and the crowd was dressed not only in folk costumes but also in brown shirts that looked remarkably like SA uniforms. When they started to get really drunk, everyone joined in a raucous rendition of the "Horst Wessel Song," the original Nazi anthem. It was surprising to see such a well-heeled group of neo-Nazis. Having grown up under socialism, I wasn't always as good at assessing a person's financial status from appearance as people in the West were, but I could tell that this crowd was not badly off. The Austrian neo-Nazis were, on average, richer than the German. They practically all had college or graduate degrees, if they were not still in school. Hardly any were working class, as many in Berlin were.

In Austria the line between neo-Nazis and conservatives was much more fluid. And just as Küssel accepted and admired the mainstream Freedom Party, so many in the Freedom Party more or less overtly admired Küssel. This was especially true of right-wing students, for Küssel had excellent connections with the dueling fraternities, which thrived in Austria to a degree that would have been considered positively anachronistic in Germany. Many members were here tonight.

These fencing clubs were where young aristocrats and aspiring members of the upper middle class acquired, under controlled conditions, the scars that would prove their bravery and contempt for pain. Rudolf Diels, the first head of the Gestapo, had had a face full of such scars. But so had Karl Marx and Friedrich Engels. In fact, from the time of the Prussian defeat by Napoleon in 1806 to the Nazi defeat by the Allies in 1945, most German students of any social rank and ambition had joined fencing corps and acquired scars. The Nazis had encouraged Aryans of every class to fight for their honor and embrace the duel, and one of the Reich's greatest swordsmen had been the vice chairman of the SS, Reinhard Heydrich. But after World War II, when East Germany had become a socialist paradise, both nobility and dueling had been banned, so to find that these boys still slashed one another in the face with swords was remarkable. It made Austria seem even more like something out of a time warp.

The group in the *Heuriger* frankly disgusted me, for they seemed snobbish and stuck up, even as they were interested in meeting me, as the Führer from Berlin. They toyed with the Nazi legacy—many of them were like the young professionals at the German Cultural Community Meeting in Berlin, whose parents had held high-ranking posts during the Third Reich—and they liked to consider themselves militant nationalists. In the world of these fraternities, where almost everyone was a member of the Freedom Party, only the more "extreme" young men were also members of Küssel's VAPO. It was a hip, radical gesture in their little world. But I had the feeling they wouldn't do anything that wasn't completely safe.

Küssel introduced our group and said that we were pioneers of the rebirth of the Movement and that the audience should invest in the future by donating to us. The brown-shirted fraternity boys clearly admired Küssel, who belonged to a fraternity himself, but I don't know what they made of us. I got into a discussion of the economic costs of foreigners with one of them but quickly got bored.

In their careers as doctors, lawyers, and government officials, Austrians like the ones gathered in this *Heuriger* could not openly state their admiration of Hitler and hatred of Jews. Küssel was someone who took that step for them, and they admired him for it.

Still, I was always amazed by just how anti-Semitic one could be in public in Austria. There was a reason why German neo-Nazis didn't dress our dummies in concentration camp uniforms at war games practices and why they did here. The lines were more ambiguous in Austria, which after the war had been absurdly declared the Nazis' first victim rather than the main source of Nazi perpetrators. Küssel himself was quite sensitive about national distinctions. He was very offended when I once tried to explain to him that I thought of the Austrians as foreigners but German foreigners, in terms of both language and blood. "Austria *is* Germany!" he'd shouted. "Austria belongs to the Reich!" For Küssel, Hitler was not an Austrian, as most people considered him, but a German. When I would ask him whether he was going back home to Austria for the weekend, he'd bark back, "I do not leave this country. I never leave Germany!"

But this was not Germany. Much as I had to pinch myself sitting in the middle of Küssel's living room surrounded by SS waxworks or peeing on Jewish stars, here I had to pinch myself as I shook the hand of a man who was widely considered a serious candidate for prime minister in the future—and not after a seizure of power. He shook hands all around and offered some words of encouragement for our struggle. Such a situation would have been impossible in the Federal Republic of Germany. This was yet another sign that Küssel had things under control and was the right man for the job of Führer. While we were secretive pariahs back home, here he got us personal connections with the upper reaches of society.

We made the rounds of various pubs and *Heurigers* for the rest of the night. Küssel was a big man-about-town in Vienna, and most of the proprietors at these places knew him. And when they called a taxi for him, I heard them request especially that no foreign driver be sent.

24

SOCIAL WORK

IN THE NEXT few months after receiving my post in the coming Reich, I had a lot of contact with Gottfried Küssel. Though Küssel was, practically speaking, my new Führer, Christian Worch continued to foot most of the bills. In August, for example, Worch once again financed the Rudolf Hess Memorial March, just as he had financed the Rainer Sonntag March in June; this year we were banned from Wunsiedel, where Hess was buried, so we held the march in Bayreuth, already a neo-Nazi pilgrimage site because it was where Richard Wagner's *Ring* cycle was performed each year.

But Küssel and Reinthaler also made their share of financial contributions. One day, for example, they showed up with a suitcase full of money, approximately 50,000 marks, of unknown origin.

We used the money to buy weapons from the Russians—light machine guns and a number of bazookas—which we added to the stockpiles we'd been building outside Berlin. We had at least twenty new Russian bazookas, as well as more than a hundred machine guns and lots of grenades and ammo. We kept everything carefully wrapped in oiled paper. We were keeping these stockpiles in preparation for the "emergency"—as we referred to the moment when we would rise up and attack the government.

This moment seemed more and more imminent to Küssel, and his brazenness was beginning to worry me. He was not exactly a member of the *Kameradschaft*, but, as the de facto inheritor of Kühnen's status, he was of course always welcome, and he often visited. He was an excellent guest speaker and did a lot of indoctrination with us. He gave spontaneous lectures on all manner of topics, from techniques of terrorism to ways of spotting Jewish businesses.

We all knew Küssel had some money to throw around, as his little private museum of anti-Semitism made clear, but unlike Worch he did not have a reputation as a millionaire. He didn't donate money to the Cause very often, though he did finance events in Austria.

Reinthaler took the charade a step further, posing as a poor student. Little did we know that the Gauleiter of Salzburg owned investment property all over, as well as having a fortune of 60 million Austrian shillings, making him one of the wealthiest of the neo-Nazis. Reinthaler's poor-student image would hardly fit with the picture of a man who was always going to check on his real estate holdings in Barcelona, Vienna, and Salzburg, driving there in an assortment of new BMWs. Whenever anyone asked, he'd say he was simply going to these cities on Movement business and that the BMWs were leased.

But Reinthaler was best known for a weakness he had, a handicap, that had made it difficult for him to fit in and that created its special problems in the neo-Nazi movement: Reinthaler's right arm was crippled, and the hand was the size of a tiny child's. He always told people that his deformity had been the result of an auto accident. (In fact, his mother had been given some chemical during pregnancy that had deformed the arm—you could tell it hadn't been an accident because his thumb grew out of the wrong place.) Neo-Nazis don't tolerate cripples, of course, because they are considered pollutants of the race, fit for extermination. I'd heard Reinthaler's boss and idol, Küssel, taunt him about his arm: "You can't even make a respectable German salute!" And once one of Arnulf Priem's men told Reinthaler that if his arm turned out to be an inherited deformity none of the Wotan's Volk or the Vandals would have anything more to do with him.

I'd had some interesting contacts with the Gauleiter of Salzburg over the last year and a half, since the time when I had first refused to join him in celebrating Hitler's birthday on April 20, 1990. Reinthaler had invited me to Salzburg shortly after that incident— perhaps thinking that if I were to spend time in the region where Hitler had grown up, and breathe some of that good Austrian mountain air, I might see the light and give up my northern, Strasserite bias. We drove down together in a black BMW to his beautiful apartment house in the middle of the old city, and that evening we went to a gathering he'd organized for my visit. Unlike Küssel, Reinthaler didn't invite us to his apartment for meetings.

Instead, he'd rented a large room in a pub, and when we arrived there we met Jürgen Maria Lipthay, Reinthaler's deputy, who owned a large travel agency, and another man named Gerhard, an ordinary member of VAPO, the Austrian neo-Nazi party. (Reinthaler's organization in Salzburg was a branch of the VAPO.)

We sat down at a long wooden table, and Reinthaler said, "Why don't we begin now?"

"Don't we want to wait until the others get here?" I asked.

"There aren't any others," Reinthaler said.

This was the entire *Gau* of Salzburg: three people. A Gauleiter, a deputy, and a member.

Then the Gauleiter gave a dull speech whose topic was, absurdly enough, "The *Gaue* of Austria."

The fact that I paid only limited attention to his speech didn't seem to faze him at all. As I was leaving that night, even though we lived in the same house in Berlin, Reinthaler handed me his visiting card, which read GÜNTHER REINTHALER. GAULEITER SALZBURG.

The next "trip" I made with Reinthaler was in Berlin. Two days before German reunification, the Anarchist Anti-Fa blew up his black BMW. The car's Salzburg plates had simply become too well known in left-wing Berlin circles. So on October 3, 1990, the official day of the reunification, Reinthaler went to identify his burnt-up car, which was being held in a police yard on the border of Kreuzberg. I figured I'd go along to keep him company and provide a little backup in case he needed it.

He already had a certain amount of protection with him, for Reinthaler didn't go anywhere without Thor, a strapping, impressive mixture of a Doberman and a Mastino-Napolitano, a Roman attack dog. But Thor was actually the nicest dog I've ever known, a very kind, sensitive animal. He was completely fixated on Reinthaler, who'd raised him as a puppy in Spain. Reinthaler didn't have such delicate feelings for Thor, though. One time, when he was jumping out of the car, Thor tore off the seat release lever by accident. The dog couldn't help it, he was so big and had such long legs. But Reinthaler beat him furiously, and Thor let him; then he went off and lay in the bushes, moaning and howling, his face bleeding.

I knew other neo-Nazis who beat up their dogs to make them aggressive and bloodthirsty. The best way to train a dog to attack strangers is to abuse him yourself. Some neo-Nazis did things like take their puppy and hang him by his legs until he'd almost die of pain. Dogs have a great memory for pain, yet their loyalty instinct causes them to redirect their aggression at strangers, rather than their masters. That and feeding them lots of raw meat would make them into attack machines. But Reinthaler's brand of abuse hadn't made Thor nasty; he was just a sweet-tempered animal. It killed me to see him treated that way. But when I tried to make Reinthaler stop beating him, he told me to mind my own business.

In any case, on Reunification Day, we borrowed a Ford from someone in the house, and Thor and Reinthaler and I set off in the direction of the lot. We promptly got lost, and after driving aimlessly around the border area, where bits of the Wall still stood, we ended up in Oranienburger Strasse, near the Anarchist Anti-Fa central headquarters that we'd attacked so harshly only four months before—and where, at the moment we arrived, several thousand anarchists were demonstrating against German reunification, which they regarded as a bourgeois, big-business plot. The streets were packed with shouting people in black clothes with Palestinian scarves pulled up over their noses and multi-fluorescent-colored hair.

We were driving the Ford through a sea of enemies, and there was nothing to do but to try and ignore them and hope the waters would stay parted for us. We were both terrified that someone would see us who knew us personally. The only advantage of it being such a huge crowd was that we could hardly stick out much, even in our military clothes and hairstyles and even with Thor sitting in the backseat. Actually, anarchists on average had more dogs than neo-Nazis did. But theirs were mostly benign mixtures like German shepherd and collie.

While we did manage to avoid attracting any immediate attention from the anarchists, we were promptly pulled over by agents of the federal border patrol who were monitoring the protest. Our nervousness must have made us look even more suspicious, and they probably figured we were there to do something nasty to disrupt the demonstration. Protesting that we were just there to identify a ruined car didn't help. They searched the Ford, found several rubber truncheons, and arrested us on the spot. But to get us into one of their patrol cars, the cops had to walk us through the crowd of screaming anarchists. By that time the left-wing radicals had realized who we were, and the cries went up all around us:

"Hasselbach, you Nazi pig!"

"Reinthaler, you brown rat!"

"Kill the Fascists!"

For the first time I was truly happy to be looking out the barred windows of a police van. And in the van Reinthaler and I suddenly sat facing a long-haired anarchist with an anti-Nazi patch on his leather jacket. The tables turned, and we started to provoke the left-wing radical until he got really scared, so that he was practically shaking. The cops didn't interfere, and the anarchist didn't say a single word on the whole ride to the precinct in the Perlebergstrasse.

At the precinct, they locked me and the anarchist in a cell that already contained about forty left-wing radicals who'd been picked up at the demonstration. I was terrified that one of them would recognize me or that the anarchist would give me away. I couldn't close my eyes the whole night from fear. But oddly enough they all left me in peace. I was sweating, but the anarchist didn't squeal. I felt slightly guilty, thinking how fair he was being and how we'd intimidated him. I almost wanted to apologize, but of course I couldn't say anything to him. The next morning, after twelve hours, I was allowed to go.

Meanwhile, Reinthaler was never even locked up. It had to do with the fact that he had a big dog with him. They were afraid of the dog and didn't want to have to take him to an animal shelter. It was simply too much for them first to run around and find somebody who would take the dog so they could take Reinthaler to prison. So they simply told him to leave.

In the Weitlingstrasse house we had mostly had German shepherds. One skinhead had a German shepherd, for example, named Kathy. Kathy was a completely disturbed dog because he beat her all the time with a cane, and she became very aggressive. She never attacked her master because German shepherds are very smart. But anyone else who came near him got attacked. The skinhead lived one floor below me in the Weitlingstrasse house, and when I wanted something from him I would knock on the door and say, "Lock Kathy up." Kathy would have attacked me immediately because of course she couldn't tell the difference between a neo-Nazi and an anarchist, only between her owner and everyone else.

Thor's story, meanwhile, just got sadder and sadder. Reinthaler was later in prison for eight months, in 1992, and Thor went virtually blind during this time. The veterinarians said that it was a psychological problem—he'd gone blind from grief. Then, three months after Reinthaler got out of prison, the Austrian police searched his apartment in Salzburg when he wasn't there. Thor ran madly around the house, barking at the intruders. A policeman thought the dog was going to attack him and shot him dead on the spot.

REINTHALER WAS THE movement's South American expert. After high school he had studied early Spanish history and had lived for more than ten years in Spain and South America, where he had made contacts with the Cedade and other Fascist groups, including associations of old war criminals. He became fluent in Spanish and acquired a number of false passports. He also joined a kind of neo-Nazi legionnaire's troop, which he was always shy about discussing. But he often spoke of the old Nazis he'd become friends with there, especially Goebbels's press secretary, von Oven. Through his travels, he had developed a closer relationship with the old war criminals than any other neo-Nazi of our generation had, and gradually he became the one in charge of collecting donations from them.

The Gauleiter of Salzburg had a way of disappearing for months at a time on missions to our "Kamerads in South America." He was on such a mission for most of 1991, except when he attended Gottfried Küssel's seizure-of-power cabinet session in Vienna. We counted on Reinthaler to take care of the old war criminals. These people were very important for us—they were our direct link to the Third Reich—and we were important to them because we were their direct link to the contemporary world. Our dreams lived through each other, you might say. The financial contributions flowed one way—toward us—

both while they were alive and after they died, if they bequeathed some of their estates to us. I never gave this blood money a thought then, but now I realize that at least some of the money that filled our coffers came from the profits from concentration camp inmates' slave labor or gold teeth.

All during 1991 we received cards and packages from Reinthaler with return addresses in Venezuela and Argentina and Chile. He didn't send cash this way, but often, when old Nazis died or got very sick, he would get them to bequeath their library of books and Third Reich propaganda material to us. There were also private diaries and letters, as well as issues of Nazi publications. Packages from South America might contain original copies of *Mein Kampf* and *The Myth of the Twentieth Century,* or they might contain something much more personal. I kept an archive in my apartment, as did our new recruit, Oliver W., who had a keen interest in history.

While Reinthaler was gone, Küssel was always coming around to visit us in Berlin, and often we felt he was pushing things a bit too far. One day, he showed up at Pfarrstrasse when we'd made an arrangement to meet during lunch. But he came too early. Küssel strode into Michael Heinisch's office and demanded, "Where's Hasselbach?"

Heinisch flipped out. He ran Küssel out of his office and then later threw a screaming fit at us, threatening to throw everyone associated with him out of the social project. He explained that he'd been getting visits from high-level anarchists lately, telling him that we were lying about being nonpolitical in the project, that we were in fact very active still, especially since Kühnen's death, and now here was the proof.

"Gottfried Küssel is the biggest neo-Nazi terrorist in Europe!" he cried. "When the Anti-Fas see that he's coming here, we'll have a holy war. Are you crazy? You're out! All of you!"

We just smiled at him. Heinisch hardly realized it, but he had little power left in the project by this point. We'd attracted most of the other young men to our side. Nobody listened to the Christian leader much at all anymore. They listened to us.

In October 1991 the anarchists firebombed the project. The entry hallway and staircase were completely burned up. It was a blow for Heinisch, for we'd actually made a great deal of progress on the house. We'd smashed through many of the partition walls and torn out most of the ceilings. We were even erecting an entirely new gabled roof, which was then to be shingled. I was getting good practice in my masonry skills.

The firebombing attack came the day before we were to hold a *Richtfest* to celebrate the completion of the new roof and framework. We celebrated anyway and got really smashed. Heinisch tried to impart a mood of Christian equanimity and to get us to turn the other cheek. "Boys, we will come through," he said. "If we just keep working we will come through this thing." But our mood was finally at a breaking point, and I and the other neo-Nazis encouraged calls for vengeance.

The Anarchist Anti-Fascist Youth Front claimed responsibility for the attack in a letter printed in *Die Tageszeitung,* a leftist newspaper. But we didn't need to read the letter in the *TAZ* to know whom to hold responsible. We saw our scraggly enemies every day in the houses across the street, and the lingering stench of butter acid reminded us daily just how seriously they took their "peace treaty" with Heinisch.

Still, I advised people to refrain from attacking the anarchists indiscriminately. I figured it was better to wait and see if we could pick up word on the street as to who'd planned and carried out the Moli attack. Then we'd strike.

One afternoon a few days after the bombing and the letter, a few of us got into a conversation with a passing anarchist named Willy, whom I knew pretty well and got along with. "I had nothing to do with the bombing, I thought it was shit, too," he said, and I actually believed him. He was older and fairly level headed.

I was trying to get Willy into a chat about who might have been involved when suddenly one of my Kamerads fell to the ground, screaming and clutching his face. It was Frank Lutz. He had been hit in the side of the head with a rock.

Ever since Frank had been beaten so badly by the Stasi that he'd lost some of his vision and sustained permanent kidney damage, he had had a kind of psychotic reaction to pain. When someone inflicted the slightest pain on him—or looked like he was about to—he'd lose control and react like an animal whose life was threatened.

I knew that whenever he wiped the blood off his face and was able to stand up again, whoever threw the stone was going to regret it.

A fuse blew in my mind this time, too. It was such a cowardly and unprovoked act, to smash him in the head. The thrower probably hadn't even been aiming for Frank. He'd just wanted to start something, and now I'd give him his chance.

I'd seen which house the stone had come from, and in a fury I ran across the street and inside, not knowing how I'd find him but fully intending to take the cowardly punk by his green hair and pull him out into the street. Two or three other neo-Nazis followed me into the house, and I believe a couple more behind them, including Frank.

But all I knew as soon as I ran in the door was that anarchists were all over me from every side. Shit, I thought, it was really stupid to do this.

They beat me with their fists, kicked me, and hit me with a two-by-four. After a few minutes of this, six of them picked me up and carried me upstairs. They were all masked, so I couldn't tell who was doing what to me. When they got me into the room, they continued to work me over, only this time there were more of them—and they had baseball bats.

I kept trying to jump up, but they surrounded me, more than I could count, hitting me with the bats and the two-by-fours and the fists and boots, crying "Death to the Nazi!" "Take that, you Fascist!"

Would I get the one or two crucial blows that would fuck up my insides forever? I wondered. I shielded my head but it hardly helped, they'd hit below the belly and I'd have to shield my groin. My whole body was becoming one giant throbbing swollen bruise. Would they kill me? Leave me to be found, the anonymous street fight kill, an untraceable murder? Would I become the next Rainer Sonntag? Made into a martyr for the Cause? They just kept beating and beating, like horrible bees with bats for stingers . . . and what had happened to Frank?

The answer to that question hit me, and the anarchists, that instant, like a ton of bricks.

"Ingo!" shouted Frank as he came crashing through the door of the room where I was being tortured.

"Frank!" I shouted. "Get these shits off me!"

Almost every anarchist in the room threw himself at Frank and managed to push him back out of the room, into the hallway, and almost close the door. Meanwhile, I was barely conscious from the beating. I tried to move but couldn't. I saw Frank being shoved out the door. "Frank!" I shouted desperately.

But he was busy pushing against the weight of six ski-masked anarchists leaning against the door. He managed to get his arm back through the door, and he was tearing at the flesh of any anarchist who got near him.

"Aeeeyy!" screamed one of the anarchists in pain as Frank got him in his grip. Frank's arm was dangerous. They started shouting that they would smash it off with the door, but Frank didn't let up.

Then I saw another anarchist pull out a long, flashing blade and begin to slash Frank's hand with it, no doubt thinking this would make the beast finally pull his arm back.

That was really the wrong thing to do.

Feeling his blood gushing and the pain in his hand, Frank slammed against the door with his crazy strength and it flew open, blowing the anarchists aside like so many swatted insects.

His head and hand gushing blood, Frank lifted me over his shoulder and helped me out of the room, kicking and punching anarchists who got in his way as he went. I got in a couple good ones myself, though I felt like I might not make it down the stairs. Every part of my body was part of a giant pain.

Frank had saved my life. It felt like any number of organs might stop functioning any minute, and I could barely see out of one eye, but I was alive.

Outside, the sun was going down and all hell was breaking loose. A huge street fight, the one that had been brewing all year, was going full force. It seemed like everyone who might have had the vaguest Left or Right affiliation in the neighborhood was out in the street, pounding away at one another with every weapon they could get their hands on. There were also police and ambulances and fire trucks. I saw flashing blue through the red film in my eyes. Everything was getting darker by the moment.

I heard sirens. Frank laid me down on a sidewalk. "You're okay, Kamerad," he said. I heard huge explosions. Screaming. More sirens. Firemen. I later learned that my enterprising younger brother, Jens, had gone into the house, fetched a jug of gasoline, and set two of the anarchists' cars on fire, a VW bus and an Opel. All I knew at the time was that I heard big explosions. And sirens. And water cannons. And shouting I couldn't understand. It was very noisy in the street. Then it started to become very quiet. . . .

As I lay on the sidewalk drifting into unconsciousness, I heard a bizarre, ferocious sound rise above the rest. I forced myself to look up, and the last thing I saw before passing out was a crazed skinhead charging into the crowd of anarchists waving a chain saw.

WHEN I WOKE up in the hospital, I learned that the police had managed to break up the fight and that Heinisch had managed to disarm the man with the chain saw and that I was under suspicion of having "started it." Needless to say, there'd been many seriously wounded on all sides. Many hospitalizations. I myself had two dislocated shoulders, a torn eyelid, a bruised ear, two broken ankles, a broken nose, and a concussion.

I was arrested on the X-ray table.

I was lying there, waiting for the pictures that were supposed to show if I had serious head injuries, when the police pushed their way into the room and said, "Ingo Hasselbach, you are under arrest. You must accompany us immediately."

I couldn't walk because my ankles were broken. They turned me around on my belly and cuffed my hands behind my back. They sort of dragged me by my handcuffed hands, with a little extra propping beneath the arms, out of the room and brushed off the supervising physician, who protested, "No, he cannot go with you, he has to stay in the hospital." I didn't protest, though. I had been drugged beyond caring. I figured that if I was going to be put to bed by cops, it might as well be in jail.

I was in jail for only a day or so, though. Then Frank Lutz, Auschwitz, and I were all released and taken back to the hospital. The cops didn't want us dying on their hands. Besides, what charges did they have against us? People had tried to crack our heads open with rocks and baseball bats. We'd defended ourselves. It had been a perfectly honorable way to spend an afternoon.

THE NEXT AFTERNOON Frank Lutz and I hobbled into the Pfarrstrasse project to work as usual. The anarchists were walking through the streets, caring solemnly for the remnants of their cars. They looked flabbergasted that we were back.

Inside, we found a completely wrecked Michael Heinisch. He seemed lower than I'd ever seen him. The eternal optimism and turning-the-other-cheek were gone.

"Look, it's okay what happened yesterday," I said. "It simply had to happen. We've just been sitting by for a year while they destroyed everything we did and kept giving us worse and worse shit. They hit Frank in the head with a rock."

Heinisch didn't look at me.

My whole body still hurt like it never had before, and I couldn't forget being locked up in that room with them. But in a way it was so terrifying I didn't want to even mention it. I would have been happy if we'd burned the bastards' houses down at that moment. I couldn't understand Heinisch's depression.

"Look, Michael, we had to give them something back. At least now things are evened up a bit. We can get back to work."

Heinisch looked at me uncomprehendingly, with what I might have taken to be a glint of unfamiliar anger in his eyes. Then he said wearily, "You're all suspended. We'll meet again in a week and discuss how things can continue here at the project."

Heinisch seemed near tears, but Frank agreed with me that there was no reason to mourn. All the Berlin newspapers reported that week about the riots on Pfarrstrasse in Lichtenberg. We hadn't made such headlines since the Rainer Sonntag March. We were physically hurt, but it was a media success for the Movement, for the new *Kameradschaft*.

The following week we had our big crisis meeting at Pfarrstrasse. Heinisch was back to his familiar placid, self-righteous self. He beat around the bush for a while, while the full membership of the project was there, but it was clear to Frank and Auschwitz and me what was going to happen. Everyone except us three was sent away after Heinisch's speech. Then the good Christian who'd tried to help us said quietly, "Boys, you're being sent away from the project." As a justification for his decision, he told us that we had been the "ringleaders" of the street fight, even though he must have known perfectly well it had been spontaneous.

A couple of months later, Heinisch admitted in an interview that he'd thrown us out of the project because of the strong pressure from the anarchist house occupiers on the other side of the street. Looking back, I think it was probably the right decision. We were simply using the project as a base to recruit the younger kids. And while we were a thoroughly corrupting influence on the other members, hardly any of Heinisch's Christian message had gotten through to us. We were too deep into the Movement. Even though I'd at first appreciated the chance for some peace and quiet in the wake of Kühnen's death, I'd soon rediscovered my zeal.

TERRORISTS

TV INTERVIEWS WERE often a neo-Nazi's best weapon, but they backfired on Gottfried Küssel. Shortly before New Year's Day, 1992, Küssel gave PrimeTime Live a tour of his VAPO paramilitary camp, bragging about his new Brownshirts and predicting a "violent war on the streets" and a mysterious "great bang." On *Nightline,* Küssel praised Hitler, called the gas chambers a hoax, and taunted a Holocaust survivor on the air, prompting Ted Koppel to wonder aloud, "I don't know, when I listen to this kind of trash, whether to think it's frightening or just to think it's silly." The Austrian government stopped wondering. Küssel was arrested on January 7, 1992.

The role of "Führer" of world neo-Nazism had just gone to his head. Maybe it hadn't helped living in an apartment filled with wax SS soldiers and gigantic caricatures of the Evil Jew.

He did things that he had only recently warned us against, such as calling for the restoration of the Nazi Party. "Never say that in public," he'd advised me quite earnestly. Then he'd said it on ABC! And his advice had been right. Those televised statements alone were enough for the Austrian authorities to charge him with attempting to propagate national socialism.

They also discovered a large cache of weapons in his apartment: grenades, pistols, explosives. The Austrian political police discovered the arsenal when they tore up the floorboards. Of course, they also carted off all his treasures.

Another complete violation of every rule of operation was that he had the diskettes for the neo-Nazi computer network sitting around his apartment. When the authorities found them, they were able to use them to expose a number of key players in Germany and Austria, as well as budding NSDAP/AO cells in Hungary. The Hungarian neo-Nazis were all busted as a result of Küssel's carelessness.

With his arrest, Küssel became perhaps an even more important leader than he had ever been in the Movement. Hitler had also first achieved his superhuman status among the original Nazis when he was sent to prison for an attempted putsch in 1924. Küssel was now the Führer-martyr of the Movement.

He was reserved in his appearance before the court, and he pretended to be a completely ordinary Viennese graduate student, denying any "serious" involvement with the neo-Nazis. His statements had been taken out of context. He wasn't trying to bring down the government. He was a law-and-order type. It was the old Mafia trick: "What, *me* extort protection money? I can barely put my own kids through school . . . it's tough being in the olive oil business."

Günther Reinthaler fled the country immediately after Küssel's arrest, and the VAPO began to function like a headless organization that gets its inspiration from the memory of the dead leader. And the memory of Küssel would turn out to be even more dangerous than the man himself.

Küssel's arrest on the heels of our getting kicked out of the Pfarrstrasse Project sealed our course. Frank Lutz and Auschwitz felt the same as I did. The time for legal work and patience was through. The only thing to do was to turn our *Kameradschaft* into a real terrorist organization. We would never make the kind of idiotic statements Küssel had made because our statements would be made under cover of night or in anonymous explosions—and no one would ever trace them to us. They would, however, come to know the name we had chosen for our group: the Social Revolutionary Nationalists, or SRN.

WE PLANNED OUR first big action for January 1992. Every January there was a big demonstration to commemorate Karl Liebknecht and Rosa Luxemburg, the Communists who had been murdered by rightist soldiers in 1919 in Berlin and whose bodies had been dumped into the Kreuzberg Canal. The demonstration began in Kreuzberg, where they had been killed, but the marchers always ended up in Lichtenberg, in the Cemetery of the Socialists, where their graves lay alongside those of other famous German Communists.

On the night before the demonstration, Auschwitz and I sneaked into the cemetery. We had no weapons other than two cans of white spray paint. Frank couldn't come because he had to baby-sit his kid. Auschwitz and I would have to take care of all of Germany's most famous Communists ourselves.

The spot we were interested in was a big round piece of grass in the middle of the cemetery, in the middle of which there was a big stone. It read THE DEAD ADMONISH US.

There were nine or ten graves arranged in a neat circle around this monument: Ernst Thälmann, the leader of the German Communist Party who had died in the Nazi concentration camp at Buchenwald; his successor, Walter Ulbricht, who had founded the state of East Germany; and seven other major figures, including of course Luxemburg and Liebknecht.

We began spraying. It was a simple design. On the big stone, over the solemn phrase THE DEAD ADMONISH US, we sprayed a white swastika. Then, on each of the gravestones, we sprayed a Star of David. That was all. A simple message but one everyone would understand. To my knowledge, Rosa Luxemburg was the only Jew buried there, but that didn't matter a whit. Communists and Jews were all the same to us.

There was an interior, decorative wall nearby, and on this wall we wrote VOLKSGEMEINSCHAFT STATT KLASSENKAMPF ("Community of the *Volk* Instead of Class Warfare").

It became a huge media event and was reported everywhere. It was only the second grave desecration in the cemetery since 1933. The Nazis had desecrated it, then we had. Between the two events it had been the most famous Communist cemetery, so it had been well protected by the GDR government. I suppose the reason that it wasn't better protected had to do with the facts both that it had not been attacked in so long and that it was one of the most important monuments of Communist East Germany and therefore, in united Germany in 1992, not high on the agenda.

More than eighteen thousand people protested our little action on the streets of Berlin in the following days. It made headlines around the world, and Gary Rex Lauck wrote about it in his newsletter. We considered this a huge success in itself. For an hour's work we'd gotten the full media blitz. In the wake of Kühnen's death and Küssel's arrest, this was important. We'd shown everyone that we weren't defeated, that in fact we were back at full strength.

I had always dreamed of becoming a terrorist, and I must admit that my ideas of a life as a terrorist were romantic. I saw terrorists as idealists who fought for a better and more just world as they saw it, against the overwhelming forces of the State and conventional society. For years I had collected everything I could find about the Red Army Faction, the Maoist terrorists who had forced the Federal Republic into a state of emergency and suspension of the constitution in the late 1970s. The RAF fascinated me, and now my Kamerads and I planned to base our group on their structure, which had been remarkably successful, considering they had had half the cops in Western Europe trying to track them down for twenty years.

The RAF had brought terrorism to modern Europe, and, even though they could not have been more opposed to our ideology, we respected them for their fanaticism and skill. Some of us, like the excitable anti-Semite Nero Reisz, even openly supported the RAF and called for a union between extreme Left and extreme Right to bring down German democracy.

While the RAF specialized in kidnapping or assassinating high-profile leaders of industry and government (most recently, in 1991, they had assassinated the head of the Treuhand, the largest corporation in world history, formed to sell off the industrial and manufacturing holdings of the East German government), neo-Nazi terrorists had always unleashed much more indiscriminate violence against much less prominent targets. In 1980, for instance, West German neo-Nazis had exploded a bomb during the Oktoberfest in Munich, killing a dozen people and injuring more than two hundred; that same year, another neo-Nazi operative had murdered a Jewish couple in the same city. Most recently, of course, neo-Nazis had mainly been identified with carrying out terror attacks against refugee shelters and anarchist houses.

We wanted to bring neo-Nazi terrorism up to the level of that carried out by the radical Left, striking at targets that would be both better guarded and more significant—targets that would do serious damage to the democratic German state while driving home our racial message. There was, for instance, talk of assassinating Gregor Gysi, the head of the reformed Communist Party, the PDS; he was East Germany's most prominent Jew and a leader of the Communists to boot. He was not only a major politician but the political representative of the former GDR system. We also considered hitting Ignatz Bubis, the new head of the Jewish community, as well as a number of politicians in Bonn—including the interior minister and Chancellor Kohl himself.

There were about twenty people in my NSDAP/AO cell by then. We did a lot of weapons training, silent killing, war games stuff. But we weren't interested in going to fight in the former Yugoslavia just because the Ustashe had once fought alongside the SS. My group wanted to rip apart the Federal Republic, not some foreign country.

I organized required reading and homework on terrorism in the *Kameradschaft* evening meetings. Using books and magazines, we gradually informed ourselves about how to blow up bridges, tanks, train tracks, and cars. We discussed potential targets of right-wing terrorism, which were first of all socialist and Jewish monuments in the former GDR.

We lifted a lot from a book entitled *The Total Resistance,* by Major H. von Dach Bern, a former Swiss Army officer. It was divided into two parts—"Organization and Conduct of Guerilla Warfare" and "Organization and Operation of a Civilian Resistance Movement"— and contained sections on "Basic Rules of Terror" and "Behavior in Concentration Camps." Von Dach wasn't a Nazi at all; as far as I know, he had written *The Total Resistance* for military intelligence experts. He had done a research project, for example, about how terrorists could work in Switzerland against the government. It was an excellent manual from beginning to end, showing the basics of how to live underground, handle explosives, build timed bombs, and ambush vehicles, as well as how best to confuse the police when being interrogated. It was not written for terrorists—quite the contrary, it was written from the perspective of the authorities, to tell them what to expect—but it certainly helped many a terrorist find his footing.

The way it came into our hands illustrates the fluidity of terrorist circles and the de facto cooperation between ideological extremists and fanatics, even when their only common goal is to upset the status quo. The RAF got *The Total Resistance* first, and we eventually got it from a spy in anarchist circles. Now there are photocopies everywhere, and both extreme leftists and rightists have it. The first copy probably came from some American GI, as did practically all the material on weapons and explosives circulating underground in Europe.

Another very useful manual was actually printed by the U.S. Army and was called *Explosives and Demolitions*. It still had the TOP SECRET stamp across the title page. Lauck sent us this manual, which was more technical and precise than *The Total Resistance,* and we photocopied it and mailed it to neo-Nazis all over Germany.

The most modern handbook for terror we received was sent from Nebraska via the Internet. It was called *A Movement in Arms* and described how to wage a war of right-wing terrorism against a democratic government. (Gary Lauck made the information available in printed pamphlets for those without access to the information superhighway.) Once again, there was much material that was repeated from *The Total Resistance,* but there was also much that was new and more specific to our purposes.

Of course, while we studied terrorism, we also continued to distribute hard-core Nazi propaganda material from Nebraska. It usually had a little swastika flag with a saying like "Germans protect yourselves, don't buy from Jews!" These professionally printed swastika signs from Gary Rex Lauck's NSDAP/AO had a tremendous impact in a country where Nazi propaganda had once been ubiquitous and had then been banned for fifty years. The swastika was both shocking and utterly familiar, and the anti-Semitic sayings Lauck chose for his stickers and flyers reminded people of when the German government had itself erected the same signs. I think it was far more powerful when the swastikas and sayings were printed officially, rather than just graffitied in an uneven hand. It conjured up memories of the Nazi-controlled state.

Sometimes the man in Nebraska or someone else from out of town would suggest some "action" to us involving violence. Violence was usually only hinted at indirectly, and there would also be talk of finding "solutions." Consciously or not, we were mimicking the methods of the original Nazis, who had used code words and euphemisms to describe the need for a "final solution" to the Jewish problem, so that no written order could ever be found.

* * *

IN APRIL FOUR of us from Berlin—Schweigert, myself, and two others—decided to participate in a protest event in Vienna calling for the release of Gottfried Küssel. On the way, we decided to make a pilgrimage to Adolf Hitler's birthplace in the town of Braunau, on the Inn River, on the border of Bavaria and Austria.

But no sooner had we pulled out our cameras in Braunau to snap some pictures of the south German landscape than we were arrested by the Austrian political police. At least fifteen of these stiff-looking men in dark suits surrounded us, like we were trapped in some businessmen's convention, only these businessmen flashed badges and pistols. They must have thought we four were pretty dangerous, though we were only armed with cameras. They were polite but insistent that we go with them.

I found it amusing at first—with all the things we had gotten away with, now they were arresting us for trying to take a picture of Hitler's house? But then one of them broke police procedure, for when I grinned a bit too widely he shoved his pistol into the side of my neck; they were allowed to point the pistol at the kidneys or chest, but not the neck or the head. "Hey, that thing could go off, be careful," I said. He was a stone-faced type. He didn't seem to give a shit if it did go off. I just hoped his trigger finger was as placid as his face.

They handcuffed us, covered our heads with black cloths, and pushed us into the car. I have no idea why they covered our heads because it was no secret where they were taking us. I suppose they wanted to keep some bystander from taking a picture of who they were arresting.

We drove over three hours to the main office of the political police in Vienna. There we were held for a week. They tried to interrogate us, but we took the line that we'd been kidnapped by a foreign government. "We are German citizens and you must speak to our ambassador," we all said. "We won't talk with any Austrian cops."

The German ambassador said that for the time being he could not do anything. We'd looked suspicious as tourists, and the Austrians had had the right to take us into custody. But the Austrians couldn't issue an arrest warrant because we hadn't committed any crime. If they'd wanted to, they could have tried to get us simply for visiting Hitler's birthplace—if they could prove we'd done it as a pilgrimage, that would have been an offense under Austria's laws against reviving national socialism.

They had very complete records about the others; they knew which organizations they belonged to, for example. But with me they were in the dark, and that made them particularly suspicious. "I'm not with any organization," I said. "The last organization I was with was Michael Heinisch's Christian Youth Project. I'm trying to get clean." They didn't believe me for a second, and I knew they had an instinct that I was plotting something underground. But I didn't say a word, except that I only wanted to speak to a German attorney and to the German ambassador.

The Austrian political cops had been following us since we had crossed the border. Right-wing radicalism was reaching an all-time high that spring, with more than 50 percent of Austrian and German teenagers and many older people expressing support for us. The level of right-wing violence in Germany was higher than at any time since 1945, and the Austrian authorities were eager to keep it from slipping across the border. Anyone with short hair was looked over carefully by the passport officials, and they'd obviously done a computer search on us and come up with a book of offenses. Normally you could pass this border very quickly; we were held up for nearly an hour before being allowed to cross. After we got our passports back, I think they followed us by car.

Unable to extract anything from us and unwilling to keep us locked up in Vienna, the police expelled us from Austria as undesirable aliens and dropped us over the border in Bavaria. In Freilassing, a town on the Bavarian side, the same dark suits who had arrested us handed us over to the German suits, the BKA, the Federal Office of Criminal Investigation. We were taken to a nearby police station and interrogated some more. What did we want to do in Austria? Were we plotting to spring Küssel from jail? Were we planning some plot based in Braunau?

"We were visiting Hitler's grave," we said, consenting to reply to them because at least they were German cops. "We were in Austria strictly for tourism."

The week in the Austrian prison had given me an idea what Küssel was dealing with. It was the lousiest West prison I'd ever experienced—filthy and bug ridden. You slept on a sack of straw, like the fucking Middle Ages. When you wanted to leave the cell, you had to stick your hands through a little opening in the door, and they put handcuffs on you. Only then would they open the door.

I got messages from Küssel in jail. He knew immediately that we were in custody. We had arranged a meeting point in Vienna with several people from the VAPO, and, when we hadn't shown, they had found out what had happened and reported to Küssel. He offered us a few words of clichéd encouragement. But it was impressive that he'd known so fast, as though he'd read about our arrest in the evening papers.

In jail Küssel knew a lot of things.

ON MAY 1, 1992, at the same time as the traditional May Day demonstrations by the leftists and anarchists were going on, I took part in a demonstration of the Free German Workers' Party, the FAP, in the Ernst Thälmann Memorial Park in the former East Berlin.

Ernst Thälmann had been a resistance fighter during the Third Reich who had headed the underground Communist Party until he had been shot by the Nazis in Buchenwald. Thälmann had been one of the GDR's absent Founding Fathers, the most famous of the exclusive group who'd died in Nazi concentration camps fighting for socialism. He was a very important symbolic figure as we were growing up. From age eleven to fourteen, following my compulsory stint as a Young Pioneer, I'd been a "Thälmann Pioneer," which was also compulsory. But my group of former Thälmann Pioneers and our West German Kamerads were hardly there to honor Ernst Thälmann.

When the left-wing organizations told their participants about the radical right demonstration in Prenzlauer Berg, more than a thousand of them streamed into Thälmann Park. There were no more than a hundred neo-Nazis in the park, mostly from the FAP. Most of the FAP men were in their mid-twenties, some a bit older. They were neatly dressed in their faux–storm trooper uniforms, looking as close to original Nazis as the Constitution would allow, with red armbands that looked like the real thing but for the black letters "FAP" rather than a black swastika in the white center.

These young Brownshirts were led by Kühnen's old enemy, barrel-chested, white-haired Friedhelm Busse; at least twice the age of most of his followers, he looked robust and powerful as any of them, his flushed red face getting redder by the minute as he shouted slogans into the crisp May air. He was in Berlin to stir up a fuss and was look-ing forward to it.

"Red Front, die! Berlin free at last from Moscow's bloody hand!" he cried.

I stood next to Busse, holding a black, white, and red imperial Ger-man flag. With Kühnen dead and Küssel in jail, Busse had ideas of getting me to come over to his organization. I wasn't really inter-ested—the FAP were the most impressive looking of the neo-Nazis, but in a way they also seemed the silliest, in their brown uniforms and red armbands, like cartoon Nazis—but I didn't mind coming along for the ride. With my current status as a cell leader in the NSDAP/AO, by necessity an utterly secret enterprise, I missed mak-ing big public displays the way we used to. I got a kick out of stand-ing there next to the defiant old man, staring down a mass of leftists at least ten times bigger than our group.

Suddenly, rising out of the opposing crowd, I saw my old nemesis and black-haired doppelgänger—the dark beast of anarchy and sometime designer-jeans model, Olaf Arnwalt.

"Hasselbach, you Nazi pig!" Arnwalt shouted at me with what amounted to a sarcastic but friendly gesture. He knew he'd just put five hundred people onto me.

The anarchists began to shout, in rhythm, "Hasselbach, the Nazi pig! Hasselbach, the Nazi pig!"

Arnwalt grinned at me from the other crowd and shouted. Then I was bombarded with cobblestones, one of which barely missed my head.

One of the FAP Brownshirts passed me a knife. "Looks like you're going to need it more than me today!" he said.

I saw that Arnwalt was chucking stones at me. The big black-haired bastard. I started hurling stones back. At the moment I let the first stone fly, I thought: I hope I hit someone in the head—especially Arnwalt, but another anarchist swine would do. But it's an odd thing about throwing stones—as soon as one stone was airborne, I stopped thinking about whether I'd hit someone with it and my whole being became absorbed in picking up the next stone to throw.

Standing next to me but somewhat out of the line of cobblestone fire, Busse looked flabbergasted and rather upset. I could tell that he couldn't believe that these people would be interested in me instead of him. I found it a bit amusing myself, considering that, though he'd been in this game for forty years, I was the more recognizable "Nazi pig" in Berlin. (Busse was much better known in the south of Germany. His headquarters were in Munich, where he published the FAP newspaper and printed it on his own presses.)

But I had a bad feeling, mostly because of the disparity in numbers that was becoming apparent. If there was trouble, which we'd had every intention of assuring, we'd get clobbered. The only thing to offset the mass of anarchists was the police, who had begun to emerge from all sides into the park. A few groups of cops began to set up water cannons.

In no time the anarchists had us encircled. The police stood between us and them, but if they were planning to keep things calm, it didn't work. The police tried to close off the roads around the park so no more anarchists could get through, but they must have found other places to park nearby, because more and more of them kept coming in.

Now it began to hail stones from all sides. A female member of the FAP, one of only two women at the event, caught a stone on the side of the head. She fell to the ground, bleeding all over her white dirndl.

In the meantime, it turned into a regular street battle, with both sides chucking cobblestones at each other and the police standing in between firing water cannons. I noticed many injured policemen lying around me, which was probably why they started firing the cannons mostly at the anarchists, who were the ones who'd started throwing the stones.

There were lots of FAP flags around me, but I was still holding the black, white, and red flag of the German Reich. I decided I had to raise it.

I ran up onto the Thälmann monument itself, like it was the hill at Iwo Jima, and planted my flag, letting it flutter in the wind.

This was the symbol of everything antithetical to this leftist monument, and the left-wingers went wild. They raged behind the police chains. You have to imagine a thousand masked people completely flipping out. When they saw me they exploded and started throwing rocks at me and attacking me up on my perch. I used the flagpole as a weapon to beat them off. Meanwhile, the other woman at the event, whom I had once dated, started putting stones into my hand so I could throw them down from the monument.

A cop came over and shouted at me, "If I see you throw another stone, I'll take that flag away, son."

"Yeah, okay, okay."

But he was serious. A minute later he was back.

"I saw that," he said. "Give me the flag."

"Hey, everyone is throwing stones, all hell's breaking loose," I said.

"But I told *you* not to," said the cop.

He grabbed the flag on the bottom and tried to take it away from me. I wasn't about to let go. It became a tug-of-war between me and the cop.

"The flag you will never get!" I said, thoroughly carried away by the absurd spirit of mock battle. The flag was holy, I'd never give it up as long as I could stand. *"Die Fahne hoch!"* ("Raise the flag high!") I shouted, cribbing a famous line from a Nazi movie about a Hitler Youth street fight, in which the hero dies after having defended the flag.

The policeman had to laugh at what a stubborn idiot he'd come up against.

"The flag you will never get!" I repeated with a fanatic's grin and a surge of adrenaline.

"Okay, you idiot!" he said, laughing and letting go of the flag.

The anarchists also had flags—the white skull and crossbones on black field of the Edelweiss Pirates. A lot of the Edelweiss Pirate anarchists were carrying chains that day, and I saw them running up to neo-Nazis and smashing them with their chains. I had to admit I respected their fighting technique. Completely hard and in your face.

Another trademark tactic the Edelweiss Pirates were using was to form a human chain and run, knocking down everything in their path. They were such big, strong fighters, like Olaf Arnwalt, that it worked. Woe to anyone who got in the way of one of their chains, metal or human.

The water cannons were running the entire time now, from all sides, the flood mixing in with the more deadly hail of rocks, sometimes catching them in the stream and propelling them forward with even more deadly effect. Everyone was soaking wet. It was total chaos. This was when I noticed what a fit and courageous old man Busse was, for all his defects.

I wouldn't have thought it, but he was out in front of his younger troops—this white-haired, pot-bellied old guy, fearlessly dodging rocks and throwing them. With the other FAP people, one noticed immediately a certain cowardice. They were looking around anxiously and observing what we, the Berliners, did so they could copy us. While we'd had years of street-fighting experience with the toughest anarchists in the country, the FAP were from the provinces and mostly only had experience attacking remote foreigner shelters in the countryside, terrorizing people who couldn't or wouldn't fight back. Now they had to look to us, and their old leader, Busse, for a lesson in active self-defense.

At some point, one of the cops ran up to Busse and me and explained that we'd just lost our right to demonstrate. The meeting was forbidden, and we had to clear out of the park immediately. We didn't protest.

The cops provided us an escort to try to make it to the closest S-Bahn station. The anarchists, who just kept growing in number with hundreds more streaming in from Kreuzberg and other surrounding areas, followed, getting in their potshots at the neo-Nazis. I helped someone pick up the FAP woman, who obviously needed a doctor badly.

The water cannons were making it all more chaotic. There was only one road, which was very narrow, and eighty men in total panic were running down it.

The anarchists were blasting the ultimate anarchist street-fighting song, "Die Letzte Schlacht Gewinnen Wir!" ("We'll Win the Last Battle!") by the anarchist rocker Rio Reiser. I personally loved Reiser's music—it was enough to make anyone, even a neo-Nazi, want to become an anarchist. It was probably the best German rock music ever recorded, a thousand times better than any right-wing band. The anarchists had it going on a loudspeaker wagon. I had to restrain myself from singing along with them: "Out of the way, capitalists, the last battle we will win. Throw the gun away, Mr. Policeman, the first fight, and the last fight, we will win!" It rocked!

But I was on the other side. I wasn't supposed to be getting into it.

The music gave the anarchists a huge advantage in morale. It made them want to bash heads—neo-Nazis, cops, whoever was the enemy in the "Last Battle."

But then they started going into chants like "German policemen protect the Fascists, Nazis go away, Nazis go away!" and I was somewhat less inspired.

We tried to counter with our own chants: "Beat the Reds where you find them!" and stuff like that. But it was pretty pointless to sing anything, because we were only eighty guys and we couldn't make ourselves heard. We walked behind a bunch of cops and made *"Sieg heil!"* salutes—nobody could drown that out. We also yelled "Red Front perish!" which had a sort of resonance to it when eighty men shouted it.

But the anarchists were really well organized. They would sneak toward us through the bushes, and then they would suddenly be standing, right where you were walking, with cameras. "Say cheese!" they'd yell, jumping out of a bush. Or "Over here, Fritz!" Then they'd get you. They were making a photo archive of all the neo-Nazis in Berlin. The Anti-Fa Youth Front and Edelweiss Pirates were becoming real intelligence pros, accumulating material on all of us.

Meanwhile, a cameraman from a TV station, SAT 1, didn't have such luck. He thought he'd run ahead of us and film us as we were running away—neo-Nazis in retreat chased by friends of Ernst Thälmann—but I didn't see him until I was right on top of him. He was rather small, after all, and there were fire hoses going all around me. I smashed into him with tremendous force, knocking him at least thirty feet across the asphalt.

We were almost at the S-Bahn station when we saw we'd have to cross a bridge. The problem was that anarchists were already on it. They used flares, Molis, everything they had as we charged the bridge. What a battle. Then a group of "Union Men Against Nazis" suddenly showed up and started mixing in. I was still carrying the flag and started beating up a union man with it. We couldn't get across the bridge, so we found a way to go under it, only that exposed us to incredible casualties from the anarchists, who threw things down on top of us. The loose stones made the area all around the S-Bahn station look like the ruins of an ancient city.

With so many flying that day, it was amazing that I never got a stone in the head. But of course, from our troop, Silvio Baumann was the only one who got a stone in his head that day. I'd tried to keep an eye out for him and my brother Jens throughout the fighting, but, just as we reached the entrance to the train station, Silvio got a huge

stone in the head. It was only a couple of inches shy of the spot where
the steel plate had finally been implanted in his skull. The guy just
had no luck at all. He was a magnet for stones.

At Ernst Thälmann Park station we ran as quickly as we could into
a waiting train, which was full of ordinary people. Luckily, the police
had stopped one and ordered the conductor not to leave the station
until we were all aboard. It took a damned long time to get eighty
wounded, scrambling people on board, but when we were finally all
on, the train rolled slowly out of the station. As it did, stones rained
down like hail on the top of the car, frightening all the passengers
even more. The windowpanes all started to break as stones flew in
through the windows. Everyone was on the floor or had their heads
between their knees. Women were screaming.

As the train pulled out of the station, there was one flag that could
be seen fluttering out the window—the black, white, and red banner
of the German Reich. I could hear the furious screams of hundreds of
stone-throwing anarchists, shouting "Hasselbach, you swine! Nazis
die! Nationalist scum, rot in hell!"

It was a wonderful feeling. It reminded me of old times. The train
was wrecked. We were wrecked. The Cause was hopeless. But I had
the flag high! This was what neo-Nazism was about to me, far more
than all the terrorist business I'd been planning. It was the thrill of
this defiance, of snatching victory from the jaws of defeat. In 1932
the SA and the Communists had battled for these very streets, I told
myself. Horst Wessel and Heini Völker, the young martyr in *Hitler
Youth Quex*, and all the trumped-up heroes had been here, holding
the *"Fahne hoch"*! At the next station, everybody had to get out and
most were loaded onto ambulances. Nothing mattered. "The Last
Battle We Will Win!"

But what did the flag really mean anymore? Why was I holding it?
Why the hell had I just risked shattering my skull like a coconut for
the honor of holding the pre-1918 Reich Flag on top of the Ernst
Thälmann monument?

A certain person had entered my life who would make it difficult
for me to continue to avoid confronting these obvious questions.

26

THE MOVIEMAKER

AT THE BEGINNING of September 1991 my brother Jens had told me that some guy from France had been snooping around the Pfarrstrasse house wanting to make a movie about the scene. Jens had met him a couple of times for a beer, and now the Frenchman also wanted to get to know me. I wasn't interested, though, and advised my brother to be careful. "You can never tell what these press idiots really want. He was obviously just using you to get to me." But my brother met with the filmmaker a couple more times and took along Stinki the skinhead, who was also working on the Pfarrstrasse social project with us. Both Jens and Stinki seemed to like the guy, or at least the fact that he bought them beer. One day the Frenchman simply showed up at the house and persuaded me to meet him at a café on Weitlingstrasse.

In addition to our "no politics" pact, we'd also promised Heinisch not to have any more contact with the press; he didn't want his social project to be portrayed in the media as the new vacation home for neo-Nazis. But Heinisch wasn't around when the filmmaker came by, and I let my guard down.

The Frenchman seemed like an amusing guy. Only he wasn't actually French, he was German. His name was Winfried Bonengel. He had lived for more than eight years in France, and he said he'd come back to Germany now only to make a film about neo-Nazis. He showed up in a beat-up Volkswagen that he said he'd driven all the way from Paris. I liked that he was immediately frank about his dislike of Germany, not a position that would ingratiate him with me. I didn't know if he was being straight about any of this.

At least it was clear he'd lived in France, for he had an accent and mannerisms that were squarely between the two cultures. He talked with his hands, rather excitably, his big greenish eyes bugging out, bloodshot and huge, like someone who took speed or coke or at least drank too much coffee. He was quite tall, but it was hard to see it because he was always bending and twisting his large body, as though he were mildly uncomfortable with it. It made me aware of how straight I always stood. He had a few days' beard growth and talked excitedly as he chain-smoked Marlboros. All in all he gave the impression of someone who lived and worked in erratic, energetic bursts. I felt instantly that he was someone who could go a long way on sheer force of will—and, judging from his clothes and appearance, he'd have to.

I was sure this guy was sincere—about something. The problem was, what? Was he an Anti-Fa spy? BKA or *Verfassungsschmutz*? An undercover cop? Interpol? The Mossad? He could have been any of those things, for the strangest people sometimes work as spies and narcs, and the better the secret service, the stranger and less likely the spy. My own country, the German Democratic Republic, had specialized in making narcs out of the most disheveled, wild-eyed romantics and dissidents. I wasn't above suspecting anyone.

Nevertheless, I liked him, even if I still suspected him. There was something appealing about him, in his disheveled way, and I could see why Jens and Stinki had enjoyed going drinking with him. If Winfried Bonengel was a low-down scumbag of a headline-grabbing, lying, left-wing narc, he was one with personality.

I agreed to meet with him to discuss the possibility of filming. Only discuss. Nothing more.

IN THE FOLLOWING weeks I stood him up regularly. Though I'd been enthusiastic at first, from a distance I reconsidered. I didn't have any desire to do anything for television anymore, and some of my friends stoked my suspicions about him.

Frank Lutz especially had hated Bonengel from the beginning and urged me never to speak with him again. He kept asking me for his address so he could "finish him off." I told him to forget it. The moviemaker lived in Paris. I didn't have his address, and he was not listed. I only had a number where I could leave a message when I was ready to begin filming.

"That guy will be your demise!" Frank warned about him.

"What do you want with him?" Auschwitz seconded. "For sure he's from the State Security Service, and if not, this left-wing, fag journalist is working for the Anti-Fa."

Others thought he was a Jew.

Normally it wouldn't be a problem to work with any of these types—even a Jew—if they seemed useful as a means for transmitting our propaganda. The "voice in the middle"—the journalist or other person asking questions—was hardly more important to us than the camera. We were well versed in the art of getting our message across through the mediation of a hostile questioner to those in the public who would be susceptible.

What worried Auschwitz and Frank Lutz was that they could see that I'd gotten to be friends with this filmmaker—that I wasn't using him as merely a microphone for my propaganda. But even they probably never guessed what grave consequences this friendship would have—not only for the moviemaker and for me but for all of them.

WE HAD PEOPLE who were in charge of collecting reports and articles written about us and building files on both Anti-Fas and reporters who took a special, therefore suspect, interest in our activities. We kept an archive of all Anti-Fa publications, of course, including the British magazine *Searchlight,* which was the most prominent internationally but rather sensationalistic and inaccurate. All these publications had a strategy of publishing the addresses and phone numbers of known neo-Nazis, and, if we could find out about it in advance, it could be very helpful to help someone defend his place or temporarily move. They also took lots of photos of us at our rallies and published these as well.

Of course, we used the same techniques, publishing the addresses as well as photos of our enemies, both in print and on the Internet. It tended to be even worse for the leftists and anarchists to have their names published by us. When they knew a street where a neo-Nazi lived, they'd put up a sign or graffiti saying so by his house, and this would often prove embarrassing, especially for our older, respectable supporters. As leftists usually didn't mind being exposed as such, we tended to launch straight into violence against them—bombing or some other direct attack. Christian Worch had organized an "anti-Anti-Fa" task force especially for this purpose.

With the anti-Anti-Fa task force, Worch consolidated the archive about all known anti-Fascists: their names, addresses, families, everything that could be found out about them. It included photos we'd taken of people and tracked new faces that appeared at Anti-Fa rallies. It was a huge research project, like making a telephone book. In Berlin alone, we archived detailed material on more than three hundred people. These lists were made in each city. Oliver W., the young man we'd so successfully indoctrinated into the scene the previous year, was especially good at ID photographing. He worked with a high-powered zoom lens and enjoyed it because it was like playing spy. Frank Lutz also appreciated getting to follow in his parents' footsteps.

Frank checked out Bonengel in our archive as thoroughly as he could, but nothing had ever been published about him. No one had ever taken his picture. He'd never been mentioned in an Anti-Fa magazine. He was an utterly unknown, mysterious stranger.

Still, Frank took him for a left-wing snooper. But the more I thought about it, the more I decided that the director was being honest—that he had nothing to do with either right-wing or left-wing politics. He kept calling me from France and asking if I was ready to do the film with him, and sometimes he'd appear unexpectedly at the Pfarrstrasse project, having driven half the night to get there. He was like a dog with a film camera, always waiting there with his messed-up hair and determined expression, knowing he would finally, someday, get me to come out and play ball with him.

Finally, after I was thrown out of the Pfarrstrasse project, I couldn't dodge Bonengel anymore with the excuse that Heinisch wouldn't let me speak with the press. Also, now that I was focused on neo-Nazi work again, with a face full of battle scars and a couple of broken ankles, I felt the urge to get myself back into the media and to prove that I was still an important fighter for the Cause. I began to see this film as a way to document my unbroken loyalty to national socialism and my central role in the scene. I knew that any film had tremendous propaganda value. I thought I knew what to say before the cameras and what not to, and Küssel's arrest had only made me more cautious in that department.

Vanity also played a part in my decision to go ahead and work with him. I was flattered by his interest in making me the central figure in a film about the entire German neo-Nazi movement. The young Führer. It was true that, since Kühnen's death, most neo-Nazis, especially in the north of Germany, had taken me for their Führer, even if I'd let Küssel claim the title for himself. If Bonengel asked Worch and Heinz Reisz and a lot of other German neo-Nazis, they'd all pronounce me their new Führer of the East.

In November 1991 I allowed Bonengel to come for the first time with his camera to my place on Wotanstrasse. He came alone, with a borrowed camera. He asked me a couple of questions on camera. He let me know that he had no contract for the film and therefore no money but what he himself could put in from his personal savings, which wasn't much. After two hours he stowed the camera back in his VW bug—one window had been broken in since the last time I'd seen it—and drove back to Paris.

I still had no idea what would come of it, but I didn't mind talking with him. He was different from other journalists. They only wanted to get their story and then disappeared. Bonengel seemed interested in me as a person. He listened carefully to the answers I gave to his questions and then asked even more probing questions. He was able to go quite deep, yet I could tell he had little background on Nazis or neo-Nazis. We were simply a bizarre phenomenon for him—like people who thought they'd been picked up by UFOs or some other cult—and he wanted to explore our motives and beliefs on film.

He told me that I didn't fit his clichéd image of a young Nazi, and precisely because of this it was interesting for him to make a film about me. At the time I figured he thought I didn't look like the cliché—I didn't have a shaved head or a brown shirt with an armband—but later he said he'd meant I seemed too sensitive and intelligent to be a neo-Nazi. Either way his impressions were fine with me—I didn't want to fit any clichés of neo-Nazis.

I was skeptical, to say the least, because it wasn't clear how he was going to make a longer film with no money and no equipment. But his enthusiasm and way of asking questions impressed me. He really seemed to want to capture the truth, not just some quick, sensational images.

IN JANUARY, ABOUT two months later, Bonengel returned. He explained to me that he had borrowed some money and now things could really get going. I had no job and nothing better to do, so we set off with his little team, crisscrossing Germany. I found that the team he'd selected also didn't fit the clichés I had of film people and journalists. They were very loose, plainspoken guys.

Bonengel had a brash sense of humor and didn't restrain himself from making light of my Kamerads. And he was constantly making fun of our rituals and ideology. I now see that this was part of a strategy to make us seem less intimidating to him, but at the time I thought he was really crazy. Sometimes he even succeeded in making me smile about the grim, overbearing poses of my Kamerads as they spoke about their hatreds, plots, and plans.

We drove to Langen to speak with Nero Reisz and "Knight's Cross Bearer" Otto Riehs. Reisz showed up at the station in his big Mercedes and drove us to his house, proudly showing off the countryside as though it were his Reich.

"I was sitting next to a man at an event about the Third Reich in Frankfurt the other day, sponsored by the city," said Riehs. "This man said he was an Auschwitz survivor. But in the Frankfurt paper that very morning was a photo of the gate at Auschwitz concentration camp, and the caption read 'Whoever went through this gate never came out alive again.' So I said to the man sitting next to me, 'How is it, if everyone who went through that gate never came out again, how is it that you are sitting next to me today? And how is it that the community of Frankfurt invites four hundred Holocaust survivors back every year if they were all gassed?' He couldn't answer properly, and that's why I say it's all a big hoax to extort money from the German taxpayer."

Reisz spoke about how he would personally erect concentration camps for Jews, fags, political enemies, and the Jew-influenced politicians in Bonn. He said that he supported the RAF, the left-wing terrorists, because they also attacked the democratic politicians and that if the radical Left and the radical Right could only concentrate, they could solve Germany's problems together. Then he sang a little anti-Semitic song, jumping up and down with glee in his seat, his huge potbelly and walrus mustache jiggling as he sang and took sips of beer.

This was the first time that I'd ever listened to people talk like this with someone else in the room whom I respected but who was entirely outside the Movement. All my friends for as long as I could remember had been in the Movement in one way or another.

Now, to hear my Kamerads talking in the presence of *my* new friend—as I now thought of him—I actually began to feel ashamed. I was ashamed to be associated with these hate-filled drunken pigs. Reisz's worst Jewish jokes practically made me ill. I didn't say another word.

As I listened to them go on and on for the camera, I began to identify more with Bonengel and his team than with my Kamerads. It was a terrifying moment, for I suddenly felt cut loose and adrift. My home was in the Movement. Outside was nothing. Yet now the Movement seemed to be closing to me, the doors closing at the end of a tunnel, and it was much too far to run fast enough to slip out in time. If my Kamerads were revealed as devils, that would leave only one person I could talk to . . . and if this one person was the Devil? He had arrived as a stranger, but now he had made my Kamerads seem stranger than he.

Obviously the situation had made Bonengel uncomfortable as well—having to ask rabid anti-Semites serious questions when he knew he was getting poisonous dreck for answers—and on the drive back from Langen he seemed to try to relieve his discomfort by making fun of the Movement in an almost frantic way. He couldn't stop. He made fun of Reisz and Riehs and Stinki and my brother. He talked about how he'd seen photos of Michael Kühnen at a gay S & M party in Paris, and wasn't it funny that the top Führer of our homosexual-hating Movement was gay himself.

He was going too far. While I'd been enjoying his sense of humor before—and his jokes about the Movement had probably helped to give me some new perspective—now he was pushing too hard. He was pushing me, goading me . . . to what? Did he want me to snap and attack him? So he could get that on camera?

I just managed to restrain myself, sitting back, brooding, steaming with shame and anger. At one point, he leaned over and told me, secretively, that he was in fact not just a filmmaker, as he'd claimed. He had been sent by an organization. My eyes lit up—so there was some lousy plot afoot! Why was he telling me this? What did he want? The thoughts raced through my mind.

"What organization?" I asked, controlling my shock and anger.

"I am the chief—" he said, pausing for effect, his greenish eyes boring into me in the dim light of the van "—of the NDKS."

I searched my memory for the meaning of this acronym. A government agency? An Anti-Fa group? Another neo-Nazi group? What was NDKS? I had no idea. But I knew one thing: I'd made a mistake to trust him so far. I began thinking, in the back of my mind, what I might have to do to get rid of him and his films. . . . I shrugged my shoulders, giving him a cold stare.

"What!" he shouted, looking stricken and furious. "You don't know the NDKS? Kamerad!"

"Kamerad"—a right-winger, then? What was this?

"You have to get in contact with them!" said the director, slapping me on the shoulder. "No, I'm serious—the kid doesn't know the NDKS."

"What is it?" I asked, smiling awkwardly.

"The NDKS is the 'Neue Deutsche Kolonialstaffel'—the New German Colonial Command—in Paris," he said, with a conspiratorial wink. "We have exactly as many members as the *Gau* of Salzburg—namely two!"

The cameraman and the soundman burst out laughing, as if on cue. The director kept me fixed with his bloodshot eyes for a moment more before a grin took over his face and he, too, burst out laughing. They all laughed themselves half to death as I stared out the window, a debilitating mix of adrenaline, fear, outrage, embarrassment, and secret amusement keeping me from saying anything.

Thinking about it as we sped down the dark highway, staring out the window to avoid their glances, I tried but couldn't keep myself from also breaking into a wide grin. It was all pretty silly, when you saw it from the outside looking in.

DURING THE REST of the filming we sometimes talked seriously about the murder of the Jews in the Third Reich. This was the central intellectual issue that kept me tied to the Movement, and I believe Winfried—I'd taken to calling him by his first name now—knew that if

he could make me begin to question my views on this, then my ideological moorings would really come undone. And I know now that
that's fully what he intended. He'd gotten the idea that I was not like
the others—as he'd said, that I didn't fit the cliché of a neo-Nazi—
and he was determined to carry out a little experiment in pulling me
away from it.

Of course, I was still a neo-Nazi. I still defended the idea that mass
murder had never occurred in Auschwitz or any other German concentration camp. Jews and other prisoners had died of epidemics and
malnutrition, but our spiritual forefathers had not deliberately murdered them with cyanide gas. The truth was that I already had some
inner doubts at that point. Hearing people like Otto Riehs talk about
sitting next to an Auschwitz survivor and asking him absurd questions intended to point up the logical flaws at the heart of the Holocaust had begun to chip away at the foundations that had been laid
when I had first read the Holocaust denial literature in the refugee
camp only two years before.

When I had escaped from the Communist system into the West, the
revelations in the Leuchter Report about the impossibility of gassings
at Auschwitz had seemed like my final mental freedom from the anti-
Fascist state I'd grown up under. At last, I could be proud to be a German, free of all guilt. Hans Coppi, the man whose mother's head had
been chopped off by the Nazis, was suddenly just a self-righteous
jerk, rather than the representative of six million admonishing souls.
The Nazi worldview was the righteous one, not the Communist one.
It was the view of a resistance movement that would fight against the
lies and hegemony of both the East and West superpowers, which
were, after all, in the last analysis under the thumb of Wall Street and
Jerusalem. . . .

It had all made so much sense when I was only thinking defensively, building up this alternative view of history in which the Holocaust was merely a Jewish trick used to divide Germany. The key to
the power of the Movement was that it always caused you to think
"defensively," rather than ever considering the issue from the outside, from a foreigner's point of view, or a Jew's, or simply that of a
hypothetical person from Mars. You always thought about it from
the perspective of an embattled German man. There was a world
conspiracy against the Nazi Party, which made us the most persecuted group in history—"today's Jews," as some neo-Nazis ironically

put it. But it was a sentiment we all shared. We were the most persecuted minority in Europe, so there was hardly a moment to stop to
think objectively, when every minute had to be spent in a defensive
struggle against our enemies.

Winfried had given me that moment to think objectively, and that
had given my doubts—which I believe had always lain inside me,
dormant seeds—the light they needed to begin growing again. I felt
strange to have these things growing inside me. It was like a child, another creature.

But I was still a neo-Nazi. This was my role, my meaning, my
mission. The French moviemaker was attacking my very being. I
wouldn't expose anything to him—I would drive him away! He was
damaging me. I hated him and wanted to put him and these doubts
out of my mind.

At the end of January, after the end of the filming, Winfried invited
me to come visit him in Paris.

"I think you'll like the capital of French culture, even if it is a little
'foreign,' " he said to me. "Come on, the German Colonization
Command will put you up, all expenses paid by the Reich. We can
practice goose-stepping down the Champs-Élysées!" Despite his sar-
casm, he was serious about the invitation.

I turned the offer down. I thought it would be better if I avoided
him for a while. I was beginning to feel manipulated. Meanwhile, I
was building myself and my *Kameradschaft* up to be terrorists, learning about how to cause mayhem and destruction. My mind was rac-
ing in two utterly divergent directions, toward opposite goals
—getting deeper into the violent side of the Movement or gaining a
mental and emotional distance from the Movement itself. This conflict was mirrored in my increasing contact with two Germans who
lived abroad: Gary Rex Lauck in Nebraska and Winfried Bonengel in
Paris.

27

PROFESSIONAL NEO-NAZI

ONE DAY SOMETIME after the Thälmann Park riot and months after I'd filmed with Winfried, I opened up a letter from a Mr. Feldstein or Mr. Zuckerman or Mr. Rabinowitz . . . I don't recall which and it didn't matter, for these letters with Jewish surnames always came from the same sender: Gary Rex Lauck of the NSDAP/AO.

When I decoded it, I was holding in front of me an order for terrorist action to be taken on a target that had nothing to do with our usual objectives: the Berlin Olympic Committee, which was in the middle of a huge publicity campaign to bring the Games to the city in the year 2000.

Lauck's reasoning was that the city of Berlin, and by extension the Federal Republic, stood to gain a great deal of money and prestige by hosting the Games. The last time they had taken place in Germany was in 1936, at the height of Hitler's prewar power. By staging the Olympics at the millennium, no less, the Federal Republic would finally eclipse the Third Reich. Democracy would win out over dictatorship. The Movement could not afford to let this happen, the letter stated, and it called for all efforts to be taken to help scuttle the bid for the Olympics to come to Berlin. Public events that were going on all over the city in favor of the Games were to be "disturbed." The attacks would show that the German state could not effectively combat terrorism and that it would be too dangerous to hold the Games in Germany. Continued attacks on foreigners would also add to this climate.

Another reason to fight the Olympics was that they would give a windfall to German big business. Like the rest of us, Lauck was oriented in a Strasserite, anticapitalist direction. Hindering the Games would hurt the State financially and prove its incompetence to an ever-growing number of discontented Germans and in that way win them over to national socialism. The federal government and especially Berlin were fighting very hard for the Games. It was a matter of great prestige for them.

Oddly enough, the question of the Olympics was a conflict where the extreme leftists and the neo-Nazis agreed. The leftists protested because it would change the city's demographics and architecture, requiring the building of a huge number of new housing units and putting added stress on the environment.

With the forces of Left and Right both gearing up to hinder the Olympic effort, the government was soon presented with an insoluble problem. There were attacks on all the sponsors, both corporate and individual, of the Games, as well as an atmosphere of escalating anti-foreigner violence. It was almost continuous, because when the left-wingers weren't doing anything, the right-wingers took action, and vice versa. (The attacks went on until fall of 1993, when the International Olympic Committee decided that the Games would not be held in Germany. All committee members had received threatening letters from both sides.)

I helped orchestrate much of this, but my heart wasn't in it the way it would have been a year before. Even as Lauck was trying to make me his main conduit in Germany, I was having second thoughts almost every day, wondering if this was really how I wanted to spend my life, trying to bring down democratic society.

For me, violence had been my way of establishing a distance from a society I couldn't stand. Anarchists and neo-Nazis had this in common—we rebelled against peace and order. The point when I passed from being a victim to a perpetrator was hardly clear. I still thought of myself as a victim of the anti-Fascist state.

During the last few years, I'd closed the door on a normal life, and the idea of forming an NSDAP/AO cell meant I'd close it forever. But let's say I wanted it back to some degree, I began to think: What would a "normal life" for me look like? I thought of Winfried and his film crew: they were utterly nonviolent and nonmilitant, yet they weren't bourgeois suck-ups any more than the rest of us. By making films they were able to remain at a kind of distance from society, and by living abroad Winfried had even more distance from Germany. I was beginning to wish I'd followed a path like his, where I could express my dissent in a more individual way.

But where could I go from here? I was in an apprenticeship to be a terrorist. My former career as the party chairman of the National Alternative was over. So I decided to stick by my ideology and continue the struggle I myself now sometimes saw as ridiculous and absurd.

In the meantime, in July, I celebrated my twenty-fifth birthday.

THE NEXT TIME Winfried contacted me, it was about a new documentary he was filming about the Movement, *Profession Neo-Nazi*. This time he'd gotten more money and it was to be shot for film, rather than television. (He was still editing the previous one, which now bore the title *We're Back* and was to be broadcast on television sometime in the next year.) *Profession Neo-Nazi* was to focus on Ewald Althans, the so-called yuppie Nazi of Munich, and in August 1992, I drove down to Munich with Winfried to meet him.

I'd never met Althans, though we'd extended a number of invitations to each other in the past. One reason we were curious to meet was that we looked somewhat similar—he was the only other person in the Movement who was as tall and blond as I was. We were both "Aryan poster boys," in a sense, and both of us had used our looks to gain support. But the resemblance ended there. Althans's game was Holocaust denial, rather than street fighting or electoral politics. He treated it all as a business. He wore designer suits and generally projected a slick, ad-exec style.

This was appropriate because rather than a political party or a *Kameradschaft*, Althans worked for the Movement through his own publicity firm, which he called "Althans Company and Public Relations" (AVO). He had a number of full- and part-time employees who ran the office for him, especially as his calendar filled up with Holocaust denial meetings all over the world. He was constantly shuttling back and forth from Canada, where he worked with the middle-aged German-Canadian Holocaust denier Ernst Zündel. AVO was almost exclusively interested in Holocaust denial, or "revisionism" as it was called in polite neo-Nazi company. There were a great many people willing to donate to "research" in this field, some with very deep pockets.

The yuppie Nazi had a similar relationship with middle-aged sympathizers and old Nazi widows as I had, only Althans invited his pigeons to lunch, rather than vice versa. His was a strictly professional act, and he liked to keep control over every detail of it. He usually invited them to a big hall, where he made a presentation about revisionism, reported news about recent "Holocaust lies," and brought personal greetings from his fellow deniers in North America, Zündel and Fred Leuchter. Althans was a charismatic speaker who was good at putting himself on the intellectual level of his audience. He was appreciated equally by the professor and the truck driver, the Nazi war widow and the college student.

In July 1992 Winfried had filmed him in Munich giving a reception for young men "just back from the former Yugoslavia." He had concluded at the end of this meeting, "These young Europeans from Germany, Austria, England, France, Italy, and Spain went to the war in Croatia as idealists, and they came back as men." Two hundred mostly old people in the audience had applauded and taken money out of their wallets. Althans had a close connection to Michel Faci, the French Fascist mercenary, and he was known in the scene as a master fund-raiser.

He had created something rather unique in the scene. He had a firm circle of donors who were loyal only to him. He didn't allow any influence from the outside. Christian Worch could not call and give his opinions, nor could Gottfried Küssel. The only boss was Ewald Althans, and he worked with young people who followed him unquestioningly. Most national groups constantly tried to recruit more members. With Althans this wasn't the case. He emphasized working perfectly with the people he had.

In an interview Winfried conducted for the movie, he captured Althans's personality and strategy perfectly: "These people come to me because they are looking for a model," said Althans. "If I say to them, 'Stand up straight!' they do it, and this is quite fascinating nowadays. I want to have these people completely. These young people without orientation should, with me, enter into a living community in which they have everything. These people are an easily kneaded mass, very easy to form. Everywhere the young people cry out for help, I gather them together and make orderly National Socialists out of them."

Althans liked to be based in Munich because it had been the original capital of the Nazi movement: it was the "Brown City," while Berlin was the "Red City." Berlin was a good place for a neo-Nazi to be if he wanted to pick a fight, which was why it suited me. Munich was better for someone who wanted to run a yuppie Nazi publicity office and a mail-order company specializing in Holocaust denial literature. My Kamerads and I wouldn't have lasted ten minutes in Munich with our methods, for, of all German states, Bavaria had the strictest law enforcement about rioting and street violence. Even though Bavaria was the capital of many right-wing groups, from Althans's to the far-right party the Republikaner, it always had the lowest incidence of right-wing violence. Bavarians hated foreigners as much as other Germans did, but they would not tolerate having their shelters burnt down. Bavaria was a quiet, orderly place.

Althans gave tours of Munich like Küssel did of Vienna. This also revealed the more bourgeois atmosphere in the South—nobody in the Berlin scene gave tours. But Althans's tour was much more political than Küssel's. He always took people first to the site of the original Brown House, the ideological center of the old Nazi movement, and then on a tour of all the classic Nazi sites, more or less bypassing the aspects of Munich that interest most people.

Althans's office was on Herzog-Heinrich-Strasse. When you entered, the first thing you saw was a display case where you could buy revisionist material. In the rear you could go up the stairs to another office or downstairs to the conference room. Whenever he was in Munich, he would receive guests upstairs, as he received Winfried and me.

If inquiring journalists told Althans that they were from the United States, he would tell them point-blank, in a flat voice, "You're Jewish." It was his way of testing them. Most people were a bit shocked. If they protested, "No, I'm not Jewish," he would say that he didn't believe them. He was very allergic to Jews. He often got reactions like "Yes, I'm Jewish, so what? Is that a problem for you?" To which Althans would reply smugly, "No, I always speak with my enemies."

He liked to face off from the beginning. Then during the discussion he would pump you full of anti-Semitism until you lost your cool. He loved to unload his soul about Jews to whomever would listen—they were freeloaders, they took advantage of the German people, they had committed the biggest deception in the history of mankind with the Holocaust and had done it all to finance a war against the Arabs. But he said these things without the burning conviction—fear even—of Nero Reisz or Gottfried Küssel. It was simply his considered opinion. He'd say very calmly and clearly what he thought.

In the scene there was always the feeling floating around that Althans had taken over a few too many of Kühnen's qualities. At one point a letter from Althans would appear in the gay magazine *Magnus* (which comes out in the Netherlands and Germany): "Stop making ass fucking into politics; everyone does what he thinks is right." He was repeatedly asked whether he was homosexual, and to my knowledge, he never directly contradicted the rumor.

He had good practice skirting the boundaries of truth and saying things indirectly. He had to constantly be careful not to overstep Germany's strict laws about Holocaust denial—at least while he was on German soil. During the filming of *Profession Neo-Nazi*, Winfried followed Althans to Ernst Zündel's house in Canada and then to the death camp memorial at Auschwitz, where he managed to film the yuppie Nazi saying things that would come back to haunt him.

IN THE SUMMER of 1992, as *Profession Neo-Nazi* was being filmed, there was news of the massive firebomb attacks on the foreigner shelters in Rostock. It was incredible. On television we saw literally hundreds of young men and boys as young as twelve throwing firebombs at a building where Gypsies and Vietnamese lived. The police were standing by and watching. The crowd chanted "Foreigners out! Foreigners out!" and the local townspeople, many of them the parents of these violent kids, stood by and applauded.

For a moment my doubts disappeared, replaced by curiosity. Althans was a rather inspiring character to be around anyway, young and dynamic, unlike older men like Reisz and Riehs. He and I decided to drive together to Rostock right away. We wanted to see what was really going on there. Winfried didn't come: he wanted to stay and film other neo-Nazis in Munich. So we left him—me and my new Kamerad—and drove ten hours up north to the famous port on the

Ostsee where all the trouble was happening. We left at night and arrived early the next morning.

The attack had been going on for three or four days when we arrived but showed no signs of stopping. This was the superbattle, the arson attack to end all arson attacks. In fact, we had arrived on the last significant day of rioting. The area was full of police with water cannons. We went downtown first and had breakfast; then around noon we went over to the apartment complex where the attacks were happening and waited for the night's mob to assemble.

The morning was fairly quiet as firemen and police picked up rubbish from the night before and put out the flames and the arsonists caught some sleep. Young people met around noon there and didn't begin rampaging again until after five in the afternoon. I'd never seen so many cops in one place in my life. But nobody interfered with us, so Althans and I began recruiting among the kids milling around us.

I was impressed with Althans's ability to handle young people. I could see he inspired them, which was no easy task considering how simpleminded and immature most of them were. A thirteen-year-old with five Molotov cocktails stuffed into his jacket pocket was hardly in the mood to hear about Holocaust revisionism.

We didn't bother with propaganda because lots of the kids knew who we were already—the Führers—and they respected us. Almost before we'd finished breakfast, the media circus that was already in Rostock fell on us. They automatically viewed us as the string pullers. It was ridiculous. We'd only just gotten there, and it was obvious that we were meeting these kids for the first time. Rostock hadn't been organized; it was a spontaneous affair that had escalated. Certainly members of the NSDAP/AO and various German neo-Nazi parties were participating in the violence, but they were no more the "leaders" of the attack than I was.

But we did manage to recruit people there—I for the Berlin scene, Althans for the Holocaust denial movement. We both distributed fliers and took down people's addresses. To older people we suggested that they work with the HNG, the old ladies' group that supported neo-Nazi political prisoners.

We gave a couple of interviews—mainly saying that the government was incapable of solving the "foreigner problem" and that's why there were these riots. "We are here to try to help bring the situation under control," said Althans. "Wherever German youth is in trouble, I'll go." Personally, Althans told me that he thought the kids at Rostock hadn't been violent enough.

I LEFT ALTHANS and drove back to Berlin, where I found that the local papers were writing—based on my appearing in news footage of the riots—that I must have been the string puller behind the operation. It was a joke. But it had been a fertile field to recruit in.

I actually didn't know what to think of the events in Rostock. I wanted to understand the kids who were throwing stones: they had zero perspective, no chance of getting an apartment or a job, unemployment had gone up more than twenty times in the area since the fall of the Wall. The youth clubs had been closed for lack of money, and the young people thought it was going into putting foreigners into brand-new buildings. For these kids the solution was to burn them out. As in our case in Berlin, the method worked. After a few days of burning buildings, the foreigners in the shelter were marched out like prisoners in a chain gang and loaded onto German government buses for resettlement.

The old people told me that the foreigners were eating neighborhood cats, raping women, and stealing, not to mention living in filth. Everyone in Rostock told us how the Gypsy camp next to the shelter had originally caused all the local fury. It wasn't purely the old clichés that people used against minorities. Even people who were utterly opposed to right-wing radicals admitted that conditions at the camp had been terrible ever since the government had sent so many foreigners there. But I didn't realize yet that this wasn't the fault of the foreigners and that they didn't deserve to be firebombed. Only later did I realize that it was nonsense to punish foreigners for their horrible conditions, that in effect you are adding insult and pain to their troubles because the sight of them offends you. But even at the time, watching the fires upset me. I didn't tell Althans that, of course.

For some time I had found violence against foreigners unjust. At *Kameradschaft* evenings I tried in vain to explain to people that many foreigners in Germany had been here for three generations. I saw violence against them as idiotic and also cowardly, for we were always going after the innocents, often women and children. For these opinions I only got blank looks.

My opinion about foreigners at this time was still oriented toward neo-Nazism, but I questioned the ways and means, which I found cowardly. I tried to talk about how rightist terrorism should really be executed. I thought we should take action against those who employed foreigners, big companies like Mercedes-Benz and Opel.

Althans was so pleased with my way of recruiting—and he'd heard of my skill in running the Weitlingstrasse house—that he asked me if I would run his office in Munich for him when he was away. Althans had a terrible problem with employee attrition; he was bossy and used to making all the decisions himself. That always got to be too much for his employees, who never stayed with the firm long. He offered me a fairly sweet deal, at least as far as things in the scene went—a salary plus an apartment.

I turned him down politely. The last thing I wanted to do now was to expand my neo-Nazi horizons further and add another hate-propagating job to my résumé.

No MATTER WHAT my doubts about the ideology, I found myself irresistibly drawn back by the raw psychological and physical power the Movement unleashed. Shortly after my return from Rostock, in fact, I experienced what I can only describe as one of my all-time "highs" as a neo-Nazi—the ultimate Führer Feeling, a moment when ideology and violence came perfectly together to give me utter control over a group of violent followers. It was the kick we were all reaching for in the Movement, and I finally achieved it only when I was on the verge of getting out.

It was the end of September 1992. I'd arranged a raid together with many people and planned to storm Pfarrstrasse on Saturday. It was to be the final battle. I told ten people I trusted about this meeting and they told ten more and soon the whole circles of hooligans, skins, and neo-Nazis all knew. They even got the message to the neo-Nazis in Bremen, a couple hundred miles away, and they sent their contingent.

The word of mouth about the attack was so good, unfortunately, that the police somehow heard about it as well. When we met together in front of the disco on the corner of Pfarrstrasse, the cops were waiting, blocking the entrance to the street. Two undercover cops I knew, Thomas and Martin, drove up in an unmarked car and called out to me, "Hey, Ingo, we've heard you've organized this thing here. We won't arrest you now, but nothing better happen today. You get your people to go home."

I was there with a big girl with butch-cut blond hair named Ulrika. She was going with another neo-Nazi then, but I'd been sleeping with her just the same. (She was involved with the neo-Nazis only because they were the people she'd grown up with; since I've gotten out of the Movement, she's switched over to the anarchists, where she continues street fighting much as she did with us.) Ulrika was a real special girl: you could steal cars with her, have gang fights or go dancing. She was a little masculine and huge—over six feet tall—with short hair and a great body she knew how to use in more ways than one. She was a tough girl, but I didn't realize how tough until that night.

Ulrika and I were standing in front of a crowd of maybe three hundred keyed-up right-wingers—hooligans, skins, and neo-Nazis—all hungry for blood and cracked bones. We looked out at them, this mix, and Ulrika and I agreed they looked just right, like a perfect batter ready to be popped into the oven—for these people were ready for heat, ready for violence . . .

And yet Thomas and Martin had told me to send them all home. It made me sick to my stomach to waste all those good people, to say to them, "Hey, we're not going to do anything today. We came for nothing."

"No," I said to Ulrika. "We can't waste this enthusiasm. We have to do something with them!"

I led Ulrika away from the crowd into a dark corner, where I put on my black mask. Ulrika put her mask on as well. But when we came back to the front of the crowd, though our faces were disguised, everyone in the crowd knew exactly who was behind these masks. Then, taking the energy of all these angry followers into our arms, Ulrika and I started picking up stones and hurling them at the crowd of cops. "Die Letzte Schlacht Gewinnen Wir!" (We'll Win the Last Battle!), the anarchist anthem, started going through my head.

I don't know who was more shocked—our people or the police. Ulrika and I were throwing so fast that they couldn't rush us without risking severe injury. But the real reason the cops must have held back then was that they were thinking: these two are so crazy we'd probably have to shoot them to keep them down, and that would start a riot. In any case, they were so shocked by our behavior that they didn't react.

At this moment, seeing that the cops were totally helpless against just us two, the crowd felt its chance, and suddenly all of them were with us, seething ahead, hurling stones at the cops and pressing into the little cordoned-off street. I had this surging feeling of my power being multiplied three hundred times—of a great angry mass following my every movement. "Okay, now, okay!" I thought. "With *these people* you can really do something, you can let loose." I led my mass through the lines of cops, sweeping them aside to get into the street where our enemies lived.

Ulrika was still with me, charging right in front, when the anarchists came out into Pfarrstrasse with their own stones. We beat them down their street, our anger being harder and more perfectly honed than theirs this time. The cops had stopped trying to intervene and were instead living by their usual maxim in such matters: "Let them go at each other, we'll pick up the corpses." (In fact the only people from our side who were busted were the neo-Nazis from Bremen, out-of-town pussies who'd entered the fighting last and were therefore the easiest to catch up with; the cops were so angry to have been stoned that they beat up on these Bremen kids extra hard.)

But for me the main high was to have dared to throw the first stones, to start the storm, and then to be followed into battle by a crowd that had hesitated but was now let loose to express its passions. It was the feel of overcoming odds and circumstance through the most basic, primitive sort of leadership: point out the enemy, throw the first stones, the people will follow. A biological process acted out on the stage of human events—the Führer Principle in action.

When we'd fought our way through to the other end of the street, Ulrika and I took our masks off, threw them away, and walked down another side street to the corner we had started from. Ten minutes later, when Thomas and Martin stopped us, we were walking out of the disco on the corner as though we had no idea what had happened in the street. They had no proof. It was dark, I had been masked, they couldn't recognize my clothes. They only knew it had been a tall masked man.

"Hasselbach, we know damned well it was you," said Martin.

"What?" I said, giving my best innocent look.

"There was a lot of trouble here. There was a big street fight."

"Hey, I'm sorry, that's not my problem. I'm glad I was able to avoid it."

"You're such an asshole," said Martin.

They put me and Ulrika up against the wall and searched us for the masks, which of course we'd ditched by then. Then they made us show our hands, because if you've been in a street fight, you have dirty hands. But we knew this, so Ulrika and I had washed our hands in the disco, even being sure to check under each other's nails for any traces of dirt or blood.

A COUPLE OF months later Winfried showed me his completed film *We're Back*. He'd added practically no commentary, yet he'd succeeded in presenting me at the beginning of the film as a sympathetic figure who turns into more and more of a neo-Nazi Pied Piper by the end. I was shocked at myself. The film was somehow completely different from others in which I had appeared. The other films had simply let us present our ideas in a scary way; the narrator had repeated to the audience how scary we were and had then let us go on our way. Winfried had repeatedly and skeptically questioned me about my neo-Nazism; my attitudes and goals thus came to seem ridiculous, as well as frightening. At least that's how I saw the film.

But Winfried's film didn't sell at all in Germany. If it had, I would have panicked, because I had really let Winfried reveal more about my ideology than any other filmmaker or journalist had before. I had allowed him to film me standing in front of an enormous swastika flag, discussing my ideology. I'd stood next to Worch, who was wearing an ascot and a leather blazer, with his hand around my shoulder declaring me the new Führer.

Since I liked Winfried personally, I had let down my guard. He'd had that effect on some of the others, as well—even the irascible skinhead Stinki, for example. On the drive back from filming Stinki with his parents, they had stopped for coffee at a highway rest stop. Winfried had constantly slapped Stinki lightly on the head and shouted, "Behave yourself, you boor!" Almost anyone else might have gotten a broken rib or a concussion for that, but Winfried had got away with it.

I saw Winfried fairly regularly in Berlin that fall. He'd gotten an apartment in the city, I didn't know where. He was afraid to tell me then—and with reason. The filming of *Profession Neo-Nazi* and my subsequent trip to Rostock had brought home how much I still had a foot in both camps.

Winfried always seemed to arrive at my place on Wotanstrasse on *Kameradschaft* evening, when the whole gang was gathered there. There was no way I could let him in, because most of the guys couldn't stand him. He didn't want to film them—he knew that wouldn't work—he just wanted to hang out. He may have been trying even then to set up a clear competition between me and them— trying to goad me into rejecting one or the other.

I gave him a couple more interviews for *Profession Neo-Nazi*. I was no longer thrilled to represent the Nazi ideology before the camera. Nevertheless, I made a couple of racist statements for the camera that earlier would have come much more easily from my lips. I played my role to the end.

Winfried sensed my reservations, and he asked me if I would prefer not to appear in the film at all.

This impressed me: because of my doubts, which he'd had no small part in creating, he was ready to endanger the project.

At that moment I gained total trust in him. He became the first person completely outside the Movement whom I'd trusted in ages— maybe, even, since my grandparents. This alone was a dangerous move for me—a kind of heresy.

I knew that actually to have such confidence in somebody outside the scene was almost a way of dropping out. Our friendship really depended on my no longer being part of the scene. A neo-Nazi could never truly be friends with an outsider.

In the meantime Winfried had also brought me into contact with some of his acquaintances, and I liked feeling accepted by these apolitical people. I was still active in the scene, but the old enthusiasm was gone. Something had changed. If so many smart people rejected national socialism, where did that leave me?

Before, everything had been simple and I had really felt good to be a neo-Nazi. I missed that feeling, that confidence and momentum, but I didn't know how to get it back. I didn't even know if I wanted it back.

28

LAST ATTACK

A NEW YOUTH club had recently opened on our turf in Lichtenberg, not far from my apartment on Wotanstrasse, where we held our *Kameradschaft* evening meetings. A bunch of us went over there early on and worked out a deal with the mostly anarchist contingent in the club: if they didn't do any political work in Lichtenberg, we'd leave them in peace. These young people were tied to the Anti-Fa Edelweiss Pirates, the tougher of the two anarchist organizations, but they really didn't seem to want any trouble around their club. When we visited, they had pirate flags all over, which alone was a political statement, but we'd agreed to overlook them if they didn't do further work. We felt pretty slick that they'd apparently caved in to our strong-arm tactics without our having to start a big street fight about it.

Then one night, during a *Kameradschaft* meeting, Oliver W.— who by this point had become more militant than most of the older Kamerads—came running in and held up a poster for us to see.

"Hey, look at this, the swine are doing political work against us here in Lichtenberg! They've broken the deal."

We all looked at the poster, which read "Big Anti-Fa Meeting in the Youth Club, Against the Memorial Service for the Nazi Soldiers in Halbe in 1992."

"We've got to do something to the swine!" Oliver said furiously.

Silence. Everyone was waiting for me, the Führer, to say what we'd do.

"Okay, shit, they broke their promise," I said. "We have to do something. We'll go smash some windows at their club."

"Breaking windows is shit!" said Oliver. "They need to burn! We'll do a fire attack."

"No one needs to burn for this," I said. But I could see that everyone was agreeing with the young fanatic. I didn't want to lose face, and besides, they had broken a clear promise and they had always firebombed us in the past.

"Okay, let's go, men," I said. "We use Molis, but no one gets hurt. Just throw them in one window of the club and leave them all to run out in panic. We don't burn anyone."

We picked out two other people to go with us—two skinheads whose names were Spinner and Messer—Spider and Knife. Oliver would come, of course, because it was his idea, and I would go because I was the Führer.

We sent Spinner and Messer home to prepare some Molis, because we decided something had to be done that same day, and we went ahead to the youth club on bikes. We had things planned out clearly beforehand: there would be no attempts to block any exits or set anyone inside on fire, just furniture. It was also agreed that because I was so big and easy to recognize, I couldn't throw any Molis. I would serve as a lookout, standing on one end of the street to make sure no cops were coming; Messer would stand at the other end of the street to watch for cops. Spinner and Oliver would then run in and throw the Molis. We would all wear masks, like the kind you wear on a motorcycle or skiing, so they could only see our mouths and eyes.

When we got there, we saw that, to our advantage, they'd left one window of the club open. We could see lots of anarchists hanging out inside, among the pirate flags, smoking and drinking and listening to punk music. They'd probably left the window open because it was so hot inside. It would soon get a lot hotter.

Standing at my lookout post, I reflected that I didn't really want to be in this situation. I wasn't in the mood to pull off any more firebombing raids. What would Winfried and his crew think of such childish idiocy? On the other hand, this was a matter of honor. By breaking their word so deliberately, these anarchists were spitting in our faces. We had to teach them a lesson, I thought. Oliver was right.

Just as Oliver and Spinner had sneaked up to the open window and were about to light their Molis, I noticed something moving on the dark street. It was a drunk, a bum walking down the street toward us. I signaled to Spinner and Oliver to wait, and I watched to see if the bum noticed anything funny. Spinner and Oliver were covered in darkness, waiting by the wall of the anarchist house.

Then the bum began to act suspiciously. Spinner and Oliver looked at me and motioned as if to say, "Shit, he's onto something!"

The drunk looked up and down the street in both directions. He looked over to the house wall but didn't seem to see Spinner and Oliver. He looked over to our bikes, which we'd leaned against the wall of a house across the street. He looked up and down the street again. What's this bum doing? I thought. Damn him! Then suddenly he sprang into action, and it was clear what he'd been on about.

He ran over to the wall, looked around again, grabbed one of our bikes, and started pedaling off down the street.

I immediately ran down the street toward him, calling, "Hey, you, there are people here. Piss off." Oliver ran him down before he could pedal thirty feet, jumped him, and started beating the hell out of him.

"Hey, man, be cool," I said. Then I noticed another of the coincidences that was always happening to me: the drunk was an old classmate of mine from Lichtenberg—Jörg.

Jörg was a poor pig. In 1986 he'd lost three fingers in an industrial accident, lost his job, and become an alcoholic. He'd never been in any trouble—never been involved in politics or anything else in the GDR, as far as I knew. He'd just become a complete bum, a homeless type, because of his fingers.

"Don't beat him up," I said, pulling Oliver off him. My drunken former classmate looked like he was going to shit in his pants, with three masked men holding him down on a dark street.

I said to Jörg, "Hey, just get lost." And he ran away head over heels into the darkness. He hadn't been able to recognize me in my mask and army parka.

Then at last there was quiet on the street and we could get back to our business. Spinner lit his Moli, threw it in through the open window, and it landed exactly on the bar. It was perfect. The bar went up in flames and you could see chaos breaking out inside, everyone screaming and running.

Then I wondered, Why haven't I heard Oliver's Moli? I looked around, thinking, What's he doing? Then I saw that the nasty little Kamerad had indeed not thrown his Moli but had instead opened it up, taken out the fuse, and tipped the gas-and-oil mixture out onto the doorway. He grinned at me, jumped back a few feet, and lit a match. I gestured to him not to, but in a second he'd thrown the match and the doorway was in flames. He was a total swine.

We all jumped onto our bikes and took off. When we got back to Wotanstrasse, I screamed at Oliver, "You asshole! Are you trying to murder people? We agreed just to throw them in the window. Spinner threw his perfectly. We never talked about trying to block the escape route. You're really fucked in the head!"

"It's all the same to me, man, burn up a couple Communists," Oliver said. "I told you they had to burn. Throwing stuff in the windows is no good."

I worried about whether I was going to be an accessory to murder then, and I scanned the headlines nervously the next morning. But luckily there'd been a second exit in the club, and everyone had got out in one piece. It was a pure stroke of luck that had saved them, because they never would have gotten out through the wall of fire Oliver had left them. He had no scruples, and I admit I was even somewhat afraid of him myself.

TWO DAYS LATER I was at my mother's and the doorbell rang. I answered it, and there stood three plainclothes cops who flashed badges that showed they were from the political crimes unit. "*Ja, guten Tag*, we're looking for Jens Pfannschmidt," said the leader.

"He's not here," I said. "He's at work." This was the truth. I wondered why in hell they'd be looking for my little brother.

"Where's his work?" they asked. Every German citizen had to register where he lived, so the cops had at least one home address, but you didn't have to register your place of work.

"Well, you need to go down to the third light from our house, cross the S-Bahn tracks, go right and walk as far as you can go till you pass a drugstore, and then to the end of the next block and turn left and then to the corner and turn right . . ." I gave them directions to Jens's job that were correct but so confusing and intricate that they would never find it.

"We'll never find that," said the leader.

"So?" I said. "That's not my fault."

"Please come with us and help us find it," he said, calmly.

"I'm afraid I actually don't have any time."

"It's very important. It can only help Herr Pfannschmidt."

I thought, Shit, what can this be about? But it didn't seem like I would help by stonewalling. "Okay," I said.

I changed and went downstairs with the cops. I stood a head taller than any of them. As we were getting into the car, one of them said, "Hey, by the way, show me your papers. Who are you, anyway?"

I showed him my ID.

"Ah-ha, that's funny!" he said, chuckling. "We were looking for you, actually, Herr Hasselbach. We went first to your house on Wotanstrasse, but you weren't there. We thought your brother could tell us where you were."

What bozos, I thought. Then they made me put my hands on the roof of their car, searched me, and shoved me inside.

The car drove into central West Berlin, in the direction of Tempelhof Airport. I guessed that they were taking me to the special BKA headquarters for counterterrorism, which was in that area of the city. One cop said to me, "You know damned well why you're coming along with us, eh?"

It had to be the youth club firebombing, I thought.

"No idea," I said.

For the whole ride I tried to remember what exactly my alibi was. I was having trouble. I had so many alibis all the time, for so many things, that I often got them confused.

We arrived at the Platz der Luftbrücke, near Tempelhof Airport, at the special building of the BKA for fighting terrorism in Berlin.

Shit, I thought as we got out of the car, I can't remember my damned alibi!

"What did you do the night before last?" one of them asked me when we'd made ourselves comfortable in one of the sparse, modern interrogation rooms. The hum of the air-conditioning system was bothering me as I racked my brain to remember the alibi. He was a cool guy, this counterterrorist cop, he didn't put the pressure on me directly, but his calm was making me even more nervous. I stalled, smoking a cigarette, looking at the ceiling . . . then I remembered!

"We were watching soccer!" I said, trying to hide my sense of triumph.

"Who played?" said the cop placidly.

I thought hard. "Mexico-Germany," I said, remembering correctly.

"Who played on each team?" said the cop.

"Now, that's a dumb question," I said, knowing I'd gotten through it okay. "I'm not too interested in soccer. I'm not a fan. I just watch. I can't remember those things."

"Okay, who can verify what you're saying?"

And I gave them the names of my coconspirators. The cops called up Oliver and Spinner, who had no official record as being neo-Nazis, and they came in and verified my alibi. As they were verifying my alibi, the cops, of course, had all their perpetrators but one sitting right there in the counterterrorism building. We pulled this shit all the time, using one or more perpetrators to clear the others. It was an absurdly reliable technique, especially if you had young people like Oliver W. who didn't have criminal or political records. Once a cop even caught us red-handed in the act of doing something, but so many bystanders on the street were neo-Nazis, and we'd had alibis all planned out ahead of time, that they'd simply said the cop was lying and it had worked.

THE ATTACK ON the youth club was my last violent act. After that, it all began to disgust me even more. I wished Winfried would come by more, but he was busy with his film about Althans and we didn't stay in as close touch. In fact, Althans kept trying to contact me to get me to come work in his office. Then there were the letters from the "Jewish men" in Nebraska and Illinois asking how my terrorist efforts against the Olympic Games were going.

I'd grown tired of meeting with my *Kameradschaft,* and Oliver W. was beginning to take over some of the functions of Führer, for he was the one with the most zeal and determination. He or Auschwitz led readings from *A Movement in Arms,* our instruction manual about how to wage an urban terrorist war. Since Rostock the mood in the scene had been euphoric. There seemed to be no limit to how far we could go. Everyone from teachers to social workers to journalists was dubbing this the right-wing generation, acting as though they'd given up most teenagers to the maw. And it was true that you felt a change. A critical mass had been reached. When I went through the streets of East Berlin, junior high school students—kids of only twelve or thirteen—would salute me and call me the Führer.

And come Friday night, instead of going to a movie or a party with their friends, the older kids would drink beer, make the bottles into Molis, and go off to terrorize a refugee shelter. It had become the accepted way to cut loose after school—to go "light a few Gypsies" or "pack a Fiji up the side of the head." I was in large part responsible for this atmosphere. I had helped hatch it. And in this atmosphere of weekly firebombings, NSDAP/AO cells were spreading at an incredible rate. Of course, none of us knew precisely how fast or far, for only Gary Rex Lauck, back at headquarters in Lincoln, Nebraska, was privy to that information. One thing was for sure: thousands of pamphlets, stickers, and video games from the NSDAP/AO were being disseminated by our cell alone, and these played an obvious part in creating the climate of prejudice and violence.

Arnulf Priem, the chief of Wotan's Volk, also held more gatherings at his apartment that fall. These tended to be more on the "recreational" side of things—films, parlor games—but of course every meeting was a chance for indoctrination. We'd go sit in his booklined apartment, with its huge altar to Reinhard Heydrich in the living room, and watch movies.

Most of the movies at Priem's house were from the 1940s, but they were all preceded by a particular short of more recent vintage that he'd grafted onto them. The short film began with an empty room and a bed with an enormous Nazi flag behind it. Then a woman appeared, very pretty with long black hair and gray eyes. The woman was nude and had a more-than-decent figure. She grinned provocatively at the camera and then began to touch herself. It went on for about five minutes, I'd guess, until she'd apparently masturbated herself into ecstasy. As you watched, you couldn't help associate her ecstasy with the swastika flag that covered the whole wall behind her.

This perfect piece of neo-Nazi pornography had been a gift from one of Priem's many girlfriends. She'd made it for his birthday, as a surprise, and he had started adding it to Nazi propaganda films after she broke up with him, as revenge. This very personal "political" act was shown not only to us but to thousands of people all over Europe, for Priem ran a sort of clearinghouse for Nazi videos. He had a lot of dubbing equipment, and he sold the videos for only 10 marks apiece, at cost, in order to get them out to as wide a public as possible. He had a sort of internal catalog that he circulated within the Movement. You could order *Nuremberg Party Day,* for example, and all the feature films from the period, like *Hans Westmar* and *Hitler Youth Quex.* And whenever you ordered a Nazi video from Priem, he tacked his old girlfriend masturbating in front of the flag on at the beginning, like a cartoon.

During Priem's get-togethers, we'd watch some film like *The Eternal Jew,* and then often we'd play a computer game. Priem's favorite was a modification of the most popular German board game, "Man, Don't Bother Yourself," called "Jew, Don't Bother Yourself." It was another goody you could order from Lauck, though I don't know where Priem got his copy.

There were four colors—red, green, yellow, and black—for four players. Each player got four figures: three figures were Jews and the fourth figure was an SS man. You moved your Jews around the board by rolling dice, and the object was to get your Jews into the center, which was the gas chamber. There was a gray gate painted on the center of the board—the screen—with the words *Arbeit macht frei* ("Work will make you free"), the words above the gate at Auschwitz, and the chemical symbol for Zyklon B, the gas used to murder the Jews.

The name for this little diversion meant "Jew, don't get so upset that you're getting sent to the gas." There was a perverse irony to it: when someone won, they said, "Jew, don't bother yourself!" Don't bother yourself that you're now dead.

The game was popular because it gave the players total power over the Jews, who became just little board-game pieces, or computer symbols. They couldn't chastise you for being German because the title of the game was saying "Relax, let yourself be murdered."

It was part of the total indoctrination, which always made clear that there was a master race and that those who were inferior were of no value. It gradually built up such an aggression that you could get yourself into this whole trip. Of course, it was especially useful for those who felt inferior themselves. They came into the group, and we gave them a feeling of specialness, of superiority, of belonging.

Many in the original SS death's-head divisions during the war, especially in the concentration camps, had been no older than I was. They'd also learned to treat Jews and others like pawns and to laugh at their extermination—while at the same time taking their own superiority completely seriously. It was a deadly combination. It still is. I don't think those people were sadists from birth. I think they were made this way from 1933 to 1940. I think that in order to bring off this perfect mass murder they had to be perfectly trained.

Of course, there were also always people who were naturally sadistic. Priem himself was a sadist. It was well known in the scene that he liked to beat women up during sex. There were some people who could just play around with S & M, but Priem was reputed to be really brutal. His sexual sadism must have been a way of expressing his whole identity as an SS fanatic and basically his whole political worldview.

As they played "Jew, Don't Bother Yourself," my Kamerads would reminisce fondly about desecrating Jewish cemeteries. I'd never done this myself, though I'd desecrated the Cemetery of the Socialists and painted a Jewish star on Rosa Luxemburg's and Karl Liebknecht's graves. But I understood why they loved it: to attack the "Jewish lobby"—to smear swastikas on the gravestones of Jews—was the ultimate game of symbols. The power of our symbol was magnified when it was on a Jewish gravestone.

And that's why we watched *The Eternal Jew* over and over at Priem's house. It showed all the Nazi stereotypes of the Jews: they were rats, parasites, they knew how to get money. It convinced us again of the truth of our leaflets, stickers, and graffiti: "Don't buy from Jews." What Jews? you might ask. There were no Jews to buy from in Germany. The idea was not to buy from the Eternal Jew the idea of his truth, the idea of his importance as a human being. The Eternal Jew was a piece in our board game who needed to learn not to take so seriously what we'd done to him.

The game was really the perfect comment on the Holocaust denial movement and why it was so crucial. The basic message was that the Jews had gotten way too bothered about it all. Don't worry, relax while you're gassed, it's just a game, calm down and inhale. It showed the utter schizophrenia of the Movement that we could deny the Holocaust and then play this game, cheering when we got "our" Jews into the gas chamber.

Yet any of the people playing this game would have gotten up at a moment's notice and argued that the Holocaust was a lie. This was the psychological horror at the heart of everything we did: you held both ideas in your head at once. By doing so, you lived in a realm that was beyond rational thought.

In the past, I'd often found "Jew, Don't Bother Yourself" amusing. Of course, I'd seen the Jews as my enemy, too, just like all the others did. But I'd also liked it simply because it was modeled on a game I remembered playing with my mother when I was a little boy. A harmless game. But now it had been changed, perverted, as though its real meaning had been uncovered—this was really what the most popular German board game was about. And suddenly I found myself in Arnulf Priem's house, surrounded by my pals, "playing my Jews" around the familiar, colorful board on the computer screen, and I wanted to cry, thinking that this was the same pleasure I had had with my mother when I was a boy, now irrevocably corrupted and evil. Would the game ever end?

MEANWHILE, THE NATIONWIDE response to the neo-Nazis was peaking, as was radical right youth violence. Hundreds of firebombings and beatings were taking place each month. Every day brought news of a new firebombing of refugee shelters. Rostock had focused international pressure on the German government as never before to do something about neo-Nazism, but Chancellor Kohl was also being careful not to alienate the millions of German voters who were saying in polls that they agreed with the neo-Nazis' goal of driving out the foreigners. There were daily arguments about neo-Nazism and the foreigner question—which were really the same issue, talked about from two opposing political points of view—on the editorial pages of every major newspaper, on television talk shows, and in bars and restaurants.

At the beginning of November, one of the leading members of the government, Finance Minister Theo Waigel, announced that "the next election will be won on the Right" and led the call by a number of the more conservative people in the government to incorporate some of the demands of the neo-Nazis into their platform and tighten Germany's asylum law.

An opposing, liberal current in the government was building at the same time behind President Richard von Weizsäcker, whose father had been a high-ranking figure in the Third Reich, to take a stronger stand against neo-Nazi violence and to support the foreigners. At the beginning of November, von Weizsäcker appeared in a march in Berlin designed to show solidarity with the embattled foreigners and condemn the neo-Nazis. The demonstration gathered tens of thousands from around the country, but the chancellor and many of his conservative allies refused to come. Standing next to the new president of Germany's Jewish community, the charismatic Frankfurt businessman Ignatz Bubis, President von Weizsäcker was pelted with eggs and fruit—not by the neo-Nazis but by the anarchists, who thought it was all too little too late.

I found myself at the center of a movement that was tearing the Federal Republic apart. Kühnen's vision was being fulfilled beyond his wildest dreams. I was finally seeing the results of years of careful propaganda work—a nation of youths enflamed with racist hatred and the lust for violence.

And for the first time I really thought about quitting.

I was disgusted with all of it. I didn't know myself anymore exactly why or how I'd gotten involved with this hate-filled crusade. It now seemed to me that I'd been looking for a father figure, which I'd first found in Kühnen, and that had given me strength. Now, in some ways, Winfried had taken that role and was giving me strength in the other direction—to become independent, to stop hating, to stop the violence—to leave Germany.

But also, in the midst of this national orgy of violence, I could see so clearly how we'd made the foreigners pawns for our politics. I could no longer act like we neo-Nazis were a persecuted minority, for it was clear to me that much of the country was behind us in the crusade against foreigners. The chancellor himself was using the violence we'd caused as an excuse to build support for a vote to change the Constitution and ban most foreigners from receiving political asylum in Germany. I hadn't completely switched sides on the issue—I wasn't a hard-core leftist by any means—but I now questioned the righteousness of our position and the point of going on as an underground terrorist in a cause that I was beginning to find more and more repellent.

Who were my enemies? I asked myself as I went to bed at night. Who were my Kamerads? The answer had never been less clear in my mind.

*   *   *

I TRIED TO think of people I had been friends with before I became a
neo-Nazi, anyone from outside the scene I could talk to. I remembered
a woman who'd been my girlfriend in the mid-1980s, when I was a
punk in the GDR. I'd been her first great love, but we hadn't seen each
other for seven years, and I think she'd avoided seeing me because of
my neo-Nazism. I made some inquiries and figured out that she was
living not far from me and working in a beauty parlor, one of those
people the fall of the Wall hadn't affected much one way or the other.

I went to her address and rang the bell. She was really shocked, but
I quickly saw that she had kept the old flame lit for me all these years.
We went for coffee, and she confessed that she'd been in love with me
all this time but that it had made her sick that I had become a neo-
Nazi. She was completely leftist, though she'd never belonged to any
party.

"You know, Inken, this Nazi shit makes me want to puke now,
too," I said. "I'd like to get out of the scene, but I don't have a clue
how to do it."

She was thrilled to hear this, but then, as we talked, we scared each
other.

"Will they try to do something to you, Ingo?"

"I don't know if they will. I suppose so," I said. It was odd. For the
first time, I had referred to my Kamerads as "they" rather than "we."
The Movement seemed much darker and more sinister when you
weren't part of it. But actually, the worst violence was reserved for
those who tried to quit. It was the same as in the Mafia or in a cult.
Quitting wasn't something you talked about because it wasn't something that happened. Your whole life was the Movement, so quitting
meant death, metaphorically or literally or both.

I told her about what had happened to Johann Bügner, who had
told his Kamerads, including Michael Kühnen, that he was planning
to quit. He had been found in a forest near Hamburg with twenty-
seven stab wounds in his chest. The word was that Kühnen had ordered it, but nothing could be proved against him; Kühnen had been
in jail at the time. Bügner's killer, however, had visited Kühnen in
prison the week of the murder.

I speculated that now, with Kühnen dead, the two most dangerous
people for me if I quit would be Gottfried Küssel or Günther

Reinthaler, the Austrians, who were truly ruthless and fanatical. Once Reinthaler had offered me a lot of money to kill someone, a man who owed him money, and I was sure he'd have better luck hiring someone to finish me off. With his many connections in South America and Spain and his deep pockets, it wouldn't be hard to hire a professional, a foreigner, to come in, do the job, and leave.

As I told Inken all this, I brought her practically to the brink of tears.

"Oh, no, Ingo, stop. This is awful! I'm so afraid for you if you try to quit. It's too dangerous, you mustn't."

Fear of the consequences had made her go from enthusiastically supporting my quitting to rejecting it within the space of half an hour. But I was not about to make fun of her reaction. I felt the same way myself, once I got past the barrier of thinking about leaving the scene and losing practically all my friends. I was terrified of the physical consequences.

Perhaps if I just made a clean break of it, I reasoned, without informing on anyone but just walking away . . . I wouldn't be a hero, but I might have a chance of leading a normal life again. And maybe they'd just forget the Führer of the East. There were already much more ruthless people rising to take my place, like Oliver W. That guy would be trouble, I imagined, if I quit. The kid I had indoctrinated would not hesitate to tear me apart with his new teeth if he thought it would feed his ambition for power or leadership in the scene.

Over the next few weeks of November I went to the movies with Inken a lot. We weren't having a romantic relationship, but at the time it seemed like something better: a normal friendship. I hadn't really had one in five years. I started making excuses not to hold *Kameradschaft* evenings at my apartment. I hadn't quit, though, and I still held the meetings, just less frequently. Then came an event that drew us all together and forced me to face my Kamerads rather than just avoid them.

29

ROCK BOTTOM

AT THE BEGINNING of December, Winfried Bonengel's film *We're Back* was scheduled to air on German television. It was to be shown during prime time. The last week in November, Winfried came to Berlin and we went out for a beer and talked about the film. I wanted to stop it from airing because I knew I had made statements in it, nearly a year before, that I now doubted and that I knew I'd find painfully embarrassing to hear. But it was impossible; the film had already been sold to TV. Winfried sympathized with me and was pleased that I was rethinking some of my positions. He also said he thought I'd need to be careful because I'd said certain things in the film that were highly self-incriminating.

I woke up the next morning to the news on my clock radio: three people had been burned alive in a neo-Nazi arson attack in the town of Mölln in northern Germany.

Two skinheads had thrown firebombs into a middle-class Turkish home. Two young Turkish girls and their grandmother had died in the fire. Oddly enough, considering the thousands of attacks that had occurred in the last couple of years, this was the first with fatalities. One reason was that we usually threw the Molis against the outside walls, causing the flames to leap up and scare people without actually setting the place on fire. But these boys had thrown their Molis so they would set the house on fire and block the exits. It was an utterly cowardly and deadly act.

I felt a certain boundary had been overstepped. The boys had not been from any organized party, but surely they'd been people who'd been influenced at least indirectly by our work. Our work had been successful, I thought as I listened to the news. Gary Rex Lauck and Gottfried Küssel would be rubbing their hands with glee. I felt sick, like I was waking from uneasy sleep into a living nightmare from which I knew there was no escape.

At the next *Kameradschaft* evening, I told my Kamerads point-blank that this was a sad and awful event and we must at least re-think our methods if they were to lead to this. I tried cold political arguments as well—this was the worst possible publicity for the Movement, killing innocent women and children—though I was no longer thinking as a cold strategist myself. The act itself really sickened me. I didn't give a damn how it made the Movement look. I cared what it turned the Movement into.

It was utterly naïve, but I still thought there was some way to re-deem our ideology or at least some of the people in the *Kamerad-schaft*. I thought I could get some of them to agree with me that this was bestial and going too far.

But on the contrary, they didn't show the slightest understanding of my attitude. In fact, they celebrated Mölln, giving spontaneous speeches about what a brave and righteous act this had been, striking a blow against foreign infiltration in Germany and the "Jewish gov-ernment in Bonn." They spoke of the perpetrators, whom I took for criminals and cowards, as martyrs and heroes.

"I think it's great what happened in Mölln," said Oliver W. "We only talk, always talk, talk, talk. They had the guts to act."

"What guts does it take to set innocent women and girls on fire?" I said.

"Shit Turks! What are they doing here anyway? That's what I want to know," said Oliver. There were general murmurs of agree-ment. "If they want to be safe in their homes, let them stay home—in Turkey."

"You're entitled to the opinion that they shouldn't live here," I said. "You're entitled to vote that opinion. But you're not entitled to sneak up in the middle of the night and *kill* them! That's cowardly and immoral."

"*You're* cowardly, Hasselbach," said Oliver.

I really lost it then. But instead of hitting him, I tried to attack his ideology, which was also mine. And in the deaths of those three people that I felt indirectly responsible for, I had an inkling, for the first time, of the real violence of the Holocaust—of what it would mean to burn people alive.

It was a humbling experience trying to get even one person to side with me, the so-called Führer, in this crowd. They all preferred the view of young Oliver, and some people threw back into my face my own words from previous meetings, when I had said the foreigners were simply a vehicle for politics.

It was true. I'd thought like that not too long ago. But something had permanently snapped inside me, and I couldn't think that way anymore. I couldn't think of these Turks just as foreigners. They were also people—dead people with families.

Winfried's film *We're Back* played two days later on prime time.

My mother rushed to my apartment right after seeing it. "What have I raised for a son?" she asked me, her voice shaking from shock. It was as if her world had collapsed. I'd never seen her like this. Around her I'd always tried to make my involvement with the neo-Nazis seem harmless. Now she knew otherwise. In the film she'd seen me together with Michael Kühnen, whom she knew to have been Germany's most notorious neo-Nazi leader and fanatic.

Among other things, I talked on camera about how I was prepared to become a right-wing terrorist. Winfried had certainly been a brilliant interviewer. He'd gotten me to do and say things so self-incriminating that the legal consequences alone could have been disastrous for me—things that I never otherwise did because they were too risky. In one scene, I was sitting with my brother Jens in front of an enormous Nazi battle flag from World War II, rather than the usual black, white, and red flag of the imperial Reich. I could have been prosecuted for just that scene—for displaying an anticonstitutional symbol.

It was almost physically painful to watch myself rattling on, a somewhat drunken grin on my face—whether from liquor or simply from the power of being a Führer it was hard to tell anymore—going on about the Jews: "I met a Jew once. I didn't like him. He was slimy, not really honest." Such lies. I hadn't ever met a Jew. I had literally created things, people, and places to fit in with my worldview.

It hurt me a lot to see my mother so upset. While watching the film, she had grasped for the first time what a dangerous neo-Nazi I was. "This is the wrong movement you've chosen, Ingo!" she said, crying. "This is human-despising and cruel ideology. It can only lead to something like what happened in Mölln, to innocent families being killed. How can you endorse that?"

Before, she'd told me she couldn't comprehend how I could support what the Nazis had done. I'd never listened to her when she'd talked to me like that. I'd simply pushed her away and said, "Mom, you don't know what you're talking about. You don't know what neo-Nazis are. We're not the old Nazis. You don't know what my friends and I do." I couldn't use that argument anymore. She'd seen exactly what my friends and I did—in Winfried's film and in the constant television reports showing the dead bodies from Mölln.

Once before, she had thrown me out of her house for being a Nazi. It was in 1990. I was visiting her and had brought a book for Jens: *My Father, Rudolf Hess,* by Hess's son, Wolf-Rüdiger Hess. My mother saw that it was autographed by the author and threw me out of the apartment. She said she didn't want to have a Fascist as a son and she didn't want to see me anymore. And indeed I hadn't seen much of her for the next three years, but I'd always been able to go home. I'd never really felt thrown out for long. I could always count on a mother's unquestioned support.

Could I now? I supposed she would still love me, but maybe the way the mother of a convicted murderer loves her son. I tried to console her. This film hurt her more than any of my various arrests and convictions. I had no friends outside the scene—now I had to wonder if I had a family.

ABOUT A WEEK earlier Oliver Schweigert, the new chairman of the National Alternative, had moved in with me at Wotanstrasse. His girlfriend couldn't stand him anymore and had thrown him out. People were in the habit of using my place as a crash pad when they found themselves temporarily homeless. I really didn't particularly like the swaggering, brutal West Berlin neo-Nazi, but it would have seemed odd not to let him stay awhile. As I was unemployed and hardly in a position to pay my rent all by myself, I agreed to let him stay on a semipermanent basis.

Living with him was fairly problem free. He got up every morning at four o'clock, because he had to be at work at six. He was a metalworker at a truck-manufacturing company. I got up at noon, so I didn't see much of him. At six in the evening he came back home. Then he always drank a liter of beer and played video games for four hours. Punctually at eleven, he went to bed. In the whole time he lived with me, he was always reading the same book, a Nazi biography of the National Socialist "martyr" Horst Wessel, written and published during the Third Reich. Schweigert was such an eccentric loner that he hardly got into my hair. Of course, he wasn't a friend either. If anything, his stupid face playing those video games and always reading the same dumb book about Horst Wessel was just a daily reminder of what a pathetic bunch of people I'd built my life around. When he wasn't playing computer games or reading, he wrote ridiculous manifestos and plans for terrorist operations on his computer.

I began trying to do things with some of my Kamerads without talking about rightist politics. Not Schweigert, who was a brute, but people like Auschwitz, who were quite intelligent. But it was impossible. They always came back to "politics." If we went for a coffee, they'd say, "It's not German coffee." If there was trash in the street, they'd say, "Damned foreigners." If they didn't have enough money for a drink, they'd curse the "Goddamn rich swine Jews!" They'd use every little thing as an excuse to bring the topic back to some person or group they condemned.

Meanwhile, I noticed how normal people suddenly pointed at me on the street when I went out. I wasn't served in many pubs and cafés anymore. Before, I'd always liked to go to certain pubs or cafés that weren't explicitly neo-Nazi, just to read the paper or a book or meet someone without feeling like I was surrounded by people from the scene. Now when I went to these places, I was stared at coldly and politely asked to leave. Before, they had known I was a neo-Nazi, but they had never known exactly what I was actually doing or what it meant. Winfried's film had laid bare the connections with the paramilitary camps, the arms smuggling, the international plots. No ordinary person wanted to have anything to do with that sort of thing, even if they hadn't minded the idea of a neo-Nazi leader in their establishment. "We don't want terrorists here. *Out!*" they'd say. Someone like Schweigert would have said, "To hell with you. Throw me out, and I'll flatten your store!" But I couldn't. Already now, when they called me "Nazi pig," I thought, "Yes, you're right, I am a Nazi pig." Not "What do you want to do about it, buster?" but "What can *I* do about it?"

I ALSO HAD to deal with the fact that the militant Anti-Fa was now plotting actions against me. Already on the same evening as Winfried's film played on television, I was attacked by anarchists in the courtyard of my apartment house with baseball bats when I came home. I was able to fight them off—I shot one in the back with a flare stick—and ran upstairs with only minor wounds. A few days later an anarchist car circled in front of the building for hours. I began always carrying a weapon for self-defense.

Just a few days later, a pair of left-wing radicals got to the main gas pipe of my apartment house. It wouldn't have taken much for the whole building to go up in flames. The basement wasn't locked, and the gas line ran along the door hinge. The anarchists set the door on fire. An elderly lady who didn't sleep well told me later that she had heard some noise in the house. She had gone downstairs, and, when she had seen that the door was burning, she had called the fire brigade. The flames were already very high, less than two feet from the gas main. The fire department said that if the door had burnt for two more minutes, the pipe would have started to glow and then would have exploded. The anarchists would have blown up the entire apartment building and all the tenants inside just to get at me.

WINFRIED GOT IN touch a couple of weeks after the film aired and, hearing what bad shape I was in in Berlin, invited me to come spend Christmas with him at his parents' house.

Winfried's parents' house was in a little village in the Rhineland where he had grown up. It added another incongruous wrinkle to his already odd persona that the sophisticated filmmaker from Paris was from a conservative little town named Wolfstein in a remote rural part of southern Germany. His parents had recently died, and he had inherited the little house. But he only ever went back there at the

Christmas holidays, when he and his high school pals had a tradition of gathering in the town where they had grown up.

He invited four of them over: a couple who were now architects in Munich and another couple who were both in the art world and lived in Berlin. I immediately got on well with this second couple, Otto and his girlfriend Karin. Otto was a painter, and Karin worked in the theater.

I couldn't help noticing that Karin looked at me longer than was necessary when we were talking. She liked me, that was obvious, and I liked her, too. She was so unlike any of the women I knew—rather thoughtful and creative and very emotional. Otto was even more so—the complete possessed artist type—and I liked both of them very much. I hoped he wouldn't notice her looks and become jealous. For his part, Winfried seemed to enjoy bringing such radically opposite people together.

The Berlin Otto and Karin lived in was a city I didn't know at all: a city of art galleries and exhibits and concerts and plays, a multi-ethnic city of gays and lesbians and people from around the world. They were equally strangers to my Berlin—a city of occupied houses, police raids, and gang wars where everyone was on one political side or another. This was exactly what I needed—to be with people utterly outside the scene who didn't confront me as a Kamerad or a Nazi pig but simply as a person.

Then, in the next hour, this unburdened atmosphere was shattered. Winfried proudly pulled out a video copy of *We're Back,* which his friends hadn't seen yet, and popped it into the VCR. Yes, the moviemaker was proud—and why shouldn't he have been?—he had exposed a bizarre, dangerous movement and gotten its leaders to say absurd, dangerous things for the camera. A triumph. The only problem was that I was the star, the central figure in this nightmare web, and I could not have been more ashamed. I watched with horror as I appeared on the screen spouting neo-Nazi ideology and sitting with my Kamerads like Nero Reisz as they said even worse things. I could feel an almost chemical change in the room as Otto and Karin watched me become an evil Nazi plotter before their eyes. Karin watched riveted, occasionally shooting glances at me that became colder and colder.

When the film was over, I was a different person to them. I was now like some diseased specimen that they wanted to examine. Otto tried to bury the awkwardness a bit with humor, and the architect couple were also trying to be polite about it, though I knew I was now more or less a freak in their eyes. Karin seemed especially rattled. I was now probably the embodiment of everything she hated and feared about her country, everything that was threatening to make Germany an international pariah once again.

As soon as the film was over, Otto and the architect couple started asking me questions like "Why did you join the Movement? What do you think is good about neo-Nazism? Why do you consider terrorism an option?"

Karin didn't say a word. She acted like I was not in the room.

I didn't answer the others' questions directly. I talked a lot, but I didn't really say anything. I was so disappointed that things had turned like this, that I was now forced to meet them on this clichéd, political basis, as a representative of an ideology I didn't really believe in anymore. I'm not the man in the film, I wanted to say, but I couldn't say that. Because I was. But I didn't believe any of the shit anymore, and I didn't want to explain it.

I answered their questions indifferently. When they asked, "Why did you become a neo-Nazi?" I simply said, "Because I was sitting in prison in the GDR and the Communist system made me want to puke." It wasn't totally untrue, but of course there was much more to it than that. Not everyone who hated the GDR or rotted in an East German jail went on to be a neo-Nazi Führer. I didn't want to give them a false impression, but I also made it clear that I wasn't able or willing to talk about it.

Eventually they stopped asking questions and went out to a bar. They invited me, but I said I was feeling tired and preferred to stay in. I didn't go out of the house again for the rest of my visit to Wolfstein.

I sat in the house alone, and to block out all my thoughts I tried listening to music. I desperately wanted to hear some Neil Young, what I'd always listened to when things were hard and I needed to take a break from reality, but there was no Neil Young in Winfried's collection. There were many old albums from the '60s and '70s, though, music he'd had in high school: Rolling Stones, Beatles, Roxy Music. It was stuff that I hadn't heard for years and that I'd once loved. I listened to it all, blasting it into the empty little house in the middle of the empty provincial landscape to try to erase everything from my far from empty mind.

When I couldn't stand that anymore, I tried going outside and walking around, but the tiny German village seemed horrible to me. An ugly, cold place, utterly dead, because this was a very religious area and everyone was probably inside or at church. The emptiness felt eerie and frightening to me, a city boy, who'd grown up in apartment buildings and prisons. I'd never spent much time in our glorious German countryside, though I'd preached its virtues. Now that I was in it, it gave me the creeps.

As I walked around, I thought about how I'd so badly screwed everything up. I had done only shit—and not merely worthless shit, as so many do. Evil shit. Shit that was getting women burned alive in their homes. Shit I couldn't even begin to explain now, when ordinary people asked me why I'd done it.

I went back and sat alone in the living room, that film of Winfried's sitting by the recorder, and I wanted to take it out of its cassette and tear it to shreds. I hated the film. I hated it. But tearing it up wouldn't have helped. The sickness wasn't in the film.

I started to think of hanging myself that night. I looked around for places to do it, thinking that, just as it was a disadvantage to be as tall as I was in a firefight, it was equally a disadvantage when you wanted to hang yourself. Where could I find a place that would be high enough to sling the rope? And what could be worse than a botched suicide? To have them come home and find me choking and struggling from the rope, not high enough to die and not low enough to get myself down. After pitying myself about the method for a while, I got even more self-pitying about the results, thinking about how there would be no one who would care if I did succeed in killing myself.

But then I realized how wrong I was: nearly everyone would care if I was dead. They'd be happy. The anarchists would rejoice in my death, and so would my old Kamerads, for they'd have a great new martyr, far more useful and plausible even than Rainer Sonntag. Whatever else I did, I decided that Christmas night, I would not give any of them such pleasure.

QUITTING

When I came back from Christmas in the Rhineland, I knew that, before I could do anything else, I needed to explore some hard questions. All across Germany the winter of 1992–1993 brought hundreds of thousands of people into the streets in candlelight marches to protest the violence my Kamerads and I had instigated; these were the first mass protests against the weekly firebombings that had been happening for over a year now. But the questions I needed to ask myself were not about the firebombing of foreigners but about far more fundamental aspects of my ideology—questions that began and ended with the Holocaust.

These were not things I could talk about with people like Winfried and his friends. For them the questions I had were not possible. There would have been no basis for discussion. It's all nonsense, what Fred Leuchter and Thies Christophersen and Gary Lauck tell you, they would have said. You've been a fool to listen to it.

For them it was clear: the murder of the Jews by the Germans had happened, and they would not have comprehended how somebody might doubt it. It was like doubting that the world was round. And just as it would have been fruitless for a person who came from Europe in the fourteenth century, before Columbus's discovery, to talk with a group of people from the twentieth century about the earth's shape, it would have been fruitless for me to discuss the Holocaust with these ordinary people.

As a neo-Nazi, I needed to talk over the Holocaust with someone who was more "open minded"—someone who was ready to consider doubts and thus deal with them. Of course, most neo-Nazis would voice no real doubts: they accepted the dogma that the Holocaust had never happened, and all discussion could only lead to proving that point. But in an odd way the other side seemed the same to me. I wanted someone who could talk about it all openly.

This person turned out to be my brother Jens. It turned out he was grappling with uncertainty at the same time I was.

We talked about Thies Christophersen's book *The Auschwitz Lie,* one of the central texts of our belief—or should I say disbelief?—system. The former German SS concentration camp guard and now Danish citizen wrote that in Auschwitz the prisoners had been allowed to go out every day after work to go to a brothel, for example, or, if they liked, they could stay in and listen to beautiful music in "their rooms." He should know, he wrote, because he had been a guard there. Even hard-core neo-Nazis sometimes privately laughed at Christophersen's book. Most of us argued that concentration camps had existed and had been harsh, only that there had been no mass murder and no gassing. Christophersen maintained that Auschwitz had been like a hotel, complete with swimming pools to cool off in during the summer. I had been with Worch once when he'd said that Christophersen was an old idiot and a liar. But it was only now, as Jens and I discussed all this, that the holes in the arguments seemed to assume importance. Before, we'd just rolled right over them as if they weren't there.

Now we realized that Christophersen had never even been inside the main camp at Auschwitz where the Jews were because he admits it in the book. He had been in the part of the camp reserved for professional criminals and political prisoners, which was completely separate from the main camp, where the Jews and the Gypsies were being murdered. The prisoners he supervised had had more freedom and better conditions because they were not considered "race enemies" and because they were needed to run the extermination camp. I even read a book that later confirmed part of Christophersen's account—it described bonuses the regular prisoners had got in exchange for working harder and upping their production—that is, killing more Jews.

But the Leuchter Report was even more important because it claimed to refute technically and scientifically the possibility that mass annihilation had taken place at Auschwitz between 1942 and 1945. It relied not just on the account of an old man but on the word of an "outside expert," an American engineer named Fred Leuchter who supposedly had built gas chambers in the United States, the only country in the world that still executed people with a cyanide solution similar to that used by the Nazis at Auschwitz.

For the first time, Jens and I examined the Leuchter Report in detail. We saw that it was written in a ridiculous style and that the evidence didn't seem scientific except in the most superficial way. We looked at the original sketches by the Americans, which they had made of the camp after the war, and made comparisons with Leuchter's sketches. Leuchter wrote that he had proved from soil and water samples that cyanide gas had not been present at Auschwitz. But he had collected the samples from areas where there had been no gassing or burning of corpses. More important, the entire premise of the "experiment" was absurd, since the gas residues would have had fifty years to disperse into the groundwater; of course he hadn't found any.

Jens and I were shocked at how shoddy and absurd this cornerstone text of the Movement actually was. The secret was that nobody ever looked at it in detail. It was simply a prop, useful for dazzling a young person eager to hear that Germans were not, in fact, guilty of the worst crime in history. A neo-Nazi could thump his hand on the report and say, "Look, here an American engineer, a disinterested expert, has determined that the so-called gassings were a lie . . ."

Leuchter also examined crematoria that had been built after the war as a memorial (the SS had blown up the original ones) and asked why there weren't proper chimneys and, if there weren't, how they could have functioned to burn hundreds of thousands of bodies. But of course there weren't because the crematoria had been built after the fact as memorials, so why would they have connections to working chimneys? Only in the interest of making a more realistic model, but that was nonsense.

I tried bringing these things up with some of my Kamerads, but they didn't want to hear them. They were happy with their view of the world. Afterward I often asked myself why I had not sat down sooner and read this thing thoroughly. The answer was that I had not wanted to. I had seen in national socialism something both humanitarian and heroic. In order to maintain this view, I'd had to look the other way from the truth.

Much later, I found out that Christophersen had once been videotaped saying that he had told lies about Auschwitz in order to protect the Germans—to free them from guilt. He hadn't realized that the camera team filming the interview was from a normal television station; he'd thought they were Kamerads filming for internal use. He'd said it very matter-of-factly, as an afterthought, something like "Hey, pals, I only did all this in order to help Germany, of course it all happened but it's better to forget about it." He later said that the film crew had tricked him and put words into his mouth.

These conversations and readings with Jens were the first concrete steps I took toward freeing myself from the ideology that had held me in its grasp and that I had used to grab others and reel them into the Movement. I was pleased that Jens, whom I'd pulled into the Movement, was rethinking the ideology with me, so that he would start to emerge from under its weight as well. In January Jens went into the army and I was left alone again, living with the brutal idiot Oliver Schweigert, with his video games and biography of Horst Wessel.

BY THE END of January 1993 I'd had enough. I announced to my roommate that I was throwing him out and quitting the Movement. It was more an expression of raw frustration and anger than it was a thought-out decision. Schweigert treated it like a bout of temporary insanity.

"Hey, Kamerad, relax for a few days, then you'll feel better," he said. "Everyone gets a little nuts in winter, being cooped up."

"If you're still here in a few days, I'm sure I won't feel any better," I said.

Then, as he just sat around the apartment staring at me, I decided I needed to make a more definitive statement. I went over to the shelf where we kept most of our neo-Nazi propaganda, magazines, and books and began dumping them into a large cardboard box.

"Okay, Kamerad, do you want any of this? Or should it all go into the oven?" I asked.

Schweigert grinned at me and could barely hold back a giggle. "It's okay, you'll still need all of that."

I took the box, walked over to the coal oven, and started throwing the propaganda in, watching satisfied as it quickly caught on fire.

Alarmed, Schweigert threw himself onto the carton: "Stop it, Kamerad, think what you're doing!"

The idea that I'd send all that precious propaganda into the fire really scared him: to burn up our ideology!

"I know exactly what I'm doing, and don't call me Kamerad!" I shouted at him.

Schweigert looked really shocked. I handed him the rest of the material, told him he had two days to clear out, and grabbed my jacket. I drove aimlessly through the city, wondering what the consequences of that little scene might be.

The next day Schweigert asked me if I was feeling better.

"I've never felt better!" I said, disappointing him. "Nothing has changed."

"That's impossible, a convinced National Socialist doesn't simply quit from one day to the next!"

"Anything is possible, as you can see."

"I can't accept that," answered Schweigert threateningly.

"That's your problem, you'll have to deal with it," I said.

"But it can also easily become your problem."

But I had no fear and also no desire to discuss it with him further. The next day he picked up all of his things from my apartment. Of course, Schweigert was right about one thing—my decision hadn't happened from one day to the next.

Schweigert probably thought it best to leave me for a while so that I could come to my senses. Though he must have told the rest of the Kamerads, nobody threatened me. Instead, they just gave me some breathing space, probably figuring it was just a temporary lapse.

To tell the truth, I myself was worried that I might have trouble "staying out" once I quit the Movement. It was my whole life; practically everyone I knew was in it, I had a position of authority, and many people looked up to me. What would I find on the outside?

And if it wasn't enough, wouldn't I want to get back in? I decided that, for it to work, I'd have to find some way of quitting that would keep me from ever letting myself get sucked back into it. There was always a danger of going back out of boredom or loneliness.

I decided the only way to do it would be to quit publicly and to renounce the Movement in such a way that I wouldn't have the choice of returning.

I CONTACTED WINFRIED, told him of my plans, and asked if he could arrange to get my announcement aired on television. I could do it like an interview, with me making a public statement condemning the Movement and its ideology in no uncertain terms. He said it could be arranged. Afterward I would need to leave Berlin and preferably Germany immediately. Winfried agreed to let me stay with him in Paris. No one in the scene knew his address there—he was always subletting from someone—and it would be safe at least in the short term. He was thrilled by my decision, and I could tell he felt at least somewhat responsible for it.

Winfried met with the producers of the SAT 1 political magazine *Akut*. They sent a TV journalist to Berlin to meet me and do an interview with me; it quickly turned out that this guy was interested in uncovering as many secrets as possible from me about the right-wing scene. All he wanted to hear about was names, connections, weapons caches—all the supercriminal stuff that gave the Movement its media cachet. Like so many journalists I'd met—and unlike Winfried—this guy was so obsessed with getting a sensational insider story that he barely saw the real story in front of him.

But the segment got filmed and the station told us it was scheduled to air on March 15, 1993, almost a month away. Winfried and I explained to the journalist and everyone else who knew about the film that it was a matter of life and death that nothing about it be disclosed until then. At the end of the interview I burned a picture of Hitler and some other propaganda material for the camera. To outsiders, it might seem a little silly. But I knew that, within the scene, for the Führer of the East to burn a picture of Hitler would be an utter provocation.

*   *   *

AROUND THE TIME we taped the interview, I was being prosecuted for the street battle in 1991 on Pfarrstrasse. I was accused of "breach of the public peace" and "inflicting multiple bodily injuries." This was the last possible obstacle to quitting, because, if I'd been sent to prison then, it would have been extremely difficult to get out of the scene. The right-wing atmosphere in prison alone would make the whole thing more complicated and dangerous. Also, I had no idea if I could have psychologically stayed out if I'd suddenly been plunged back into that kind of environment.

The case against me was ridiculous. It was true I'd run into the anarchist house, but someone had thrown a stone out at us first. And then I'd been beaten to unconsciousness and come away with more injuries than almost anyone else that day. It was actually a time when we had been on our best behavior. I didn't feel any guilt for what we'd done to the anarchists that day. If Frank Lutz hadn't rescued me, who knew if I'd even be here?

But it was so strange in the courtroom because I felt a twinge of guilt in the opposite direction, toward my Kamerads, who were getting up in court and testifying in my favor: Stinki, Frank Lutz . . . none of them had a clue that I was about to run out on them and the Movement for good. On the other hand, I told myself, I wasn't going to squeal. I had just decided to leave and speak out against the neo-Nazi philosophy in general. I had vague ideas of helping other right-wing kids steer clear of the Movement somehow, but not of getting all my old Kamerads busted.

I WAS ACQUITTED for lack of evidence that I had instigated anything. It was now just a matter of waiting until the interview aired. This was an especially hot winter for neo-Nazism, what with all the mass response to our violence, and many of the Kamerads wanted us to make plans for even more radical actions. "Now is the time to really strike terror into their hearts" was the sentiment in the *Kameradschaft*. I had banned the regular meetings in the last few weeks, and when the Kamerads came over to my place to visit, they looked suspiciously at my blank shelves and walls, where previously swastika flags and Nazi books had been. They'd heard about my incident with Schweigert and how I'd burned everything. They were holding back from condemning me, but I could feel the rumors swirling around.

I decided that, to buy myself time, I'd have to make up a story to explain my strange behavior. I said that I'd gotten an offer to go work for a year abroad as a tour guide for German tourists. I said I needed to get out of town because of various police investigations against me and because the pressure was getting to me. That's why I'd blown up at Schweigert. The pressure was getting to me. I'd let things cool off, I'd make good money, then I'd be back, a better Führer than ever. It would be a one-year exile, nothing more.

I visited almost all the Kamerads individually and told them this story. The visits served two purposes. On the one hand, they allayed suspicion. On the other, they gave me a chance to bid farewell to these people without their knowing it. I knew it would probably be the last time I would see any of them. It was like leaving your buddies from the war, the people you'd fought and sweated and lived in close quarters with, but now the war was over and you knew you'd follow different paths in civilian life. Only this time the war was over only for me, and I was about to betray the Cause.

I think many of them thought I was taking my one-year absence a little too seriously. "Lighten up, Kamerad," they'd say. "You'll be back before you know it."

THE DAY MY announcement was to air, I was at my apartment on Wotanstrasse putting some things in order. A knock came at the door. It was my old pal Freddy, the guy with the two hundred swastika tattoos all over his body. I hadn't seen him since the storming of the Weitlingstrasse house, almost two years before. He didn't invite himself in. His car was running outside, and he actually had the strange idea that I should go with him.

"I'm reporting to Hoyerswerda, Hasselbach. It's much better there," he said, referring to the grim factory city near Dresden that had the odd distinction of having been the first German city to become "foreigner free" after a series of neo-Nazi actions there in 1991. I could tell that the last couple of years had not treated Freddy well. I'd heard rumors that he'd killed somebody.

"What do you mean, you're 'reporting' to Hoyerswerda?" I said.

"Report there, then next time we'll get sent to Bautzen. It's good for us there, Hasselbach!"

Bautzen was a large prison near Hoyerswerda that had had one of the worst reputations during GDR times. In Germany, wherever you live, you're required to register with the police, and if you're sent to prison, you're sent to prison in the region where you're registered. It would have been deadly for Freddy in prison in Berlin, where he was so well known and hated by so many people, but Bautzen was farther away and they didn't know him so well. Also, it no longer had its horrific reputation.

"I'm actually not planning to go back to jail," I said.

"*Ach,* come on, Hasselbach, we all go back to jail."

It was odd that Freddy would pop up at that moment—the one I'd begun my career in crime with would be the last person I'd see before getting out of this shit forever. I told him so long and went on to a new life.

I HAD NO idea how fast and how hard my quitting would affect the scene.

The day after the interview was shown on TV, my *Kameradschaft* dissolved. I heard later that some of the Kamerads had been so shocked and upset that they had actually cried when they saw my announcement. I didn't realize until I quit just how seriously they all took the idea that I was their Führer. Some, like Oliver W., were hard and self-sufficient enough that they were more or less independent, but far more in the scene saw me as their leader in a very personal way. During the previous six months, as my doubts had grown, I'd forgotten many of those who were looking up to me—but they hadn't forgotten me. I had been a father figure for some of these young men, and now I was abandoning them forever.

I watched the film with Winfried and Inken in an apartment Winfried was renting. Then we went out to a bar and had a beer. It was insane on our part. If we'd met someone from the scene, there would have been big trouble. But none of us quite realized the dimensions of it then. Inken and I had spoken about Bügner's murder, but at the moment we were all naïvely relieved that I was out, and none of us was thinking about the consequences.

The next afternoon Winfried and I were getting ready to drive to Paris, where we figured we'd stay until things cooled off a bit. About two hours before we were going to leave, I went out to buy some cigarettes near his apartment. On the way back, I stopped to make a telephone call. When I walked out of the booth, someone from the *Kameradschaft,* the beefy young idiot Johannes Hochstetter, was standing there looking at me rather expressionlessly.

"That film yesterday was really too much," he said placidly. He seemed in shock, waiting for me to tell him it was all a gag or something. Hochstetter always needed a little help with interpretation.

"Everyone does what he has to, Johannes," I said and shook his hand before walking quickly away, not looking back.

I was scared shitless, for Winfried's apartment was in a leftist area of Berlin and it was very unusual that one of the Kamerads would just show up there by chance. He could have had friends waiting around the corner. I also realized by the look on his face what a blow it had been to Johannes personally, and I suddenly knew he wouldn't be alone. No one in the scene had ever done anything like what I had just done. I quickly crossed the street, entered a building, and escaped out the back. When I got to Winfried's, I had my stuff packed and down in the car in five minutes. I wanted to get the hell out of occupied Berlin and over to liberated Paris as fast as his car would take me.

PARIS WAS THE most amazing thing I'd ever seen. Winfried lived in Montmartre, in the northern part of the city, where we were surrounded by people of every race and color—many of them black Africans and Arabs. Here I was the blondest and without doubt the tallest one on the street. But people were friendly to me. They didn't stare at me as we would have at a black person in East Berlin. This was a cosmopolitan world, and they were used to seeing people from all over. For the first time in my life, I was a foreigner.

It was a strange feeling, to live in a part of the city where there were so many blacks. Winfried was the only European in his six-story building. I felt as though a heavy weight had fallen from me; for the first time I had the feeling I had a future. I could once again have a clear thought, without always being on guard against an attack by this or that left-wing radical and without having to avoid my Kamerads.

I got used to buying a baguette in the morning and having my coffee at a café where the Arab waiter would greet me. After a few days he began offering me a free coffee now and then. We had to speak in sign language because we didn't know a word in common. In Germany you'd never go to a coffee shop and have the person become familiar with you; all German coffee shops were part of the Tschibo chain, which was as uniform as McDonald's, though a good deal less friendly, and which seemed to hire only Germans. In Paris half the employees in shops and restaurants seemed to be from other countries, even in the best stores. I'd hardly ever seen a foreigner, not to mention an African or an Arab, working in a German department store or coffee shop.

We ate delicious food every night. Winfried made a point of taking me to different ethnic restaurants: Vietnamese, Moroccan, Algerian, Italian, French. The splendid diversity of the world was brought home to me in a way it never had been before, when the foreigners had been like cartoon characters, much as they appeared in films. It was the reason why *The Blues Brothers* could be our favorite movie, because we didn't really see the black people in it as people.

Here they were real people—an entire world taking place in many languages and skin colors—a world as real as my own lily-white neo-Nazi world. It was as though I'd stepped out of a cartoon universe into real life and was seeing it before me in its staggering complexity. Where before I'd seen everything in terms of certainties, I now saw it as an endless string of questions.

Winfried actually opened my eyes about many things. He had experienced things I couldn't conceive of. He would say, "Check this out, you'll like it." He'd wanted to take me to Paris when I was still a convinced neo-Nazi. But I'd blocked him out. I'd said I didn't have any time. He'd say, "You need to, you'll like it." But I'd been afraid I might like it! That another culture could please me had been the most threatening idea in the world to me until just last month.

The only time I'd ever been abroad before was in Barcelona with the Spanish Fascists, the Cedade. But with their perverted worship of Hitler and national socialism, they were even more German-fixated than I was. They shut out Spanish culture and worshipped Austria and Germany. Adolf Hitler, not Francisco Franco, was their model.

Most neo-Nazis talk about cultures they've never experienced. They talk about Jews when they've never met a Jew. And don't want to. Firsthand experience is their archenemy, because it is the one antidote to their ideology. Arguments and counterarguments only cause them to fight harder. The best thing that could happen to the scene would be if all the neo-Nazis could get sent on a long vacation to Africa, I thought. Not the hard-core, ideological ones but the younger ones, sixteen-, seventeen-, eighteen-year-olds. Before they really get stuck in their belief system, that's when I'd try to open their eyes.

But it's a complicated thing, of course. Many factors play a role in whether you let influences in or not. Winfried was the deciding factor for me—at the very least, he was the catalyst for an unstoppable series of events that would transform me into someone barely recognizable by those who had known me before.

31

THE BOOK

Michael Kühnen always said, when somebody left the group, "That separates the wheat from the chaff." In other words, the wheat remains. I came to think the opposite, of course. But it was true that a hard core remained. One person leaving just seemed to make that core harder.

I spent two weeks in Paris. When I went back to Berlin, I found that my place on Wotanstrasse had been sprayed with calls for "Death to the traitor!" I'd only come back to that neighborhood because I'd left my car near the apartment, a Russian car that I'd recently acquired and that wasn't known in the scene. And indeed, I found the car just as I'd left it, no smashed windows or slashed tires, everything was fine . . . except no gas tank. Someone had stolen it.

Winfried wasn't with me, and I had to walk from my place to my mother's. I was lucky I didn't see anybody. My mother seemed greatly relieved to see me in one piece. We hadn't had any contact since just after she'd seen the interview on television. She was overjoyed at my change of heart, but I quickly discovered she was terrified as well. We sat down for coffee, and she told me about what my former Kamerads had done during the time I was in Paris.

The *Kameradschaft* had re-formed themselves into a so-called Kommando Horst Wessel whose sole stated purpose was to take my life or exact whatever revenge they could on my friends and relatives. They had put up posters all over East Berlin, bearing my picture and the words "Ingo Hasselbach—State Spy." One of the people who most wanted to kill me, apparently, was Frank Lutz, whom I'd known for more than twenty years and who had probably saved my life when they were beating me in the anarchist house on Pfarrstrasse. But the one who was most active was our little Frankenstein monster, the cold-blooded nineteen-year-old West Berliner Oliver W.

Oliver had led the Kommando in putting up the wanted posters. He himself had never been photographed, and no one in the police or the media knew anything about him. He always wore a ski mask when he did anything connected with the Movement, because he was training to be a terrorist; he wanted to be a man with no face and no record. During street fights Oliver was just as dangerous as Frank Lutz, but, while Frank actually lost control, Oliver was simply a cold-blooded, calculating sadist. He was the type who would have volunteered to work in the death camps.

The Kommando Horst Wessel had been terrorizing my family in the weeks I'd been gone. They'd practically destroyed my mother's front door and sprayed disgusting graffiti against my family all over her building, calling for revenge. My teenage sister, Jana, had been threatened by skinheads and hooligans and then beaten by skins who said they were "exacting revenge" for the traitor. She was now scared to walk down the hall from the elevator to the apartment door, because she'd been jumped once in the dark. There were now plain-clothes police keeping an eye on the building, but they weren't there all the time. And when they weren't, men with short hair and boots were often lurking in the bushes and the stairwell.

I called Inken and found that the Kamerads had put her apartment under surveillance as well. They had asked her where I was, and when she'd said she had no idea—which was the truth—they had tried to scare her into telling. After that there was always a skinhead standing near her door, waiting.

As my family described these incidents to me, the hatred rose up in me. My former friends knew I was refraining from going to the cops and ratting. Yet here they were trying to get all of East Berlin to hunt me down and kill me and terrorizing my family. But then what should I have expected? The posters and graffiti were similar to what we had done against foreigners, only I was the only "traitor" here. Traitors were not welcome in Germany. The Kommando Horst Wessel wanted traitors to go back to their native land—or ten feet under the topsoil.

While the neo-Nazis were more than convinced by my conversion, I soon found out that the anarchists weren't convinced at all. When I went to stay at the apartment of a Berlin acquaintance, I was attacked by Edelweiss Pirates, who put up their own wanted posters on my door, announcing that I was "Ingo Hasselbach—the Nazi Führer."

Luckily, I wasn't staying in Berlin long—just long enough to make another film about my quitting, a more detailed one than the first. The first interview had been only ten minutes long and had contained very little and very superficial explanation. This next one was thirty minutes long with a lot of background. Winfried did the interviews and during them played sections from his film *We're Back*. I watched on a monitor and commented. I found I could get distance and perspective on my own behavior—watching myself as a neo-Nazi in action and then giving my thoughts about it—about what I thought of the person on the screen and the things he was saying.

I wanted to go out and strike back at all the people who were attacking me, most especially my Kamerads. But I knew I couldn't take on all of Berlin with my fists and my boots. For the first time in my life I came to rely on some cops.

THOMAS AND MARTIN were cops in a special undercover unit in Berlin called the "Working Unit for Group Violence." They had been recruited for this elite unit to fight crimes committed by gangs, from hooligans to neo-Nazis to foreign thugs. Its members were all hard, tough guys. They had to be to work with such people. Both Thomas and Martin were built like American football players, and in fact they played American football in their free time, on the Berlin semipro team.

But aside from being physically tough they were somehow more relaxed than ordinary cops, and in the case of these two I really trusted them. To be in this unit, they had to be not only strong but street smart. What I liked about them was that they never seemed like idiots, you could talk with them and they talked with you intelli-

gently, while the regular cops were just there to either take advantage
of you or manipulate you. They also never showed any favoritism to
the neo-Nazis over the anarchists—they were equally straight in dealing with trouble from the Left as with trouble from the Right—and
oddly enough, as a neo-Nazi, I respected that. I knew they weren't
full of shit, these guys. If I had to guess their politics, I'd figure they
were slightly to the right, law-and-order types, but they didn't let
their politics influence how they worked. They were real pros.

Thomas and Martin had tried to bust me many times in the past.
But when I'd called Martin up the day before my interview was to air
on TV and told him I had something heavy to talk over, he'd been
very friendly and invited me to come down to the precinct for a cup
of coffee. So I went by, and over some lousy coffee I told him my
plans for quitting the Movement. He didn't believe me. He thought I
was fucking with him.

"The film is playing on TV tomorrow," I said. "It won't seem like
a joke then."

He laughed but then looked serious for a minute. "Okay, I hope
you're not fucking with me. If something happens, I'll know what's
up." He called up a central number for security agencies in Berlin and
told someone what I'd just told him. Then he gave me his private telephone number. "If something happens, you can call me whenever
you want," Martin said.

After I got back from Paris, I stayed in the apartment Winfried was
renting, and the cop came over and brought me things because he
knew it was dangerous for me to go out. He brought food, cigarettes,
money, and books. He had a huge collection of books about the Red
Army Faction that he'd had to read during his days learning about
counterterrorism techniques. I'd never told him that I'd had a lot of
interest in the RAF as a model for right-wing terrorism, but I think he
guessed this sort of stuff would interest me. I was nearly going out of
my mind then, feeling so cooped up and anxious and angry.

Over the next few weeks, he also helped me by getting information
about the scene and the plots against me. "You really weren't kidding
about quitting, kid," he said. He knew all my old friends, and talking
with him was always one of the best ways of getting information
about what they were up to.

*   *   *

IT WAS A good idea to stay inside. One day I was with Winfried near his apartment, getting something out of his car trunk, when he poked me and said nervously, "Look, there's a lunatic across the street. A nut you should have recruited."

When I looked I saw this guy walking down the street in full Nazi battle uniform.

"Hey man, that's Bendix!" I said quietly.

"Bendix?" Winfried practically turned green at the mention of the man who played with SS skeletons; before I could say anything, he had literally jumped into the trunk of the car. I had told him that Bendix always carried a sawed-off pump-action under his army jacket and usually had a couple of hand grenades hidden somewhere in his clothes for emergencies.

Spotting the Movement's biggest traitor and his accomplice would certainly have been an "emergency."

Bendix was just back from Bosnia and Croatia, where he'd worked as a mercenary and finally gotten to kill people and increase his expertise in blowing things up. Before that he had tried to enter the French Foreign Legion, which was a common course of action for men of his tastes. They'd taken him into basic training but then kicked him out because he'd insisted on being allowed to fight in an SS uniform. I'd heard about it from another German guy who'd traveled with Bendix down to Marseille to join up. They wouldn't take the other guy because he'd had swastika tattoos on his neck and face. Ironically, Bendix was more of a Nazi fanatic than he, but it didn't show so much at first because he didn't have any tattoos except the traditional SS brand—his blood type under his arm.

I ducked down behind the open trunk, but Bendix was walking in the other direction and didn't seem to notice us. As he rounded the corner, I could hardly keep from cracking up at the absurdity of it— a guy walking through Berlin in 1993 dressed in a Nazi uniform. It seemed to capture the whole lunacy of my youth, which was now over. It didn't occur to me that Bendix's training with the foreign legion and his year of fighting in Yugoslavia could have the gravest consequences for me and my family.

ONE DAY WE got suspicious that someone was watching Winfried's apartment and that they might be waiting for me to come out. In the middle of the night, we sneaked out of the building. Winfried had gotten hold of another apartment I could use through his friend Karin, the woman I'd met at Christmas. She was renovating the apartment for a friend—she was trained in theater design and knew a lot about carpentry—and I offered to help with the masonry.

Though Karin had been completely cold to me at Christmas after she'd found out who I was, she was now very open and willing to see that I'd changed. "I can see you have a good heart," she said to me, "and that's more important than your past."

We soon became lovers. It was like having a relationship with a foreigner; through her, I got to know an unknown land beyond neo-Nazism and anarchism and violence. Forgetting my situation to some extent, I dared to go out more—to go on dates, to go out to eat. Karin took me to a little Italian restaurant she loved. I had never been inside an Italian restaurant, even though there are many in Berlin. I'd preferred to eat the German brand of frozen pizza, Dr. Oetker's.

Through Karin I soon met all sorts of people who were from the other city I didn't know—people in the theater, in the arts community, people who'd never been near a street fight.

She made up an odd pet name for me—I was her "Führer-Ex"—the big bad Nazi who had changed overnight. I think it was her way of making light of the whole thing so it didn't scare her too much that my former Kamerads were out looking for me and that I was on the run. "I think we should go to the movies tonight! What do you think about that, Führer-Ex? Do we have permission?"

I wasn't thrilled with the joke. I felt especially awkward when she called me Führer-Ex in public. In a supermarket, for example, heads would invariably turn.

"I'm trying to put neo-Nazism behind me. Besides, it's really not a good idea to make jokes like that in public. It could be a problem sometime."

"Oh, my Führer-Ex! Pardon me, I wouldn't want to do anything to displease the Führer-Ex."

"Just think up a different pet name for me, okay?"

"It's hard—you're my first former neo-Nazi leader boyfriend. I want it to be something appropriate."

She came up with "F.E."—the initials for Führer-Ex—which she pronounced "Fey." It had the advantage that no one could ever know what the hell it meant. And it meant she didn't call me Ingo in public, which was also safer. If we were shopping together, she'd just say, "Fey, should we get some melons?"

One evening, Karin and I were attacked by anarchists. We had just eaten at an Indian restaurant near her apartment, and we were about to open the door to the lobby of her building. They were fit-looking guys, and they'd obviously been lying in wait. They taunted me with shouts of "Nazi asshole" and tried to push me into the doorway of Karin's apartment building. I tried to hold them back, but somehow I couldn't get myself to punch or kick them. I just blocked their blows as best I could.

I was impressed how well Karin handled herself. After her initial shock—I'm sure she'd never been physically attacked in her life, at least not since grade school—she screamed, "Fey! Get back!" Then she stood in front of me to protect me from them, for she saw that they were trying to avoid hitting her in order to get to me. When I tried to push her aside and get both of us inside the door and lock it, I was too slow. The anarchists broke in behind me, and Karin slipped out into the street and started screaming.

Inside the doorway my one advantage was that I knew the stairway and they didn't. It was totally dark—I could see them in the moonlight, but they couldn't see me—and we could all hear Karin's screams just outside the door: *"Polizei! Polizei! Hilfe!"* I'd never figured I would be in this situation, hiding from my opponents and counting on a lefty young woman to get the police to save me. The anarchists bumped around in the dark for a couple of minutes, but then they must have felt their plan was blown and they bolted.

I realized then that I really hadn't missed the feeling of fighting over these past months. And when the anarchists attacked me, it had been hard to even muster the urge to defend myself physically. For me physical violence was so associated with being "inside" the Movement that to throw a punch, even in self-defense, was a little like an alcoholic taking a drink—there was the risk that I'd want another. I didn't ever crave even one drink, truth be told, not even an occasional one. When I escaped and got back to the restaurant, I was trembling, shaking all over. I'd never shaken after a fight before. I was a different person.

ONE DAY MY new girlfriend and I went in to the Police Presidium to speak to an expert on personal security for people in danger. It was the equivalent of marriage counseling for fugitives. The police had recommended we go have such counseling, and, especially since Karin was completely innocent about the ways of the street, I thought it couldn't hurt.

We were sent to see a cop named Frau Plottnitz. She was very tall, about six foot two, and rail thin, with close-cropped hair and a severe, strict expression. If you saw her on the street, you'd guess she was a cop. Even her stride was stiff, with hands held precisely at her sides to cover the weapon under her arm. This was always one of the most obvious ways of telling a cop, when they walked like that to protect the weapon under their arm. They were afraid someone would grab it out of the holster or that they would fall on it and it would go off. Almost all the Berlin plainclothes cops had something of this walk.

Frau Plottnitz sat in back of her huge desk, looking like a Supreme Court justice, and proceeded to give us the sort of advice you might get in first grade: when you're walking in the street, turn around and look back often. Don't go down dark alleys. Stay where there are lots of people. If you sense trouble, try to find a uniformed policeman or guard.

We talked for three hours and she only gave us one really useful piece of advice: never walk in the direction of traffic, always against it. It's harder for someone to drive alongside and shoot you that way.

After the session, Karin was really shocked. "But any child knows most of what she told us," she said as we left the presidium. She'd never had anything to do with the police before, so she'd been sure that what they'd say would be important. There's a sort of belief that most people have in the omnipotence of the police that's almost always shattered by real contact with them. I tried to explain to her that the authorities' strong point was arresting people who'd committed crimes, not protecting potential victims. I could see that her trust in their ability to protect her was deeply shaken.

We were supposed to continue to report to Frau Plottnitz for tips every few weeks, but we never went back. The next time I saw the huge woman, it would be a little late for her advice.

ONE DAY IN May, someone pointed out an article to Karin in *Der Prinz,* an alternative leftist magazine in Berlin, which included a list of the fifty most famous neo-Nazis in Germany. I was right there on it. The anarchist scene didn't believe I'd truly had a change of heart. And for a moment neither did Karin. She was worried. I was able to reassure her, but it still made me uncomfortable that her confidence in me could be shaken so quickly.

It reminded me of what I knew already: it wasn't so easy to get out. My love affair with Karin was making me forget much of the anxiety of being hunted, as well as the mental shock of having rejected my entire ideological universe and all my old pals. But even if it lasted, my relationship with her couldn't cure the problems of being a Führer-Ex. I needed to confront those myself. And that reminded me of an idea I'd played around with in France with Winfried: writing a book, a complete account of my experiences and my motives for being a neo-Nazi—why I'd joined and why I'd quit—and what kind of person I was now.

I talked over my idea for a book with Winfried. It would be in essence a more detailed version of my statements on video. I wasn't a writer, but he agreed to help, and, though he wasn't a writer either, it seemed as though between the two of us we could get my basic thoughts onto paper.

We decided that it would be too difficult to write the book in Berlin, always looking over our shoulder and worrying who was at the door. He had some friends in London and thought that would be a good place to work. I talked it over with Karin, and soon I was saying good-bye to my new girlfriend; I'd see her in a month.

In London I stayed with Winfried on the second floor of a big apartment building. We started to work on the book, and at first it was a great meditation, a way to calm down, to think about my whole life from beginning to end.

I'd realized earlier that most of my life I'd been searching for a father figure, and in the Movement Michael Kühnen had been happy to fill the role. I'd been proud to be photographed with him, to have him smile his sly grin and approve of my work. Like my own father he had mostly been absent, but his influence and fame had given me the feeling that I was important myself. I could also talk about other things with Kühnen. I'd told him how my mother was very important to me, and he'd said he understood and wished it had been the case for him as well.

For Kühnen the Movement had been more important than any individual, but nevertheless on a personal level he was totally reliable.

This was the paradox of the man that had made him so fascinating. At some point I had not separated the two things anymore—the personal from the political and ideological. But Kühnen could always separate them. For him, convictions had always had priority.

Kühnen had embraced me because I had come to him with convictions. I decided that I had swallowed all the anti-Semitism and race education and such things largely because they had originated from somebody I admired. It is often so: a particularly inhuman ideology needs a particularly human face to make it function. Hitler was that way for my grandparents' generation—he was a fascinating leader whom Germans found warm and sympathetic. All the women who were always running around the Third Reich worrying about "the Führer's health," we did the same for Kühnen and his illness—this almost gentle, sympathetic side is required to make people swallow inhuman ideas. In a democracy you can have very bland leaders and the system will keep functioning, because it is not so inhuman.

Kühnen had been a dazzler. On a political level he had been evil—perhaps devilish is more accurate. And I had been like Faust, he had seen the weakness in me, how to tempt me. He had seen that I was somebody who values humaneness, and so he had seen how he could use me. He had recognized my weak points and exploited them. And I had used the same method in indoctrinating young men into the scene.

If Kühnen had not died, I reflected, if he were still alive, the friendship with Winfried might never have happened. Kühnen would have prevented it. He would not have permitted Winfried to shoot his film, and he would have recognized a competitor in him.

In a way, I wish Kühnen had been alive when I quit. Because he died, I could never quite see him clearly the way I saw the rest of the Movement. He still seemed so likable, even if he had supported a horrible ideology. I couldn't entirely separate the two. I later came to see how he had used his own deep and complex humanness to make others embrace an inhuman and cruel ideology. But I didn't understand any of this as I wrote. I wrote to figure things out. It was like an extension of the discussion I'd had with my brother Jens in January.

*   *   *

ONE NIGHT I locked the front door, not realizing that Winfried was outside. He got frustrated and smashed a pane of glass to get into his apartment. He could have just rung the bell. He was drunk and in kind of an agitated state. When I spoke to him, he blew up and said, "Okay, just hit me in the face if you're such a tough guy, street fighter, hit me," he said.

"Leave me alone," I said and tried to go back to bed.

But he just continued to provoke me. I don't know, but I suppose he wanted to test how far he could go. As I stood there and let him provoke me, I thought how if somebody had done this before, I would have hit him in the face immediately. I realized I had a certain abhorrence of violence now that I'd thought about some of its associations and consequences. Before, it had impressed me. Now it disgusted me. The idea of even having a fistfight with this guy repulsed me. I'd simply given up violence. It wasn't a tool I wanted to use anymore, under any circumstances, except in self-defense. I knew if I saw a gang of neo-Nazis approaching me to attack, I would run away. I wouldn't take up the challenge. The whole idea of fighting had lost its connection to honor.

Personally, in a fight, I'd always screamed loudly before I struck someone. This scream had taken away my fear. It had made it possible to be ever more easily violent. It was like being a samurai warrior. We all used this method in street fights. Everyone was always shouting—or playing music. It was so loud that you blocked out your scruples and your thoughts. You just attacked.

Now I was trying to get all my thoughts back, and I didn't have time for violence.

With all the thinking I was doing about "father figures," I decided to write the whole book as a long letter to my father. I hadn't spoken to him in years, and I concluded my small, chaotic manuscript with an invitation to reestablish contact:

> I have presented to you the deciding moments of my life. I'm also interested in your life. That's how both of us could better master the situation. Neo-Nazism doesn't solve any problems, it only deepens them. It is too simple to join this or that group and to believe that it is the solution. One is responsible for oneself, and no one can take this responsibility away. . . . My life can now become better. Every person can change himself at any time. We

think we need to hate each other, but perhaps you and I should simply talk with each other, without prejudice. . . . That would possibly be useful.

At any rate it would really make me happy if I could buy you a cup of coffee sometime.

Ingo

Back in Berlin Winfried and I found a small East German publisher who was eager to rush my extended private letter from the heart of the neo-Nazi movement into print. The book, which we'd written in less than a month, hit the bookstores in October, with the title *The Reckoning: A Neo-Nazi Gets Out.*

Almost as soon as it came out, I began to get invitations to read and speak from all over Germany. Not only journalists, but teachers and young people and people in the Jewish community started writing me to request that I come speak to their groups. It was wonderful to come into contact suddenly with such a diverse number of people and to be treated with respect and appreciation even by Jews, whom less than a year before I had considered my greatest enemies.

My other enemies, the Anarchist Anti-Fas, were not so inviting. Once I tried to participate in a public discussion with them and they chased me off the stage. Even with my book out—a clear and very personal statement against the neo-Nazi scene—they still didn't believe I had quit. Or at least they still held a grudge so strong it kept them from hearing what I had to say.

That's why I was so pleased when one day I got a letter at my mother's address from Rainer Fromm, one of Germany's leading anti-Fascist authors. He wrote how much he had enjoyed my book, how he respected my courage in quitting, and how interested he would be to meet me and discuss the problem of neo-Nazism. He also wondered in the letter whether I had read his most recent book, *A Lexicon of Right-Wing Radicalism,* which, in case I hadn't, he was sending to this address. I was very flattered that Fromm had written to me, and I looked forward to meeting him. I happened to already have bought the book, so I told my mother that when it came she could open it and keep it.

*   *   *

ONE AFTERNOON THE following week, I was filming with a team from Dutch television, a brief segment on my life, when my beeper went off. It was my mother's number. I found a pay phone and called her. She was frantic. The book from Rainer Fromm had arrived that day in the mail, she said, and she'd taken it out of the envelope and had opened it to leaf through it.

But when she'd opened the book, instead of a title page, she'd seen a fuse, a battery, and a large gob of what sounded from the description like plastic explosive. She'd taken the book out on the balcony then, thinking it might be safer to leave it outside. There was an odd calm in her voice. I suppose it was the sound of someone who knows she should be dead but isn't, the eerie flatness that comes over a person who walks away unscathed from a ten-car collision and wonders what to do next.

"Ingo, I'm so scared," she said.

"When you hang up," I said, "I want you to call the police immediately and ask for Thomas or Martin." I gave her their numbers. "Second, Mom, whatever you do, do not touch that book again."

32

THE BOMB

I PICKED UP Karin and drove to my mother's. By the time we got there, there were cops everywhere and everything was closed off. Three large apartment buildings—my mother's and the two next to it—had been evacuated. The street was closed. A uniformed cop told me I couldn't go any further because there was a bomb alarm.

"Yes, the bomb was sent to me," I said.

"Oh, well, then naturally you can go through."

Karin and I found my mother, and we stood comforting her on the street. She'd been all alone when the bomb had come. My sister Jana was at work, my brother Jens was at the army base, and my stepfather was also out.

A policeman who recognized me came up to us and said in a very friendly way, "Good evening, Herr Hasselbach and family. I know you can't stand police, but there is so much press here who've heard about the bomb that we need to take precautions for your own sake."

Thomas was in fact the first one on the scene, so I had a real friend among the cops. I could see they were there from various branches, but most were dressed in combat uniforms, with helmets and boots and automatic pistols. Thomas and his friends from the Group Violence Unit wore T-shirts and jeans with automatics hanging off their belts.

"Seven hundred fifty-five grams of plastic," one of the cops explained to me. The book bomb had been filled with plastic explosives that looked like clay. Plastic explosive has various colors. This one was nut brown. It had been pushed into the hollowed-out book with cables and a little fuse. "The bomb would have been strong enough to take out four stories of the building. Maybe three because they're pretty strong, these new concrete buildings."

The men from the bomb squad said they'd never seen anything like this device. Normally book bombs blow when you open them. This one had been built with a real sense of perversity. The person who receives it opens it and sits there looking at the explosives and wires, wondering why he's still alive. First you get scared—oh, no, a bomb, oh, God—but nothing happens and you close the book in horror. Then it goes off.

There was a battery inside, and it was isolated with paper. On this paper was a tiny scrap of aluminum foil that you could hardly see. This piece of aluminum, which the bombers must have overlooked, had completed the circuit and drained the juice out of the battery. It was pure luck.

"I believe this is the biggest book bomb that has ever been sent to an individual in Germany," said one of the cops from the bomb squad, an older guy who looked like he'd seen his share. "Certainly I've never seen such a large amount of explosive sent to a private person's house before."

His name was Herr Dörte. He was a small, doddering little man who was about to go into retirement. He always spoke in cop slang with me. "Where's your POM?" he demanded. POM was the cops' expression for the domicile where you were registered, as required in Germany, but under all the stress I couldn't think what he meant. "Huh?" I said.

"Your POM, young man!" he barked. "Don't you know your own POM?"

"No, what the hell are you talking about?"

"POM, young man, POM!"

He was kidding around. He was really quite nice. He noticed how upset and scared and angry I was that they'd tried to kill my mother.

He patted me on the shoulder and said, "Don't worry, young man, we'll get the guys. Don't you worry about it."

To pass the time while I waited in the squad car, he told me stories about his career, anecdotes about all the bombs he'd defused. He'd seen a lot but never this size, he kept saying. We also talked about how this was the most technical and sophisticated incident of right-wing terrorism since the collapse of the Wall, how it represented an escalation of tactics and techniques.

When I was allowed to enter my mother's apartment again, there were lots of plainclothes cops all around. One of them came up to me, another older type like Herr Dörte, and said, "Hello, my name is Wien."

"Like the city."

"Yes, young man, like the city. I'm from the BKA central office, Meckenheim. I'm taking over everything. I'd like you to accompany me to the Police Presidium at the Platz der Luftbrücke."

Herr Wein was about fifty-five, I guessed, with a little beard and gray hair, friendly. He addressed me in the informal form—*du*—from the first conversation, just as Herr Dörte had. He smoked a pipe. I loved the smell of a pipe. He really reminded me of my dad. As we were leaving, he put his arm around my shoulder. This was a night full of fatherly cops.

WE ARRIVED AT the Police Presidium at 1:00 A.M. All important interrogations in the city were held here, at the office of the Berlin Security Service at Tempelhof Airport. The style reminded one of the '30s, but also of the '50s, since the office had been renovated. It was very disconcerting. On the outside there was a big column where it said POLICE PRESIDIUM OF BERLIN. Inside, none of the doors said anything. You went up stairs and came to a steel door where it said STATE SECURITY, and then inside you saw only numbers. If you were told to go there by yourself, you had to be given a little slip of paper by the police that said where you were supposed to go. Of course, I was escorted.

A sense of constant movement and activity was created by the fact that the elevators were the open kind that never completely stop— you had to spring on or off at your floor. The last time I'd seen these was at the Keibelstrasse jail, when I'd been arrested in the GDR. I remembered how the cop leading me then, just to be obnoxious, had sprung in too suddenly. I had been handcuffed and chained to him, and I hadn't reacted quickly enough, so my arm had got stuck as he pulled me onto the elevator. Later, my skin had been all sore and red from the pulling. When we got out he'd done the same thing, not telling me which floor we were going to get out at, so I'd caught my arm again.

I suddenly had the sinking feeling of being brought back into prison.

HERR DÖRTE APPEARED again as my interrogator, along with another friendly cop who was somewhat younger. Through their friendliness, I could see how happy they were finally to have an excuse to have me on the examining table—to be able to interview me. I was actually surprised that no one had tried to talk to me sooner since I'd quit. I would have been willing to talk to the police to some extent. This was the first time they'd made contact.

I was asked if I could name any suspects. I said I'd recently received a threat from Arnulf Priem. I'd also gotten threats from Oliver W., Frank Lutz, Auschwitz. I told them about the wanted posters. I also named Ekkehard Weil. He was described in my book as someone who knew a lot about explosives and building them, I said, and I also knew he sometimes stayed in Göttingen. The package containing the bomb had a return address in Göttingen. The final reason I had for suspecting Weil was his close friendship with Priem. The questioners then became fixated on the idea that Weil might have sent the bomb to prove his competence with explosives. On this and other points, I began to see that they were putting words into my mouth, but I was so exhausted and at the end of my rope that I just accepted whatever they said. Weil would send a bomb to me because he was pissed off at my quitting the Movement, not because he wanted to prove he could build one, I said. But they insisted:

Q: Herr Hasselbach, couldn't it be *possible* that Herr Weil thought he needed to build a bomb and send it to you to show he could do it?
A: No, I don't think he's that weird.
Q: Yes, but it *could* be true? It's *possible*?
A: Okay, it *could* be true.

Q: Thank you.

A: If you're so sure of things, don't ask me!

They asked me if I was aware of any bomb practice that had gone on within the scene. I explained that bomb practice was conducted along the lines of the book *The Total Resistance* by the Swiss Army specialist and also according to *Explosives and Demolitions,* the manual from the U.S. Army. They asked me who'd taken part in these bomb trainings, and I gave them the list of names again—Oliver W., Auschwitz, Hochstetter, Lutz, and so on—the usual names. Who do you know who collected explosives? Bendix Wendt, I said.

Then they began to ask me about the NSDAP/AO, which they seemed to know very little about. Then about Eite Homan and the organization in the Netherlands. We talked a long time about these groups. They were always very friendly, but I remained rather distant because I suddenly found myself in such a strange situation. I didn't trust cops, but they told me they could help me only if I told them everything—absolutely everything—I knew. They swore the information would never be used against me. They were only trying to catch the people who'd tried to murder me and my family. These psychopaths were out there. Didn't I want to help get them?

JUST BEFORE THE bomb came, I'd been doing a lot of press work. I'd been going from one interview to the next, and during all this running around I'd met two public figures who were very important to my quitting and who supported me during all the trouble ahead. One was Ignatz Bubis, the head of Germany's Jewish community.

I met him on a talk show called "Gespannt auf Ignatz Bubis" which means "Curious to Meet Ignatz Bubis." Each week on this show a different celebrity turns up and various people get invited to have conversations with him. Next week the show might be called "Gespannt auf Helmut Kohl." I think this encounter was equally fascinating for Bubis and me. For Bubis, it was his first encounter with a neo-Nazi; for me, it was my first encounter with a Jew. After the show we went out to a restaurant and talked for three or four hours. He asked me about Kühnen, about what kind of person he'd been to start such a movement and spend so much time in jail—and why he'd had such charisma. Bubis told me a lot about Auschwitz, where he had been sent with his family as a young boy.

And then the thing that made me most respect Bubis: while everyone else was always asking me why I had quit the Movement—in a way that suggested they didn't really believe I had, that it was just some sort of hoax or stunt—Bubis said, "I won't ask you why you quit the Movement because to me that's quite obvious, I can relate to you perfectly on that. But what puzzles me and what I most want to know is why a young man like you would ever get *into* such a movement." It was not really an unusual question, but the way he got into it was rare and made me feel much better, like there was someone who understood me after all—and that someone was the head of the Jewish community!

He asked me what neo-Nazis thought of Jews. I explained to him how, no matter what they said in interviews, about how they didn't feel one way or another about the Jews, how they were more concerned about foreigners, that they were in fact always obsessed with the Jews, just in a different way from the original Nazis. Nowadays, the main position was that the Jews should be forgotten, at least publicly. This was why they all hated him, Bubis, so much—because he was the public face of Judaism in Germany. Before the Holocaust the greatest anti-Semites had wanted everyone to notice the Jews, so they couldn't assimilate—they wanted to identify and attack them. Now, after the Holocaust, the goal was to forget the Jews and what the Germans had done to them. "The Jews are too much in the media. Too much in German politics. Never moving on and putting a line under the past" was the official neo-Nazi line. But in fact they never forgot either, as well they couldn't because painting a swastika was anti-Semitic, not to mention the fact that they were always desecrating Jewish cemeteries and throwing darts at Jewish faces and pissing on Jewish stars.

I was in an airport a few months later when a heavy hand clasped me on the shoulder. I swung around to see the short, corpulent figure of the head of the Jewish community beaming at me in his ruddy way. "Hello, Hasselbach! How've you been?" Bubis said, and I can't tell you how good it made me feel.

ANOTHER PERSON I met by doing talk shows was Horst Eberhard Richter, Germany's leading psychoanalyst and head of the Sigmund

Freud Institute. I had been invited to appear on a talk show three days after the bomb came, and I didn't go because my nerves were shot and I didn't want anything to do with the media. Winfried went in my place. The other guest on this program was Dr. Richter; he is especially interested in people who are or were extremists, and he'd written a book about extremism entitled *The Group.* It's the best thing I've read on the subject.

The program was called *Riverboat,* and the moderator was angry that I hadn't come. He said I hadn't come because I was scared. He didn't even *mention* the bomb. He even said on the air, "Mr. Hasselbach is probably a liar and a psychopath."

Dr. Richter spoke up and said, "I think I should be a better judge of who is a psychopath than you" and that while he didn't know me personally, based on everything that he'd heard and read about me, he thought I was quite sane and trustworthy. He said that one must have a little consideration and that there are certainly situations in life that one shouldn't jump to conclusions about. I was very impressed that he'd do this even though he didn't know me.

FOR THE FEW days after the bomb came, I could barely think. I had misjudged everyone I knew so badly; I hadn't thought they could be so unscrupulous. I couldn't sleep anymore. I was having nightmares where, as I was falling asleep, closing my eyes, my mother was suddenly holding the book in her hands and closing it and then, before I could wake up, it would blow up.

Frau Plottnitz suggested Karin and I visit her again. Desperate for anyone's help, we went. This time the stern woman ended her speech with a piece of advice that made Karin almost burst out laughing: "And Herr Hasselbach," she said in deadly earnest, "please don't open any mail that seems suspicious looking to you."

"Thank you very much, that's very helpful," I said. There was something almost reassuring about her earnest incompetence. At least one could be sure of Frau Plottnitz's motives—she was just trying to protect us from further harm. I wouldn't walk down any dark alleys that week.

The cops gave my mother round-the-clock protection, but I wouldn't accept it myself because I didn't want to let them know where I was living and all my movements. I would guard that one bit of autonomy.

Nearly every day I had to go to the Federal Office of Criminal Investigation, the BKA, for questioning. They had me in every day supposedly because they wanted to look for the offenders, but later I came to doubt they had ever been serious about this.

At first I was willing to give them whatever information they wanted about the scene and anyone in it. Before, I'd thought I would fight ideologically against my former Kamerads, exposing the problems of neo-Nazism, but I wouldn't betray them personally. I'd still had some naïve idea that they would value our friendship as something separate from our ideological connection. But now a clear line had been drawn, and I understood which side I was on. Also, I wanted to catch whoever had sent the bomb. But now I can see that, from the very first, the cops never really investigated the bomb. They were only after information about the right-wing scene. But I figured that out too late. Herr Wien had really made me trust him.

Wien had me flown to the head office of right-wing terrorism of the BKA in Meckenheim, near Bonn. He was a specialist in right-wing terrorism, trained by the FBI. He showed me proudly the awards he'd gotten from the FBI on the wall of his office. I was there each day for twelve hours. (Once we took a break and I was put into a helicopter and flown down to Karlsruhe to talk with a federal judge.) The formal interrogation in Meckenheim began on November 29, 1993, almost exactly a year after the firebombing in Mölln.

Meckenheim is between Cologne and Bonn. There is BKA Wiesbaden, which is responsible for left-wing terrorism, and then there's BKA Meckenheim, which is responsible for right-wing terrorism. The BKA complex was huge with double barbed-wire fences all around, watchtowers, machine-gun posts. You went over a tire killer on the way in so you couldn't back up and leave. Video cameras were everywhere. There were Mercedeses with superreinforced bulletproof sides. It was like a fortress, and as soon as we went through the gates I started to be afraid.

I'd been flown there from Berlin in a government plane. Just me and a couple of BKA types. They were all friendly, gave me food, cigarettes, whatever I wanted. I tried to talk with them about other things, but they wouldn't make small talk. Only about business. Real hard cops. There were also a couple of guys from the GSG9, the elite West German counterterrorist force, there. One of them told me that.

Otherwise I wouldn't have known. They all looked like ordinary guys in jeans, leather jackets, sneakers. There was one woman, a secretary, taking notes.

All the buildings were supermodern, with computer hookups everywhere and windows of thick, tinted bullet-proof glass. Next to the main building, there was a smaller one where the people who did night work lived. I stayed in there. My room was spartan and small, a combination of cheap hotel room and prison cell.

I ate in the canteen, and it was really strange because I was the only one there who wasn't with the BKA. And everybody—every one of these hundreds of people—immediately knew who I was. They all looked up when I came in; when I walked near a table, people stopped talking. I could tell they didn't trust me. I was never allowed to be alone in the complex. I was always with one or two cops. They'd come to eat with me.

AT THE BEGINNING of December the mayor of Vienna received a mail bomb that blew off three of his fingers. Various other politicians and left-wing activists in Austria also received bombs. This was clearly the work of neo-Nazis. Ten bombs were sent. A bomb for each of the ten years of Gottfried Küssel's jail sentence. There were similarities between the mail bomb I'd received and these, which appeared less than a month later in Vienna. I suspected the work of Bendix Wendt and an Austrian named Peter Binder.

I'd introduced Binder and Bendix in 1992, the evening we'd gone out with Küssel in Vienna after plotting the seizure of power. I'd met Binder for the first time that evening. Küssel had introduced him as a "loyal Kamerad looking for some materials." Binder had just said calmly and quietly that he wanted to get his hands on some explosives and weapons. He'd seemed a practical type. Bendix had better connections for stuff like that than VAPO had because of his contacts with the Russian soldiers, and when Binder had later came to Berlin, I'd put them in touch. Binder was known to have been spending a lot of time in Berlin in the months before I received the book bomb.

I tried to explain to the BKA the connections between the neo-Nazis in Austria and those in Germany. That we'd got the Austrians explosives, that we'd done war camps and indoctrinations together— that we'd always worked together. They seemed uninterested in these connections and said I exaggerated. I got excited then, and I said, "Look, I'm just telling you what I know. If you don't want to hear it, don't tell me I exaggerate—just don't ask! Let me go my way if you don't want to hear what I have to tell you—because sometimes I have the feeling that you don't *want* to hear these things."

They backed off then, but I thought it was fishy. They only told me I was exaggerating when it became a question of connections with Austria. They didn't want to see it, somehow. I suppose the connection bothered them so much in part because, until then, Chancellor Kohl and the government had said that neo-Nazis here in Germany were just "asocial kids." A simple solution that clears the problem off the table.

Then along comes someone who says, Be careful, gentlemen, it's all a very well planned structure with international connections. I threatened their whole approach, their appearance of competence. They had always said that here in Germany the neo-Nazis were just some messed-up individuals, while in Austria there was a solid structure. Something like that had never existed in Germany, they insisted. Küssel was an Austrian phenomenon. In Austria, it was clear that everything was well planned.

The Austrian government had made a mistake. Küssel had always had a fanatically loyal group of followers. After his arrest, they had gone underground, into cells, to work illegally. Many of them went to Croatia to practice killing and using explosives. The authorities had known all this, but they hadn't done anything about it. Ultimately they had to admit that they had simply missed the boat.

Then, at certain moments in the interrogations, something even fishier started happening: the questions seemed to be going in a way that could be used against me—like when the cops asked, "Have you had anything to do with explosives yourself, Herr Hasselbach?"

The turning point came when they asked me if I wanted to be a "state's witness"—to get immunity from all charges if I'd give testimony against my former Kamerads. I said no because I knew that if I did that, I couldn't have any more contact with Karin, my mother, the people I loved. You have BKA people around you every second of the day. They practically take the garbage out for you. I couldn't live like that. For me the whole point of quitting had been to take charge of my own life and to get out from under the influence of an organization. Furthermore, German and Austrian cops had far too many ties to the neo-Nazis for me ever to put my survival in their hands.

When I turned them down, the whole tone of things changed and the pretense that the cops were working to catch the bombers slipped away. They said I wasn't honest, I hadn't really quit, I wasn't trustworthy. Then they stopped being friendly and Herr Wien stopped being fatherly. I didn't have my lawyer with me, because you have the right to a lawyer only when you are the accused, not as a witness.

I HAD GOTTEN a lawyer some years before—Susanne Kossack, a very committed woman. She was about fifty with long black hair. She made a dynamic impression, like somebody who knows what she wants both from herself and from the world around her.

I'd had her as an attorney under the Communist regime, and she had been very courageous. She had a successful law office in Berlin-Mitte, and she liked taking on difficult political cases. Before the Wall fell, she had represented many right-wing skinheads against the Communist State. After the Wall fell, she defended, among others, Willy Stopf, who was one of Erich Honecker's closest colleagues. Her law firm also represented Honecker. They got him off so he could go and die in Chile. It was ironic that I was represented by the same law firm that represented the former leader of East Germany, but by now I took the most topsy-turvy things in stride.

Frau Kossack was Jewish, but in the GDR she had seen that a lot of what the skinheads did was out of pure opposition to an oppressive state. And from this point of view she did not have any problem defending them, or me, at the time. But when I asked her to represent me now, I had to prove to her that I was really no longer a neo-Nazi. She said plainly to me that she'd lost any understanding for right-wing ideology among young people; before reunification she had understood the need for rebellion, but now she had no sympathy for it.

I contacted her when the attorney general of Germany started asking me again to be a state's witness and go into a witness protection program. Even beyond my fear of losing all contact with the outside world, by that point I refused simply out of anger at the way the authorities had manipulated me when they were pretending to try to help me. Frau Kossack advised me to stop talking to the authorities completely for a while, and in the meantime she would try to get the transcripts of our discussions, so she could see what they had said in the interrogations.

EARLY IN 1994 Karin and I moved into the apartment of a friend of hers who lived in a part of Berlin where I wasn't known. The friend was away working as a set builder at a theater festival in Bremen and didn't mind if we stayed at his place.

Steven Spielberg's movie *Schindler's List* opened in Berlin that spring, and we went to see it. I hadn't seen a movie about the Holocaust since I was fourteen or fifteen, when I had seen a film called *The Trials of Majdanek,* a documentary.

I was really moved by *Schindler's List,* especially the scene where the women are transported to Auschwitz and Schindler gets them out. When they are in the shower, expecting to die, I felt I could really put myself in their place. I knew that everyone in the scene would also be seeing *Schindler's List* but that they'd ridicule it and dismiss it as Hollywood clichés. "It's exactly like *Jaws,*" I could hear them saying. "These Hollywood Jews are so good at making frightening kitsch. Just good fun."

Karin and I also went to the concentration camp memorial in Ravensbrück in April. I'd been at Dachau twice for meetings with a man named Max Mannheimer and to speak to schoolchildren. Mannheimer was a survivor of both Dachau and Auschwitz and was responsible for giving tours of the former concentration camp at Dachau. They were peculiar encounters. He should have hated me, yet we were immediately like old friends. It was a great joy to be with Mannheimer, and we walked around the camp and had long conversations.

Mannheimer and I did two programs for television about the camp and the people who visited it, and each time I struggled with the shame I felt over my years of trivializing the Holocaust and denying it. But my visits with Mannheimer also showed me that I could have a positive influence. I could transmit things entirely differently from an ordinary teacher, and young people became more interested in the history of the place because I was there—because they could see through me how it was relevant to the present, how it was a legacy that could still screw up lives, causing people their own age to become Nazis. I also hoped they saw in me the chance to always rethink their positions.

I told Karin about how neo-Nazis had burned down the Jewish barracks at the Sachsenhausen concentration camp—the biggest camp in northern Germany—in the fall of 1992. It was the first concentration camp memorial ever burned down. Karin thought it must be difficult to protect all these monuments when there are so many across Germany.

I told her how directly in back of the Sachsenhausen memorial there was a large complex called the "Police Precinct for Oranienburg and Area." I knew because I'd cased the place out with Priem and Weil enough times, though I don't know who actually burned it down. "Yet the police didn't notice anything," I said. "There's the precinct for the entire county, right in back of the camp, and they only noticed something was wrong when the Jewish barracks were already burned to the ground. It isn't just a problem of money or men, it's a problem of interest."

"Perhaps some sort of private security guards like the ones they're using in the Munich subway system is the answer," said Karin.

"I think one protects what one wants to protect and that's all," I said.

I got the idea of putting together a book of voices against right-wing extremist politics from diverse sources. My idea was to solicit the opinions of leading politicians as well as radicals and outsiders, to get a broad spectrum of voices. Winfried would write a chapter on the media and right-wing extremism. I thought I'd write about quitting the Movement. And in order to get an entirely different point of view, I wrote to a member of the Red Army Faction named Christian Klar.

If I'd grown up in West Germany, I might well have gone into the RAF or another extreme group in the left-wing scene. I'm sure that in the West I wouldn't have been a right-wing extremist. So for me it was very important to have a dialogue with this left-wing terrorist whom I saw, in a sense, as my doppelgänger.

Christian Klar was a prisoner in Stammheim, one of West Germany's toughest prisons, where he had spent the past twelve years in solitary confinement. All RAF prisoners were kept in solitary confinement to separate them from the other prisoners. It was but another example of how left-wing extremists got harsher treatment in Germany. The young bomb throwers in Mölln had killed three people, but they'd got one life sentence apiece. Klar had killed three people and got seven life sentences. In Germany, with one life sentence, you can be paroled after fifteen years. With seven, you serve seven times fifteen years before you can be paroled. By then you're dead. Klar could be paroled in 2088.

I wrote him that I'd be very interested to exchange ideas for a book project about right-wing and left-wing terrorism. He wrote back and agreed on condition that the book not merely serve capitalism and make a profit. Of course, by corresponding with Christian Klar I branded myself a sympathizer of the RAF with the German authorities. This was worse than being a neo-Nazi. It was just one more nail in my coffin with them.

I also wrote a letter to Chancellor Kohl, describing the project and asking him if he would consider contributing an essay.

I THINK PART of the reason I was so desperate to talk with leftist extremists was that the Anarchist Anti-Fas and the Edelweiss Pirates, my old enemies, refused to exchange a word with me. They refused to believe I had changed, or else they didn't care. "The only reformed Fascist is a dead Fascist," they said. Their cynicism about my conversion hurt terribly. While Jewish people were being wonderful—really listening to my case, inviting me to discussion groups—German leftists were much less forthcoming. The exception was Christian Klar, who'd been sitting in solitary confinement for twelve years and was pretty happy to be getting postcards and letters from almost anyone, I think.

And then there was my old nemesis Olaf Arnwalt. I didn't exactly have a dialogue with Arnwalt, but he'd made it clear that he trusted my conversion when we had a chance run-in on a street in Kreuzberg one night.

It always had been a disappointment that Arnwalt and I had never gone man to man: the black-haired beast of the anarchists versus the blond-haired giant of the neo-Nazis. There had even been a sort of bet within the anarchists' circles in Pfarrstrasse and among our people about who would win the mythic match. But it had never happened. We had confronted each other a number of times, but events had always conspired to keep us physically apart. The closest we'd ever gotten was hurling stones at each other from one crowd to another.

Then, after quitting the Movement, I met Arnwalt by chance as I was driving through Kreuzberg and a carload of anarchists started following me too closely, honking and bumping into me from behind. When they finally forced me to pull over, I got out of the car, expecting the worst. Arnwalt strode up to me, slapped an enormous, dangerous hand on my shoulder, and congratulated me on coming clean. Then he brought up the fact of our never having had it out.

"We never managed to fight each other," he said. "And now we'll probably never have the chance."

"It wasn't meant to be," I said, and we parted with a handshake.

THE ANARCHISTS OFTEN tried to disrupt my public speaking engagements or keep me from taking part in discussions. In April I was invited to participate in a roundtable discussion at the Jewish community in Düsseldorf. Here I met up with the psychoanalyst Dr. Horst Richter again. He was part of the discussion panel with Herr Bubis, other representatives of the Jewish community, myself, and members of the Anti-Fa who wanted to kick me offstage. He said he was pleased to finally meet me, and I was pleased to meet the person I'd seen defend me so eloquently on television at a moment when I was really unable to defend myself.

When Anti-Fa people tried to prevent me from speaking this time, when they shouted and booed and tried to disrupt the meeting, Herr Bubis, Dr. Richter, and all us others simply wouldn't acknowledge them. There were enough police there to keep the meeting from ending. But I was fuming at the arrogance of these German leftists—their similarity in a way to Nazis—that they thought they had a right to police whom the Jewish community invited to talk.

After the meeting, Dr. Richter asked if we could speak at length privately. So we started a correspondence, and in June he invited Karin and me to his house for the weekend. He lives in Giessen, not far from Frankfurt. It was a fascinating visit. He was seventy-three years old, but he seemed much younger, always in jeans, with long hair and moccasins.

Richter was born in 1920, so he was a young man under the Nazis. He fought in the war; he was on the Russian front, where he worked as an infirmary surgeon. But he got hit in the forehead and practically died. He was sent back from the front and ultimately completed his formal studies in medicine. For a long time he was at the Free University in Berlin, before becoming chairman of the Sigmund Freud Institute in Giessen.

We talked about all sorts of things that interested him—about group dynamics and right-wing extremists. I told him how I was thinking of doing social work, working at some sort of office that the State could sponsor for young people who wanted to get out of the right-wing scene. He thought it was a good idea and agreed to help me with recommendations where he could.

ON APRIL 26, 1994, the BKA carried out a huge crackdown in Berlin based on my testimony. They searched the apartments of Lutz, Auschwitz, Oliver W.—all the guys from my terrorist cell, as well as many others I'd mentioned in my testimony. It was the first time the BKA, the top institution of the national police, had decided to strike in Berlin, and it was a major shock to the scene.

The BKA hit dozens of people at exactly the same time, practically the same minute of the day, searching through apartments, confiscating propaganda material and weapons—instructions on bomb building, kits for making letter bombs, and fuses, as well as photocopy machines and computers. Under Priem's floor they found a huge cache of munitions. They also took away his altar to Reinhard Heydrich and confiscated his videocassettes—*The Rockford Files,* his favorite television series, as well as hundreds of Nazi films.

Perhaps the most important catch they made that day was Oliver W., the ruthless young man whom I'd trained and whose one goal in life was to become a Nazi terrorist. He'd had no record before I spoke out about him; there had never even been a picture published of him without a mask. That day, they got him for propaganda. But a few months later, they would arrest him and Priem for blowing off a journalist's shoulder with a high-pressure metal catapult, and the next time they would do a house search at his place, they'd find four completed pipe bombs.

Then the authorities threw a curve. On the same day they searched the people I'd identified, the BKA searched my mother's apartment, my brother's army barracks, my old apartment, and even the apartment where Karin was officially registered. In fact, she just used it as a mailing address, and there was this guy living there named Philip, a gay painter who'd never even heard of the neo-Nazi scene and who was usually on drugs. With his house filled with federal agents, Philip called up Karin, frantic, and said, "What a trip—did you know your boyfriend is a notorious neo-Nazi?"

A few days later, the BKA contacted me and my lawyer, Frau Kossack, to say that there was now an investigation in which *I* was the chief suspect. They were building a case against me as the founder of a terrorist organization. The main evidence was the statements I'd made when they had questioned me in Meckenheim. Wherever possible, the testimony I had supposedly given to help catch the people who'd sent me a bomb was going to be used against me.

NOT LONG AFTER, Horst Richter wrote a big article in my favor in one of Germany's most respected daily papers, *Süddeutsche Zeitung*. He wrote about how the BKA had used me and gotten help from me and was now turning against me. It's unfair and crazy, he wrote, to treat those who quit extremist movements this way. It tells others that it is safer to stay in the Movement than to try to make a clean break and return to society.

While the authorities were hounding me and people like Richter were defending me, Karin and I still had to worry most about the possibility that the neo-Nazis would find us. After the raids in April, they'd see me as an even greater threat than before. My mother had police protection now and experts were checking her mail, and I'd stopped visiting her in order to reduce the danger to her and my siblings. The Movement couldn't possibly know where I was because I was constantly moving around from the house of one friend to another, all people I'd met through Winfried. But it was still harder to live as an ex-neo-Nazi than I'd ever imagined, and time only seemed to make it harder.

There were a thousand things about normal life that I had taken for granted that I couldn't do anymore: I couldn't get a job, and I couldn't collect unemployment. I couldn't do anything where I had to register and give an address. I couldn't rent an apartment, I only had addresses through other people and got my mail through other people. I could never ride public transportation, but I also couldn't rent a car. Anything could be traced—a car rental record, for instance.

The neo-Nazis had friends in the police, and any of these things could lead them to me. So I was a kind of half person. In a way, it was as if I'd gone underground to become a terrorist. All direct contact with my family was severely limited at the moment when I needed them most. As a neo-Nazi, I'd felt in control and free to do what I wanted. As an ex-neo-Nazi, all Germany had become my prison.

I got information from Thomas and Martin. Also from my sister Jana. She still went to cafés where lots of girls who knew neo-Nazis hung out. I had an informant for a while—a guy who had worked with both the Anti-Fas and the neo-Nazis. He was one of these young guys who just liked to hang out with radical tough guys, even though he wasn't one himself. He was in school with my nephew.

Karin had the hardest time of it. This woman from a small town in the Rhineland had never had any contact with criminals or the police, and here she was in the middle of one of the biggest investigations in the history of the Federal Republic, one in which the authorities kept changing the rules. She also had to live under the threat of discovery and attack by my former Kamerads, while helping me to work through my massive change of worldview.

Our apartment, which no one knew about except our friend who was off in Bremen, made us feel we had one firm thing under our feet. Then one day I was emptying the garbage, and the neighbor who lived one floor below us approached me and said, "Hey, you're quite a big number. You're really somebody—chased and persecuted by everybody. I've seen you on TV." He said he'd keep our secret, but I knew we had to leave. He was the sort of person who'd go boasting about it at the local bars—hey, I've got the ex-Führer of the East German neo-Nazis living in my apartment building—and he also seemed like someone who'd have right-wing extremist friends, if he wasn't also that way himself. We couldn't take the risk.

Now we had to look for an apartment. Everything was difficult in Berlin. We talked about leaving, going someplace where no one knew me. But on the other hand, Berlin was the best city for me. It was the biggest, most anonymous city in Germany, and at least here I knew where everybody was. In Frankfurt or Hamburg, I wouldn't know my way around, and if someone was after me I wouldn't know where to run. Here I knew all the secret shortcuts. I could also get odd jobs as a mason here—repairing the office of a friend of Karin's, little things that helped tide us over.

I kept my gas pistol with me at all times. It looked like a real 9mm pistol, and that's what counts. Your opponent wouldn't know whether it was real or not. Then again, you could also seriously injure somebody with a gas pistol if you fired when it was directly pressed against someone's forehead. Just the pressure of the gas would blow a hole in his head, especially from a heavy-caliber 9mm. For a while I had a sort of sawed-off shotgun—a pistol that fired shot—from the United States. I'd bought it on the black market, but I didn't carry it around anymore, both because I didn't want to kill somebody if I could avoid it and also because I couldn't risk getting caught with an illegal weapon.

SPEAKING ENGAGEMENTS BECAME the one semblance of normalcy in my life, the one thing that made me feel I had a purpose and a job. I'd get small stipends to cover the costs of travel and expenses. When the anarchists accused me of profiting from my quitting, however, I started donating the money to charity. I donated to a fund that used the money to bring Russian Jews into Germany, and also to a fund for the Solingen Turkish families.

In September I did a reading on the small Ostsee island of Usedom, practically on the German-Polish border, an area with a great deal of neo-Nazi activity. The event was held in an evangelical church, and it was fairly full. Usually in those events I'd say a little about myself, read a little from my book, and then take questions. This audience was divided between adults in their late forties and fifties and teenagers. After my talk they began asking fairly normal questions— what had happened to me, how did I feel about it, and so on—and then gradually I figured out that the mood in the room was moving toward provocation.

When I notice that someone is deliberately being provocative, I usually employ a strategy. I look at the person and say, "Okay, now I know who's responsible for the provocation. Thank you." Usually then I'd get most of the audience on my side. But here someone spoke up from up on the balcony, above the organ, and I looked up and saw that there was a group of ten or twenty skins up there. The heckler said, "Tell me one good reason why I should have a foreigner as a friend."

"That's as dumb a question as if you asked me, 'Why should I accept my neighbors?' " I said. "Simply because they're there, that's all. It's ridiculous to even have to consider it."

"Yeah, well, foreigners are dirty and smell and are shit," he said, flustered, and the others started repeating it.

Then from around the room various young people started to shout, "Traitor pig!" "Communist swine!" "Jew!"

The police had to smuggle me out of the church before something happened. The other people in the room just listened. There were maybe 250 people in the audience and only 20 neo-Nazis, but the others didn't say a word. The cops took me away in one of their cars so the neo-Nazis wouldn't recognize mine and drove me in circles for a while, the usual strategy, until they brought me back to my car and I took off.

THE NEXT TIME I was called to Meckenheim was in September. I wasn't allowed to stay in the BKA complex now because I was a suspect, rather than just a witness, so they got me a hotel room nearby. They'd pick me up in the morning and bring me back at night.

Herr Wien and the old crew were off the case. My new interlocutor was a Herr Rolfs, a neat-looking, athletic type in his mid-thirties with short blond hair and a casual appearance. Although he wore jeans and looked very muscular, I soon found out he was a career bureaucrat with no experience in the field. And it was only his clothes that were casual. From the first Herr Rolfs was cold and mistrustful.

His colleague, Herr Glaubrecht, was the opposite of Rolfs: short, small shouldered, and shaped like a bowling pin or a Christmas tree. Herr Glaubrecht had black hair, gold-rimmed glasses, and a giant mustache like Kaiser Wilhelm. The little man began our first day of interrogations by saying things like "I bet you know a lot more than you're telling us." Meanwhile, his sporty colleague looked on in disapproval.

I expected them to try to build a case against me as the Führer of East Germany, the founder of a terrorist organization, the ringleader of everyone I'd helped them arrest. In short, I expected them to turn my former career against me and to assert that my conversion wasn't real and that I was still a terrorist at heart. But once again the authorities surprised me because, over the summer, they'd put their heads together here in Meckenheim and come up with a new theory: I had sent the bomb to myself, in care of my mother, to create a sensation and thereby increase the circulation of my book.

Q: Herr H., for us it is no coincidence that on exactly the day the book bomb came, you were working with a film team. For us it seems to have been planned so that you could get the optimal media exposure for the event.

A: The Dutch film team suggested the appointment, not vice versa.

Q: Herr H., will you write a new book now?

A: Yes.

Q: Will Ignatz Bubis or Horst Eberhard Richter be involved in any way?

A: Yes, possibly.

Q: Have you asked any other public figures to work on this book with you? Anyone in the government?

A: Yes, I wrote to Helmut Kohl to ask him to help me write this book.

Here is where it really got wonderful. These detectives had seen a lot of old movies and had really been putting clues together. I had no idea where this was leading.

Q: Do you still have a copy of the bomb letter?

A: Yes.

Q: Do you use this copy as a model from which you write your own letters?

A: Certainly I've never used it as a model for my own writing!

What kind of moronic question is that? I thought. We'd been at it for eight hours. Then they produced their trump card. They had in their possession the letter I'd written to Helmut Kohl asking if he'd be interested in contributing to a book of essays against right-wing terrorism. Apparently, Chancellor Kohl hadn't known who I was at the time and he had given the letter to the BKA directly. The thing that had started this whole line of inquiry was the first sentence of my letter to the chancellor, which happened to bear some syntactical similarities to the first sentence in the letter the bomber had sent to me. The fatal clue was this sentence, which introduced both letters: "Dear ———, As you don't know me, allow me to introduce myself." Their reasoning would have been funny if it hadn't been so sick.

Q: Did you write this letter?

A: Yes, I wrote it.

Q: Herr Hasselbach, this letter which you wrote to the chancellor shows a surprising similarity in sentence construction with the book-bomb letter sent to you! How do you explain this?

A: I don't see the surprising similarity. If there is one, it's a pure accident. . . .

Q: Herr Hasselbach, it has been scientifically established that there are a vast variety of concurrences on many levels—for example, a similar syntactical complexity in the constructions of the first sentences or, for another example, the failure to use certain punctuation, such as commas, after certain words where it would be grammatically correct to do so. What do you say to this?

A: I think it's a pure coincidence.

Q: The preceding questions and accusations have shown that you had possession of a book with instructions for explosives, a motive for sending the bomb, which was to raise the sales of your book, and finally there is the similarity between your handwriting on the letter to the chancellor and that of the bomb sender. Can you give a concrete reason to rule out why you shouldn't be a suspect?

A: For me an absolute point that rules it out is that I would never endanger my mother.

Q: We know at this time that the bomb was functional at the moment when the fuse was built. This bomb could no longer function after five days in the mail. A skilled electrician or tinkerer could have constructed a bomb exactly so that it would not go off after this elapsed time.

A: I couldn't have any idea how long the mail would take. It could have taken ten days or three. . . . Look, I'm first of all not capable of building a bomb. I don't know how. Second, I certainly couldn't construct it to such minute specifications. Third, I don't know anyone in my current circle of friends who could help me build such a thing. . . .

Q: In the letter you sent to the chancellor, it's been established that you used right-justified margins. In the interrogation this afternoon you said clearly that you don't understand or have this function on your computer.

A: My girlfriend, Karin, can tell you that I have enormous problems with my computer. . . . I've got no idea what functions are on the machine and what aren't. I swear I wrote the letter myself without any help or any influences or models. . . .

They wore me down with ever more absurd arguments and ever more complicated and disconnected series of questions:

Q: Herr H., do you know the Red Guard?
A: Yes, it's an organization in the circles of the anarchists.
Q: What do you know about the Hoffmann Militia?
A: That was long before my time. What I know about this group, I know out of newspapers or books.
Q: Before the bomb came, did you have connections to Rainer Fromm?
A: No, I knew him as an author, from his books.
Q: Herr Hasselbach, are you aware that Rainer Fromm wrote a Ph.D. thesis?
A: That Rainer Fromm wrote about it I know from this letter announcing the bomb.
Q: Does your brother Jens have a computer?
A: Not that I know of.
Q: Herr H., do you have your own letterhead?
A: No, I just write my name and address in the upper-right-hand corner.
Q: Do you write with justified right margins?
A: What?
Q: Do you write with justified right margins?
A: I don't know!
Q: How do you write Hasselbach—Hasselbach or Haßelbach?
A: With two "S"s.

These interrogations with me as the suspect for the bomb began on September 8, 1994, and went on all autumn, until December. The cops went on to try to establish a variety of conspiracy theories, which had me killing my mother for her life insurance, sending her a dud bomb to raise the circulation of my book, and plotting to do it with my girlfriend and Winfried and my brother. Finally they introduced the possibility that it had been a plot engineered by my stepfather to kill my mother.

They also developed more and more complicated theories about the bomb itself: "Technical examinations of the bomb have shown that the safety mechanism on it was only provisional and that it could have blown up anytime during its trip through the mails," they announced one day. "We maintain that the envelope didn't hold a book bomb at all, but rather a dummy bomb. The bomb was so hot that it would have blown up in the mail otherwise. Rather, the bomb *dummy* was intercepted and substituted with a real bomb, either when it was in the mailbox at your mother's or even in the very apartment of your mother after she had received the package. Your stepfather could have done it, or you."

Finally they started to unleash the battery of evidence they'd collected against me, which consisted of statements by neo-Nazis saying that I'd sent the bomb to myself. They hadn't been using any of the testimony I gave them to really investigate these guys but had in fact been rounding them up to use as witnesses against me:

Q: In his interrogation from 4/27/94, page 3, Mike Prötzke [Auschwitz] told us that he could well imagine that you sent the letter bomb to yourself. What do you say to that?

A: I take this as a ridiculous game they're playing in order to discredit me so I can't testify or speak against them.

Q: In his interrogation from 6/20/94, Frank Lutz also said that. . . .

A: I can only repeat what I said before—that I think these people are lying in order to protect themselves.

Q: Johannes Hochstetter also testified this way and said he thought you did it not only to raise the circulation of your book but also to get more police protection. What do you say to that?

Johannes Hochstetter! My God, they'd gotten testimony from the moron I'd taken to the nationalist folk concert and given a mock quiz to afterward to prove that he was competent to be a neo-Nazi. The list went on and on. They'd gotten all of my former Kamerads to speak out against me, to say they believed that I'd built the bomb and sent it to myself. They'd interrogated Frank Lutz, Arnulf Priem, Christian Worch. Of course, they'd all spoken out against me because I'd quit. The BKA had gathered testimony from all the people I'd given them information about, even Oliver W. Oliver W.! The young neo-Nazi who was now sitting in jail for getting caught with *pipe bombs*—the terrorist whom I had exposed for the first time to the police—this same Oliver W. was now quoted to me as saying "Oh, yes, it was Hasselbach who sent the bomb himself."

There was no point to their little game—I obviously hadn't sent the bomb to my mother, and in more lucid moments, I *knew* they knew that.

Conclusion

I wrote this book not only to tell my story but to provide the first complete exposé of the neo-Nazis' international network of paramilitary camps, indoctrination, and friends in high places. Even though I am the only voice from within the neo-Nazi scene in Germany denouncing it, the German Department of Education has refused my offers to come speak in schools or community centers. Yet whenever I go abroad to speak, I find encouragement. I recently went to Rome and did an interview with Radio Vatican. This is the biggest radio station in the world, and when you do an interview, it's broadcast everywhere. It was an older man who asked me if I had something special to transmit to humanity. I was a little taken aback and said, "Hey, I'm not the new apostle." He laughed and said he appreciated that I had put it that way.

Foreign cultures have become my everyday existence, and I couldn't imagine living without them. Except for Winfried and Karin, my best friends now are foreigners. Germans often seem arrogant to me and somehow damaged in their outlook. I actually feel sick sometimes when I'm speaking to my countrymen. I was driving to the airport recently and the driver got stuck in traffic and started giving a speech about foreign drivers, like I was supposed to agree just because I was also a German. I said, "I'm sorry, I'm getting out of the cab now." And I walked out in the middle of traffic, on a sort of overpass. I preferred it to staying inside with him.

I even have problems with my family sometimes. The other day my brother Jens came back from a soccer game he'd played with the Berlin-Kreuzberg team, the Turkish team. They'd won.

"These swine Turks," Jens said.

"What do you mean, swine Turks?" I said. "They obviously played better than you."

"Nah, it makes me sick."

"What makes you sick? You should be sick at the Germans, at how badly your team played."

He thought it over, but you still have to say things like that to him. Otherwise he slips back into casual racism. The German Army is hardly a bastion of multiculturalism. They're still trained to think in terms of racial enemies. Jens tells me about how he's been trained to fight against the "yellow flood" from China. The Warsaw Pact is gone and so the only real threats that can come now are from China and Japan, so they talk about the yellow flood. I argue with him about how foolish it is to think that the Chinese would even bother to invade Europe and Germany and how transparent the search for enemies is.

IN APRIL 1995 my testimony finally bore some real fruit: Gary Rex Lauck, supplier of neo-Nazi propaganda for all of Europe and the leader of a worldwide terrorist network, was arrested in Copenhagen, Denmark. Then, in a huge operation code-named Atlantic 2, the German police raided cells of the NSDAP/AO all over Germany. More than eighty important links in the network were broken, and tons of propaganda material, indoctrination books, and terrorist equipment were seized.

Lauck's lawyers demanded he be set free and be allowed to return to the United States, where he had officially committed no crime. The German authorities lobbied equally hard to have him extradited to Hamburg. Then the Oklahoma City bombing happened, and this probably persuaded the FBI that maybe it wasn't so important to protect the civil rights of one of the world's most dangerous right-wing extremist leaders. The American authorities began unprecedented cooperation with the German government to have Lauck, an American citizen, extradited to Germany to be prosecuted for spreading neo-Nazi propaganda and terrorist training materials. The Danish courts toiled with the issue over the summer—Lauck had not violated Danish laws either—and eventually the case went to the court of the European Union, which finally allowed the extradition to go through in August.

Meanwhile, I saw ominous parallels to the string of mail bombings that had been going on in Germany and Austria since my mother first received the book bomb. In early spring a group of Gypsies were killed by a pipe bomb hidden in a sign that said GYPSIES GO HOME—it was rigged so that when they removed it, they died. That summer some liberal German politicians and talk show hosts also received mail bombs. I was terrified my mother would get another bomb. I was sure Bendix had had something to do with this bomb series—he was now in custody—and that the rest of the VAPO boys were taking up the slack.

Though I'd been out of the Movement for two years and was trying to make a difference by speaking out against the intolerance that created neo-Nazism, I decided I should swallow some of my disgust for the way the German authorities had been treating me and try to put some of my dangerous former Kamerads behind bars. And I couldn't let the "Farm Belt Führer" return to Nebraska a free man when I saw him as responsible for the biggest cancer among young Germans—the sort of casual, mail-order neo-Nazism that had been behind the Mölln bombing. Besides, if I could put him away for acts that were legal under the U.S. Constitution, I thought I'd be doing America a favor. Gary Lauck's brand of free speech was not something any country needed.

I still refused to plea-bargain with the BKA or join a witness protection program. I didn't believe they could protect me from retaliation even if they tried. That was my own responsibility. And I would help them only on my terms. I agreed to testify against those I had the most personal evidence against and those I thought were the most dangerous.

Of course, in ten years, some of my former Kamerads like Worch will no doubt be playing at being democratic politicians. They will say their neo-Nazism was merely a youthful folly, though based on the proper instincts—against foreigners and in favor of nationalism. These basic sentiments are growing in acceptability.

I WAS NOT consciously aware of the point in time when I changed from victim to culprit. During my time as a neo-Nazi leader, I never realized I had become a culprit. I still saw myself as a victim of the Communist regime. Even now, the only strong hate feelings I harbor are against all the Communist rulers of my former country. I'm still seething with hate for people like Honecker and the Stasi men in prison. It's like the hate you have for your parents if they beat you—you never forget it.

Still, that can be no excuse. I realize now that as soon as I started to work as a neo-Nazi, to incite against other people and groups, to find scapegoats, I became a culprit. After all, there are thousands of people in the GDR who were in prison, thousands of people who had to go through the same shit as I did and who worked it out in completely different ways.

The trials against my former Berlin Kamerads began in September 1995. At the end of the first trial, one of the accused stood up in front of the full court and shouted: "Hasselbach, I'm going to kill you, you Jewish pig!" Having this anti-Semitic death threat shouted at me by a boy whom I'd once indoctrinated into the Movement seemed the perfect ironic comment on my life. He was fined 150 marks for the outburst.

What my life will produce is unpredictable. In five years maybe no one in the scene will know Ingo Hasselbach personally anymore and a new leader will come along. You can't tell. Young people have short memories.

ABOUT THE AUTHORS

INGO HASSELBACH lectures frequently on right-wing extremism.

TOM REISS grew up in Texas and New England and was educated at Harvard College. He has written often about the Nazis and their legacy for *The New York Times*, *The Wall Street Journal*, and other publications. He is currently at work on a novel.

ABOUT THE TYPE

This book was set in Sabon, a typeface designed by the well-known German typographer Jan Tschichold (1902–74). Sabon's design is based upon the original letter forms of Claude Garamond and was created specifically to be used for three sources: foundry type for hand composition, Linotype, and Monotype. Tschichold named his typeface for the famous Frankfurt typefounder Jacques Sabon, who died in 1580.

The following names are aliases:

Edgar

Elke

Ulf

Frieder "Freddy" Meisel

Silvio Baumann

Christine

Oberleutnant Schuchard

Uta

Birgitt

Stefan

Mareike

Frank (the Stasi guard)

Meyer

Stemp

Mike "Auschwitz" Prötzke

Stinki

Joachim Modrack

Valeria Krebs

Johnny

Raider

Olaf Arnwalt

Johannes Hochstetter

Claudia

Inken

Karin

Otto

Thomas

Martin

Spinner

Messer

Frau Plottnitz

Herr Dörte

Herr Wien

Herr Rolfs

Herr Glaubrecht